D0772704
CALGARY PUBLIC LIBRARY
SEP / / 2008

FIGHTING TECHNIQUES OF THE NAPOLEONIC AGE

FIGHTING TECHNIQUES OF THE NAPOLEONIC AGE

1792 ~ 1815

Equipment, Combat Skills, and Tactics

Robert B. Bruce Iain Dickie Kevin Kiley Michael F. Pavkovic Frederick C. Schneid

THOMAS DUNNE BOOKS
ST. MARTIN'S PRESS NEW YORK

Fighting Techniques of the Napoleonic Age

Copyright © Amber Books Ltd 2008

THOMAS DUNNE BOOKS
An imprint of St. Martin's Press.
All rights reserved.
No part of this book may be used or reproduced
in any manner whatsoever without written permission except
in case of brief quotations embodied in critical articles or reviews.
For information, address
St. Martin's Press, 175 Fifth Avenue, New York, N.Y. 10010.

www.stmartins.com

ISBN-13: 978-0-312-37587-4
ISBN-10: 0-312-37587-5

Editorial and design by
Amber Books Ltd
Bradley's Close
74–77 White Lion Street
London N1 9PF
United Kingdom
www.amberbooks.co.uk

Project Editor: Michael Spilling
Design: Zoe Mellors
Picture Research: Terry Forshaw

Printed in Dubai

10 9 8 7 6 5 4 3 2 1

CONTENTS

CHAPTER 1

THE ROLE OF INFANTRY

In the summer of 1789, the political, social and economic upheavals that had plagued the French state finally erupted in crisis. The French Revolution would bring not just political and social changes but also a dramatic transformation in the conduct of war.

Unlike the revolution in military affairs that began in Europe in the late fifteenth century and which was heavily influenced by the adoption of gunpowder weapons, the French Revolution altered warfare without introducing any major technological innovations. Indeed, the standard weapons, the smoothbore musket and cannon, had changed little in more than a century. It is true that there were minor incremental changes that made the flintlock musket and artillery more efficient, but a soldier in the army of Marlborough would have easily been able to handle the weapons and tactics used by the army of Wellington. Instead, the major changes

THE CHÂTEAU OF HOUGOUMONT *became a focal point of French forces during the battle of Waterloo, drawing troops away from the attack on the British centre. Here, troops from the Coldstream Guards engage French troops assaulting the outside of the château.*

were in the ways in which armies were recruited, commanded and supplied, and these, in turn, led to significant changes in the fighting techniques of the armies themselves.

The Revolution may have been the catalyst for this transformation, but the French Army was certainly ready for change. For more than a century, French officers had been debating a number of military questions. There were two significant trends that influenced this debate, one pragmatic, the other philosophical.

The pragmatic concerns that dominated French military discussions centred on the performance of the French Army during the course of the late seventeenth and early eighteenth centuries. From the wars of Louis XIV through to the American War for Independence, the army's performance had been mixed, to say the least. Several major defeats had cost the monarchy dearly, especially in terms of its overseas possessions, including territory and influence in North America and India. Like many institutions with a tarnished reputation, the army recognized that such a lacklustre performance required serious self-reflection to overcome the deficiencies that had led to so many defeats. The fundamentals of military organization and tactics began to be discussed, and a number of officers wrote treatises that dealt with all manner of subjects, including equipment, the organization of military units, unit formations and methods of manoeuvre and combat.

The second factor that generated writings on military theory was more philosophical and was embodied in the major intellectual movement of the period, namely the Enlightenment. For the first few decades of the eighteenth century, its proponents, the *philosophes*, dominated all areas of French thought. The basis of the Enlightenment was the synthesis of reason, including the belief in natural law, the importance of classical models and systems, and the mathematical accuracy derived from Newtonian science. The confluence of these two trends – the self-reflection of the French military and the Enlightenment – led to a tremendous surge in the number of works of military literature produced as the century progressed. This is particularly true of the period from the Seven Years War through to the outbreak of the revolutionary wars. In keeping with the spirit of the age, many of these publications attempted to discern an orderly 'system' that could be applied to the conduct of war.

L'Ordre Profonde

One of the most heated topics in military works of the period concerned the proper formation to be used in warfare. In the course of the latter seventeenth century and throughout most of the eighteenth century, the trend had been to thin, linear formations, which had been generally standardized to a depth of three ranks, allowing the largest number of muskets to be brought to bear when firing. During the War of the Austrian Succession and the Seven Years War, Frederick the Great (1712–86) and the Prussian Army had shown themselves to be the masters of this fighting technique. Some French military writers

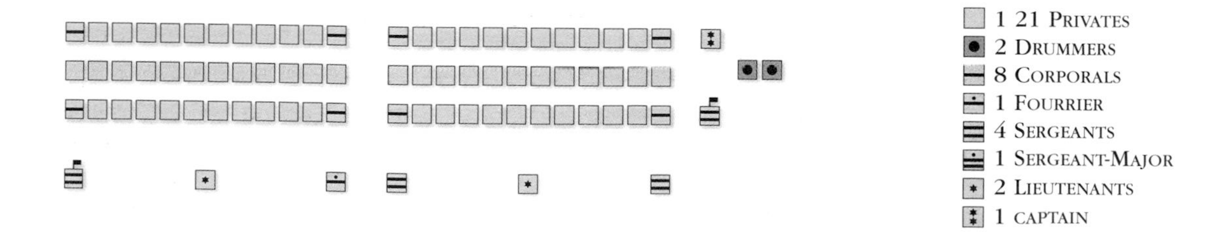

French infantry companies *from 1791 to 1808 deployed in three ranks as shown in the* Règlement du 1er Août *1791. This formation was the building block of French tactical formations. Lines were formed by placing companies one beside another while different columns were created by placing companies in deeper formations, usually nine or 18 ranks deep.*

argued that this form of manoeuvre was well suited to the stolid and dull Prussians but was not appropriate for the more imaginative and hot-blooded French soldiers. They argued that it would be better – and more fitting to the French temperament – for troops to form up in deeper formations, *l'ordre profonde*, allowing for a tactical system that emphasized movement and attack with the bayonet.

One writer who addressed this tactical question was Lieutenant-Colonel Paul Gideon Joly de Maizeroy (1719–80), who was also an avid student of ancient warfare. In his multi-volume study on tactics, he advocated the use of deeper formations. Acknowledging that these did not provide as much firepower, he insisted that they made up for this with an increase in morale and cohesion.

'It is well known with what gallantry the officers lead and with what vehemence the [French] troops follow...'

— WILLIAM NAPIER, BRITISH OFFICER AND HISTORIAN OF THE PENINSULA WAR

The most vocal advocate of the deep formations of *l'ordre profonde* – so much so that he referred to such formations as *l'ordre française*, the French order – was Baron François Jean de Mesnil-Durand (1729–99). He had served in the War of the Austrian Succession, and in the wake of defeat in the Seven Years War his work on tactics generated tremendous acrimony over the direction of tactical formations in the French Army. Mesnil-Durand argued that three characteristics were required for a successful tactical doctrine: solidity, security of the flanks and speed. To meet these requirements, he developed a new formation, the *plésion*, a formation of 768 line infantry arrayed 24 across and 32 deep. The *plésion* was supported by two platoons of grenadiers, 96 in all, and a small unit of 50 horse grenadiers. The formation was divided, for purely tactical reasons, into different vertical and horizontal sub-units, which allowed the *plésion* to face in any direction. The *plésion* was thus both solid and had secure flanks. To address the need for speed, the formation was compact and thus easily manoeuvred.

In 1778, as France prepared for war with England, a French army of some 44 infantry battalions with supporting cavalry and artillery was encamped at Vaussieux in Normandy, under Marshal Broglie (1718–1804). There it drilled according to Mesnil-Durand's ordinance. The results were less than impressive, as certain manoeuvres were shown to be very difficult in practice. Moreover, as two brigades were put through their paces – one using current doctrine and the second Mesnil-Durand's – it became clear to many of the officers assembled that the former was superior. Marshal Broglie, a proponent of *l'ordre profonde*, nevertheless held some eight manoeuvres with the new ordinance over nearly three weeks – and his official report was positive.

Rethinking Tactics

Much of the military literature dealt primarily with the infantry, the largest and most important part of most armies, but there were also those who focused on what had traditionally been a supporting arm, the artillery. Key among these was an artillery officer Jean du Teil, who published a treatise on the use of artillery in 1778. This work would greatly influence Napoleon since both men both served in the same regiment under the command of du Teil's older brother Joseph, who became one of the future emperor's chief patrons. Du Teil was able to think of artillery in a new way thanks to the introduction of a new artillery system into the French Army by General Jean Baptiste de Gribeauval (1715–89).

As inspector general of artillery, Gribeauval introduced canon that were far superior to those in use during the Seven Years War. He shortened the cannon barrels to make them lighter, introduced improved elevation screws, and improved the carriages and methods of harnessing the guns to their teams. All of these improvements made the French guns more manoeuvrable. Du Teil capitalized on this and called for the artillery to be regarded no longer as a mere adjunct to the infantry but as an independent arm that would be capable of attacking alongside it. It should be deployed to cause the greatest damage to the enemy, rather than hanging back as the battle developed. As a battery took casualties, it should be relieved by a fresh battery, as surreptitiously as possible, so that the pressure could be maintained at the point of attack. Finally, du Teil broke with the common wisdom by arguing against counter-battery fire. Rather than attacking the enemy guns, artillery should make enemy troops their main target, bringing themselves to bear against enemy artillery only when there was no other target or if the enemy guns were causing great damage to their own troops. The culmination of this

intellectual discourse was perhaps best personified by Jacques Antoine Hippolyte Comte de Guibert (1743–90). He served in the French Army during the Seven Years War and distinguished himself in the French campaign to annex Corsica. He attained the rank of colonel and is often considered the archetypical military *philosophe.* While he held a relatively modest rank, he was fortunate to have a father who was an eminent soldier and who had served on the staff of the Marshal Broglie and the War Minister Choiseul (1700–70), and who took pains to educate his son in the key issues of the day.

Guibert wrote extensively on military affairs. His most famous work is probably his *General Essay on Tactics*, published in 1772 and dedicated to his father. For Guibert, tactics were at the heart of the theory of war, whether elementary tactics like those of basic units or the grand tactics that dealt with the movement of armies. Although more of a supporter of traditional linear tactics (*l'ordre mince*), Guibert was also pragmatic. He advocated that tactics needed to be flexible: it should be possible for units to manoeuvre in one formation and yet attack in another. He is also credited with the concept of a mixed order, in which part of a unit was formed in a deeper formation for manoeuvre and possible shock action, while the remainder was formed in a more traditional linear battle line.

Although he would die in 1790, Guibert's ideas on tactics formed the basis for the *Règlement concernant l'Exercice et les Manoeuvres de l'Infantrie du 1er Août 1791* (henceforth abbreviated *Règlement du 1er Août 1791*). These were a set of regulations that represented the culmination of nearly a century of debate for the French Army of the *Ancien Regime,* and they would serve as the basis of drill for the armies of the Revolutionary and Napoleonic periods.

Infantry During the Revolutionary Wars

The outbreak of the Revolution had a deleterious effect on the French Army. Although there had been much debate concerning doctrinal changes and even some actual reforms, the army was beset by a variety of internal problems that made it vulnerable to the forces of Revolution. The process of self-reflection and orderly reform would come to a halt with the Revolution, and although many of the seeds planted by the intellectual debates of

THE EVENT MOST *commonly associated with the beginning of the French Revolution is the storming of the Bastille on 14 July 1789. Here, members of the French Guards join the mob, bringing with them a cannon.*

the preceding half-century would take root and eventually sprout, they would not necessarily do so in an orderly fashion.

In the middle of 1789, the French Army was still a formidable force, numbering some 180,000 men under arms and more than 70,000 militiamen who could be called up. While this was a significant reduction from its structure earlier in the century, when the army could deploy well over 300,000 men, it was nevertheless a force to be reckoned with, at least on paper. Moreover, some of the military reforms, such as Gribeauval's new system of artillery, made that arm one of the best of its kind in all of Europe. However, the social, political and economic problems that beset France also took their toll on the army. For example, the officer corps was divided over issues of political reform – so divided that duals between liberal and reactionary officers were not unknown. There were also problems within the ranks of the non-commissioned officers. In their case, one problem was that of limited opportunities. Promotion within the non-commissioned ranks was very slow, and virtually non-existent when it came to receiving an officer's commission. It has been estimated that the chances for a non-commissioned officer to be promoted into the ranks of the aristocratically dominated officer corps was around 1 in 2000. This served to undermine order and discipline within the enlisted ranks.

When the Revolutionary sentiments that had been simmering in France finally boiled over in the summer of 1789, the effect on the army was devastating. Members of the King's Royal Guard deserted and some actually took part in the storming of the Bastille. The 20,000 line troops brought in fared no better. Some units were passive in the face of revolutionary activity – the most famous example being the Regiment of Flanders, which allowed a mob of women to remove the royal family from Versailles to Paris

THIS BRITISH INFANTRYMAN *is shown in the uniform of the Revolutionary period. This uniform has much in common with those worn throughout the century. The bicorne hat is worn cocked over the right eye so that it would not interfere with carrying the musket in battle.*

MARSHAL JEAN-BAPTISTE BERNADOTTE had a mixed career as one of Napoleon's leading generals, performing well at Limburg, Austerlitz, Mohrungen, Spanden and Linz, but falling short at Jena and Wagram, where he was dismissed by the emperor.

without offering any resistance. The breakdown of discipline meant that units suffered greatly increased desertion rates. Interestingly, units that might have been expected to support the revolutionaries - veterans who had fought in North America in support of another revolution - actually suffered fewer desertions and maintained a higher level of discipline than other units.

As the situation degenerated in and around Paris, the lack of discipline spread to other units garrisoned throughout France, and several units mutinied. The officer corps was also disillusioned. One famous example is the Comte de Rochambeau (1725-1807), who had commanded French forces in North America during the American Revolution. He took command of the troops in Alsace in the summer of 1789 but was so dismayed by the breakdown of discipline that he resigned his post and retired to his estates. By August, it was clear that the monarchy, which had held the monopoly of power thanks to the royal army, was no longer capable of maintaining order. Nor, though, was the National Assembly able to exert itself over the army, relying instead on its own military force, the National Guard, which first took over the security of Paris and, after the decrees of 11 August 1789, all of France.

The situation continued to worsen throughout 1790 and 1791. The National Assembly placed its hopes for security in the National Guard, numbering more than 65,000 full- and part-time troops under the Marquis de Lafayette (1757-1843), while the army continued to deteriorate. The abolition of feudal privileges opened up the officer ranks, to the consternation of officers of noble background.

Many of these, especially those above the rank of captain, left the army. Indeed, by the end of 1792 more than 6000 officers had left the army, which, of course, accelerated the deterioration of discipline. While regiments attempted to restrain the political activities of the men and discharged troublemakers, they were less than successful. The most stunning example of the breakdown of the army was a virtual pitched battle at Nancy in August of 1790 between three mutinous regiments and some 4500 loyal troops. By the end of 1791, the army had lost perhaps 40 per cent of its effective strength.

Building the Armies of the Republic

In an effort to rebuild the armed forces, the Revolutionary government began to establish a new army. A call for recruits went out in the summer of 1791. The resulting 100,000 men were known as the Volunteers of 1791, and would prove to be some of the best recruits the revolutionary armies received; many had prior military service in the army or the National Guard. But even with these volunteers, the army was far short of the numbers required for national defence. Indeed, it was not yet near its pre-Revolutionary levels by the beginning of 1792. That spring, with the threat of war looming on the horizon, a levy for additional troops yielded 200,000 men, the Volunteers of 1792. These men did not have the military experience of their compatriots from the

AN IDEALIZED DEPICTION *of a French camp during the Revolutionary Wars. Most French troops during this period were not nearly so well equipped as those shown here, neither were they able to engage in training with live ammunition.*

previous year, but they were soon supported by the addition of some 20,000 *fédérés,* politically reliable men who were to represent the National Guards from the various *departments* (administrative regions) of France.

Even this considerable influx of men did not meet the military needs of the Republic, which would soon be fighting in no fewer than six separate theatres of operation. This included the need for troops to fight counter-revolutionaries within the borders of France itself. In February 1793 came an additional levy, calling for an additional 300,000 men but yielding only half that number. This call was followed by the famous *levée en masse* legislation of August 1793, which established universal conscription and mobilized all of the resources of the Republic for the war effort.

All of these factors made it extremely difficult to develop an effective method of fighting for the armies of the new Republic. In particular, there was a dearth of experienced officers at certain levels. Junior ranks such as lieutenant and captain, however, were easily filled with experienced non-commissioned officers; indeed, some 60 per cent of captains had prior service and 55 per cent had been corporals. Some of these men would eventually reach the highest ranks. For example, Marshal Jean-Baptiste Bernadotte (1763–1844) and André Masséna (1758–1817) had both held the rank of sergeant-major in the royal army. Such men provided a valuable cadre for training recruits in the basics of military drill but were less likely to have expertise at manoeuvring larger bodies on the battlefield. That duty fell to officers of field grade and higher, but there were few in the army of the Republic since many had fled as a result of the Revolution.

Another problem was the influx of such a large number of recruits, initially volunteers and later conscripts. Many of these men had little or no prior experience and yet had to be trained and made battle ready in a short time. It has been suggested, however, that the raw numbers do not tell the whole story, especially for the volunteers who arrived between 1791 and early 1793. Many of the Volunteers of 1791 did, in fact, have some experience, and even the later volunteers had the advantage of being sent to the army in entire battalions. Many of these units therefore had the time to train or even do garrison duty before being asked to take part in major combat operations, sometimes as long as a year. This was clearly considered more than long enough – Napoleon would later say that infantry should be able to manoeuvre well and be able to withstand enemy fire after only three months of training.

Training began as soon as the men were mustered into the army and continued while the new recruits were marching to their depots and again when the unit moved to join an army in the field. Such training clearly made the men competent at a certain level or drill, such as the 'school of the soldier, basically, the manual of arms and the basics of marching' and the 'school of the *peloton* (platoon)', which dealt with close order drill in ranks and files, and the manoeuvres and firing scheme of an individual platoon.

The platoon was the smallest tactical unit of the battalion, and each platoon usually drew its men from one of the nine administrative companies although this was not always the case. This was similar to the earlier practice of platoon fire, which had been adopted by most European armies by the 1720s. The French had retained the earlier fire by rank system, but had gradually adopted platoon firing as well.

It is less clear how effective such training was at the level of the 'school of the battalion', which dealt with manoeuvres of the entire battalion and even the regiment. The fragile nature of French armies during the Revolutionary Wars, particularly in the dark days of late 1792 and early 1793, is demonstrated by how often French armies were panicked and broken – with the exception of the Battle of Valmy, fought on 20 September 1792. This must be due, at least in part, to the lack of cohesion at the higher levels such as battalion, regiment and beyond, which is probably a reflection of insufficient training at those levels. It may also be due to the varied nature of the recruits, some with significant military experience and others with virtually none.

Organization of the New Armies

Given the bewildering variety of units and sources of manpower, it became necessary to impose, at least in theory, a uniform organizational structure for the armies of the Republic. By 1793, there were regiments of regulars from the royal army – the *blancs*, so called because of their white Bourbon uniforms – as well as battalions of volunteers, or *fédérés*, and conscripts, or *bleus*, who were clothed, at least in theory, in the blue coats of the National Guard.

According to an ordinance of August 1793, battalion organization was to remain similar to that of the royal army prior to the Revolution, namely eight companies of line infantry, fusiliers

THE CAMP AT BOULOGNE *played an important part in the maturation of the armies of the Revolutionary period into the* Grande Armée *of Napoleon. It was particularly important for the training of French soldiers in everything from the manual of arms to grand tactics. On the right, officers and non-commissioned officers supervise soldiers' drill.*

and one company of grenadiers numbering 777 men.

Under the *Amalgame* of 21 February 1793, new units called demi-brigades were created to replace the older regiments. Each demi-brigade was to be formed from one battalion of *blancs* and two of *bleus*. There would be other *Amalgames* and organizational realignments over the next few years, and the number of demi-brigades would fluctuate between 94 and 205, eventually settling in at 100. Unlike earlier formations that were identified either by territorial names (Flanders, for example) or by personal names (the King's), all units were now given a number instead. The *Amalgame* also created 14 independent light infantry battalions; once again, the number varied, rising at one point to 35 and eventually being established at 30.The light infantry battalions were organized like their counterparts in the line, but their regular companies were known as *chasseurs* and their elite company as *carabiniers*.

Given the size of the French Army, it was also important for the armies of the Republic to have a higher level of organization. The French had been experimenting with larger combat organizations dating back to the 1740s and these reemerged during the Seven Years War. By the 1780s, the French Army created 17 permanent territorial divisions, each of which had a number of regiments permanently assigned to it. In time of war, these could serve as the basis for large combat organizations. In 1791, this system was replaced with 23 military divisions that oversaw recruiting as well.

Drawing upon this tradition, the Revolutionary armies routinely formed divisions, often made up of all arms. As early as 1792, French campaign regulations required that an army move in separate columns. When comprised of infantry, cavalry and artillery, this provided significant operational flexibility. A number of factors contributed to the development of this system. Firstly, the large number of troops required to fight on so many fronts meant that such an organizational structure provided a great degree of flexibility.

Moreover, concentrating the large number of troops gave the French a real advantage over their enemies, who were often spread out in an effort to defend key towns and fortresses. Such large numbers, however, also caused severe logistical problems for the French, especially since their logistic system could not support such troop concentrations for any length of time. The divisional system allowed the logistical burden to be spread out over a larger area, with troops concentrated only when battle was imminent.

OPPOSITE: A YOUNG NAPOLEON *shown at the Battle of Arcola in November 1796. Having seized an Austrian standard, he is depicted leading his troops in their attack across the bridge. This image by Baron Gros helped to establish the myth of Napoleon.*

Tactics of the Revolution

The tactical discussions and self-reflection of the royal army had a profound impact on the tactics used by the armies of the Republic.The generals of the Republic were still discussing the merits of *l'ordre mince*, thin linear formations, versus *l'ordre profonde*, deeper columnar formations. In addition, there were both practical and political concerns to consider.The pragmatic concern was that the soldiers of the Republic were not the long-serving regulars who had taken to the drill field at the camp at Vaussieux to experiment with the competing systems. The soldiers of the Republic were a mix of the remnants of that army and new recruits, many of whom had little or no prior service and whose training at the battalion level – so important to effective manoeuvre on the battlefield – was suspect.

On the political level, the revolutionary governments were great advocates of *l'arme blanche*, the use of cold steel to win victories. It was assumed that such weapons suited the highly motivated *citoyens* of the Republic.This sentiment was so strong that in the summer of 1792 the Minister of War, Joseph Servan de Gerby (1741–1808), advocated the organization of battalions of pikemen, and nearly half a million pikes were actually produced.

It seems clear that most of the Republic's generals preferred the system of tactics proposed by Guibert and embodied in the *Règlement du 1er Août 1791*, namely the three-rank line of *l'ordre mince*. But the *Règlement du 1er Août 1791* was not an inflexible treatise. It allowed for the use of columns for a variety of tasks, including manoeuvring to position a battalion for a firefight as well as to assault positions such as fortifications and built-up areas such as towns or villages, which might need to be taken at the point of the bayonet. One famous example of a general who intended to follow Guibert's doctrine and the *Règlement du 1er Août 1791* is General Charles François Dumouriez (1739–1823).

On 6 November 1792, at the Battle of Jemappes, Dumouriez's 40,000 troops attacked 13,000 entrenched Austrians. The French advanced in open columns and began deploying into line as they approached the enemy positions. The French centre was roughly handled by the Austrians as its columns attempted to deploy into line under fire, but their left drove the Austrians from their positions. Such tactics may have been beyond the level of training that the French forces possessed at the time, although changing formation under the enemy's guns is difficult for even well-trained troops, not to mention ill advised. But Jemappes also demonstrated other influences on the tactics of the Revolutionary forces. First is the extensive use of light troops operating in open order. On the French right, the terrain was ill suited to the use of heavy columns.

As a result, the French troops there advanced in skirmish order. This shows the willingness of French commanders to modify the *Règlement du 1er Août 1791* to fit their capabilities, and the use of entire battalions and demi-brigades deployed in open order is a perfect example.

Light Troops

Most of the French treatises pre-dating the Revolution are relatively silent on the use of light troops, focusing instead on the line-versus-column question. Yet revolutionary armies made extensive use of this formation. This can be viewed as an example of tactical flexibility based on the capabilities of the available troops.

Actually, a screen of skirmishers meets the spirit of Guibert's doctrine in that it is an imperfect linear formation – and one that might be employed by troops who are highly motivated, rather than well trained. Jemappes also demonstrated the advantage to be gained by superior numbers. Dumouriez was able to concentrate more than three times the number of his enemy. In combination, these two elements allowed French forces to keep up near constant pressure on their enemies at the tactical level. Unlike the eighteenth-century model of grand tactics, in which individual units were not considered to matter, this system understood the significance of individual units, in differing formations, often fitting the terrain or circumstances, and fielded in sufficient numbers to provide critical mass at a decisive point on the battlefield.

Another example of the flexibility of Republican forces can be seen in the tactics developed to deal with the uprisings in the west of France. In addition to fighting the standing armies of states such as Austria, Prussia, Russia and Great Britain, the Republic also had to deal with irregular forces raised by various counter-revolutionary factions in areas such as the Vendée and Brittany. The insurgents were initially poorly armed but became better armed as they defeated the first units sent against them – ill-trained units of National Guardsmen and hastily raised units of regulars. Later units were better trained and they were able to defeat the rebels, whether in open battle or in the attack or defence of towns or cities.

However, in what would foreshadow a number of actions against irregulars in places such as Spain and the Tyrol, the army struggled against the ambushes and small actions perpetrated by the insurgents. Despite the fact that the French Army had considerable experience of irregular warfare, gained in regions such as North America, there was no commensurate interest in the study of tactics of 'the little war'.

Tactics and doctrine were developed in the course of the conflict. For example, General Louis Lazare Hoche (1768–97) wrote and promulgated his *Instructions for those Troops Employed in Fighting the Chouans*, the latter term used for the rebels in Brittany. These instructions emphasized the importance of unit cohesion, reconnaissance and force protection against the rebels, who often used numbers to overwhelm small, disorganized units of regular troops. On the tactical level, the instructions emphasized linear tactics to bring the maximum amount of firepower to bear against the rebels. Indeed, Hoche mandated not only that his troops fight in a line but that it be a two-rank line to make use of all of the battalions' manpower in the combat. Skirmishers were also to be used, but in small numbers and always supported by formed troops, thereby ensuring that they were not lured too far from their lines and cut off.

Finally, the Revolutionary armies made extensive use of artillery, as advocated by Guibert and especially Chevalier du Teil. This was possible thanks to the work of Gribeauval, who had introduced lighter artillery pieces, and the fact that the artillery, of all the combat arms, had probably weathered the strains of the Revolution the best. It had, for example, retained a larger percentage of its officer corps than either the infantry or cavalry.

Artillery Innovations

The revolutionary forces built on earlier improvements and theories – and made innovations of its own. One was the reintroduction of battalion guns. Two of these light 4-pounder cannon were attached to each infantry battalion. While these may have impeded the speed of the battalion, they did potentially add to the unit's firepower. Equally importantly, they reduced the fragility and vulnerability of the battalion, both by boosting morale and by serving to deter pursuit in

A STYLIZED PRINT *showing the Battle of Rivoli. Here, French reinforcements arrive at the key moment and engage in combat. To the left, Austrian prisoners are escorted from the battlefield. During the battle, more than 3000 Austrians were taken prisoner.*

the even that the unit panicked. The second innovation was the introduction of horse artillery. While very expensive to maintain, both in terms of horseflesh and logistical requirements, the horse batteries provided significant offensive punch.

Initially it was thought that they might stiffen the cavalry, much as battalion guns did for the infantry, but soon these gunners considered themselves to be an elite unit.Their speed, mobility and *élan* allowed them to provide direct fire support and, in the words of General Foy (1775–1825), a horse artilleryman himself, 'to get up close and shoot fast'.

The armies of the Revolution were thus able to draw on nearly a century of military self-reflection and intellectual developments. But, they could do so only in a loose fashion since many of the developments were intended for the old royal army. What made the armies of the Republic successful, at least in part, was their ability to be flexible and to modify these developments as the capabilities of their forces allowed.

'The men...who had fought for nearly five hours with distinguished bravery, were much dispersed by the nature of the ground, and...eagerly pursued the enemy...where they were attacked by a few horsemen: when these men returned, calling out "French cavalry", a sudden panic spread like wildfire.'

– COL. THOMAS GRAHAM, OBSERVING THE AUSTRIANS AT RIVOLI

The Battle of Rivoli: 14–15 January 1797

In November 1796, the Directory, created by the constitution of the previous year, hoped to end the war in Italy on favourable terms. As a result, negotiations took place, but any hopes of ending the war were dashed over a single issue, the fortress town of Mantua. In September, the Austrian Field Marshal Count Dagobert von Wurmser (1724–97) was holed up with more than 18,000 troops. These troops were besieged by elements of Napoleon's Army of Italy. Mantua was the strongest of the so-called Quadrilateral Fortresses used by the Austrians to control northern Italy, and was the last major town controlled by the Austrians. As part of the terms for negotiation, the Austrians demanded that they be allowed to reinforce the garrison, terms that were unacceptable to the French. Negotiations therefore broke down and both sides prepared for war.

The Austrians were determined to lift the siege and reinforced their army in northern Italy under Baron General Jozsef Alvinczy von Børberek. Alvinczy's forces were brought up to a strength of 50,000 men. To counter this, Napoleon had more than 55,000 men, but he was in a much weaker position. Firstly, he needed to detach over 10,000 men for the siege and a further 10,000 for occupation duty in scattered garrisons, leaving him a field force of some 34,000 men for the upcoming operations. Secondly, Napoleon did not know when or in which direction Alvinczy would attack, and so he was forced to further divide his army into three separate combat divisions. General Pierre François Charles Augereau (1757–1816) had nearly 9000 men at Legnano in order to hold the lower Adige. General André Masséna had a similarly sized force at Verona to protect the upper Adige. General Barthelemy Catherine Joubert (1769–99) had a division of 10,000 men, placed north of Rivoli. Given the disparity in numbers and a lack of intelligence concerning the Austrians' plans, it was impossible for Napoleon to take the offensive, and these three divisions allowed him to cover the three main routes that Alvinczy might have taken to relieve Mantua.

On 7 January, Napoleon left his headquarters and headed to Bologna to deal with some diplomatic and military matters relating to the arrival of 6000 papal troops in Tuscany. He seems

French Infantryman (1797)

This French infantryman is representative of the soldiers who fought in the armies of the Republic in Germany and Italy during the latter part of the 1790s. While the ability of French armies to live off the land, and make use of 'requisitioning' for basic necessities such as food, allowed them incredible speed and mobility, it did cause problems in maintaining a proper uniform. Items such as trousers and shoes were often the first to wear out and, as a result, this unfortunate individual is forced to march barefoot. He maintains his coat and plumed bicorne, which distinguish him as a grenadier in a line unit or carabinier in a light infantry battalion, although he lacks other regulation distinctions of such elite soldiers, such as the sabre. Also, like many Republican soldiers, he does not have a scabbard for his bayonet, with the result that this weapon was permanently fixed. He carries a number of non-regulation pieces of kit, including the spoon carried in front of the cockade on his bicorne.

Battle of Rivoli

14–15 January 1797

In January 1797, an army of some 50,000 Austrians under Baron General Jozsef Alvinczy advanced against Napoleon's Army of Italy in order to relieve a besieged army in Mantua, one of their key fortresses in northern Italy. The Austrians launched a complicated assault with six separate columns against Joubert's troops, who occupied high ground. The numerical superiority of the Austrians allowed them to outflank the French left, but they were countered by the arrival of fresh troops. The battle went back and forth along the heights, with Austrian troops finally capturing a gorge on the French right wing, although a column trying to cut off the French rear was defeated by troops arriving to reinforce Napoleon. The Austrians on the heights pushed forward, but were disordered by their pursuit and the terrain; a timely French counterattack pushed them off the heights. The next day, Napoleon took a part of his army to support his forces under attack from the west, while Joubert defeated the disordered Austrians at Rivoli.

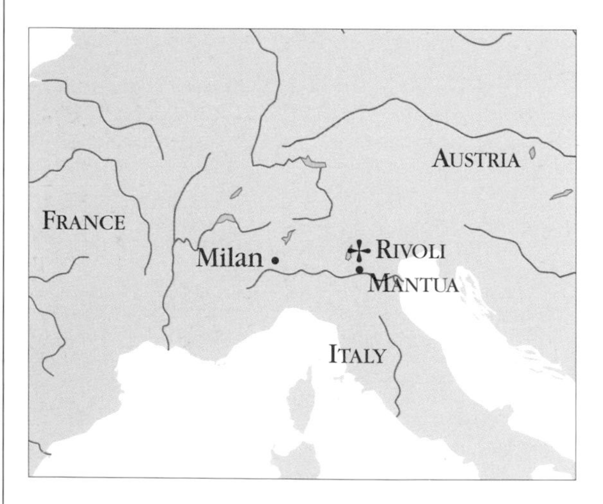

The Austrians under Alvinczy collected their forces to attack Napoleon's forces in Italy, thereby relieving one of their armies trapped in the key strategic fortress of Mantua.

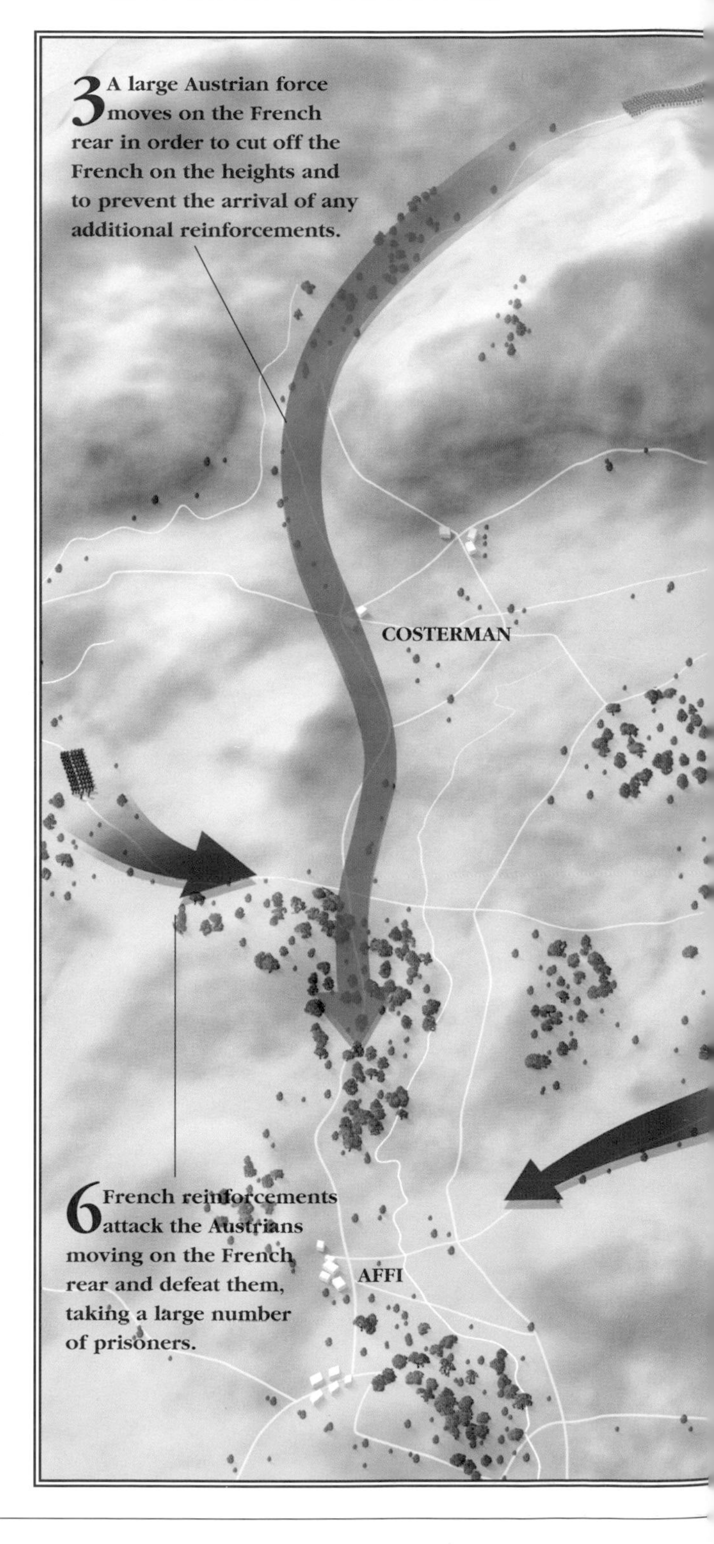

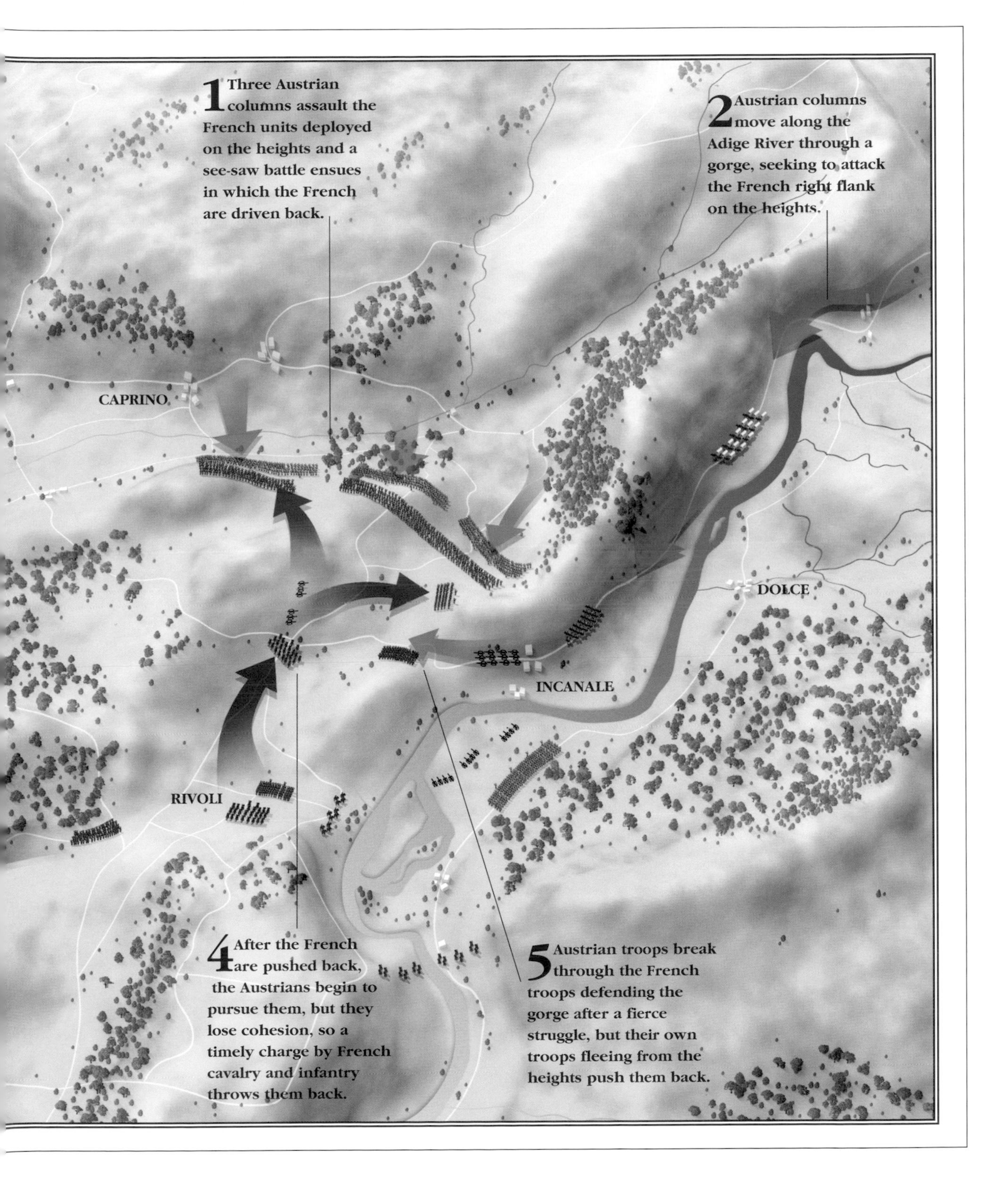
1 Three Austrian columns assault the French units deployed on the heights and a see-saw battle ensues in which the French are driven back.
2 Austrian columns move along the Adige River through a gorge, seeking to attack the French right flank on the heights.
CAPRINO
DOLCE
INCANALE
RIVOLI
4 After the French are pushed back, the Austrians begin to pursue them, but they lose cohesion, so a timely charge by French cavalry and infantry throws them back.
5 Austrian troops break through the French troops defending the gorge after a fierce struggle, but their own troops fleeing from the heights push them back.

AT THE BATTLE OF RIVOLI, *General Joubert seized a musket and took the lead of some of his troops at a key point in the conflict. This allowed the French to enfilade retreating Austrian troops, turning their retreat into a rout.*

to have believed that the Austrians were not yet in a position to launch their relief expedition since it seems unlikely that he would have deigned to leave otherwise. But on that very day the Austrians did indeed put their troops into motion. Their plan was for the main army of 28,000 men under Alvinczy himself to come down the Adige valley from the north, forcing the narrow bottleneck in the mountains near Rivoli. There were also two secondary, and diversionary, efforts under Generals Provero and Bajalich, totalling some 15,000 men. Although they made slow progress on 11 January, the columns of Provero and Bajalich were skirmishing with Augereau's troops, and on the same day Alvinczy made his push south towards Rivoli. The news reached Napoleon, who had just completed his business by signing a convention with the Duke of Tuscany. He immediately returned to his headquarters, from where he proceeded to Verona and found Masséna under attack. He also learned that enemy troops were bearing down on Joubert's division north of Rivoli. Napoleon was not yet ready, it seems, to commit all his forces to face these attacks, although he did call in additional troops from some of his smaller outlying detachments. Instead, he wrote to Joubert, asking his commander if he was faced by more than 9000 enemy troops.

On the morning of 13 January, he heard from Joubert that the Austrians had attacked in force, forcing Joubert to retire to Rivoli. Napoleon now ordered him to prepare a defence and, at the same time, ordered Masséna to send troops to Rivoli, and to proceed there with all haste. Napoleon himself arrived at 2.00 a.m. on the morning of 14 January, finding Joubert in church, writing his orders for the day. Napoleon decided to prepare for an immediate attack.

In the meantime, the Austrians were encamped, awaiting the assault. Alvinczy, who had a love of manoeuvres of Frederickian complexity, had divided his force into six separate assault columns – unfortunately his army was not that of Frederick the Great. Three columns, under Generals Lipthay, Köblös, and Ocksay, totalling 12,000 men, would attack the height to which the French had retreated directly. Two columns under Generals Quosdanovich and Vukassovich, numbering 15,000 men, were to march along both banks of the Adige and attempt to scale the gorge on to the heights. Finally, a sixth column of 4500 troops under General Lusignon was to undertake a lengthy flanking maneouvre along the French right, coming in on the rear of Napoleon's army and cutting off their escape.

Napoleon Deploys

Napoleon and Joubert made a reconnaissance that night and deployed their forces. One demi-brigade, the 39th, which had fewer than 1000 men, was sent to hold the gorge against Quosdanovich's column of more than 8000. Fortunately, the 39th was able to occupy some field fortifications and had artillery support as well. The remainder of Joubert's troops, including 18 artillery pieces, were on the heights, and attacked the Austrians at first light. Despite being outnumbered by a factor of 4:3, the French attack went well at first, with the French capturing a key village from the Austrians.

But as the attack slowed, the Austrians were able to attack the exposed left on the French line, which was formed by the 85th Demi-Brigade. This unit had been severely handled by the Austrians back in November and was afterwards shamed by Napoleon. Despite this, they broke and fled again. Fortunately, before the situation became hopeless, General Masséna arrived with nearly 6000 reinforcements, who were intended to protect the vulnerable left flank. Indeed, they were able to stabilize the left side of the line.

But things were still difficult in the now exposed French centre. Here, the 14th Demi-Brigade put up a valiant defence against some excellent Austrian troops, including a battalion of grenadiers and one from the elite Hoch und Deutschmeister Regiment. In a famous episode, the Austrians overran one of the French batteries in front of the 14th. A French officer cried: 'Fourteenth! Will you let them take your guns?' This inspired the 14th Demi-Brigade to charge in with the bayonet and recapture the battery.

On the French right, the 39th, now under bombardment from Vukassovich's column, were

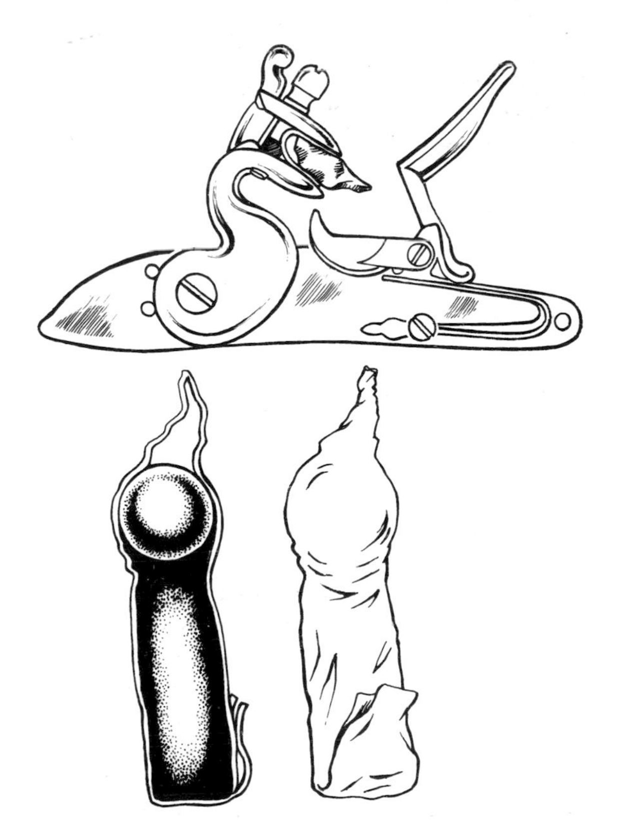

THE STANDARD INFANTRY *firearm throughout the period was the smoothbore flintlock musket. The musket was fired when the flint struck the frizzen cover, pushing it open and igniting the priming powder in the pan. Most armies used prepared cartridges to increase the speed of loading. In order to load the weapon, a soldier bit the cartridge, poured some powder in the pan and then closed the frizzen. The remainder of the powder, the ball and the paper were loaded via the muzzle and rammed into place.*

A VERY HEROIC PORTRAYAL OF NAPOLEON *at the Battle of Rivoli on 14 January 1797, where he is directing the action. In the background is the gorge forced by the Austrians earlier in the morning but later recaptured by the French.*

finally forced from their defensive works. This opened the French right flank as well, although the difficult nature of the terrain slowed the advance of the Austrian forces; a number of forces were even driven back. Fortunately, most of the French units were able to rally once they had disengaged from the combat. A house provided with a large enclosure served as a rallying point for the units. And there were some reinforcements recently arrived from Lake Garda.

Just as things looked bleak for the French, they got worse. Volleys were heard from the French rear – Lusignon's column had finally made its way around the French rear, blocking not only the line of retreat but also the route that much-needed reinforcements would take. Some of Napoleon officers were dismayed, but Napoleon is reported to have said simply: 'They are ours.' Napoleon and Masséna addressed some of the newly arrived reinforcements, encouraging them before they moved off to engage Lusignon's column. On the plateau, the French were able to sway the situation in their favour.

A small body of 200 cavalry launched a desperate attack against the Austrians troops, who were now pushing through the French centre. The Austrians were tired, and had lost much of their cohesion now that they were in pursuit. As a result, they were easily overthrown by this small body of cavalry. The panic that ensued spread from one column to another, some even fleeing into the gorge, thereby pushing back the troops trying to ascend the heights. This allowed Joubert to lead a regiment to the edge of the gorge and pour fire on to the troops below, driving them back. Shortly thereafter, fresh French reinforcements arrived, trapping Lusignon's hapless column between two enemy bodies. This tide had quickly turned in Napoleon's favour.

The battle had been won by the late afternoon, but Napoleon was still in difficult straits. News reached him that Provera was pushing forward, so he and Masséna's exhausted troops were forced to leave the field to deal with this new threat. Joubert would have to finish the battle the next day. Although Alvinczy still had a large number of troops at his disposal, his troops had been driven off the heights, so their morale must have been very low. The next day, Joubert won a signal victory.

'Nothing could shake them. They had no other memories, no other future, except warfare. They never spoke of anything else. Their officers were either worthy of them or became it. For to exert one's rank over such men one had to be able to show them one's wounds and cite oneself as an example.'

– Philippe-Paul, Comte de Ségur, refering to the veterans of the Grand Armée

Infantry in the Age of Napoleon

The various elements of the French Revolutionary armies' way of war reached their apogee under the direction of a brilliant young officer who had risen quickly through the ranks, Napoleon Bonaparte. A captain at the beginning of 1793, he was promoted to brigadier general by the end of the year for his pivotal role in the siege of Toulon. In October 1795, he proved his political reliability to the government, the National Convention, when he dispersed an angry mob with the legendary 'whiff of grapeshot'. By February of the following year, he had been named to command the Republic's Army of Italy, and it was there that he brought together the various tactical and operational innovations of the Revolutionary armies into a truly impressive system of warfare. These campaigns are particularly noteworthy given that he achieved so much in what was a secondary theatre of operations; the primary focus of the Republic was Germany. In a series of campaigns and battles beginning in March 1796, Napoleon defeated the Austrians and within a year had forced them to sign an armistice.

After his successful campaigns in Italy, Napoleon sailed for Egypt, where he hoped to win glory and threaten British possessions in Asia. He had some local successes, but his strategic position was untenable since his British enemies had virtually unchallenged control of maritime commons. He returned to France and began his rise to absolute power, taking part in a coup against the Directory in 1799. Subsequently, he served as First Consul of France. Shortly thereafter, Napoleon fought in his second Italian campaign, where he won a signal, if close-run, victory over the Austrians on 14 June 1800. Peace with Austria followed the next year and with England in 1802.

During this period, Napoleon demonstrated that he understood how the various changes wrought by the Revolutionary Wars could be used to greatest effect. In the Italian campaign, he saw, and used, the potential of the newly organized combat divisions. Napoleon organized the Army of Italy into four large combat divisions and several smaller units. The size and make-up of these divisions varied from campaign to campaign, depending on the situation. Moreover, these divisions allowed him to utilize the two methods of manoeuvre that would become his hallmarks. The first was his use of interior lines, which allowed him to concentrate his forces quickly, often against superior numbers of the enemy. The second was the *manoeuvre sur les derrières*, an outflanking movement designed to bring his forces against the flank or rear of the enemy army. This latter manoeuvre was, in part, due to the poverty of the Revolutionary armies, which did not have the supply trains that were common in other European armies of the time. While this forced the French to live off the land, Napoleon recognized that a system of 'requisitioning' gave him a much higher degree of mobility than his adversaries.

He used this operational mobility to great benefit, often striking his enemy long before they were able to concentrate for battle. Some of the operational principles used by Napoleon, however, also show a pre-Revolutionary influence, tracing their roots to the work of earlier military *philosophes*. One clear influence is General Pierre de Bourcet (1700–80), whose work on the planning of campaigns had such an impact that Napoleon often quoted him verbatim when discussing the importance of planning operations.

L'Ordre Mixte

Tactically, Napoleon likewise drew on the developing 'revolutionary art of war'. One of the tactical formations used extensively by Napoleon was *l'ordre mixte*, or mixed order, which combined lines and columns. Indeed, it has been seen as a way of coming to a compromise after the lengthy debate between the linear battle formation of *l'ordre mince* and the columns of *l'ordre profonde*. This was, of course, not really his innovation, since Guibert had certainly hinted at it. Moreover, one can see in a variety of earlier battles a kind of *ordre mixte* deployed by the French. In it purest form, *l'ordre mixte* would have had a demi-brigade of three battalions formed up in two columns, with the third battalion arrayed in a line between the columns.

This formation provided significant firepower from the battalion in line and at the same time allowed for shock from the columns while also protecting the vulnerable flanks of the battalion in line. But this formation required a high level of training and proficiency, as detailed in the *Règlement du 1er Août 1791*. A more informal version therefore appeared in earlier battles, one in which the battalion in line was replaced by a looser firing line made up of troops formed in skirmish order.

Napoleon was, however, closer to the ideal version of *l'ordre mixte* in a number of his battles during the Italian campaign. At Arcola, for example, General Pierre François Charles Augereau's division was formed up in a single line of battle. This was formed of battalions in both columns and in lines, with a battalion or two in line placed in between the columns. This type of deployment may have played an important role in the battle, since it provided not only a great deal of firepower but also manoeuvrability in the form of the columns. Indeed, at one point in the battle, when the Austrians were beginning to push through the French centre, Napoleon was able to order one of his demi-brigades to wheel in and attack the flank of the advancing Austrians, thereby halting the advance. This type of manoeuvre is likely to have been carried out initially by the demi-brigade's

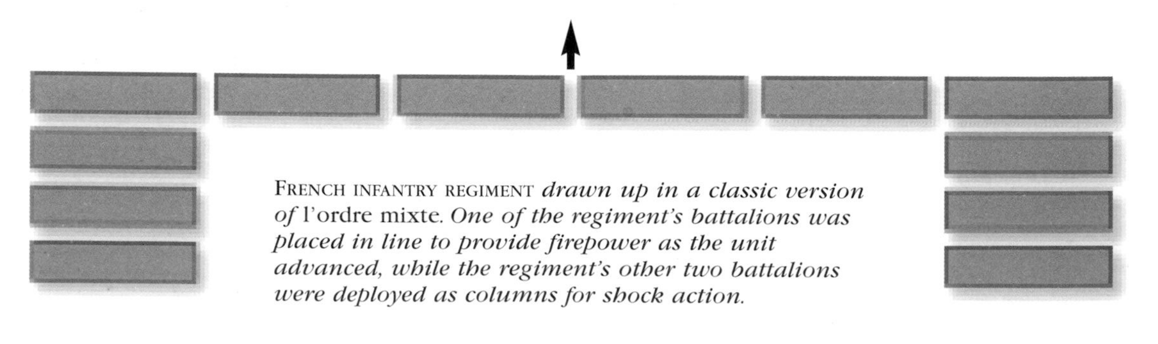

FRENCH INFANTRY REGIMENT *drawn up in a classic version of* l'ordre mixte. *One of the regiment's battalions was placed in line to provide firepower as the unit advanced, while the regiment's other two battalions were deployed as columns for shock action.*

columns, since these would have been quicker in carrying out a wheel than the battalions in line.

By the time of the battle of Marengo, we see demi-brigades under General Louis Charles Desaix (1768–1800) formed in classic mixed order with a central battalion flanked by two columns, and these units were instrumental in turning back the attack of the Austrians later in the day. No doubt one reason Napoleon was able to employ *l'ordre mixte* more and more frequently was that the proficiency of troops in performing drill manual manoeuvre improved as the Army of Italy campaigned together as a cohesive unit under his successful and energetic command.

The real leap forward, however, in the development of Napoleonic fighting techniques, both at the operational and the tactical level, would come after Napoleon had risen to become the undisputed master of France. In 1802, he was named Consul for Life, and later, on 2 December 1804, he was crowned Emperor of France. This coincided with a time of relative peace, which allowed him to codify and institutionalize his ideas about warfare.

The Napoleonic synthesis embodied itself in the *Grande Armée*. This was the main French military force, including the forces of allied states, and was always under Napoleon's direct command.This force was made up of several *corps d' armée*, and invariably included the Imperial Guard, which grew from a relatively small formation of four infantry regiments, two cavalry regiments, and some artillery to a virtual army within an army by the time of the 1812 campaign.

Le Corps d' Armée

At the operational level, one of the most important developments was the creation of *le corps d' armée*. This administrative unit grew out of the divisional system that had been employed by the armies of the Republic. Indeed, although it was larger, it did share much with the earlier divisions. *Le corps d' armée* was a combined arms unit that included the infantry, cavalry and artillery as well as necessary support units such as medical personnel and engineers.

The various *corps d' armée*, like the divisions employed by Napoleon in the army of Italy, were not of uniform composition. The make-up of a *corps d' armée* could vary with its mission and the overall strategic situation. Numbers could vary greatly. In 1805, for example, the largest corps numbered some 41,000 men while the smallest had only 14,000. On the eve of the 1809 campaign, III Corps, under Marshal Louis Nicholas Davout (1770–1823), mustered more than 60,000 men while VIII Corps, under General Dominique Joseph René Vandamme (1770–1830), had fewer than 13,000 soldiers. Nevertheless, some general points can be made concerning the organization of a 'typical' *corps d' armée*.

The heart of every *corps d' armée* was its large infantry contingent. Normally this would be based around two to four divisions, each of two or more

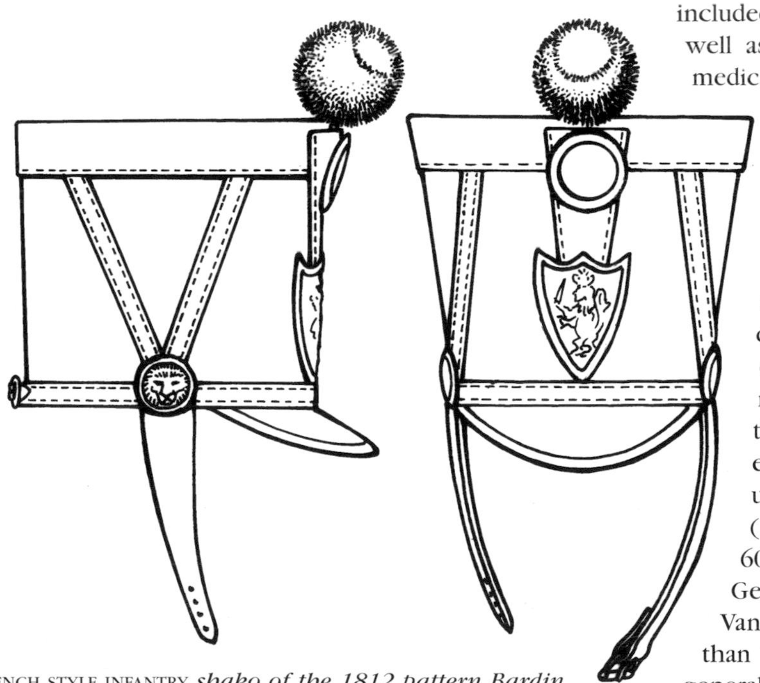

FRENCH STYLE INFANTRY *shako of the 1812 pattern Bardin regulations. This particular specimen belonged to a unit from Hesse-Darmstadt, since the shako plate carries the Hessian lion. The shako was made of leather and felt, and carried a pompom – in French units, the pompom's colour denoted the company.*

brigades, which in turn had at least two regiments. Moreover, each division had its own integral artillery contingent of medium field guns. *Le corps d' armée* also possessed its own cavalry, either a brigade or division of light cavalry such as chasseurs, hussars or lancers. In addition to the artillery assigned to the divisions, there was also a corps artillery park that usually included at least one battery of heavy-artillery 12-pounders. Finally, there was a variety of support troops, including pioneers, a pontoon or bridging unit, artificers, a medical company and a small unit of *gendarmerie* to act as military police for the corps. *Le corps d' armée* became the smallest operational unit and was designed to be able to operate on its own or as part of a larger organization of several corps.

This organization allowed Napoleon a great deal of operational flexibility as well as mobility. Napoleon could move his various *corps d' armée* along different routes, minimizing his logistical problems, yet have them concentrate for battle.

Moreover, a *corps d' armée* could, if necessary, be detailed to fight on its own since it possessed all of the combat and supporting arms to fight a

DURING THE BATTLE AT ABOUKIR, *French troops launched a night attack against the British. The British line was hard pressed by French infantry and cavalry. Here, the 42nd Regiment, the Black Watch, launches a bayonet attack on the flank of one of the French columns. In the event, they pursued too far and were themselves attacked and badly mauled by French cavalry later in the battle.*

Private, Chasseurs à Pied

The two regiments of Chasseurs à pied *of Napoleon's Old Guard were the elite of the* Grande Armée. *Along with the two regiments of Grenadiers, they were nicknamed 'the Grumblers', (*les grognards*). Each of these men had to possess at least 10 years' service, have served in the field during several campaigns and be at least 1.7m (5ft 6in) in height to qualify for service in one of the two regiments of Old Guard* Chasseurs. *Moreover, each member of the Guard had to be personally approved by the emperor himself.*

They received the best uniforms, equipment and supplies and were the Grande Armée*'s knockout punch in battle. The uniforms of the* Chasseurs à pied *were very similar to those of their colleagues in the Grenadiers. The main differences were the lack of a front plate on the bearskin bonnet, along with a plume and epaulettes in green and red to mark them as elite light infantrymen.*

battle – as, indeed, Davout's corps did at Auerstädt in October 1806.

One important thing to remember about *le corps d' armée*, and something that distinguishes it from the earlier divisions of the Republic, is that it was not only an all-arms organization, but also possessed a mass that the earlier units did not, which thus gave it a sustainability in combat. The cessation of major combat operations on the continent after 1801 gave Napoleon and the French Army an opportunity to create a formal military establishment for his infantry.

The demi-brigade was one again replaced by the regiment in 1803, although still bearing numbers as opposed to the older regional or personal names. In 1804, the number of regiments was established at 90 *Régiments d'Infanterie de Ligne* (line regiments) and 26 *Régiments d'Infanterie Légère* (light infantry). Until 1803, the organization of the regiments remained relatively constant, with three battalions per regiment, each of eight companies of regulars (fusiliers and *chasseurs* for line and light regiments respectively) and one elite company (grenadiers for the line and *carabiniers* for the light infantry battalions).

In September of that year, Napoleon initiated a change in the battalion organization. The number of companies was decreased from nine to eight, and one company was also designated as a 'light' company of *voltigeurs*. For many units, this seems to have been a mere formality, as they had already designated one of their companies to serve as skirmishers on a regular basis.

Finally, there would be one more internal organizational change in 1808, when regiments were, in theory, to maintain their strength at four field battalions and one depot battalion. In each battalion, the number of companies would be reduced still further to six: four companies of fusiliers and *chasseurs*, depending on the type of regiment, one of grenadiers, or *carabiniers*, and one of *voltigeurs*. Depot battalions had no elite companies. Interestingly, this reflects a steady increase in the proportion of elite troops within the battalion – 11 per cent in the nine-company battalion, 25 per cent in the eight-company battalion, and 33 per cent in the six-company battalion.

Training Camps

The army also had the opportunity to train under peacetime conditions rather than attempting to master the complexities of the manoeuvres described in the *Règlement du 1er Août 1791* while on campaign. This was particularly true from the summer of 1803, when Napoleon activated *L'Armée des Côtes de l'Océan* in preparation for renewed hostilities with Britain. These troops, who would later form the basis of the *Grande Armée* in the great campaigns of 1805–1807, were encamped in six major concentrations along the Atlantic coast, around towns such as Boulogne, Brest and Utrecht. For nearly two years, the various camps, which later formed the different *corps d' armée* of the *Grande Armée*, underwent a rigorous regimen of drill and observation. Each camp was commanded by one of Napoleon's senior officers, who was

AFTER 1803, *every French infantry battalion was authorized to establish a* voltigeur *company. These companies included the smallest and most agile men in the battalion and were expected to form the unit's skirmish screen. They were marked by the green and yellow plumes and cording on the shako and similarly coloured epaulettes.*

charged with training the men. During this period, units spent time drilling and learning the various portions of the *Règlement du 1er Août 1791,* from the manual of arms to the manoeuvres of their battalions. To ensure that training was to a high standard, inspectors were sent out to review the troops as they went through their various tactical evolutions and to quiz non-commissioned and junior officers on their knowledge of the *Règlement du 1er Août 1791.* In addition, there were regularly scheduled meetings at the regimental level, where the regulations and instructions of senior officers were discussed and studied. It was expected that the junior and non-commissioned officers would pass on this knowledge to their men during training exercises.

Weekly routines were instituted for each camp. At Boulogne, for example, two days per week were given over to the school of the battalion and target practice - an exercise that was unknown in armies of the period, with the exception of the British. Three days were spent at higher-level manoeuvres involving the various divisions of the corps, while Sunday was reserved for exercises by the corps as a whole. Twice per month, manoeuvres were conducted that involved what today would be called 'live fire exercises', using combat munitions against targets.

As well as the types of training to be expected for infantrymen, the soldiers at Boulogne and other camps were preparing for the invasion of England. As such, men were also expected to learn the rudiments of embarkation and boat-handling. Some troops were also instructed in manning the ships' guns. Napoleon was clearly serious that this army was destined for the invasion of England, and insisted that the men go to sea for manoeuvres in their vessels.

'We camped at the port of Ambleteuse, where a fine camp was formed; General Oudinot was in command of us with 12,000 grenadiers, who formed part of the reserve force. And every day we drilled and drilled. We were brigaded for training in embarkation.'

– Jean-Roch Coignet, Grenadier of the Guard on the Camp at Boulogne

On one occasion, ignoring a warning from his admirals of an impending storm, he ordered 20 sloops out to sea. The result was the loss of many of the craft and 2000 soldiers and sailors.

Such constant drilling over a period of two years might have been dangerously monotonous. To keep up morale, Napoleon made efforts to visit the camps and also held large-scale reviews that were great military spectacles filled with pomp and ceremony. On one famous visit in August of 1804, some 1300 drummers beat the *Aux Champs* to assemble the entire army. After the army was in formation, Napoleon distributed the *Legion d'Honneur* to deserving officers and men, the first mass award of those awards. As he said, 'it is with baubles that men are led'.

The intensive training that the nascent *Grande Armée* received while stationed along the Atlantic coast paid huge dividends when the army was deployed to fight in central Europe in the latter part of 1805 and throughout 1807. One thing that most clearly differentiated the *Grande Armée* from its adversaries was its training. In particular, the manoeuvres and evolutions that had been carried out at both the tactical and grand tactical levels gave French troops a decided advantage in battlefield flexibility. One major benefit was that the French units were more capable of coordinating different formations within their command structure as the situations dictated.

During the campaigns of 1806–07, it was not uncommon for the battalions within a French brigade to operate in a variety of formations as dictated by battlefield conditions. For example, if a brigade of four regiments, with a total of eight battalions, was required to assault a defended position, it would not have been problematic for

Prussian Infantryman

This Prussian infantryman is a member of the 1st Silesian Infantry Regiment. He wears the field uniform that the Prussian Army adopted in 1808, which consisted of a dark blue coat, the Kollet, with collar and cuffs in the provincial colour, and shoulder straps that distinguished individual regiments from the province. His shako and pompom are covered with an oilskin cover in the Prussian style. His white belts mark him as a member of one of the two musketeer battalions in the regiment rather than a light infantryman from the regiment's fusilier battalion. He also carries his greatcoat rolled over his left shoulder and supported by a leather sleeve as protection from sabre cuts. He also carries a short sabre, which was more for decoration than combat.

that brigade to deploy one or two of its battalions, and its *voltiguers*, as a skirmish screen for three or four battalions in assault columns. The remainder of the brigade could easily have been kept in reserve or even deployed in line to provide fire support or flank protection for the assault force. The key is that the brigade commander could assign tactical formations for each individual unit under his command without any concern for maintaining an artificial integrity of formation at the regimental or brigade level.

The Battle of Auerstädt: 14 October 1806

King Frederick William of Prussia was in a difficult position in the summer of 1806. He had remained neutral during the great campaign in 1805 and had, in fact, allied with France in exchange for Prussian occupation of the Electorate of Hanover in north Germany, which was dynastically tied to the English crown. It did not, however, take long for Frederick William to learn that his alliance with France would last only as long as Napoleon willed it. In early 1896, he learned that the terms of the alliance were to be renegotiated: Prussia would retain control of Hanover but at the expense of other territories in Germany and Switzerland. A few month's later, Frederick William heard that Napoleon was in negotiations with England, offering the return of Hanover, now occupied by Prussia, in exchange for a peace accord. This would leave Prussia with less territory than she had held before her alliance with the French Emperor. The situation was obviously unsatisfactory, and Frederick William was now convinced that war was the only option by hawks within his government and by his wife Queen Louisa, whom Napoleon called 'the only man in Prussia'.

In July 1806, the Prussians forged a new alliance, this time with Russia, and began to mobilize their army on 10 August. The French did not react to the mobilization for nearly a month. The emperor finally ordered reservists to be called to the colours and new groups of conscripts to be called up for training. In the middle of September, Napoleon learned that the Prussians had begun to occupy Saxony to prevent that state from joining the new *Rheinbund*, an organization of German states under Napoleon's protection. On 26

OPPOSITE: MARSHAL LOUIS NICHOLAS DAVOUT *had served in the army as an officer before the Revolution. He served with distinction during the Revolutionary Wars. Perhaps his greatest moment was at the Battle of Auerstädt, where he and his III Corps defeated the main Prussian Army.*

September, Frederick William sent an ultimatum to Napoleon, demanding he evacuate Germany or face war. But the die had already been cast, since Napoleon had left to take command of the *Grande Armée* in Germany five days earlier. Although Napoleon knew of the alliance with Russia, he also recognized that it would be some time before any Russian troops would be available to aid the Prussians in the upcoming conflict.

On 6 October, the Emperor took command of the *Grande Armée* at Bamberg and quickly began to move against the Prussians. The commander, the Duke of Brunswick, had intended to move against the French before they could mass, but now the tables had been turned on him. Most of the Prussian forces were concentrated around Erfuhrt, on the outskirts of the Thuringian Forest. Napoleon had been advancing with his various *corps de armée* along a direct route towards Leipzig, from where he would continue on to Berlin. His army was arrayed in the *bataillon carré*, the battalion square that provided him with incredible operational flexibility.

On 13 October, when two corps on Napoleon's left flank, those of Lannes and Augereau, encountered the Prussian forces in the vicinity of Jena, the battalion square allowed Napoleon quickly to change his line of advance by 90 degrees and concentrate most of his army against what he believed to be the main force at Jena.

To crush the Prussians completely, Napoleon ordered Davout's III *corps d'armée* to move to Naumburg and then to move against Apolda and the Prussians' rear. Bernadotte's I *corps d'armée* was ordered to move to Dornberg, securing a line of communication between the main army and Davout, and then joining Davout's advance to cut off the Prussians' retreat. In an appendix to his original operational order, Napoleon suggested that Davout and Bernadotte march together. At 1:30 a.m. on 14 October, Davout met with Bernadotte to propose this, but the latter chose to

ignore him and march to Dornberg via Camburg instead. This decision would leave Marshal Davout and his III *corps d'armée* of 26,000 men to face the main Prussian Army, which numbered perhaps 63,000 men.

Davout set off with his corps in the direction of Apolda before 5:30 a.m. His progress was rather slow since there was heavy fog and the terrain was a difficult climb. Moreover, he was without the great majority of his corps cavalry, three regiments of *chasseurs à cheval,* who were off on a raid in search of horses. The entirety of Davout's scouts consisted of only 80 troopers, probably a single company from the 1st *Chasseurs à cheval* under the command of his *premier-aide-de-camp*, Colonel Bourke. At approximately 7 a.m., there

Battle of Auerstädt

14 October 1806

In the summer of 1806, Prussia forged an alliance with Russia against France and by September war was imminent. Napoleon took the initiative and mobilized the *Grande Armée*, moving towards Leipzig with the intent of marching against Berlin. In the course of this advance two of his corps contacted the Prussians and he gave orders to engage the Prussians at Jena. But Napoleon had contacted only a small portion of the Prussian Army with his main force. In the meantime, a *corps d'armée* under Marshal Davout - which had been sent to attack the enemy's rear - met the main Prussian Army under the Duke of Brunswick at Auerstädt. The battle was essentially a meeting engagement as units from both sides arrived on the battlefield. The French troops formed around the village of Hassenhausen. The Prussians launched a series of attacks, but they were poorly coordinated and gave valuable time to Davout. By late morning, with his entire corps on the field, Davout was able to take the offensive against the disordered Prussians and rout them.

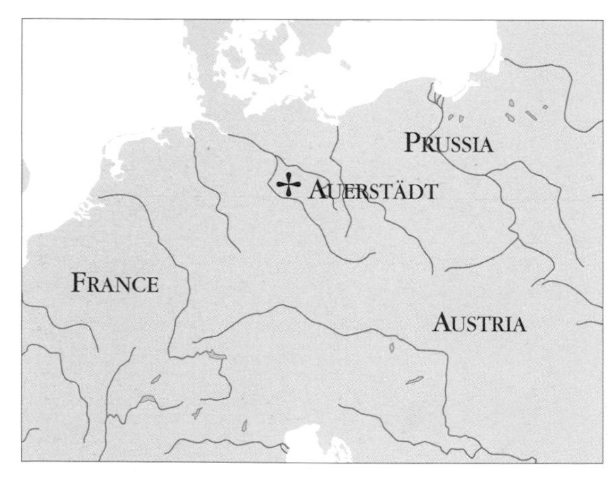

The Battle of Auerstädt demonstrated the flexibility of Napoleon's corps system on both the operational and tactical levels as one corps d' armée was able to not only stand on its own against a superior force but defeat it.

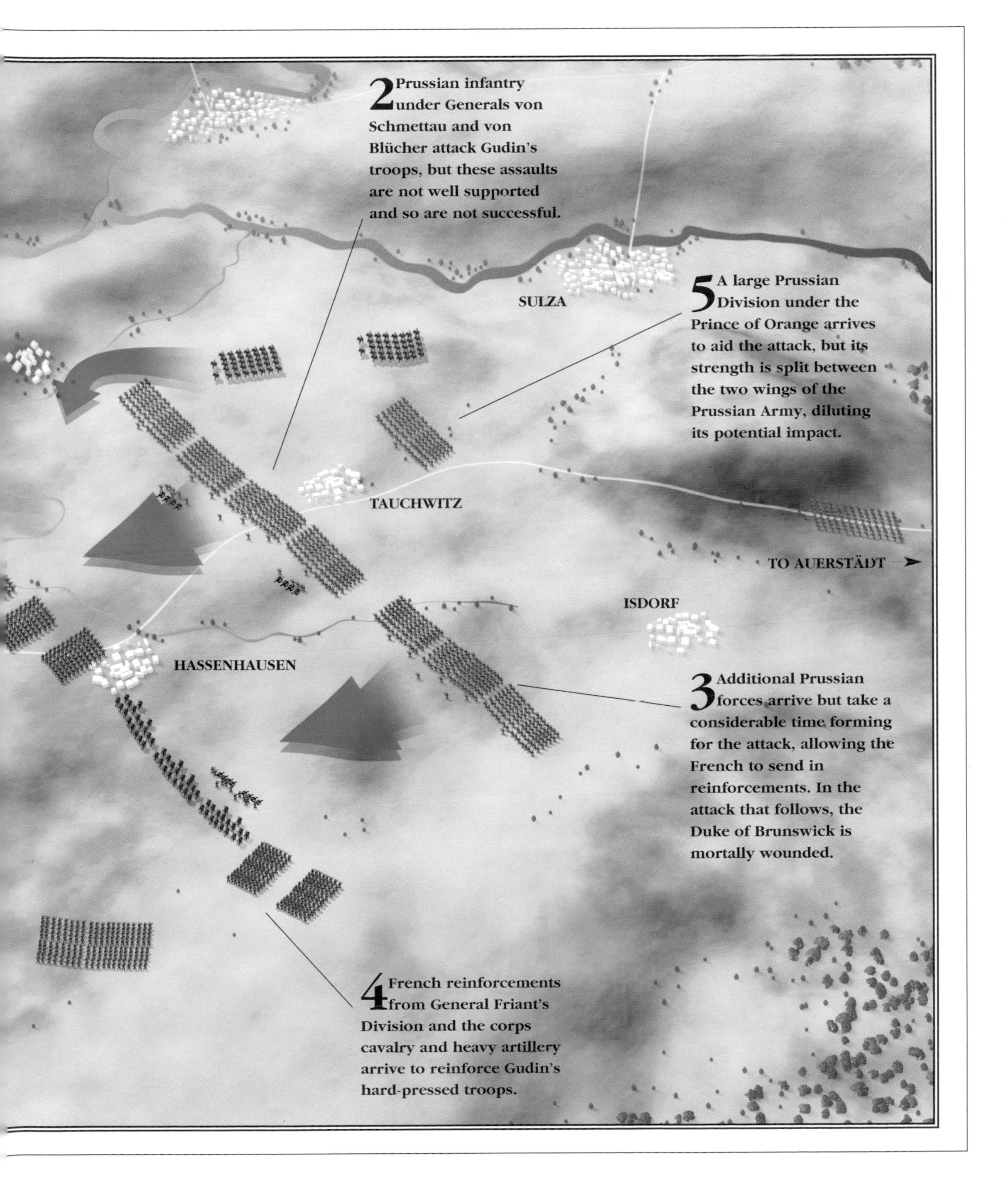
2 Prussian infantry under Generals von Schmettau and von Blücher attack Gudin's troops, but these assaults are not well supported and so are not successful.
SULZA
5 A large Prussian Division under the Prince of Orange arrives to aid the attack, but its strength is split between the two wings of the Prussian Army, diluting its potential impact.
TAUCHWITZ
TO AUERSTÄDT
ISDORF
HASSENHAUSEN
3 Additional Prussian forces arrive but take a considerable time forming for the attack, allowing the French to send in reinforcements. In the attack that follows, the Duke of Brunswick is mortally wounded.
4 French reinforcements from General Friant's Division and the corps cavalry and heavy artillery arrive to reinforce Gudin's hard-pressed troops.

was a brief break in the fog, so Bourke and his 39 who had engaged a superior force of Prussian cavalry and horse artillery, retired back to the safety of their infantry.

First Contact

The leading division was led by General of Division Etienne Gudin (1768–1812), and contained eight battalions of line infantry and a battery of horse artillery, a total of 8400 men. Davout ordered one brigade to form square – a fortuitous decision since two squadrons of Prussian Dragoons from the Queen's Regiment launched an impetuous charge, which was easily repulsed by the four infantry squares. The remainder of the division's infantry formed square as well and, as the fog lifted, Gudin's horse battery knocked out a Prussian battery and drove back some of their horse and foot. Davout then ordered Gudin to occupy the village of Hassenhausen. Unfortunately for Davout, and particularly Gudin, the remainder of the corps was still en route, most having 3–5km (2–3 miles) to cover.

Fortunately, only one of the three large Prussian Divisions, led by General von Schmettau, was in a position to attack, along with the Prussian Advanced Guard under General Gebhard Leberecht von Blücher (1742–1819). The other Prussian divisions were slowly making their way towards the battlefield. Gudin's battalions formed up to defend Hassenhausen, supported by the divisional artillery, and drove back several attacks by Prussian infantry and cavalry, none of which were mutually supported. Several Prussian field pieces were captured and hauled back to French lines by Bourke and his *chasseurs à cheval,* who were aided by a small detachment of *gendarmes*.

By about 8:30 a.m., another Prussian division, led by General von Wartensleben, appeared on the Prussian right. At this point, Blücher launched a large cavalry attack made up primarily of *cuirassiers* to the north of Hassenhausen. Gudin's battalions smartly formed square and handily drove off the Prussian troopers, who were without support from either infantry or cavalry. Blücher,

AT THE BATTLE OF AUERSTÄDT, *the Prussians launched a number of large, but unsupported and unsuccessful cavalry charges against elements of Davout's III Corps. The well-trained French troops formed squares that were placed obliquely in order to bring the maximum number of muskets to bear on the approaching cavalry.*

impetuous as ever, had his horse shot out from under him but was able to return to his lines unharmed. This attack was followed by a major infantry attack against the French in the village by Schmettau's division, which was supported by a flanking movement against the French left by Wartensleben. The fighting was fierce, but Gudin's troops held on. Fortunately for Davout, the Prussians took a long time to manoeuvre their troops into position, and this helped the French. At this critical moment, the advance elements of General Louis Friant's 2nd Division arrived, as well as the corps reserve artillery of 17 12-pounders under Colonel Geoffroy and the wayward corps cavalry.

Around 10 a.m, the Prussians launched attacks against both flanks of the French position – particularly hard hit was the 85th Line Regiment, which was the only unit left to the south and west, the remainder of Gudin's troops having redeployed further to the north in support of Friant's division as it took its position on the French right. The 85th was driven back through the village. Fortunately, Marshal Davout was there to rally them and sent in two of Gudin's regiments to retake Hassenhausen.

At this point, the Prussians launched major infantry attacks, this time attacking the village itself and ignoring the open French left. The attack was very costly – both the Duke of Brunswick and General von Schmettau were wounded, Brunswick mortally. And it cost the Prussians even more time until the command structure was restored, Frederick William himself now taking command.

FREDERICK WILLIAM III *was strategically indecisive during the 1805 campaign and tactically incompetent at the Battle of Auerstädt in 1806. The result was a near disaster for Prussia, which lost significant amounts of territory and population. Fortunately, he was served by a number of excellent officers who were able to reform and reforge the Prussian Army to play a key role in the downfall of Napoleon.*

Reinforcements

At 11 a.m., both sides received reinforcements. William Frederick, the Prince of Orange, arrived with his division. Unfortunately, rather than keeping the division together and bringing its mass to bear or one of the flanks of the French Army, King Frederick William ordered Orange to divide his command between the two flanks of the Prussian Army, thereby denying the opportunity to apply mass at a decisive point. On the French side, Davout's final division, under General Charles Antoine Morand, arrived and began to deploy on the French left.

Morand's division demonstrated its flexibility as it moved forward to join the battle line. Initially, the division was formed in three lines. The first had two battalions of light infantry in columns screened by skirmishers and supported by some artillery. The second line was four battalions of line infantry, their *voltigeurs* being deployed as a skirmish screen. The third line was the same as the second except that it had only three battalions. As the division prepared to join the fight for Hassenhausen, the first line re-formed. The left-hand battalion, which was the most vulnerable to attack (especially by Prussian cavalry), went into closed column, a formation that would allow them

NAPOLEON, IN THE FOREGROUND, *watches as his V Corps moves to attack the Prussians at the Battle of Jena. Marshal Lannes' V Corps was the first unit on the scene and pushed forward to hold the Prussians and provide time for reinforcements to arrive.*

to repel a cavalry charge but still be able to move and even attack while the right-hand battalion formed a line in preparation for the fight.

Finally, as the light infantry moved off obliquely to the right in order to join the fighting in and around Hassenhausen, the left-hand battalion also formed line. These units joined one of Gudin's regiments and together drove back a major Prussian infantry assault.

In the meantime, a massive force of 30 Prussian squadrons galloped to attack the remainder of the division, which promptly formed squares, driving off repeated Prussian changes. Seeing the Prussian cavalry abandon the field, these seven battalions formed into line and joined the attack against Wartenleben's troops. The rout of the Prussian cavalry, combined with the advance of fresh

enemy troops, took the fight out of the Prussian infantry, which began to retire. Reinforcements from Orange's Division were coming up in support, but they were not numerous enough to stem the tide of the retreat. Moreover, Frederick William was no longer willing or able to exercise effective control over his deteriorating army.

By noon, the French were in a position to make a general advance, turning the retreat into a rout. All three divisions advanced, with the wings of the corps slightly ahead of the centre. There was still some fighting and Prussian gunners manned their batteries to provide covering fire for their withdrawing comrades, causing heavy casualties. But the French were relentless and kept up the pressure on the retreating Prussians for nearly four hours, covering several miles before they halted, utterly exhausted.

The battle of Auerstädt was a great victory that showed the flexibility of the French at the operational, grand tactical and tactical levels while revealing the limits of the eighteenth-century way

Russian Grenadier

The Grenadiers of the Russian Army were the elite of the line infantry. In addition to forming elite companies within the line battalions, the Russian Army possessed a number of grenadier regiments, which were sometimes brigaded together and even formed entire divisions during the 1812 campaign. In addition to the grenadier regiments, there were also converged grenadier battalions that were formed from the elite companies of the depot battalions of line infantry regiments, and these, too, were brigaded together in their own divisions. The soldier illustrated wears the distinctive Russian kiwer *shako introduced in 1812, decorated with a black plume that marks him as a grenadier. He also carries his greatcoat rolled over his shoulder in order to protect him from sabre cuts. While on campaign the greatcoat was often worn without the green uniform coat as the Russian peasants who formed the army preferred loose clothing. Also in the field, the* kiwer *was provided with a weatherproof cover and the plume was fixed to the sword scabbard.*

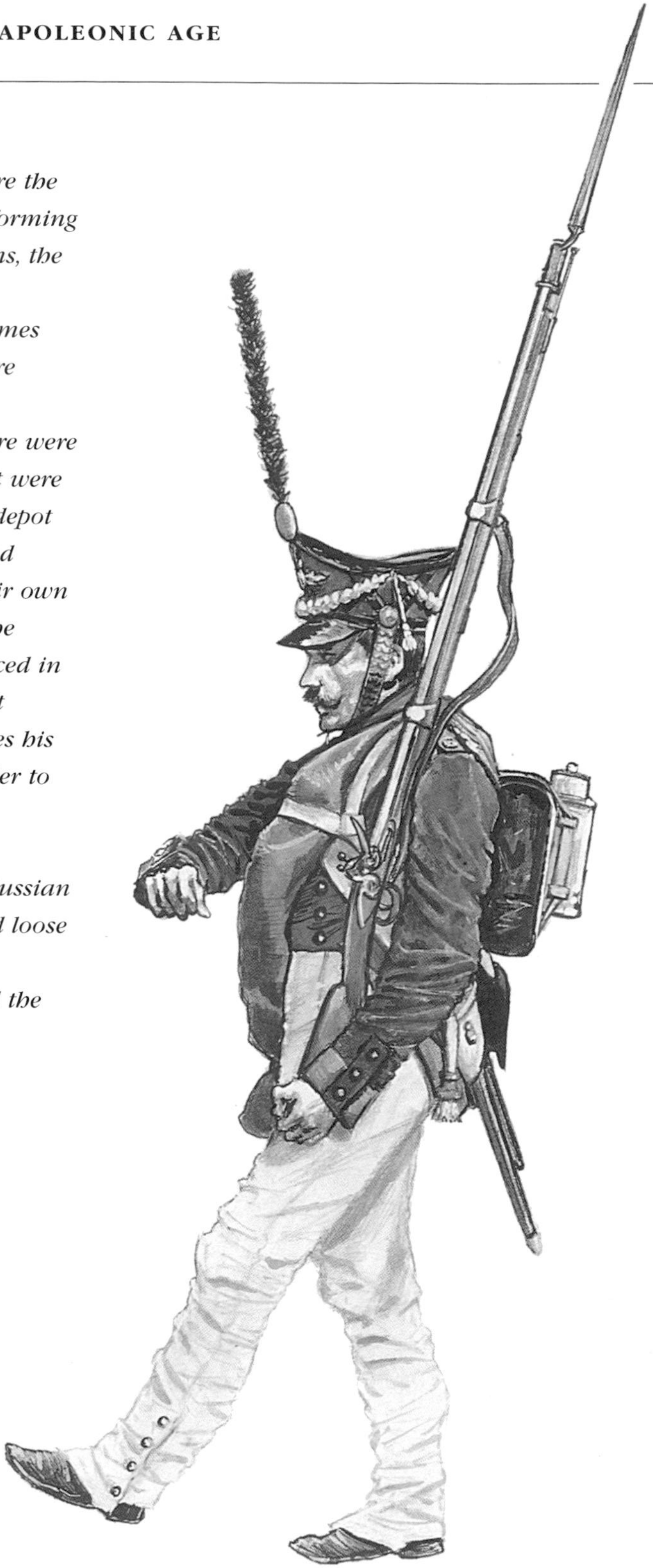

of war in all of those areas. However, the battle was very costly for Davout's corps. It inflicted some 10,000 casualties, took 3000 prisoners, and captured more than 100 cannon, but at a cost of nearly 27 per cent of its strength, with more than 7000 killed and wounded.

Tactical Evolution

Tactically, the complexity of certain formations continued to evolve. A good example is *l'ordre mixte*. During the Empire, *l'ordre mixte* became a tactical formation that could be used at a more grand tactical level. An example of this appears in a letter from Marshal Louis-Alexandre Berthier (1753–1813) to Marshal Nicolas Jean de Dieu Soult (1769–1851). In this letter, Berthier describes Napoleon's ideas on a formation to be used against the Russians: a division composed of two brigades with a total of four or perhaps five regiments. The first regiment of each brigade was to be deployed in a line formation. This line would be augmented by the division's batteries, with some gun sections deployed on the flank and others placed in the gaps between the various battalions of the line.

The first regiment of each brigade was to be supported by the second regiment. Both were to be formed into parallel columns that protected the flank of the line to their front and also provided support for the troops in the first line. If a fifth regiment was present, attached to one of the two brigades, Napoleon thought it should be arrayed in columns 100 paces behind the two regiments of the second line, to act as a reserve that was capable of supporting either brigade to its front. Finally, a squadron or two of cavalry would be placed behind the entire formation as a precaution against Cossacks, the Russians' irregular cavalry force.

The implications of this expanded version of *l'ordre mixte* are interesting. It offers a considerably greater level of firepower, with four battalions in line and the divisional artillery all capable of bringing fire to bear against the enemy. There is also considerable flank security provided by the second line of troops in columns, especially against enemy cavalry. The columns of the second line can also be used to exploit any openings made by the first line and its cannons. The same can be said of the fifth regiment and, in particular, the cavalry held in reserve. The presence of the reserve cavalry may also indicate that Napoleon may have gained some respect for the dangers presented by irregular light cavalry during his campaign in Egypt, where he fought the ferocious Mamelukes.

While the revolutionary period may have seen columns used as the exclusive formation for some units on the battlefield, it seems that during the period 1805–07 French tactical formations were much more varied. Individual units often used a variety of formations based on the immediate conditions. In particular, French units often used linear formations both for attack and defence when the situation warranted, although they may have moved about the battlefield in columns to reach the fight. On occasions, individual commanders misjudged or were prevented from deploying into line, and this has led to a misperception regarding the use of the column.

After this battle, the apogee of French tactical prowess, the *Grande Armée* was never the same. There were several reasons for this: the break-up of those higher echelon units that had spent so much time training while encamped along the Atlantic coast; and the loss of veteran troops during the numerous campaigns, who were not readily replaced by conscripts. These factors combined to erode the French tactical and grand tactical capabilities. As time went on, Napoleon's armies were increasingly forced to rely on large 'grand batteries' of artillery and massive multi-battalion, even multi-regimental, columns to batter the enemy. This decline in French tactical competence occurred at the same time that Napoleon's adversaries began to improve their own.

Responses to the Napoleonic system

Military establishments tend, by their very nature, to be conservative institutions. It is therefore not surprising that it took a considerable amount of time for the adversaries of Revolutionary and Napoleonic France to react to the changes in warfare at the operational and tactical levels. To counter the French system, they were required to transform intellectually, organizationally and doctrinally. Such a transformation took the French decades in the first place, so it is not surprising that the allied response was relatively slow to develop.

Most of Napoleon's continental opponents began to respond to his way of war after his campaigns in the period 1805–07, when the armies of France were at their peak and their armies had been smashed by Napoleon's forces. One major reform undertaken by most of the continental powers was in the size of their armed forces. Despite having to overcome social constraints about arming large numbers of men, Austria, Prussia and Russia all began to increase their militaries, often through the use of reserve or militia forces.

For example, in 1809 Austria raised a national militia, the *Landwehr*; and in 1813, both Austria and Prussia raised *Landwehr*, although the Austrians used theirs mostly as a pool for replacements. Finally, Russia raised large numbers of militiamen, the *opolochenie*, during the 1812 campaign. Moreover, virtually every European army mimicked the French *corps d' armée* structure for their armies, at least to some degree.

On the grand tactical and tactical levels, France's opponents began the period fighting in the standard linear formations of the eighteenth century. Most European nations and their officer corps had spent the last century developing the tactical principles for their troops.

By the beginning of the revolutionary period, most armies fought using a three-rank line for their units and some sort of firing system by platoons or divisions. While the infantry of most countries

THE DUKE OF WELLINGTON *is best known for his campaigns in the Iberian Peninsula and for the Battle of Waterloo. His tactics, however, were developed while he served in India. Here, at the Battle of Assaye (1803), Wellington's troops launch the kind of bayonet charge for which they would become famous.*

BRITISH LINE INFANTRYMAN *in the uniform worn throughout most of the Peninsular War. This is characterized by the short single-breasted coat and stovepipe shako, which were introduced in 1797 and 1800 respectively.*

BRITISH INFANTRYMAN *of a centre or battalion company as he might have appeared during one of the campaigns during the Revolutionary period, such as in the Low Countries in 1793–94. The uniform is similar to that worn throughout most of the eighteenth century, with a long-tailed open coat and bicorne hat.*

BELOW: A SOLDIER *from the 43rd Monmouthshire Regiment, one of the units that formed the famous Light Division. The soldier is distinguished as a member of an elite light infantry regiment by his early-model stovepipe shako with green plume, and the lace 'wings' on his shoulders.*

A GRENADIER OFFICER *in campaign dress wearing the 1812 pattern shako, usually referred to as the 'Belgic' shako. His membership in a grenadier company is denoted by his white plume and the wings on his shoulders.*

included units whose troops bore titles such as musketeer, fusilier or grenadier, these were merely distinctions in uniform or status.

All of these armies deployed those regiments in one or more parallel lines of units arrayed in three ranks. Many also had specialized units of light troops, particularly the Austrians, who used such men along their military frontiers with the Ottoman Turks, but these were not a key component on the battlefield. Likewise, although the British Army had experimented with light troops on account of its service in North America and had introduced a company of light troops for each of its battalions, it would not be until the outbreak of the Revolutionary Wars with France that the famous light infantry and rifle regiments of the British army would be formed.

This form of warfare was generally one of doctrinal simplicity, with relatively few complexities. Most of the problems facing a general as he arrayed his army for battle centred on questions such as the number of lines in which to deploy his battalions or how close those units should be placed in order best to support one another. Artillery was often placed on high ground and did not manoeuvre much while cavalry were posted on the flanks. Simply put, this form of warfare had relatively few 'moving parts' in comparison to the style of warfare the French were developing. As a result, it was very difficult for France's enemies to identify the components of the emerging fighting techniques of Revolutionary and Napoleonic armies.

WHILE EACH FRENCH *regiment possessed a regimental standard mounted on a staff surmounted by the imperial eagle, which was more important than the flag itself, this sergeant-major carries one of the battalion flags, the fanion. Unlike the regimental eagle, which was the embodiment of the emperor, the battalion flags were used primarily as a rallying point and to mark the battalion's position.*

Allied Reforms

Yet the humbling defeats inflicted by the French, coupled with a few reform-minded - or, at least, open-minded - higher officers, did lead to tactical reform in these armies. Most of the reforms centred on the two most easily identified elements of the French system of warfare, the use of deeper columnar formation and employment of skirmishers.

The Austrians, for example, had adopted new forms of closed columns for use on the battlefield by 1809. First was the 'battalion mass', in which a battalion was drawn up on a frontage of one company and with a depth of six companies. The second was the 'division mass', in which the battalion was formed up with two companies across and three deep. Neither of these formations was really new; most armies had closed columns as part of their manoeuvres, but they were not used extensively. The Austrians now began to use them more frequently on the battlefield, especially for use against cavalry, since they were easy to form. The hollow square, the more standard formation used in the face of cavalry, required complex evolutions. During the 1809 campaign, there are a number of instances of

Austrian units in these formations repulsing French cavalry.

The Russians had, even before the Revolutionary Wars, made some use of column formations in conjunction with their lines. This probably originated from their preference for hand-to-hand combat over the use of muskets. It is likely that these formations were used more commonly on Russia's 'eastern front' against the irregular cavalry they faced in Crimea and on the steppes. These tactics are most often associated with the Russian General Alexander Suvorov (1729–1800), who was a great advocate of extensive training and the use of cold steel, especially after he had observed French tactics. He famously said: 'The musket is a lazy fellow – the bayonet is a good chap.' Moreover, the Russians developed a form of *l'ordre mixte*, which they used at Eylau in 1807, where some regiments deployed one of their battalions in line with two in column formed behind.

The Prussians, who had been masters of linear warfare under Frederick the Great, were also forced to adopt new tactical methods in the wake of their army's catastrophic defeat in 1806. Prussia's reform movement was complicated by the restrictions placed on them by the Treaty of Tilsit, which greatly reduced their army.

Nonetheless, in 1812, the Prussians promulgated a new set of regulations, and these in many ways encapsulated the French system of tactics and grand tactics. This included the formation of standardized brigades with two infantry regiments, each one composed of two battalions of line infantry, musketeers, a light battalion, fusiliers and two companies of grenadiers. The grenadiers from the two regiments were converged into a single elite battalion. In addition, the brigade possessed a battery of artillery, a battery of horse artillery and 12 squadrons of cavalry. The 1812 regulations clearly drew inspiration from the French *Règlement du 1er Août 1791*. But the Prussians seem finally to have distilled more than the use of skirmishers and columns from the French system since their regulations allowed for a kind of flexible *ordre mixte*, which bears striking similarity to that suggested by Napoleon to Soult in 1807. A brigade was to have its fusilier battalions formed in line, and covered by skirmishers drawn from those battalions. These were supported by a second line of three musketeer battalions in column, flanked by the artillery that was, in turn, supported by a third line made up of a musketeer and converged grenadier battalion, also in column. Finally came the cavalry and the horse battery.

Of all of Napoleon's adversaries, only the British resisted major reforms to their army. It mobilized militia forces during invasion scares between the 1790s and 1805, and some even fought at the little-known Battle of Fishguard in 1797, where a small French force landed in Wales and was quickly defeated by British forces. However, such forces were not employed as part of their field

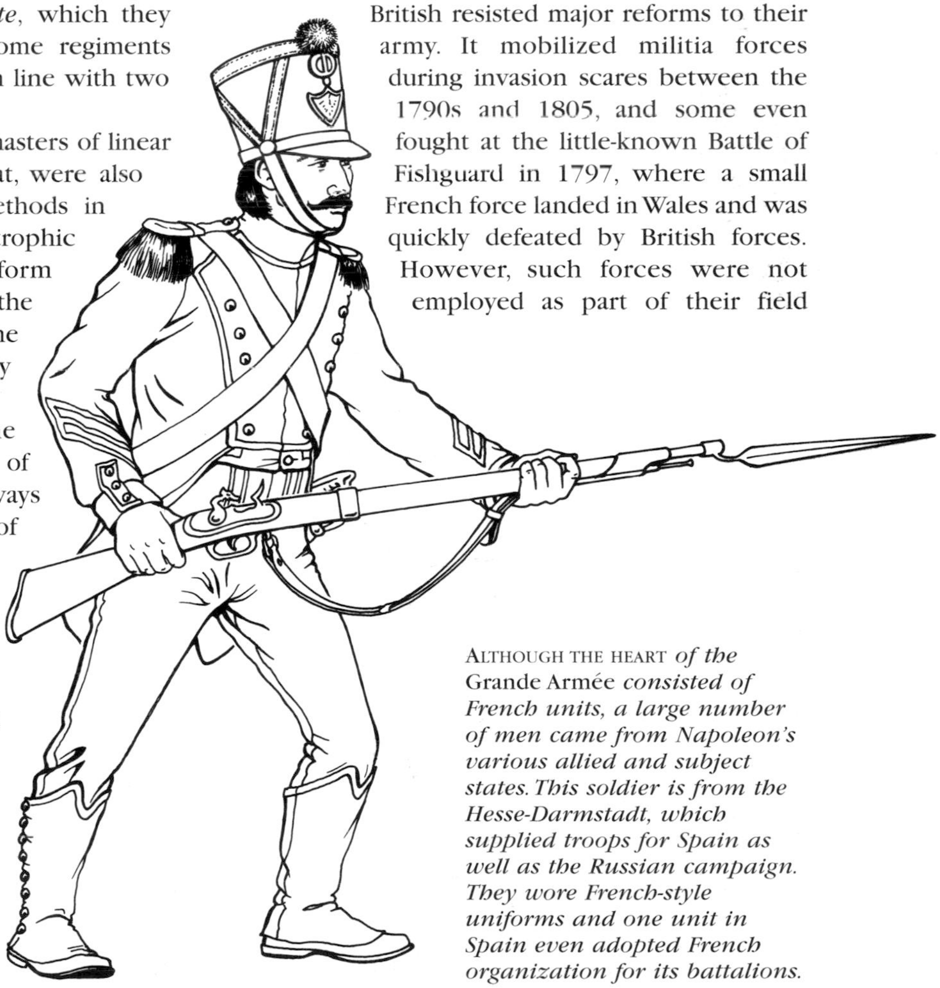

ALTHOUGH THE HEART *of the* Grande Armée *consisted of French units, a large number of men came from Napoleon's various allied and subject states. This soldier is from the Hesse-Darmstadt, which supplied troops for Spain as well as the Russian campaign. They wore French-style uniforms and one unit in Spain even adopted French organization for its battalions.*

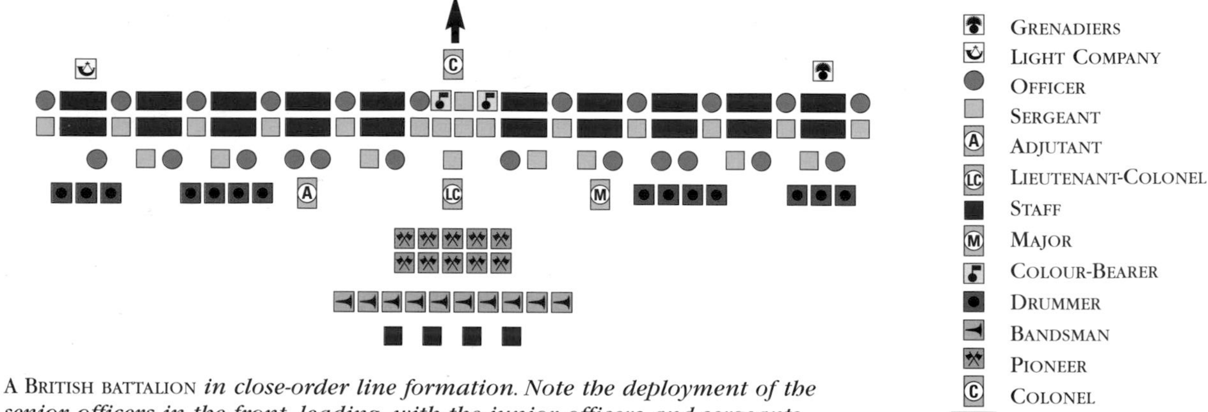

A BRITISH BATTALION *in close-order line formation. Note the deployment of the senior officers in the front, leading, with the junior officers and sergeants positioned adjacent and behind the ranks. This was done to ensure the maintenance of the formation in battle, and prevent the breaking of the ranks.*

forces. Britain was, of course, fortunate in that she was spared the full fury of the French way of war, since the Royal Navy controlled the Channel. When the British Army did deploy, it was as a kind of disposal force engaged in peripheral operations, in the sense that until the final act at Waterloo they did not have to face the *Grande Armée* and Napoleon himself, but rather his subordinates.

British tactics therefore remained essentially linear, although with some modifications to the eighteenth-century norm. First, the British employed a two-rank line rather than the more standard three-rank formation, to bring the maximum amount of firepower to bear. Other armies had discussed the use of a two-rank line in certain situations, such as the French forces against the *Chouans*, which Napoleon himself advocated in 1813.

But the British had an interesting variation on the use of the two-rank line: even though it was a formation that seems designed for fire rather than shock combat, it is clear that the British made use of it for the latter too. The standard British tactic was not to engage in lengthy firefights, but rather to use firepower to maximum effect by holding fire until a devastating volley could be delivered at relatively close range. This volley was then followed up by a charge, which often broke the enemy's nerve. Moreover, these linear formations were screened by large numbers of well-trained light infantry units, including specialized light infantry regiments and even two regiments of troops armed with rifled versus smoothbore muskets. These troops were able to provide the musketry and rifle fire necessary to attrite the enemy forces as they neared the British line.

The Battle of Maida: 4 July 1806

In the summer of 1806, the French were in the process of completing their conquest of the Kingdom of Naples, which had earlier allowed the presence of Anglo-Russian troops on its soil. By the summer, the French and their allies had defeated the Neapolitan army. The few thousand remnants of this force had fled to Sicily or were now besieged in the town of Gaeta. The British were concerned that the capture of Gaeta might set the stage for a French invasion of Sicily. At first, the British commanders in the area, Rear-Admiral Sir Sydney Smith (1764–1840) and General John Stuart, were content to be passive in their preparation for the defence of the island. They initially believed there was little chance of the French actually taking Gaeta. The French forces detailed to prosecute the siege were ill-prepared, having neither the manpower nor the firepower, since they were lacking in siege artillery. However, as time went on, the French forces at Gaeta were reinforced, and by June there were some 12,000 troops and a sufficient quantity of heavy artillery to prosecute the siege.

The fall of Gaeta now seemed imminent, so Rear-Admiral Smith and General Stuart planned an operation to land British troops in Calabria with the objective of driving out the French forces. Thus the mission of the British landing force was to seek out and engage the French forces in the area. Under the command of General de Division Jean Louis Ebénézer Reynier (1771–1814), they were believed to be numerically inferior.

General Stuart began assembling his invasion force. It was to be composed of three brigades and an advanced guard. The advanced guard was made up exclusively of light troops. It included the light companies drawn from the infantry battalions that formed the garrison on Sicily, a total of seven companies.

In addition, there was a company of 'flankers', marksmen, drawn from the 35th Foot. Finally, there were local light infantry, two companies of Corsican Rangers and one of Sicilian Volunteers. The First Brigade comprised one battalion of regular infantry, the 1st Battalion of the 27th Foot, a combined grenadier battalion of six companies and a battery of foot artillery. The Second Brigade was made up of two battalions of Foot, the 1st of the 78th Highlanders and the 1st of the 81st Foot. The Third Brigade also had two line units, the 1st Battalion of the 58th Foot and the 20th Foot. There were also four companies of Louis de Watteville's Swiss Regiment, which were unbrigaded and intended for camp guards. The unit was formed from the remains of several Swiss units in British service as well as former French *émigrés*. The landing force did not include any

THE FIRST CLASH *between the French columns and British line took place at Maida in 1806. Here, British infantry, having fired their volleys, launch a bayonet attack against the French, who have not had the opportunity to deploy properly.*

A PANORAMIC VIEW *of the Battle of Maida in 1806. The British infantry are pouring fire into the French troops and are supported by artillery who are engaged with the French at point-blank range.*

cavalry, probably because of the difficulty of transporting horses on warships. The entire force mustered about 5200 officers and men.

On 1 July, Rear-Admiral Sydney put Stuart and his landing force ashore near the town of Saint Eufemia. By landing in the middle of Reynier's area of responsibility, they hoped to catch his force divided. Stuart landed his force and established a camp. The 20th Foot was sent south as a diversion. The two companies of Corsican Rangers were sent inland to reconnoitre, but were met by several companies of Polish troops and were quickly driven back to the beachhead. There, the three line battalions were deployed and came to their aid in repelling the Polish troops. Stuart was also joined by some Calabrian guerillas, although he did not hold them in high regard and they do not appear to have played an active role in the forthcoming battle.

Reynier, who was at Reggio with his main body, soon began to march northwards, collecting units that had been in garrison along the way. He commanded the II Corps of *L'Armée du Naples,* but this was closer to a small division in terms of its numbers. His force consisted of three brigades with two light infantry regiments (1st and 23rd *Légère*) of two battalions; one line infantry regiment (42nd *Ligne*), also of two battalions; one battalion of Swiss troops (4th *de suisse*); two battalions of Poles (1st *Legion polonaise*); a regiment of *chasseurs à cheval* (the 9th); and one battery each of horse and foot artillery for a total of some 6400 men. By the evening of 3 July,

Reynier and his men had made it as far as the town of Maida and they bivouacked south of the town.

Stuart learned of Reynier's presence and gathered his troops. On 4 July, he gathered his forces and pickets and marched to meet the French, still believing that he had the French at a disadvantage in numbers. Both armies marched towards a plain on the northern side of the Lomato River and began to deploy for battle. Since Reynier had to march perpendicular to what would become the British battle line, his army ended up advancing *en echelon* as the units on the left were the first to wheel and thus advance against the British.

The units on the right, which had further to go before wheeling, were the most distant from the British. Reynier's troops were arrayed with the two battalions of the 1st *Légère* formed in column and their *voltigeur* companies thrown out along both banks of the river. Next to this elite light regiment was the 42nd *Ligne*, also in column. To the right of the regular infantry, but slightly to their rear, were the two battalions of Poles and then the Swiss.

Next came the French artillery, supported by two squadrons of *chasseurs à cheval.* To the right of the guns, and slightly behind them, were the two battalions of the 23rd *Légère* in column and

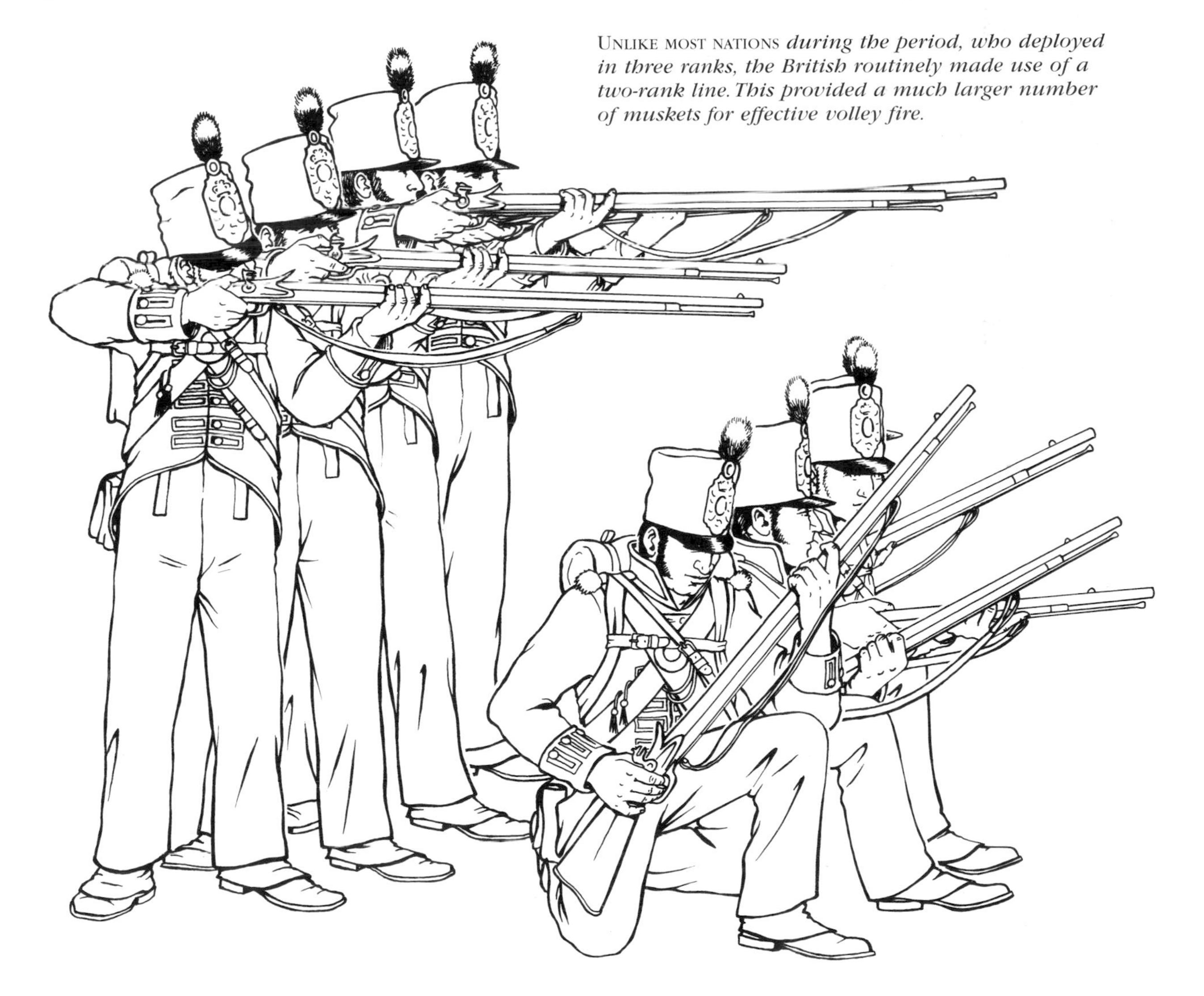

UNLIKE MOST NATIONS *during the period, who deployed in three ranks, the British routinely made use of a two-rank line. This provided a much larger number of muskets for effective volley fire.*

Battle of Maida

4 July 1806

In early July, General Sir John Stuart landed a force of some 5000 infantry supported by a battery of foot artillery in Calabria in southern Italy with the intention engaging French forces there. A French force of 6000 men under General Reynier moved to attack Stuart, and the two forces met on a plain north of the Lomato River near the village of Maida. Since the French were south of the river, they had to march perpendicular to the British line of advance. While Stuart's troops formed for battle, the French crossed the Lomato and then wheeled to advance on the British. This forced Reynier's units to advance in an oblique battle order and did not allow them to deploy from column into line. The British units waited until the leading French columns were in range and unleashed devastating volleys. As these troops were forced back, the British battalions advanced and engaged the remaining French troops as they came into range. Most of the French infantry were forced to fall back, and the British were kept from fully exploiting their victory by the presence of French cavalry who covered the retreat.

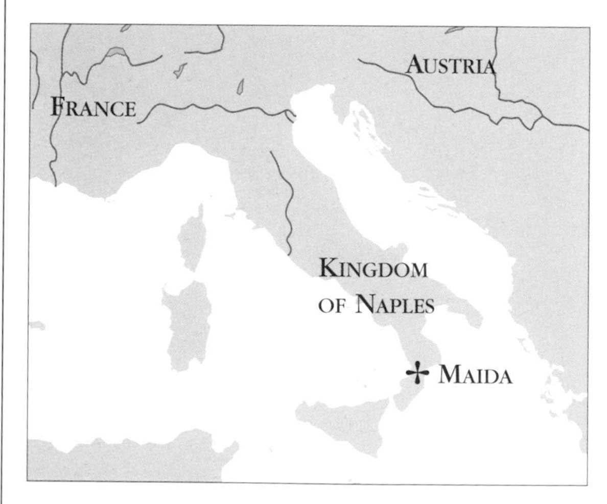

The Battle of Maida was fought when the British landed a small army that was to draw French troops away from Gaeta, where Britain's Neapolitan allies were besieged.

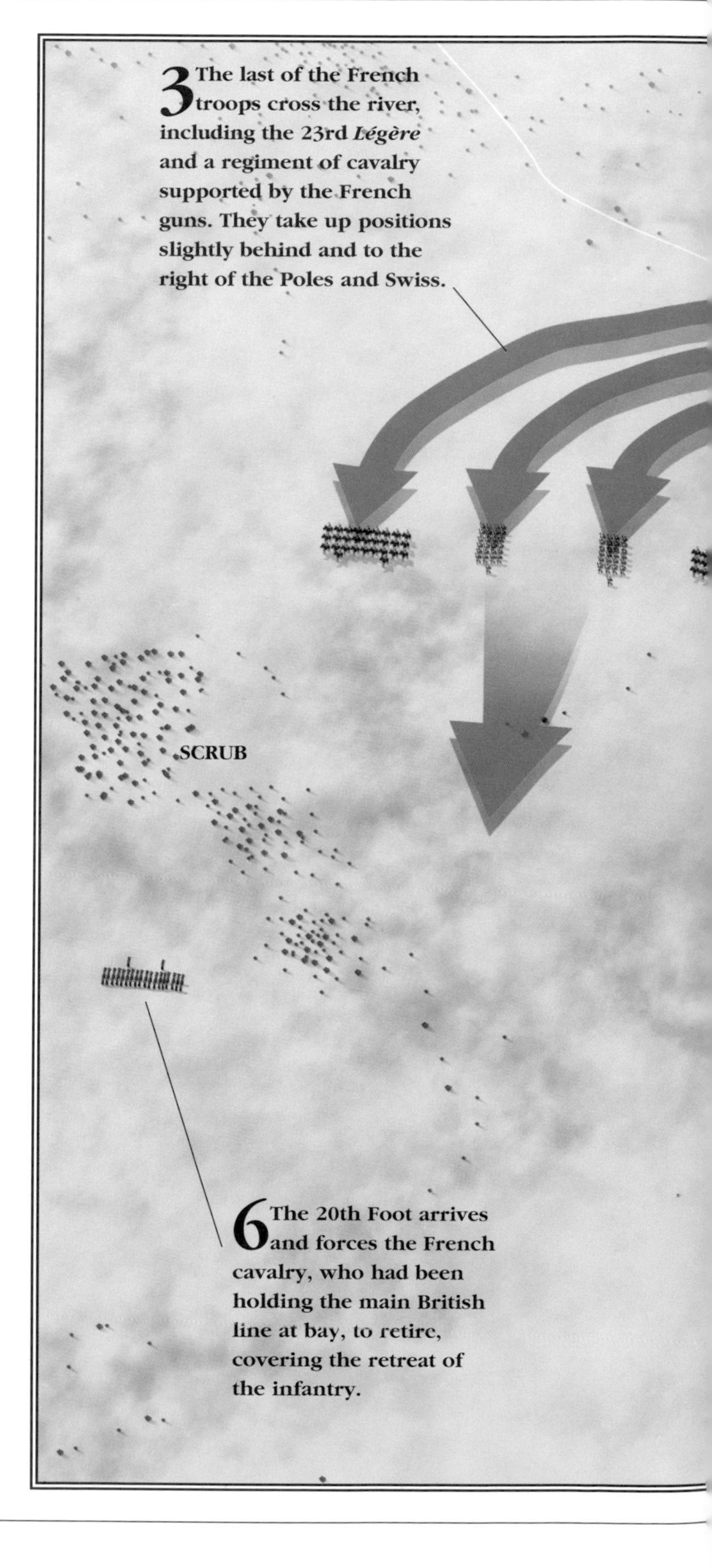

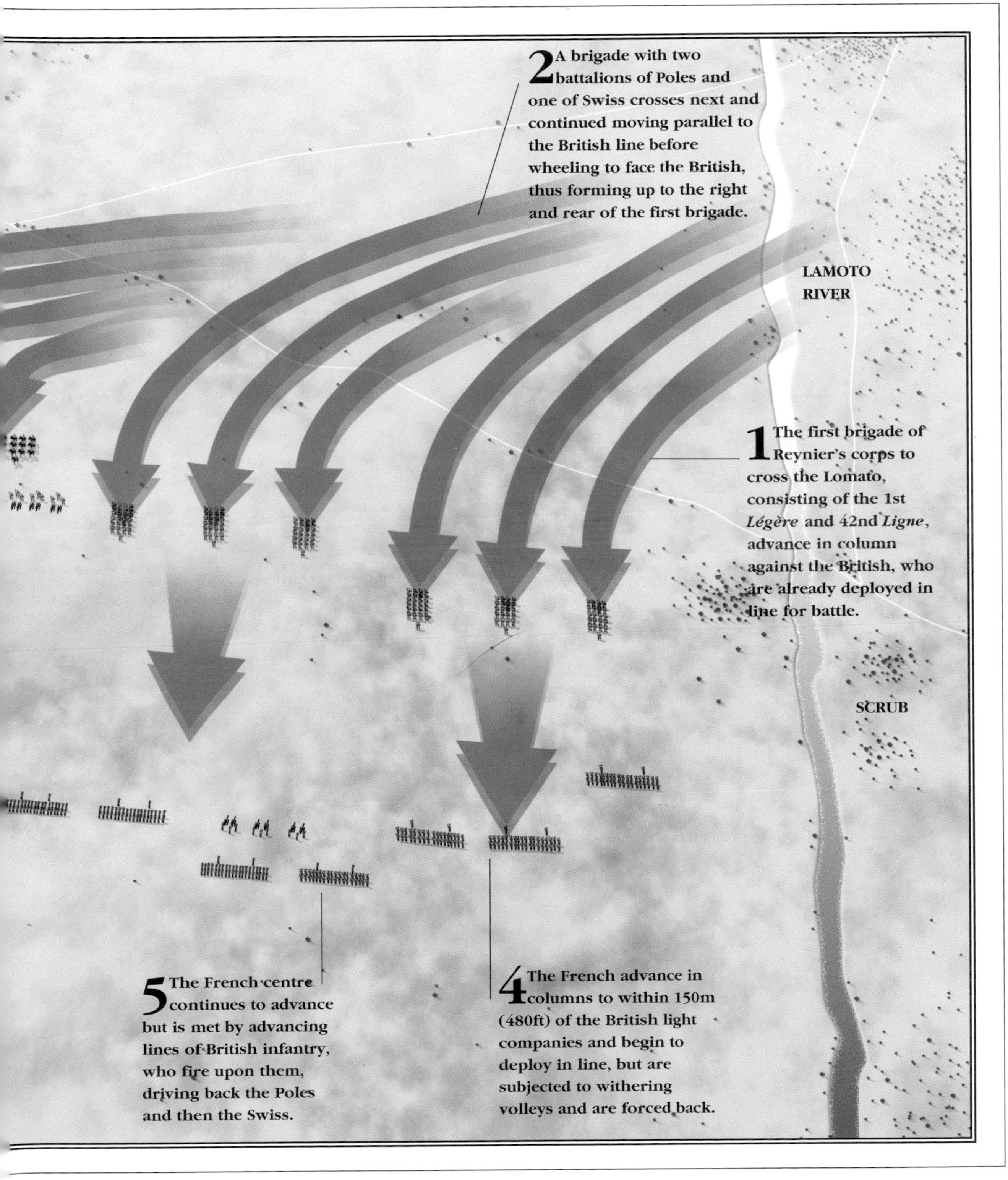

2 A brigade with two battalions of Poles and one of Swiss crosses next and continued moving parallel to the British line before wheeling to face the British, thus forming up to the right and rear of the first brigade.

LAMOTO RIVER

1 The first brigade of Reynier's corps to cross the Lomato, consisting of the 1st *Légère* and 42nd *Ligne*, advance in column against the British, who are already deployed in line for battle.

SCRUB

5 The French centre continues to advance but is met by advancing lines of British infantry, who fire upon them, driving back the Poles and then the Swiss.

4 The French advance in columns to within 150m (480ft) of the British light companies and begin to deploy in line, but are subjected to withering volleys and are forced back.

French Infantryman (1812)

While the Napoleonic period is known for its colourful uniforms, this French line infantryman is shown in the kind of dress that was perhaps most common. His uniform is covered by a greatcoat, which would have doubled as a bedroll, while his shako is unadorned and protected by a waterproof cover. The coloured pompom, however, which denoted the soldier's company, is still visible. He wears a single crossbelt that carries his bayonet scabbard in front and his cartridge box on his hip. He also has the calfskin knapsack that was used to hold the remainder of his kit and personal items. He also carries a metal canteen - these were not official issue and similar metal canteens were carried by the Russians, so this may have been 'liberated' from a Russian casualty or captive.

on the extreme right of the French line were the remaining two squadrons of the 9th *Chasseurs à cheval.*

Stuart anchored his right on the Lomato and formed his line of battle, starting with the light infantry of the advanced guard. Adjacent to the river, it was formed in the standard two-rank line, while the Corsican Rangers and Sicilians were in skirmish order along the river. Next to the advanced guard came the Highlanders and 81st foot in line. To their left was the artillery battery, with the 58th Foot drawn up to their rear. Holding the left of the line was the battalion of converged grenadiers. And the 20th Foot, which had been detached, was expected to arrive on the left flank at some point during the battle.

Opening Skirmishes

The battle began with some minor skirmishing between the units advancing in open order along the river. The French *voltigeurs* had the better of it until a couple of British light companies came up to help out. Next the 1st *Légère*, a huge regiment with nearly 1800 men between its two battalions, bore down on the advanced guard, who numbered perhaps 650 men. The British waited until the French were within 137m (150 yards) and then unleashed a devastating volley. The elite French light infantry pressed on and received yet another volley at about 73m (80 yards). This was too much for the French troops, who broke and ran.

Things quickly went from bad to worse for Reynier as the 42nd *Ligne* came under fire from the Highlanders and infantry of the 81st Foot. After several volleys, this unit also broke under the withering fire. The British line infantry continued their advance and engaged the Poles and Swiss. The Poles soon broke, but the red-coated Swiss held their ground until they too were forced to withdraw. They did so in good order, falling back towards the remaining French brigade.

The French line was stabilized by the presence of the 9th *Chasseurs à cheval*, who launched a series of charges that forced the British infantry to halt their advance and form square to receive cavalry. The situation continued until the 20th Foot made their appearance on the battlefield, coming in on the right flank of those French units that were still in good order. At this point, the field retired, yielding the field to the British, who had achieved their objective of engaging and defeating a major French force.

> *'[We] were skirmishing in the olive-groves and in a village and on the banks of a little stream.... The enemy tried several times to carry the post, but we always received them with such a sharp fire that they were obliged to drop their intention after leaving a number of dead...'*
>
> – Captain Thomas Bugeaud, battle of Maria in Spain, 15 June 1809

Line versus Column

The Battle of Maida had limited consequences on the outcome of the Napoleonic Wars, although it did slow the French pacification of Calabria. It was a small engagement, little more than a skirmish in contrast to the battles fought in central Europe. But it has had a remarkable impact on the way in which historians have understood the fighting techniques of those wars. The battle has become the model known as the 'line versus column' debate, in which some have argued for the superiority of the firepower of the line versus the shock of the column.

But things are not as obvious as they might appear, since it is clear that at Maida columns were not intended to be fighting formations at all, but rather formations for manoeuvre. There is evidence that both the 1st *Légère* and 42nd *Ligne* had, in fact, deployed into line. Indeed, Reynier himself noted this in a letter to Joseph Bonaparte the day after the battle. These two units had the shortest time to deploy before coming under fire, since they were the closest to the British line.

So perhaps what this battle really demonstrates is the importance of a unit's ability to retain its cohesion while performing evolutions under fire.

Asymmetric Responses

There was one other response to the French way of war that should be addressed, even though it falls outside the study of formalized tactics - the use of guerilla and irregular warfare. The French experience against the counter-revolutionaries has already been mentioned. More famous is the problem of Spain, where the French were forced to deal with large numbers of guerillas. The guerillas created serious problems by forcing them to devote tremendous resources to rear echelon security for the movement of supplies, protection of couriers and so on.

The Spanish guerillas were a diverse group, which exacerbated the difficulties. Not only were there true guerilla bands raised from the population, but there were also bands formed around former Spanish regulars, more in the mould of the 'partisans' of eighteenth-century warfare than modern guerillas. Indeed, as the war in Spain progressed, some of these 'guerilla' units were uniformed and could field forces the size of a division. The semi-regular nature of some of these bands can be seen in the issue of regulations

AFTER HAVING HELD *La Haye Sainte for most of the Battle of Waterloo, the men of the 2nd Light Battalion, King's German Legion, had run out of ammunition. During the final assault that captured the farm, a handful of troops sallied out and were able to reach the relative safety of the British line.*

Private, 95th Rifles

The 95th Regiment was the only regiment in the British Army to be equipped entirely with Baker rifles instead of smoothbore muskets. The 95th was formed in 1802 and had its origins in the Experimental Rifle Corps, which was founded in 1800. This elite unit was not only equipped with rifles but also received special training that emphasized small unit tactics and marksmanship. Moreover, the small-unit training of the riflemen created a level trust between officers, non-commissioned officers and other ranks that was unique in the British Army of the period.

The soldier wears the green tunic that was distinctive of rifle-armed units, including the 5th Battalion of the 60th Regiment and the two light battalions of the King's German Legion. He also carries the Baker rifle, which was a much more accurate weapon than the standard smoothbore weapon. Its main disadvantages were that it was slower to load than the normal musket and was not as useful in hand-to-hand fighting, since it was shorter and carried a rather unwieldy sword bayonet. Indeed, even today, the units descended from the 95th still give the command 'fix swords' rather than 'fix bayonets'.

for guerilla units by the Supreme Junta at the end of 1808. There were other guerilla and insurgent movements for the French to counter, especially in Germany. In 1809, the Tyrolians rose up in support of the Austrians and a savage campaign against Bavarian and French forces ensued. There were also a number of insurrections in the Kingdom of Westphalia, but these were crushed by Westphalian and French troops.

Interestingly, the only guerilla movements to have any success were the two supported from regular troops, in Spain and the Tyrol. The

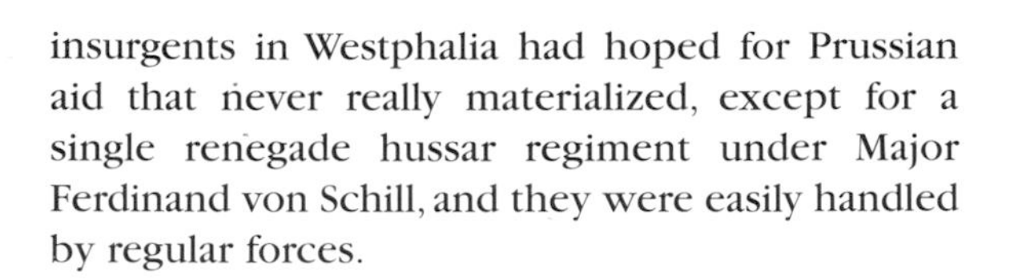

insurgents in Westphalia had hoped for Prussian aid that never really materialized, except for a single renegade hussar regiment under Major Ferdinand von Schill, and they were easily handled by regular forces.

The Hundred Days' War

In March 1815, Napoleon returned to France after nearly a year in exile on the island of Elba. There, the 'God of War' no longer had command of a *Grande Armée* numbering more than 100,000 men, only a small personal guard of one battalion of grenadiers and a squadron of lancers, fewer than 1000 men.

This was difficult for the former emperor to bear. However, news from France suggested that the restored Bourbon monarchy was less than popular with virtually every segment of society, especially the government and the military. These factors encouraged Napoleon to hope for return. He planned his escape, took ship and landed on the southern coast of France.

Beginning a triumphal march to Paris, accompanied by his Guard, he was joined all along the way by veterans and soldiers wanting to rejoin their 'eagles'. At Grenoble, there occurred what is without doubt one of the most famous incidents of the Hundred Days campaign. Here, the 5th *Régiment de Ligne* confronted Napoleon. A young officer ordered his men to fire. No one moved. Napoleon asked if there was anyone among them, the 'soldiers of the Fifth', who would shoot their emperor. Instead of gunfire, cries of 'Vive l'empereur!' rang out and shakos were raised on the tips of bayonets.

When Napoleon reached Paris at the end of the month, he may have had support at home – but not abroad. Indeed, he was declared an outlaw by the monarchs and princelings of Europe. It was

THE BRITISH-RECRUITED KING'S GERMAN LEGION *included two battalions of light infantry. These men were trained, equipped and uniformed like the men of the 95th Regiment and so carried the Baker rifle. The 2nd Battalion under Major Baring played a pivotal role at Waterloo, defending La Haye Sainte until they ran out of ammunition.*

THE BRITISH SHAKO *evolved in the course of the Napoleonic Wars. Introduced in 1799 and first issued a year later, the stovepipe model (top left) was initially made wholly of leather but by 1807 was made of felt. In the 1812 regulations, the stovepipe was replaced by the so-called Belgic shako (top right), which was made of felt and had a false front. The Belgic shako was fitted with cording, the colour of which, along with the plume, helped to mark the company.*

therefore imperative that he once again raise a *Grande Armée* to maintain himself as emperor of the French. The various states of Europe arrayed against him pledged to raise a force of 700,000 troops - and already had 400,000 men under arms.

For his part, Napoleon raised 300,000 men for the regular army and mobilized an additional 150,000 National Guardsmen. But he was in the same situation as the early Republic: he had many fronts to defend and so could spare only about 125,000 men for offensive operations. He therefore determined to strike first. The most logical targets were the allied armies located in Belgium. There stood a Prussian army of about 116,000 men under Field Marshal von Blücher and a polyglot Anglo-Allied army of 105,000 commanded by the Duke of Wellington (1769-1852).

On 15 June, Napoleon led his Army of the North, into Belgium, crossing the Sambre River at the town of Charleroi. His army was made up of the Imperial Guard, which was a shadow of its former self with a mere 17,000 men: five *corps d'armée*, four of which were of average size, although one corps barely mustered 9000 men under arms, and four small cavalry corps averaging

Battle of Waterloo

18 June 1815

In March of 1815, Napoleon returned from exile and found himself facing a united Europe. By June, he was prepared to take the offensive with more than 120,000 men against the Anglo-Allied and Prussian armies in Belgium under the Duke of Wellington and Field Marshal von Blücher. On 16 June, Napoleon engaged the Prussians at Ligny while his subordinate, Marshal Ney, attacked part of the Anglo-Allied army at Quatre Bras. Although Napoleon defeated Blücher and Ney forced the Anglo-Allied troops to withdraw, the allies coordinated their movements. Napoleon sent nearly one-third of his army to pursue the Prussians while he moved to defeat Wellington at Waterloo. The battle began in the late morning of 18 June with a series of poorly coordinated infantry attacks against Wellington's line. The French attacked in columns and suffered from the firepower of the British infantry. Prussian troops arrived in the afternoon and threatened Napoleon's rear. Napoleon made one last effort to break Wellington's line in the evening, but the solidity of the British infantry and their firepower drove back his elite Old Guard, ending the battle.

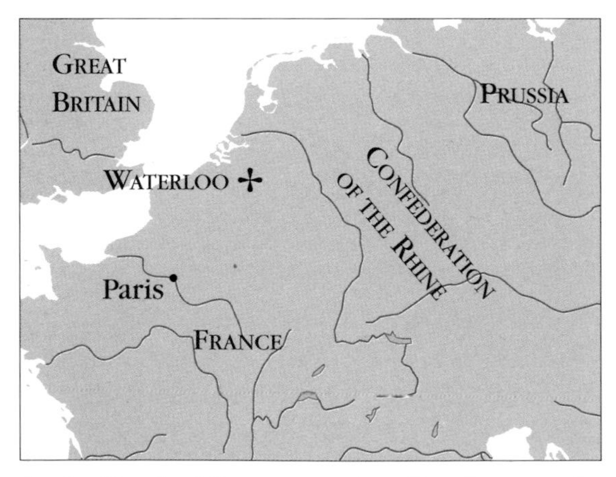

In the Hundred Days campaign, Napoleon sought to knock out the Anglo-Allied and Prussian forces in Belgium. The campaign culminated with two of the most famous and successful generals of the age locked in battle at Waterloo.

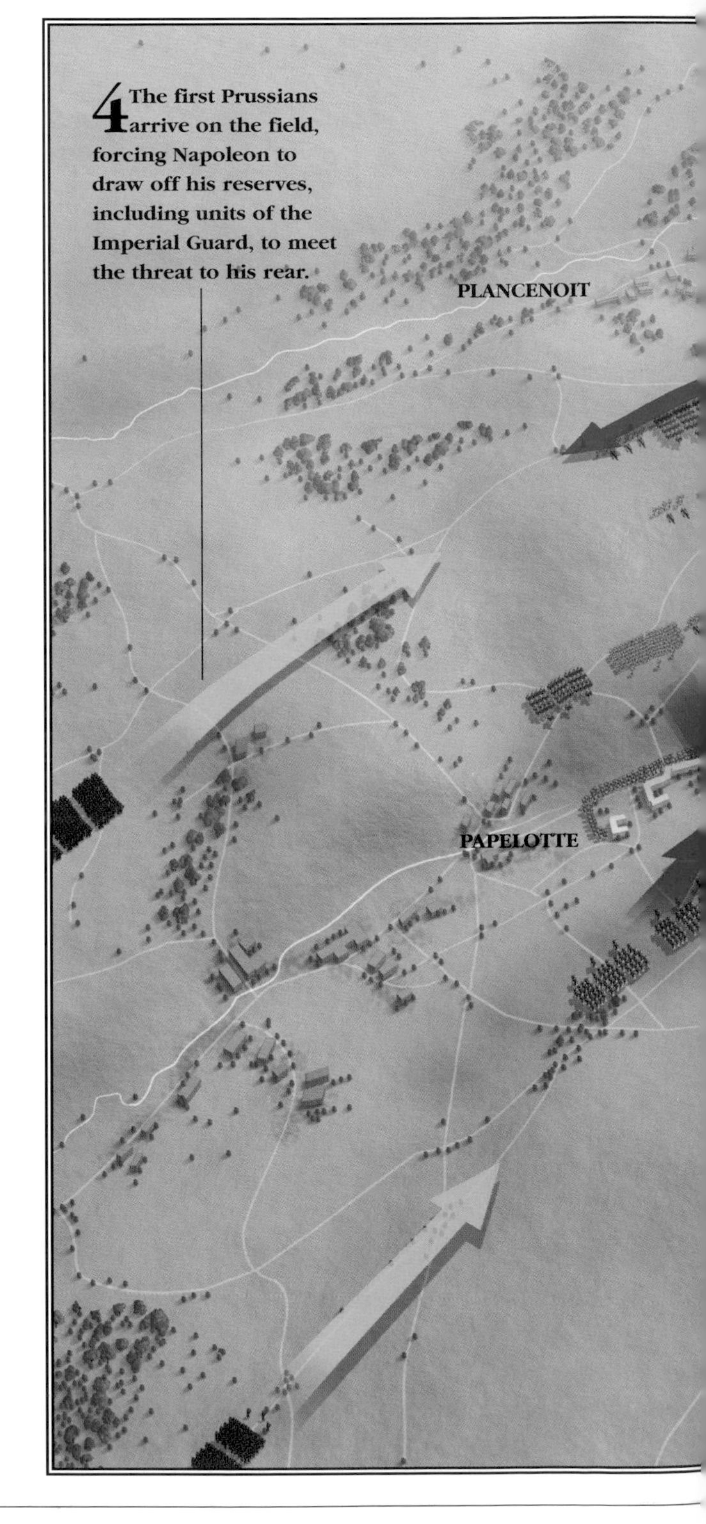

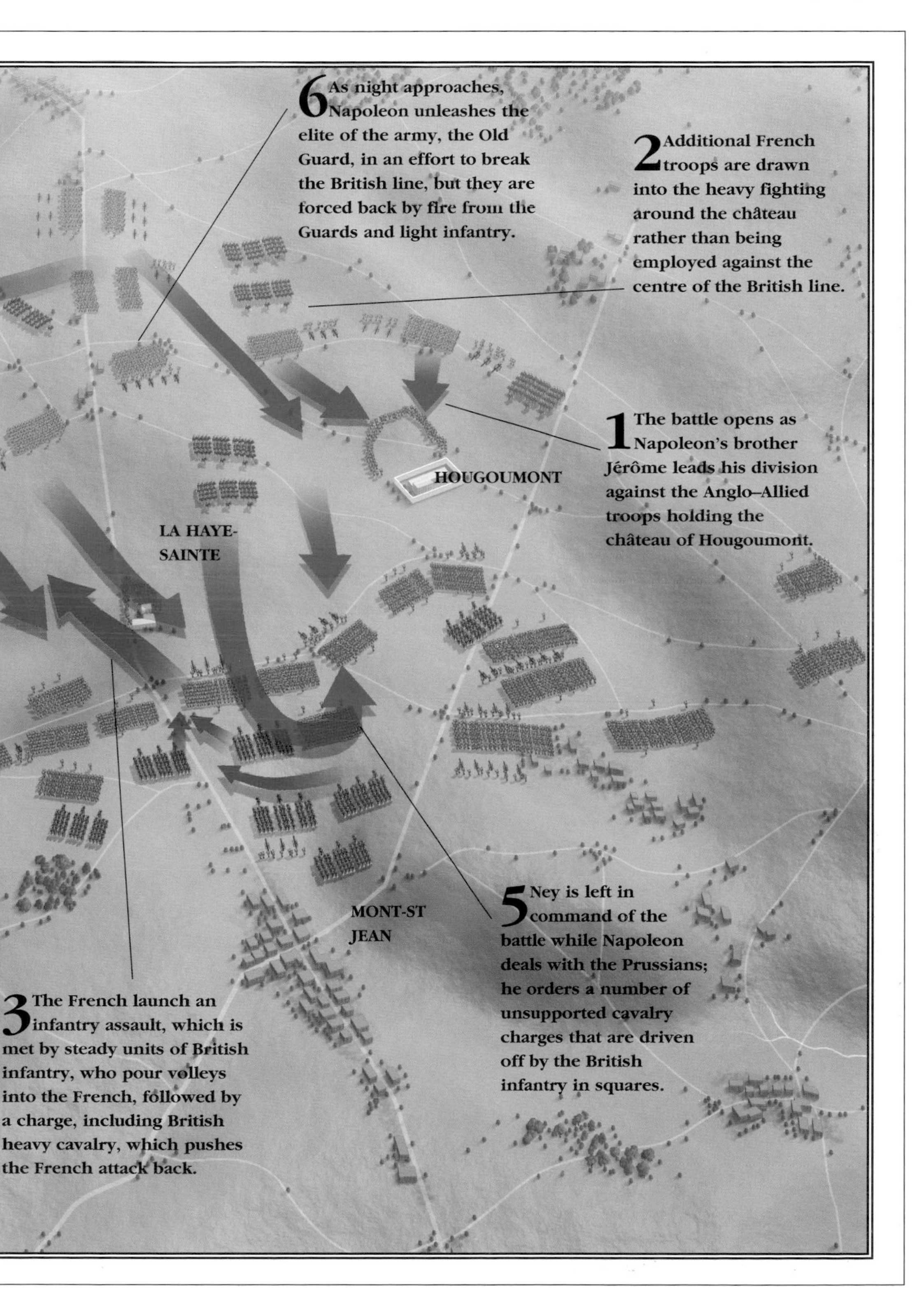
6 As night approaches, Napoleon unleashes the elite of the army, the Old Guard, in an effort to break the British line, but they are forced back by fire from the Guards and light infantry.
2 Additional French troops are drawn into the heavy fighting around the château rather than being employed against the centre of the British line.
1 The battle opens as Napoleon's brother Jérôme leads his division against the Anglo–Allied troops holding the château of Hougoumont.
HOUGOUMONT
LA HAYE-SAINTE
MONT-ST JEAN
5 Ney is left in command of the battle while Napoleon deals with the Prussians; he orders a number of unsupported cavalry charges that are driven off by the British infantry in squares.
3 The French launch an infantry assault, which is met by steady units of British infantry, who pour volleys into the French, followed by a charge, including British heavy cavalry, which pushes the French attack back.

about 2500 men each. Napoleon intended to attack Wellington's force first in the hopes that he could smash the British and force their withdrawal from the continent. On 16 June, he sent Marshal Michel Ney (1769–1815) with an advance guard of about 40,000 men towards Brussels in order to pin down the British.

However, he was then himself surprised to find that the Prussians had sought him out for battle – Blücher had an unreasoning hatred of Napoleon and dreamt of capturing and shooting him. As a result, two battles were fought on 16 June, Ney fighting an Anglo-Allied army at the key crossroads of Quatre Bras and Napoleon battling the Prussians at Ligny. While the Emperor won a victory, the Prussians withdrew in relatively good order. For his part, Ney, who had a reputation for audacity, was uncharacteristically cautious at Quatre Bras, which allowed Wellington to reinforce his troops and then disengage on favourable terms.

The Battle of Waterloo: 18 June 1815

Wellington withdrew to a prearranged position at Mont-Saint-Jean, where he planned to fight a defensive battle. Blücher retreated towards the Wavre, which would allow him to cooperate with Wellington's forces. Napoleon detailed his newest Marshal, Grouchy, to pursue the Prussians closely so that they would not be in a position to join up

IN THEIR CHARACTERISTIC BEARSKIN CAPS, *florid whiskers and sideburns, the veterans of the Old Guard were Napoleon's last reserve – one that he threw away at Waterloo.*

with the British and their allies. Grouchy was given two corps, about one-third of the army, for this important task. Meanwhile, Napoleon himself would follow and engage Wellington and his Anglo-Allied army. But he did not pursue the British with his customary vigour, even making a late start on 17 June, and the pursuit was further slowed by very heavy rains.

Both armies were in place by the morning of 18 June. The heavy rains of the day before had soaked the ground and made the movement of heavy artillery very difficult. Moreover, the soggy ground made the 'bounce' of the cannon ball less effective, and so the morning was spent in comparative quiet as both sides prepared their positions. Wellington had chosen his ground carefully. The Anglo-Allied army was deployed along a ridgeline that extended for nearly 3.2km (2 miles).This allowed the Duke to deploy many of his brigades in line and to fill the gaps between units with his artillery.

The centre of his line was held mostly by high-quality brigades composed of his veterans from the campaigns in the Peninsula.These were British units, including elite ones such as the three regiments of Foot Guards and the units of the famous Light Division, and also some excellent foreign units, most notably the Hanoverian troops of the King's German Legion. They were supported by a number of cavalry brigades deployed behind the ridgeline. There were also a couple of key strong points in front of the main British line. These included the Château of Hougoumont on Wellington's right, which was held by members of the Guards, as well as some troops from Nassau and Hanover.Also, just in front of the centre of Wellington's line was the farmhouse of La Haye Sainte, which was occupied by an elite light battalion of the King's German Legion. Napoleon placed his two large infantry corps so that each was responsible for a wing of his battle line. They were supported by artillery pieces along the line, including an 80-gun grand battery deployed in front of General d'Erlon's corps facing the centre of the Anglo-Allied line. The cavalry were drawn up behind their infantry. In reserve, Napoleon had kept his smallest corps as well as the potent Imperial Guard, both infantry and cavalry.

The Battle Begins

The battle began at 11 a.m. Shortly thereafter, the corps of General Reille sent forward one of its divisions, commanded by Napoleon's youngest brother Jérôme, the former King of Westphalia, to attack Hougoumont. It had some success. Unfortunately, the château became a focal point for massive amounts of French combat power throughout the day, sucking in troops who might have been more profitably employed elsewhere.At about 2 p.m., after a bombardment by the grand battery, a major French attack was launched against the centre of the Anglo-Allied army by the corps of Comte D'Erlon (1765–1864).

Interestingly, this attack was launched by French troops in closed columns, but unlike in earlier times there was no effort to deploy into line; the mass marched right into the teeth of Wellington's most veteran battalions, who poured volleys into the French columns. D'Erlon's troops

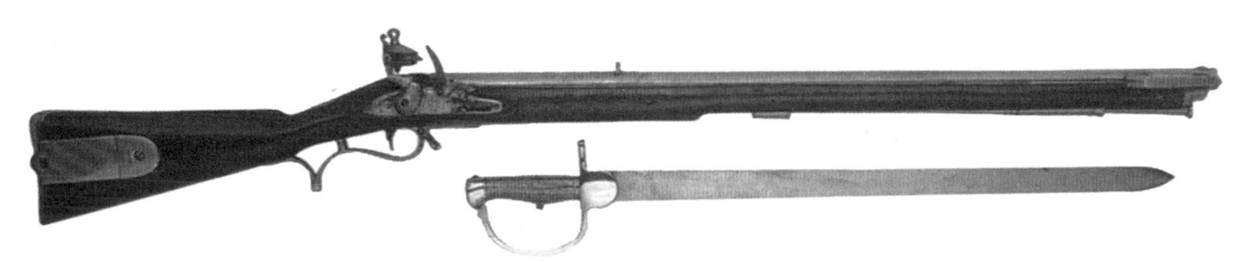

A BAKER RIFLE AND BAYONET *as used by British rifle regiments, such as the 95th Rifles. First produced in 1800, the Baker was the first standard-issue, British-made rifle accepted for the British Army.*

were badly shaken and this was exploited by a cavalry charge of the two British heavy cavalry brigades, the Union and Household Brigades. They were joined by members of the Gordon Highlanders, who launched a successful bayonet charge in support, some of the Scots hanging onto the stirrups of their mounted comrades. But the cavalry went too far and were then badly mauled by a French counterattack.

D'Erlon's corps was forced back in disorder and needed to regroup. But Napoleon had more serious problems. At 1 p.m., he learned that the Prussians had arrived on his right and were contesting the village of Plancenoit. Napoleon was forced to divert his reserve corps to meet the Prussians, leaving him only the Imperial Guard as a ready reserve. By 4 p.m., D'Erlon was ready for another assault and his troops met with the same result as before. The heavy columns were driven back with heavy losses.

Cavalry Charge

It was also clear that the Prussian threat was becoming more critical, and this became the focus of Napoleon's attention. Ney was left to command the main battle. After the repulse of D'Erlon's troops, Wellington pulled his troops off the ridgeline to protect them from the French guns. Ney took this as a retreat and launched a massive cavalry charge: 5000 troopers, including part of the guard, threw themselves against the Anglo-Allied line. Rather than an army in retreat, however, they were faced by artillery. After firing, the gunners retired to the safety of infantry battalions formed in oblique squares, which allowed them to support one another with fire without risking any 'friendly fire'. The French cavalry were thrown back with heavy losses, but Ney made them charge again and again, adding even more troopers to the mix. Finally, at about 6 p.m., he organized a supported attack using the survivors of D'Erlon's corps as well as some from Reille in a general attack, but it was too little, too late. Their only minor success was the capture of La Haye Sainte after the riflemen of the King's German Legion light battalion stationed there ran out of ammunition.

While Ney was launching his unsupported and wasteful attacks, the Prussians made headway in

THIS FAMOUS PAINTING BY PHILIPPOTEAUX *shows French* cuirassiers *attacking a square of British infantry, in this case a battalion of Highlanders. The artillery pieces in foreground and background would have been manned until the last moment, the gunners seeking protection within the square after firing one last shot at point-blank range.*

Plancenoit, forcing Napoleon to commit the entirety of the Young Guard to stabilize the situation – something they failed to do. By 7 p.m., the situation was so desperate that Napoleon was forced to gamble everything on one last attack, spearheaded by the Old Guard. By 8 p.m., the Guard was in motion, supported by the shattered remnants of the line infantry. Wellington had earlier hidden some of his elite troops from the Guards regiments, and given them the support of some light infantry. As Napoleon's guard advanced, Wellington shouted to their commander, General Maitland: 'Now, Maitland! Now's your time!' Maitland ordered his troops to stand up and fire. They issued a devastating volley and then another, which drove the Old Guard back, leaving some

THE STANDARD FORMATION *for defence against cavalry was to form a square. Here, a beleaguered British square is under attack by French* cuirassiers *at Waterloo. The British foot are in three ranks with the first rank kneeling to keep the cavalry at bay with their bayonets, while the rear two stand in order to fire their muskets.*

1200 dead on the battlefield. This was the last straw for most of the army, who simply broke and ran. A few battalions of the Imperial Guard were able to fight a rearguard action that allowed Napoleon and the refugees to escape. It was the final act of the Napoleonic Wars.

Conclusion

The fighting techniques that emerged in the course of the French Wars from 1792 to 1815 had a profound impact on warfare at virtually every level. At the operational level, the corps system and its manoeuvres became the ideal for most armies for the remainder of the century. A new generation of military intellectuals attempted to distil the principles of Napoleonic warfare, including the Prussian reformer Carl von Clausewitz and the Swiss Baron Antoine Henri Jomini, who went from being a Swiss bank clerk to a general in the Russian Army. The works of these men became standard works read by military officers for generations, right down to our own.

On the tactical level, the French *Règlement du 1er Août 1791* remained a model for drill and tactics in many nations for nearly half a century, undergoing only minor modifications to address improvements in military technology. In a famous example, Winfield Scott translated the *Règlement du 1er Août 1791* into English in 1814, for use by the American Army. It would remain the basis for tactical evolutions until the American Civil War. That these tactics were still in use then has led some to argue that the American Civil War, rather than being the first modern war, as it is so often described, was in fact the last Napoleonic War. There were, however, changes in military technology that would soon sound the death knell for the tactics prescribed in the *Règlement du 1er Août 1791,* such as the breech-loading rifle, the machine-gun, and the breech-loading steel cannon. These developments ushered in a new style of warfare that has been characterized as an 'empty battlefield' due to the increased lethality of the new weapons.

Private, 92nd Regiment, Gordon Highlanders

The British Army contained a number of Scottish regiments, including several recruited from the Highlands. This soldier is from the 92nd Regiment, the Gordon Highlanders. The regiment was formed in 1794 as the 100th Regiment but was renumbered as the 92nd in 1798. The regiment fought in many of the important campaigns during the Revolutionary and Napoleonic Wars, including the Peninsular and Waterloo campaigns. The soldier illustrated is from the Waterloo campaign, in which the regiment wore kilts. Earlier, in the latter stages of the Peninsular campaign, the soldiers of the 92nd were forced to wear trousers because of the difficulty of maintaining the kilt through the rigours of a field campaign.

CHAPTER 2

MOUNTED WARFARE

Cavalry was an integral part of every nation's army during the Napoleonic Wars (1792–1815). Mounted units performed vital reconnaissance and screening functions in the manoeuvres leading up to the battle, played a decisive role on the battlefield itself and served as a pursuit force in following up a victory.

The major armies of the era each had formidable mounted forces, and during the French Revolutionary Wars (1792-1802) there was a rough parity between the horsemen of the Great Powers. Yet, when Napoleon (1769-1821) launched his *Grande Armée* on its campaigns of conquest in 1805, the cavalry of France emerged as the best in the world. The main reasons for this dominance were the superior organization of the French cavalry arm and the excellence of the officers who led it at every level of command.

THE IRRESISTIBLE FORCE *meets the immovable object. French cuirassiers and* grenadiers à cheval *attack British infantry in square formation at Waterloo. The square formation protected infantry from cavalry attack. It was not infallible, however, and also made the infantry vulnerable to cannon fire.*

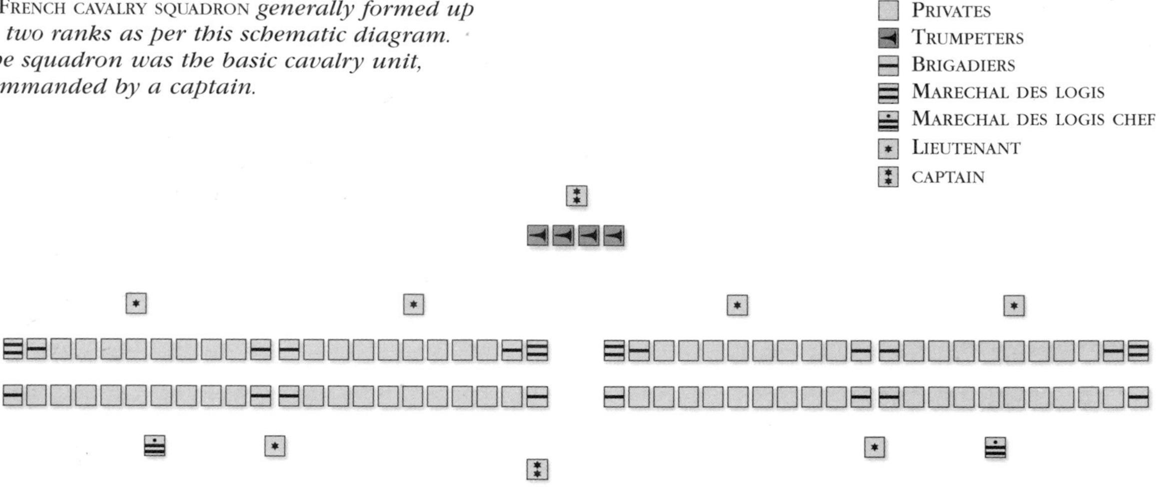

A FRENCH CAVALRY SQUADRON *generally formed up in two ranks as per this schematic diagram. The squadron was the basic cavalry unit, commanded by a captain.*

The French Army of the *ancien régime* had been dominated by the aristocracy, and in no branch of service was this more visible than the cavalry. Here the ancient tradition of mounted knights was continued through the service of the sons of the finest families in France. When the revolution erupted – and especially after the ascent of the Jacobins to power in 1793 – the aristocratic officer corps was purged, and the army was deprived of much of its senior leadership. Significantly, though, even the radicals recognized the impracticality of removing all nobles from service with the cavalry, since there was a severe shortage of properly trained horsemen to take their places, at least initially. Nevertheless, the officer corps of the French cavalry from 1792 to 1799 was a distinctly mixed bag of generally mediocre talent.

Napoleon's ascent to power, which began with the formation of the Consulate in 1799, marked a major change in many areas, including a complete reorganization and overhaul of the French cavalry. Napoleon was determined to make his cavalry a superior force to its opponents, and dedicated time, effort and money to re-equipping and reoutfitting the horse troops. In addition to promoting the best soldiers through the ranks according to his policy of 'a career open to all talents without distinction of birth', he also welcomed back *émigré* aristocrat officers and placed them in prominent positions of command within the cavalry. The result was that the French cavalry benefited tremendously in that it retained the very best aristocratic officers, who had to hold their rank based on ability rather than birth, while simultaneously taking advantage of the levelling of society, which enabled low-born troopers of extraordinary abilities to rise through the ranks. In fact, a number of ordinary troopers attained senior officer rank, with some, such as Joachim Murat (1767–1815) and Michel Ney (1769–1815), even becoming marshals of France. These men served beside scions of the ancient French nobility, such as Etienne de Nansouty (1768–1815) and Emmanuel Grouchy (1766–1847), finding common cause in Napoleon and his empire, which embraced them all.

As part of Napoleon's general army reforms, which were finalized in the training camps at Boulogne, the French cavalry emerged in 1805 as a force to be reckoned with. Within the next two years it would forcefully demonstrate that it was the finest cavalry in Europe, and would play an integral part in nearly every major victory of Napoleon throughout the Napoleonic Wars of 1805–15. French cavalry, and especially French heavy cavalry, was the dominant force on the battlefields of the Napoleonic Wars. Though there were certain elite Allied regiments who would prove to be of the same calibre, such as the Scots

Greys and the Russian Guard Cavalry, taken as a whole the French heavy horse were without peer from 1800 to 1812.

The Russian campaign changed that dynamic considerably, however. One of Napoleon's greatest losses in the cataclysm of that horrific episode was the destruction of the French cavalry. In the 1813 and 1814 campaigns that followed, the French cavalry was simply unable to dominate its opponents as it had in previous years. In the opening battles of the 1813 campaign in particular, Napoleon's lack of numbers and the mediocre quality of the cavalry severely limited his operations, and prevented him from turning his victories at Lützen and later at Bautzen into the decisive triumphs that in previous campaigns they most assuredly would have been. In his report on the battle of Lützen, for example, Marshal Ney praised the spirit and courage of his young horsemen but lamented that the attacks by the raw recruits were poorly coordinated and that they had the disturbing habit of falling off their horses during a charge.

The generally poor quality of his cavalry, and the inexperience of the raw recruits pressed into service to replace his lost veterans, had a dire effect on Napoleon's campaign. Indeed, when Napoleon decided to seek an armistice in the summer of 1813, a move generally regarded as a major mistake, he stated that while he knew the risks, he needed time to train and equip his cavalry properly since there was no point in fighting battles until it could be suitably readied for action.

AUSTRIAN UHLAN (LANCER). *The Austrian Army raised uhlan regiments beginning in 1798. They were a small, but important, component of the Austrian light cavalry. Used primarily for reconnaissance and screening missions, Austrian uhlans were mainly recruited from the Polish lands of the Austrian Empire, as the Poles were renowned for their skill with the weapon. The uhlan wears a distinctive headdress known as a* czapka*, which was also worn by Polish lancers in service with the French army.*

Cavalry Mounts

In addition to finding good recruits, acquiring proper horses for the cavalry was also a problem that concerned the armies of all countries. The armies of the Napoleonic era preferred cavalry horses that were around 15 hands (1.5m/5ft) high at the shoulder, though light cavalry were mounted on smaller animals. Horses were usually mature enough for duty once they reached five years of age and could then be relied upon for a good 10–15 years of service. Almost all cavalry horses were mares or geldings, since stallions were virtually uncontrollable around mares in season. Despite their size, horses are more fragile than humans, and have to be treated with great care. During the march into Russia in the summer of 1812, General Nansouty remarked: 'Our horses have no patriotism. The men will fight without bread, but the horses won't fight without oats.' Thus it was as important for a cavalryman to know how far he could ride his horse, and how much water and food to give it, as it was for him to know how to fight on its back. Indeed, one of the great problems with raw cavalry recruits, such as those Napoleon was forced to employ after his Russian campaign had destroyed his cavalry, was the high attrition rate of their mounts.

France alone could not provide enough horses for the needs of the largest army in European history, and thus imperial lands in Germany and Italy were relied upon to provide enough mounts for the cavalry, as well as horses for the artillery and supply services. A severe shortage of horses occurred after the disastrous Russian campaign of 1812. In addition to the loss of so many horses during the campaign, the German lands relied upon for remounts became battlegrounds and eventually fell into the hands of the Allies. As a consequence the French cavalry was a notably diminished force in size and quality during the 1813 and 1814 campaigns. The restored Bourbon regime imported large numbers of horses from other parts of Europe during Napoleon's brief first exile, and upon his return to power in 1815 the emperor took full advantage of this to rebuild his cavalry arm. Consequently during the Hundred Days the French cavalry was better mounted than it had been at any time since Russia, and as a result played a critical role in all of the major battles of the campaign.

'Cuirassiers are of greater use than all other cavalry. This arm... needs to be well instructed. It is in the heavy cavalry that the science of the mounted man should be carried to the highest degree.'

— NAPOLEON

Order and Discipline

Like all soldiers, cavalrymen were sometimes guilty of cowardice, malingering and lax discipline. Such problems included heavy cavalry discarding their cumbersome equipment and weapons on long marches in order to lighten their loads. Cavalrymen could also employ tricks to make an animal sick or hobbled – for example, by placing small rocks beneath their saddles in order to make their horses sore-backed. This provided the men with an excuse to take their animals to the rear, thus avoiding action.

At times cavalry were guilty of excesses against civilians. Sometimes lax discipline was viewed as one of the few comforts available while on arduous service, and the light cavalry seemed to take the greatest advantage of the liberty of action bestowed upon them. Light cavalry were not a welcome sight to civilians, be they countrymen, allies or enemies. The light horsemen lived, fought and marauded beyond the bounds of normal society and had a disdain for their own lives, let alone the lives of others. Looting was commonplace, and light cavalry managed always to find time for it, even when engaged in their assigned martial activities. Such activities, which could also include murder and rape, occurred with the compliance, and sometimes even the participation, of their officers. The Cossacks of Russia acquired the worst reputation of any light cavalry during the Napoleonic Wars. These wild nomads were barely controllable within the boundaries of the Russian Empire, never mind when they were set loose upon the peoples of Europe. Even Russian allies such as Austria and Prussia complained vociferously about the conduct of these marauders within their territories, so it is easy to imagine the despicable nature of Cossack activities in the territories of France and its allies.

Organization of cavalry varied greatly from army to army. The Austrians and Prussians, for example, arranged their cavalry in divisions, which were attached to their armies or, after the reforms of 1807–09, to a parent corps. The traditional role of assigning cavalry to the wings of an army/corps to defend its flanks continued in these forces. Although each French corps had a light cavalry division assigned to it, Napoleon also formed separate corps of cavalry and horse artillery. On the day of battle, Napoleon would gather the bulk of his cavalry corps into a formidable Cavalry Reserve, which was held out of battle in the centre of his position. He would allow his infantry and artillery to engage the enemy and develop the attack, and when the enemy had been properly softened up, or an opportunity presented itself, he would unleash his horsemen in a powerful charge against the enemy's weak spot. Although an artillery officer by training and inclination, Napoleon appreciated the shock power of cavalry in battle. Often it was a charge by the units of this Cavalry Reserve that decided the day; or in some cases saved it, as was the case on the snow-covered fields of Eylau in 1807.

The Battle of Eylau: 7–8 February 1807

The campaign of 1806 had ended with the Prussian Army annihilated at the battles of Jena-Auerstädt on 14 October, and Berlin, captured by the victorious French two weeks later. The Russian Army had moved to the aid of its ally just in time to be caught up in its retreat as it streamed eastwards with the French in pursuit. As winter arrived, Napoleon scattered his forces into winter quarters across the sparsely populated hinterlands of Prussia and Poland and prepared to wait out the season.

Marshal Ney found his VI Corps assigned to a particularly bleak area of the Polish countryside and, in direct violation of orders, moved his divisions out in December 1806 in search of better winter quarters. Russian scouts reported the movement to their commander General Levin August Bennigsen (1745–1826), who interpreted Ney's move as offensive in nature and sent his army forward to meet it. When he realized Ney's true intentions, Bennigsen determined to take advantage of the moment and attempted to isolate and destroy Ney's corps before the rest of Napoleon's army could react. Napoleon received news of this sudden flare-up in activity and, cursing Ney with every breath, ordered his army

MARSHAL EMMANUEL GROUCHY, *1766–1847. Grouchy was a nobleman with a long and illustrious career of service with the French cavalry. He specialized in heavy cavalry and covered himself in glory in brilliant charges at Eylau and Friedland in 1807. A devoted follower of Napoleon, he rallied to the emperor's cause during the Hundred Days in 1815 and was promoted to the marshalate. During the Waterloo campaign he was assigned command of the right wing of* L'Armée du Nord, *and commanded the pursuit of the defeated Prussians from Ligny (16 June 1815). Inexperienced at high command, Grouchy bungled the assignment. He failed to prevent the Prussians from coming to the aid of Wellington at Waterloo and also failed to reinforce Napoleon, thus sealing the French defeat there.*

French trooper, 7th Cuirassier Regiment

The cuirassiers were elite French heavy cavalry, and the finest of the age. They were large men mounted on powerful horses. Their armour included a full iron cuirass *(from which their name comes) that encased their torso and could stop bullets as well as turn aside sabres and lances. The trooper also wore an iron helmet adorned with a feather and a horsehair plume. The helmet shielded the head and also had cheek pieces to provide some protection for the face. The trooper is armed with the large straight sabre of the French heavy horse, which was designed as a thrusting weapon. The flaming grenade emblem on the saddle blanket denotes the cuirassiers status as an elite regiment, which meant better pay and rations. The cuirassiers were an imposing force on the battlefield. Their thundering charges decided many a battle in Napoleon's favour and established the French cavalry as the dominant mounted arm of the age.*

to break camp and move to meet the Russians in a winter campaign.

After a series of hard-fought minor engagements, Napoleon closed in on Bennigsen's main army and overtook the Russian rearguard at the village of Hof, where they defended a bridge that spanned a deep ravine. Hoping for a quick victory, Napoleon ordered regiments of dragoons to storm the position, but they were turned aside with heavy casualties. In spite of this, Napoleon was convinced a victory could be won here and ordered General Jean-Joseph d'Hautpoul's (1754–1807) division of cuirassiers into the battle. A giant of a man, d'Hautpoul was a battle-hardened veteran who specialized in heavy cavalry operations. At 52 years of age, he remained a formidable presence on the battlefield. He was greatly respected by his men and led from the front where he could always be found in the thick of battle with sabre in hand.

General d'Hautpoul led his ironclad horsemen forward and charged onto the prized bridge, which rattled and shook beneath the hooves of the heavy cavalry. Gaining the opposite side, the French cuirassiers slashed into a force of Russian dragoons and hussars, destroying them and putting the survivors to flight. The Russian horsemen lost all cohesion in their defeat and ran back through their own infantry, disrupting their formations and leaving them vulnerable to d'Hautpoul's onrushing cuirassiers, who were upon them in moments and rushed right through, inflicting heavy losses. The daring attack resulted in the vital bridge being captured along with four guns and two standards.

Napoleon was overjoyed at the victory, and with the battle won congratulated d'Hautpoul, embracing the giant cuirassier in front of the entire division. The normally reserved d'Hautpoul was taken aback at such high praise from the emperor, and to receive it in front of his command meant all the more. He told Napoleon: 'To show myself worthy of such an honour, I must give my life for your Majesty.' The intrepid cuirassier general then addressed his men: 'The Emperor has embraced me on behalf of all of you. And I am so pleased with you that I kiss all your arses' – to which the troopers responded with laughter and cheers. With the bridge at Hof secured, Napoleon was able to keep up his pursuit of Bennigsen's army, and late in the afternoon of 7 February the vanguard of the French forces arrived near the village of Preussich-Eylau, just as darkness was beginning to fall. With nighttime temperatures dropping well below zero, French soldiers launched a full-scale attack on the village of Eylau, urged on by their officers, who promised them that the victors of the engagement would sleep indoors. The Russians were driven from their positions at bayonet point as Napoleon and the main army closed up quickly.

Adrift in the Snow

The following morning found the two armies at roughly equal strength drawn up across from one another on opposite sides of a small valley, which was criss-crossed by streams and small lakes frozen solid and buried beneath a carpet of snow. Napoleon knew Ney's VI Corps was still en route to the battlefield but also knew that General Anton Lestocq's (1738–1815) Prussian corps, the sole survivors of the debacle of 1806, was also in the vicinity and could bring reinforcements to Bennigsen. Having determined that there was nothing to be gained by waiting, Napoleon initiated the battle by sending Marshal Louis Davout's (1770–1823) III Corps against the Russian left flank. Davout, with his customary professionalism, launched a skilful assault that hammered the Russian left flank backwards and threatened to completely turn the Russians' position. At this critical juncture Napoleon ordered Marshal Pierre Augereau's (1757–1816) VII Corps to attack the Russian left centre, thereby reinforcing Davout's success and perhaps winning the battle in a matter of hours. Yet, at this point, Napoleon's well-coordinated attack began to break down.

No sooner had Augereau put his corps in motion across the shallow valley dividing the French and Russian positions than a sudden snowstorm engulfed the battlefield. Augereau's attacking columns disappeared into the whirling storm, and his lead assault force lost its way in the white-out conditions. The other columns followed lockstep behind the lead battalions as best they could, the troops barely able to see the man in front of them, never mind the Russian lines.

As a consequence Augereau's entire corps began to drift aimlessly across the valley until it was marching parallel to, and between, the opposing lines, instead of forward. Abruptly the snow ceased and the winds died down, clearing the air and revealing that Augereau's corps had veered badly off course and exposed its right flank to the Russian main battery of 72 guns, which anchored the centre of the Russian position. The startled Russian gunners could not believe their eyes as they saw an entire French corps with its flank exposed across their line of fire. The Russian guns roared to life at the immense target presented, ripping apart the dense columns with solid shot. Officers and men fell in droves and soon all sense of cohesion was lost under the murderous fire of the Russian artillery. In less than an hour more than 5000 French soldiers fell dead or wounded, including Augereau and both of his division commanders, and the shattered VII Corps routed from the field, opening a giant gap in the French line.

At one point the battle had appeared to be a certain French victory, but it had suddenly transformed into a crisis that could spell defeat for Napoleon. Seeing this himself, General Bennigsen committed his reserves of infantry and cavalry and sent them against the yawning gap in the French positions. However, in their haste to take advantage of the situation, their attack was poorly coordinated. Nevertheless, the Russians penetrated

FRENCH CAVALRY CHARGE *at Eylau, 8 February 1807. Napoleon sent his Cavalry Reserve under the overall command of Marshal Murat against the Russian centre during a critical moment in the battle. It was the largest cavalry charge of the Napoleonic Wars, with more than 10,000 French heavy cavalry massed knee to knee.*

MARSHAL JOACHIM MURAT *at the Battle of Jena, 14 October 1806. A tavern keeper's son, Murat became a Marshal of France and King of Naples. Impetuous and brave to the point of foolhardiness, he dressed in garish uniforms of his own design and used a tiger skin as a saddle blanket. He was in his element at the front of a cavalry charge, but made poor decisions off the battlefield.*

deeply into the French positions, overrunning some headquarters and supply areas and at one point threatening to take the improvised hospital, where French wounded would have been left at the mercy of the Russian infantry. One Russian battalion, separated from the main assault, headed straight for Napoleon's headquarters.

The emperor looked on with remarkable aplomb while behind him anxious officers ordered Old Guard grenadiers forward at a run with bayonets fixed. As it became apparent to all that the Russians would be upon the emperor before the grenadiers could make it, Napoleon's personal escort squadron drew their sabres and charged the head of the Russian column. The 120 horsemen were far too few to take out the massive Russian column, but they threw themselves upon the Russians with near suicidal bravery. They suffered heavily in the attack, but the progress of the Russian battalion was greatly slowed, which allowed more French cavalry to swoop in behind the Russians while the Guard infantry, arriving at a run, slammed into them from the front. The Russians were annihilated to a man.

Murat's Charge

Nothing could have borne out the danger posed by the gap in the French centre more than this incident. Watching the Russian advance through his telescope, the emperor spied more enemy troops rushing to assist the attack. In an instant he knew that he must use his powerful Cavalry Reserve Corps to counterattack the advancing Russians. Napoleon summoned the most famous cavalry leader of the age, Marshal Joachim Murat (1767–1815), to his side.

Murat was a tall, strikingly handsome Gascon. His dress was flamboyant and included a tiger-skin saddle blanket. Napoleon once derisively compared him to an Italian circus rider but also called him the finest horseman and the greatest cavalry leader in all of Europe. Born the son of an innkeeper, Murat had enlisted as a common trooper in the cavalry at the age of 20. When the revolution erupted, his consummate skills as a horseman and reckless bravery in battle won him an officer's commission and swift promotion. Murat first encountered Napoleon in 1795, when he brought the then relatively unknown Brigadier-General Bonaparte the guns that fired the famous 'whiff of grapeshot' that preserved the Directory and won Napoleon his first major command.

From that point forward he was never far from Napoleon's side, leading the cavalry in the first Italian campaign, and in Egypt, where his wild charge drove the Turks into the sea at the battle of Aboukir Bay (1799). He participated in the *coup d'état* of 18 Brumaire, married Napoleon's sister Caroline (1782-1839) in 1800 and was named Marshal of France in 1804. Although a marshal, Murat was never more at home than in the saddle leading a desperate charge. During a battle he could always be found in the thick of the fight, charging headlong against the enemy while eccentrically armed only with a bullwhip.

Napoleon assessed his situation and quickly realized that the hole left by Augereau's shattered corps had to be cauterized before the Russians could take advantage of their opportunity. He turned to Murat and pointed towards the powerful Russian force bearing down on the French centre and demanded: 'Are you going to let those fellows devour us?' Murat immediately understood and galloped off to gather the Cavalry Reserve Corps for a supreme effort against the advancing Russians.

Murat's horsemen had spent most of the battle shivering in their saddles while they eagerly awaited their chance to enter the action. That moment had come at last as Murat moved forward d'Hautpoul's 2nd Cuirassier Division, along with the 1st, 2nd and 3rd Dragoon Divisions, with the request that Marshal Jean-Baptiste Bessières' (1768-1813) Guard Cavalry Division be prepared to support the attack. All told, Murat had in hand some 80 squadrons, totalling approximately 11,000 horsemen. They were the finest cavalry in the world with the greatest cavalry commander of the age at their head. The squadrons formed into overlapping lines, echeloned in depth, troopers pressed together knee to knee, with sabres drawn

THE BATTLE OF EYLAU, *7-8 February 1807. Fought at times in near blizzard conditions, the battle was a desperate affair in which Napoleon came close to his first major defeat. A brilliant charge by his cavalry staved off disaster and allowed him to achieve a tactical draw.*

as their horses pawed impatiently at the snow, waiting for the anticipated order to attack.

The Russians began to blaze away with cannon and musketry at this mass of horsemen forming opposite them, sending musket balls and shells whizzing through the air. The elite *Grenadier à Cheval* regiment of the Imperial Guard Cavalry, mounted on their distinctive black horses, came under a particularly galling fire. The mounted grenadiers were large men, their height accentuated by the tall bearskin hats they wore. As the projectiles hissed past, the troopers bent forward in their saddles, instinctively lowering their heads to the storm of lead sweeping over them. Their commander Colonel Louis Lepic (1765–1827), was infuriated at such greenhorn behaviour from his elite regiment. Sitting fully erect in the front rank, he turned in his saddle and bellowed: 'Heads up by God, those are bullets not turds!'

Now formed into massive lines, the cuirassiers and dragoons in the lead, the French cavalry awaited Murat's signal. When it came, trumpeters began sounding the attack, and the horsemen urged their mounts forward. This was not a wild charge, but a methodical, well-organized advance,

Battle of Eylau

7-8 February 1807

After a preliminary engagement was fought on 7 February 1807, Napoleon launched a full-scale attack on General Levin von Bennigsen's lines on 8 February 1807. Marshal Davout conducted a brilliant attack that threatened to envelop the left flank of the Russian Army, but Marshal Augereau's supporting corps stumbled blindly through a snowstorm, lost its way and wandered directly into the path of the Russian main gun line. Torn to pieces by grapeshot, the corps routed from the field leaving a gaping hole in Napoleon's line. The Russians would have prevailed had not Marshal Murat launched a massive attack with the French Cavalry Reserve and saved the day. Bennigsen was reinforced by General Lestocq's Prussian corps late in the battle, and with these fresh troops he was able to halt Davout's advance and stabilize his position. When darkness fell, the battle ended in a draw, but it was the Russian Army that abandoned the field. The campaign would ultimately be decided by Napoleon's decisive victory at Friedland four months later.

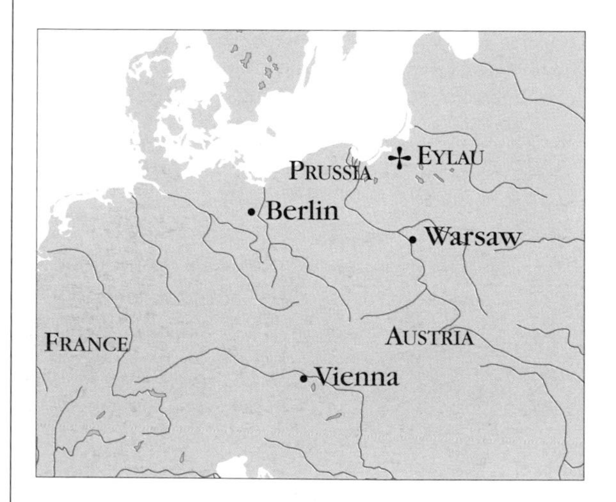

During a rare winter campaign, Napoleon attempted to destroy his Russian opponent in a major battle at the village of Eylau, in Russian Poland.

5 General Lestocq arrives on the field with his Prussian corps, reinforcing Bennigsen and enabling him to stave off defeat. Darkness brings an end to the fighting and Bennigsen's forces withdraw from the field during the night.

EYLAU

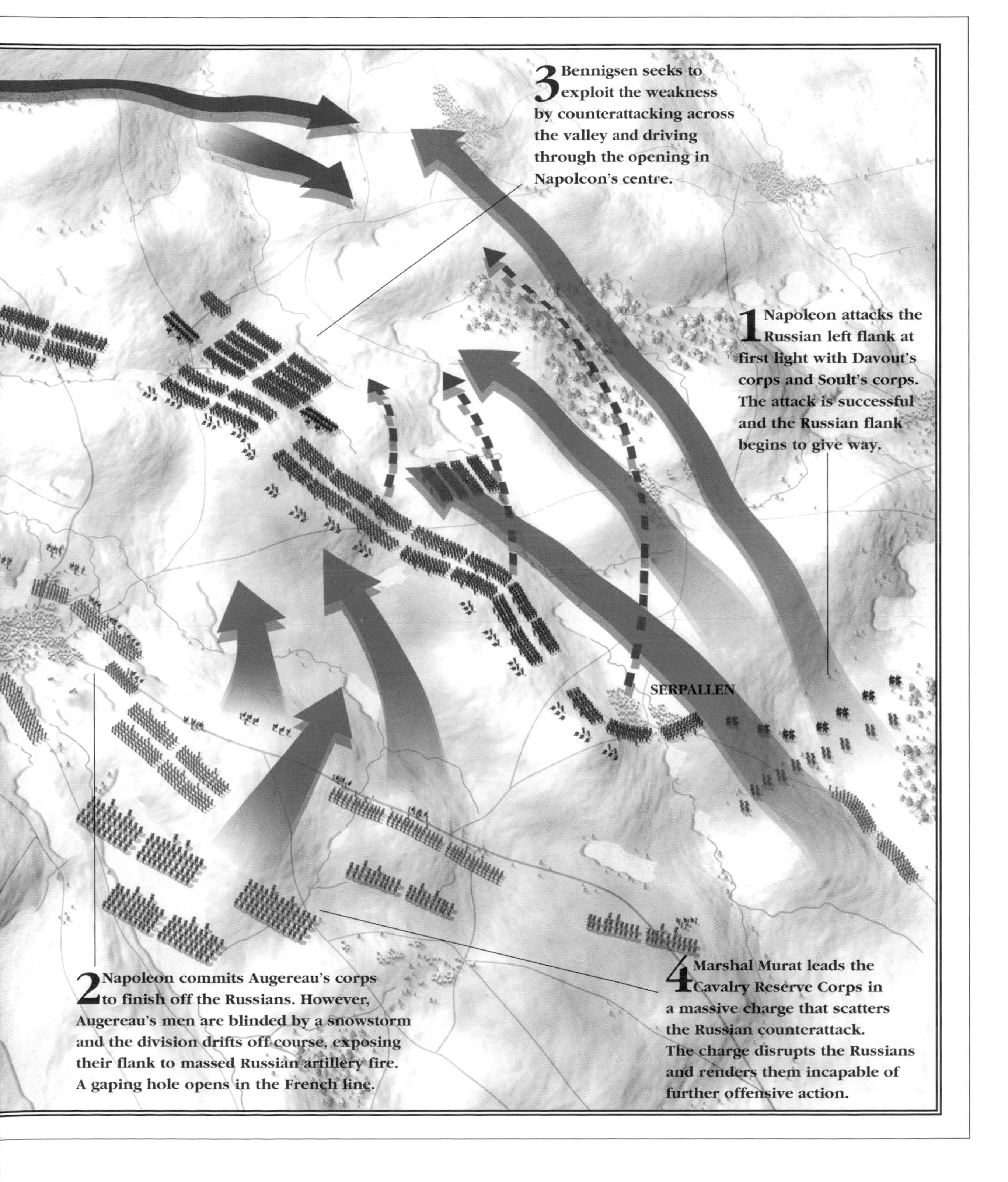
3 Bennigsen seeks to exploit the weakness by counterattacking across the valley and driving through the opening in Napolcon's centre.
1 Napoleon attacks the Russian left flank at first light with Davout's corps and Soult's corps. The attack is successful and the Russian flank begins to give way.
SERPALLEN
2 Napoleon commits Augereau's corps to finish off the Russians. However, Augereau's men are blinded by a snowstorm and the division drifts off course, exposing their flank to massed Russian artillery fire. A gaping hole opens in the French line.
4 Marshal Murat leads the Cavalry Reserve Corps in a massive charge that scatters the Russian counterattack. The charge disrupts the Russians and renders them incapable of further offensive action.

which began at a slow trot and slowly built up speed. The pace of the attack was also dictated by the ground conditions, since the horses had to struggle through snow that at some points on the field had been blown into deep drifts. Yet what the French charge lacked in speed, it more than made up for in mass – it was nothing less than the largest cavalry assault of the Napoleonic Wars.

Flashing sabres

The French horse bore down on the mass of Russian infantry columns labouring their way across the shallow valley towards the vulnerable French centre. Taken completely by surprise, the Russians were overwhelmed and went down by the hundred to the flashing French sabers, which tore through their ranks. As the infantry scattered, Murat's troopers continued forwards and ran into a few regiments of Russian dragoons who had been supporting the infantry attack. The French cuirassiers made short work of the dragoons as well, and they fled from the encounter, only to be taken in flight by the succeeding waves of French horsemen, which crashed into the flank of the dragoons and wiped them out.

The charge continued on towards the Russian gun line, heedless of the grapeshot that sent man and horse tumbling into the snow. The French cuirassiers and dragoons swept through the enemy batteries, impaling Russian gunners who stood and fought and sending others diving for cover beneath their pieces; the remainder vainly fled towards the Russian infantry, which had shifted into square formation to repel the attack. Murat's horsemen slammed into these squares, breaking many of them into pieces and inflicting grievous casualties. Nothing seemed able to stop the onrushing mass of French cavalry, which now stormed into the Russian reserve positions, breaking yet another line of resistance and threatening to split Bennigsen's army in two. Pleased with his success, Murat now reined in his horsemen, expecting the whole Russian line to give way.

Indeed, a different army might have broken under the impact of such a blow, but to Murat's amazement the Russians doggedly re-formed their lines behind his exhausted horsemen, while fresh regiments converged upon him from every side. For a brief moment the French cavalry was trapped within the mass of the Russian army. Yet before anyone could despair, the Guard Cavalry Division, which had been held in reserve for just such an event, came pounding forward. They crashed through the thin Russian front line and drove off the encircling enemy cavalry and infantry that had trapped Murat's force. Murat's men, now reinforced, went over to the attack once more, but could not penetrate the third and final Russian position, in spite of shattering more Russian infantry battalions and driving others into the nearby Anklappen Woods, which rose up like a wall halting the surging French cavalry. Meanwhile, behind them the Russians incredibly re-formed a second time and once again encircled the boiling mass of French horsemen in their midst. Eylau would forever impress upon the French the toughness of the soldier peasants of Mother Russia. After the battle French veterans would say of their adversary: 'You first have to shoot a Russian and then push him over.'

'Murat was the best cavalry officer in the world. I loved Murat because of his brilliant bravery, which is why I put up with so much of his foolishness.'

– Napoleon

The French horses were now blown, and a blown horse was almost unmovable and left his rider a virtually motionless target. Regiments of Cossacks and hussars, who would not have stood a chance against fresh cuirassiers and dragoons, took full advantage of their speed and manoeuvrability to dash into and around the French heavy cavalry, jabbing at the great horsemen with their long lances. Russian artillery batteries moved into position as well and sent solid shot and grapeshot

Grenadier à Cheval

The mounted grenadiers of Napoleon's Imperial Guard Cavalry were large men whose height was accentuated by their tall bearskin hats. Nicknamed 'les gros talons' *('the big heels'), the* grenadiers à cheval *were one of the most elite regiments in the French Army. They were mounted on powerful black horses, and armed with a heavy cavalry sabre, carbine and pistols.*

As with all Imperial Guard formations, the grenadiers à cheval *were held in reserve during a battle and utilized only at the most opportune moment to seal a victory. Their two most famous charges were at Austerlitz, where they stormed the Pratzen Heights and routed a regiment of Russian cuirassiers, and at Eylau, where they were again engaged against the Russians as part of the largest cavalry charge of the Napoleonic Wars.*

whistling through the tightly packed and virtually motionless cavalry squadrons.

General d'Hautpoul's 2nd Cuirassier Division had penetrated further than anyone into the Russian lines, and now their indomitable commander found himself and his division surrounded once more. As the cannonballs began to crash through his command, he realized he could no longer hold his current position but refused to retreat unless Murat called for it. Just then a Russian cannonball slammed into his hip, shattering the bone and sending him tumbling to the ground. He was borne from the field on the horse of one his aides and taken to a field hospital where the surgeon told him the leg would have to be amputated. The old cuirassier knew that such an operation would end his days in the saddle and therefore refused to allow the procedure, hoping somehow to nurse the leg back to health. However, without the necessary amputation, the wound proved mortal, and d'Hautpoul fulfilled his own prophecy of dying for his emperor.

FRENCH HUSSARS ON PATROL. *Light cavalry like these hussars were the eyes and ears of an army. They moved in front of the main force, scouting the countryside, screening the army's movements and probing for the enemy. Clashes between light cavalry were a common occurrence as each side's light horsemen strove to perform the same mission.*

Elsewhere Colonel Lepic's horse grenadiers were also in a tight spot, overextended and mounted on blown horses. Russian infantry began to move in, and a Russian officer called out to Lepic to surrender. 'Take a look at the faces of these men,' Lepic roared back: 'Do they look like men who would surrender?'

Meanwhile, Murat knew the charge had served its purpose and realized that it was time to pull back. Once more surrounded, Murat re-formed his squadrons into attack formation, this time aiming them back towards their own lines.

At his signal, the troopers urged their exhausted mounts to one more supreme effort and sent them rushing across the snowy fields covered by the ghastly detritus of their first charge. The battered Russians could not contain such a powerful force and once more found their improvised squares and gun positions overrun by a pounding mass of French horsemen, who hacked their way back through the centre of the Russian line before at length regaining the safety of the French positions.

French losses had been quite heavy, with at least 3000 horsemen dead or wounded on the field, including a number of senior officers. Yet the charge was one of the most brilliant in military history. It had halted an enemy counterattack and averted certain defeat, while simultaneously inflicting on an enemy force a devastating blow that under other circumstances may well have proved decisive.

The battle continued until nightfall, with neither side gaining the advantage, and ended with Bennigsen's army withdrawing , leaving the field to Napoleon. Tactically, the battle had been a draw, and therefore a disappointment to an army used to the triumphs of Austerlitz and Jena-Auerstädt. The campaign was halted until spring, and in June Napoleon achieved a triumph over the Russians at Friedland, bringining the War of the Fourth Coalition (1806–07) to a victorious conclusion.

Cavalry Types

Delivering shock action on the battlefield was but one of many functions the cavalry was called on to perform. In addition, horse troops were used for reconnaissance, screening an army's movements and for pursuit of a defeated opponent. Such widely disparate missions called for different qualities, and consequently the cavalry of the era was classified as either heavy cavalry, reserved for shock action on the battlefield, or light cavalry, charged with most other missions. Cuirassiers, carabiniers and the *Grenadier à Cheval* of the Imperial Guard were classified as heavy cavalry. Dragoons and lancers (uhlans in the Austrian and Prussian armies) were really a hybrid between heavy and light and thus were often used for shock action on the battlefield as well as

FRENCH HUSSARS DEPICTED *in the fur busby of elite companies and the universal laced dolman worn by hussars of many nations. Hussars made up the majority of light cavalry in every army.*

traditional light cavalry missions. The British Army separated their dragoon formations into heavy dragoons and light dragoons specifically to differentiate the role of a particular regiment, although even then there was some crossover brought about by the exigencies of a campaign.

Light cavalry received their general classification because they and their mounts were smaller than their counterparts in the heavy cavalry. Hussars were the most numerous of the various types of light cavalry found in the armies of the day. Their traditional braided dolmans, resplendent in a variety of bright colours, made them the gaudiest-dressed soldiers of their armies. French, Austrian and Prussian hussars also traditionally wore a moustache and long, braided side locks on either side of the face; with the Russians, facial hair varied, while British hussars were clean-shaven.

In an age in which weeks and even months of manoeuvre preceded the decisive battle, these light horsemen swarmed the countryside, probing for enemy weak points, seeking out information on strength and location and doing near continuous battle with enemy light cavalry bent on the same mission. Such a role required horsemen with a high degree of motivation and elan, as well as a natural aggressiveness that would allow them to operate independently of the main army, and often deep inside enemy country. They enjoyed a roguish image and a reputation for galloping headlong into impossible situations. This hell-for-leather attitude was best expressed by one of the most famous hussar commanders of the age, General Antoine Lasalle (1775–1809), who quipped: 'Any Hussar who is not dead by the time he is thirty is a blackguard.' Lasalle was killed in action at the battle of Wagram when he was 34 years old.

OPPOSITE: THE 2ND (DUTCH) CHEVAU-LÉGERE-LANCIER REGIMENT *of Napoleon's Imperial Guard Cavalry. Affectionately known as the 'Red Lancers' for their scarlet uniforms, the Dutch lancers became part of Napoleon's army in 1810 after he formally annexed Holland to his empire. They suffered horrible losses in Russia, and the ranks were replenished with large numbers of French soldiers. They and the Polish lancers of the Imperial Guard were the only foreign troops who served in Napoleon's* Armée du Nord *during the Waterloo Campaign in 1815.*

Aggressive pursuit of a retiring enemy force was the key to turning a tactical victory into a strategic triumph that could win a war. Although heavy cavalry was employed in pursuit operations, it was the light cavalry that excelled in this mission, nipping at the heels of a retiring enemy, picking off stragglers and raiding vulnerable supply wagons and baggage trains, never allowing the enemy to completely disengage and recover its footing. Fighting was usually limited in these affairs, and the emphasis was on speed and initiative, hence the light cavalry were in their element.

Cavalry Pursuit

The most famous example of the use of cavalry as a pursuit force was Murat's pursuit of the Prussian Army in 1806. After defeating the Prussians at the twin battles of Jena-Auerstädt, Napoleon unleashed Murat and his Cavalry Reserve to exploit the victory. Murat was tireless in this mission, overwhelming Prussian rearguard forces and rounding up masses of stragglers. With the help of Ney's VI Corps, which was predominantly infantry, he captured fortified towns that could have served as breakwaters to his pursuit but instead were taken by subterfuge or intimidation in a matter of days or even hours. Murat's cavalry kept their sabres in the backs of the retreating Prussians from 15 October to 5 November and never allowed them time to regroup or re-form.

Although the entire *Grande Armée* was involved in the pursuit, it was Murat's Cavalry Reserve that was the driving force. In approximately three weeks the French captured more than 140,000 Prussian soldiers and 800 guns. By early November the greater part of the Prussian Army had been destroyed, with only a single corps escaping by sea. Murat announced triumphantly to the emperor: 'The combat ends for lack of combatants.'

Once battle was joined, hussars usually stood aside from the main scene of action and engaged in desultory fighting along the flanks against enemy light cavalry. There were significant exceptions to this general practice, and hussars took part in notable charges at Friedland and Wagram among other battles. One of the most famous light cavalry charges of the era was made by the Polish Chevaux-Légers regiment at Somosierra, during the 1808 campaign in Spain. This charge demonstrates not only the abilities of light cavalry on the battlefield, but also the dramatic impact that a cavalry charge could have upon an enemy force and how a well-conducted charge could completely unhinge even the most formidable defensive position.

The Battle of Somosierra: 30 November 1808

In 1807, Portugal broke with Napoleon's Continental System, under which an economic embargo was placed on Britain, and a French army was deployed to force it back into line. The French war in Portugal required that Napoleon secure a long supply line across the territory of his ally Spain by placing garrisons and depots in strategic towns. The Spanish grew resentful of the large number of French troops marching across their nation with impunity.

With the situation growing increasingly volatile, Napoleon deposed the Bourbon monarch of Spain and placed his brother Joseph Bonaparte (1768–1844) on the throne, thereby making Spain a vassal state of his sprawling empire. The Spanish had no great love for their former king, but swiftly grew to revile Joseph Bonaparte – and the revolutionary political and social system which he

represented – even more. In May 1808, an insurrection broke out against Joseph's rule and he was forced to flee Madrid. The revolt spread, and soon the Spanish Army itself took the field against its erstwhile ally.

Napoleon determined to squash this uprising before it could gather momentum. He formed the Army of Spain and personally led it across the Pyrenees to restore his brother to the throne. Napoleon scored a series of small victories over the Spanish, and in the autumn of 1808 he led a main strike force of approximately 40,000 men on Madrid. His army advanced on the Spanish capital from the north, where the main road wound up through a high mountain pass, at the top of which sat the village of Somosierra.

Spanish general Benito San Juan (d. 1809) attempted to buy time for the Spanish army to organize resistance and defend its capital while hoping for British military support to arrive. Napoleon wanted to make a quick advance, seize the capital and restore his brother to the throne there as a critical first step to returning order to the country. Besides, speed was vital to the French cause, since the longer Madrid remained in Spanish hands, the more the insurrection would be encouraged and grow in strength.

On 29 November 1808, the lead elements of Napoleon's army approached the pass at Somosierra, only to find it occupied by Spanish artillery, arranged in three batteries of two guns each that blocked the road at intervals, plus 10 guns mounted in an improvised fort that straddled the road at the very top of the pass. Approximately 9000 Spanish infantry were also ensconced along the road, on the slopes of the mountains overlooking the pass and in the fort itself. Napoleon ordered General François Ruffin's (1771–1811) infantry division, part of General Claude Victor's (1764–1841) corps, to take the pass and clear the road.

Ruffin's men came under a galling fire from the well positioned Spanish and made little headway on the position. As daylight began to fade, Napoleon decided to call off the attack and resume it in the morning, when the rest of his army would have closed up and thus be prepared to exploit the anticipated breakthrough.

Early on the morning of 30 November 1808, General Ruffin's men moved to the attack, yet once more they were driven to ground by cannon and musket fire from the well-placed Spanish defenders. The steepness of the slopes forbade any rapid movement to flank the position, and the road itself was narrow and winding, twisting back and forth to help ease the ascent, forcing an

THE BATTLE OF SOMOSIERRA. *Napoleon's Polish cavalry captured the vital mountain pass that wound past the village of Somosierra in a dramatic cavalry attack that has gone down in history as Poland's 'Charge of the Light Brigade'.*

attacking army to linger under the Spanish guns. Napoleon rode forward to a point of observation, escorted by the third squadron of the Polish *Chevaux-Légers* (light cavalry) regiment.

Enter the Poles

The ancient state of Poland had been systematically dismembered in the late eighteenth century by the combined assaults of Austria, Prussia and Russia, culminating in the final blow of 1792 when Poland disappeared from the map. The kingdom was divided as spoils of war amongst the three great powers, and while Poles served in the armies of their occupiers, they yearned for freedom. When Napoleon defeated Austria, Prussia and Russia during his brilliant series of campaigns from 1805 to 1807, the Poles believed they had found their deliverer. Shortly after his conquest of Poland's ancestral capital of Warsaw, they began to flock to Napoleon's cause.

In 1808, Napoleon created the Grand Duchy of Warsaw as a satellite state of the French Empire, amidst general rejoicing throughout the Polish lands. Although Napoleon stopped short of granting Poland full independence (mainly because of his delicate relations with Russia), he was sympathetic to their cause, and the Poles loved him for it. In order to show their support for the French Empire, a cavalry regiment was formed from the sons of the finest noble families in Poland and incorporated into the ranks of the *Grande Armée*. This was the Polish light cavalry regiment, and Spain was to be its first campaign.

As Napoleon was busy reconnoitring the Spanish positions near the pass, cannonballs crashed to earth near the emperor and his staff. The enemy fire angered rather than frightened him, since he could not believe Ruffin's infantry was being held in check by Spanish troops, which he believed to be far inferior to his own. Growing increasingly frustrated, he ordered General Hippolyte Piré (1778–1850) to provide cavalry support for the attack. The French horsemen rode forward into the fight, but the combination of constrictive terrain and heavy enemy fire conspired to drive them backwards. At length an exasperated Piré rode back to Napoleon and told him it was impossible to force the pass.

An already simmering Napoleon flew into a rage at this news. He slapped his riding crop against his boot and exclaimed: 'Impossible? I don't know the meaning of the word.' He then turned to Colonel Jan Kozietulski (1781–1821), commander of his Polish escort squadron. The emperor pointed towards the pass and ordered: 'Take that position, at the gallop.'

In all likelihood Napoleon was only referring to the first Spanish gun emplacement, which had brought his staff under fire and was the only emplacement that he could see in the fog and smoke of battle. In reality, the Spanish position consisted of three successive gun emplacements spaced along the road, with supporting infantry units, crowned by a fort mounting a total of 10 guns at the summit.

The Charge Begins

Although the exact meaning of the order was unclear, Colonel Kozietulski made no attempt to clarify his instructions. Instead he saluted Napoleon then galloped to the front of his command and addressed the men. French officers overheard the exchange and thought the order madness – a single cavalry squadron to attack what an infantry division had failed to move? Yet in front of their incredulous eyes, the Poles arranged themselves into columns of four, in order to climb the narrow road they had to use, and prepared for battle. Impetuously, a number of French officers joined the Polish horsemen, as did another platoon of Polish horsemen who had just returned from a reconnaissance mission.

Officers shouted commands for the rest of the Polish regiment as well as other French cavalry units to deploy forward to back up the attack, but Kozietulski did not await this support. Instead, he placed himself at the head of his small command and shouted to his men: 'Forward you sons of dogs, the Emperor is watching.' A great cheer of '*Vive l'Empereur!*' swept through the ranks, and the Polish horsemen drew their sabres, then dug spurs into the flanks of their horses as the squadron surged forward.

A hail of musketry and cannon fire greeted the cavalry's approach. Horses and riders were sent tumbling, but onwards they came. As they wound their way up the hill, their horses laboured to increase their speed on the steep slope. Astonished Spanish gunners hurriedly shifted their pieces to place fire on this new threat as the cavalry swept past Ruffin's incredulous infantrymen.

Grapeshot whizzed through the air from the three Spanish two-gun batteries on the road, and saddles were emptied, but the charge went forward. The Poles hacked to left and right with their sabres and in a rush overran the first battery, giving no quarter and expecting none in return.

Beyond the Call of Duty

Although they had already fulfilled the mission set out for them by Napoleon, the cavalry did not halt. Instead, they continued their climb up the pass. Musketry exploded into them from either side of the road from supporting Spanish infantry and more horsemen fell. The second battery now came into view and the Poles roared through it at full gallop, scattering gunners and infantry before them as they plunged deeper into the Spanish positions. As at last they reached the crest of the pass, the ground levelled and the Poles urged their frothing mounts into a thundering gallop that exploded into the final Spanish battery. The surprised gunners were cut down where they stood, but with their horses blown and over half their number down, the Polish squadron collapsed in a heap, still short of their final objective.

Their charge, however, had unhinged the Spanish defensive positions. With all eyes fixed on the Poles, General Ruffin's infantry were at last able to move forward and they came on at the trot with bayonets fixed. Then, from the rear, the blare of bugles resounded as the remainder of the Polish

POLISH LANCERS, *depicted here as soldiers in* La Grande Armée. *The skill and success of Polish lancers sparked a revival of the lance as a cavalry weapon during the Napoleonic Wars. The Prussians and Austrians also recruited these daring horsemen from their conquered Polish territories.*

Battle of Somosierra

30 November 1808

On 29 November 1808, Napoleon's Army of Spain was driving towards Madrid in several columns. Napoleon's main column of approximately 40,000 troops found the road to the Spanish capital blocked by a Spanish force of 9000 men with 16 guns ensconced in fortified positions astride a mountain pass winding past the town of Somosierra. General Ruffin's infantry division attempted but failed to clear the Spanish from the heights overlooking the pass. The following day, Napoleon ordered Ruffin reinforced and the attacks renewed, but progress was slow. As Napoleon fumed at the delay, one of the advance Spanish batteries fired on his headquarters. At his order, his Polish escort squadron of 125 troopers charged forward and overran the first gun battery, then pressed on, capturing two more gun positions and practically clearing the road all the way to the summit before heavy casualties brought them to a halt. French infantry and cavalry then rushed forward and captured the final Spanish position at Somosierra, thus opening up the road to Madrid, which Napoleon captured shortly afterwards.

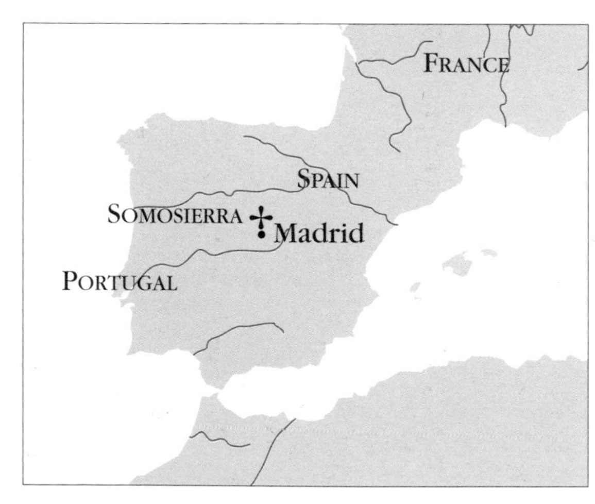

The village of Somosierra is located at the top of a strategic mountain pass along one of the main roads leading to the Spanish capital of Madrid, 95km (59 miles) to the south.

2 General Ruffin's infantry division attacks the Spanish holding the heights overlooking the pass, but is unable to dislodge them.

1 Napoleon's Army of Spain is advancing on Madrid from the north when, on 29 November 1808, they discover their path is blocked by 9000 Spanish infantry with 16 guns holding a mountain pass at Somosierra.

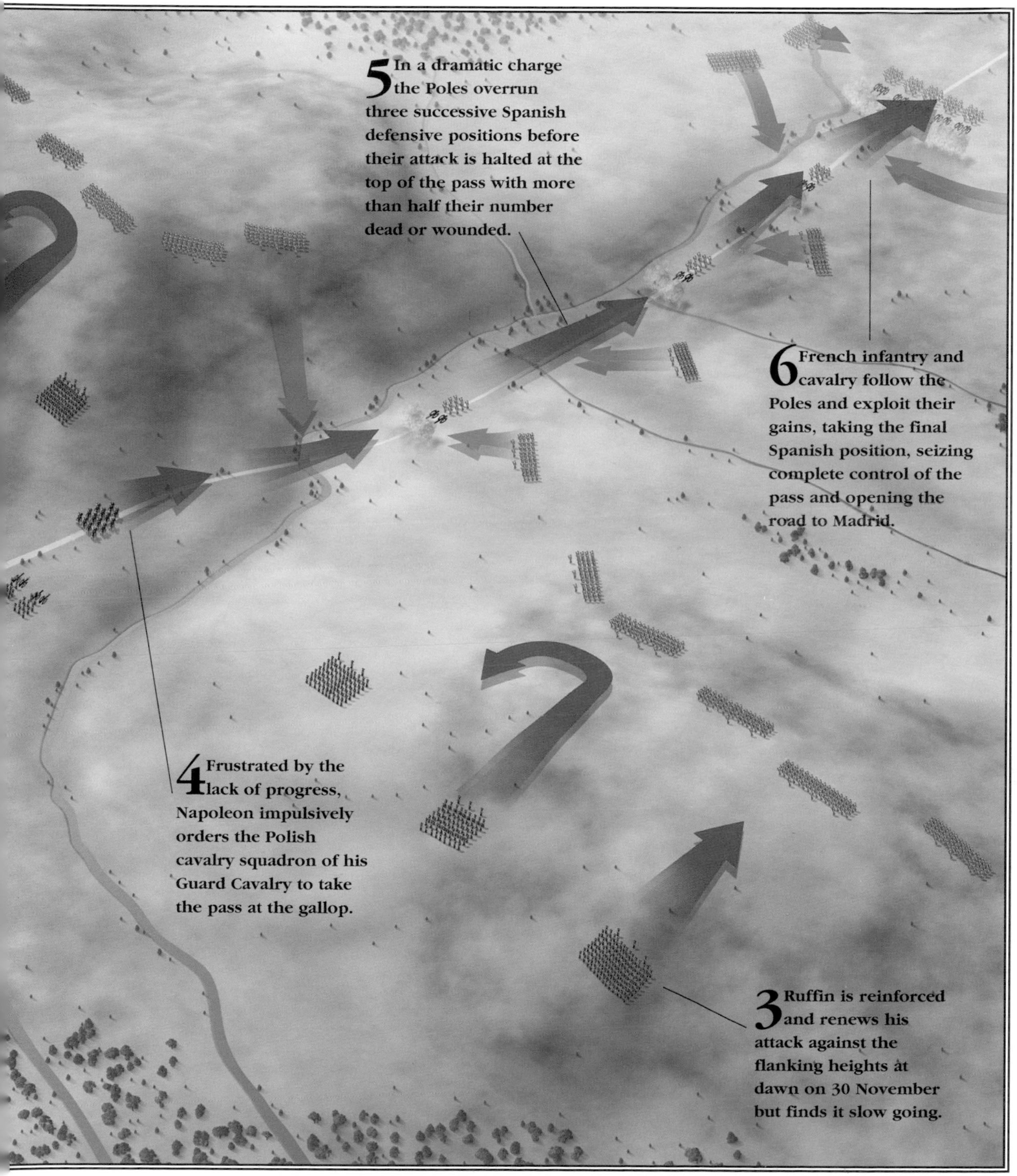

3 Ruffin is reinforced and renews his attack against the flanking heights at dawn on 30 November but finds it slow going.

4 Frustrated by the lack of progress, Napoleon impulsively orders the Polish cavalry squadron of his Guard Cavalry to take the pass at the gallop.

5 In a dramatic charge the Poles overrun three successive Spanish defensive positions before their attack is halted at the top of the pass with more than half their number dead or wounded.

6 French infantry and cavalry follow the Poles and exploit their gains, taking the final Spanish position, seizing complete control of the pass and opening the road to Madrid.

regiment and a French cavalry regiment came roaring up the road. Together with the infantry they struck the final Spanish defensive position at the summit like a thunderbolt and blew through this last line of resistance to make themselves masters of the pass of Somosierra. As the remnants of the Spanish army clambered for safety across the hills and melted away as an effective fighting force, the battle was won and the road to Madrid lay open.

Slaughter in the Pass

Napoleon had observed the attack through his spyglass, and as he saw the French colours mount the summit of the pass, he snapped his telescope shut and gave the order for a general advance. He then spurred his horse forward, as aides and cavalry rushed to keep up with him. He galloped up the winding road, noting the twisted bodies of men and horses, some still struggling for life, which lay strewn about.

Among the first of the imperial headquarters staff to arrive at the pass was Marshal Louis-Alexandre Berthier (1753–1815). A dying Polish officer lying on the ground raised himself on an elbow and, pointing to the captured batteries, gasped out: 'There are the guns, tell the Emperor.'

AT THE BATTLE OF ALBUERA (16 MAY 1811), *French lancers charged and badly mauled a British infantry brigade under Colonel Colborne. If infantry did not form a defensive square, they could be extremely vulnerable to cavalry charges.*

At length, Napoleon himself reached the pass. Amidst the debris of the third Spanish battery, the apex of the Poles' wild charge, Napoleon found Lieutenant Andrzej Niegolewski (1787–1857), who had been wounded 11 times in the course of the charge, sitting on the ground, barely conscious, propped against one of the captured guns. The emperor called for a surgeon and then dismounted. He knelt beside Niegolewski, clasped his hand and thanked him for the courage he had shown that day. He then removed the *Légion d'honneur* from his own breast and pinned it to Niegolewski's chest. The emperor stood and in a loud voice proclaimed that the Poles were the bravest cavalrymen in his army. As the survivors re-formed and moved to the rear, they passed the serried bearskins of Napoleon's Imperial Guard. Under orders from the emperor, the Guardsmen, moving with their customary machine-like precision, presented arms as the shattered remnants of the Polish regiment passed.

In his official report, Napoleon gave full credit for the victory to the Polish horsemen. In recognition of their courage, he later awarded the *Légion d'honneur* to 17 Poles who had taken part in the charge. Napoleon ordered the Poles, later reequipped with lances, to become part of his Old Guard. They would faithfully follow their emperor across Europe and onto numerous other battlefields.

Even after his defeat and exile in 1814, the Poles remained loyal to Napoleon and rallied to his cause once more during the Hundred Days of 1815. Yet none of the host of battles they would later engage in would ever remain as gloriously preserved in the national memory of Poland as the wild charge they made at Somosierra.

Modern-day Knights

The armoured warrior on horseback had dominated the battlefields of Europe for a millennium, but the advent of firearms had generally caused the disappearance of armour. By the end of the eighteenth century, most cavalry had abandoned it altogether. However, in the Napoleonic Wars armour made a comeback, especially in the French cavalry. Marshal Ney came up through the ranks as a cavalryman and was particularly fond of heavy cavalry – in spite of his early service with the hussars – and, along with General François-Etienne Kellermann (1770–1835), lobbied Napoleon to create more armoured cuirassier regiments.

Upon Ney's recommendation and Napoleon's own positive experiences with these armoured horsemen, a total of 14 cuirassier regiments were raised. French cuirassiers wore a heavy iron cuirass, which consisted of a breastplate and backplate to encase the horseman's torso in armour but leave the arms unencumbered and free for action. Armed with a large, straight sabre, heavy cavalry were the modern incarnation of knights – big men on great horses who were used almost exclusively for shock action on the battlefield itself. Besides armour, these horsemen were equipped with a brace of pistols and a carbine, though within a short time most cuirassiers had dispensed with the latter. In 1812 Napoleon ordered French carabiniers to wear the iron cuirass. The carabiniers protested the order, since they believed that it essentially turned them into cuirassiers and thereby diminished their branch of the cavalry. So, to distinguish them from their rivals, decorative copper plating was added to their iron cuirasses, lending carabinier armour a golden appearance.

FRENCH CUIRASSIER *were the best heavy cavalry of the Napoleonic era, proving their worth at battles such as Eylau and Borodino.*

These ironclad horsemen came to be a dominant force on the battlefields of Europe, and the French cuirassiers and carabiniers became the bane of the Allied armies. Indeed, in the campaigns against Austria, Prussia and Russia during 1805–07 the cuirassiers proved themselves the finest heavy cavalry in Europe. They were an almost irresistible force on the battlefield, and Napoleon increasingly relied upon their dramatic charges to finish off a shaken enemy and win the day. Napoleon lavished rewards upon the cuirassiers. They were authorized to wear the red plume and flaming grenade symbol of elite troops, and as such received extra pay. He kept their scouting and screening duties light, and avoided involving them in skirmishes in order to reserve them for action in major battles.

Although the Austrian, Russian and Prussian armies contained regiments of cuirassiers, they never quite matched the skill and audacity of their French counterparts and were routinely bested on the battlefield. Indeed, many Allied regiments even dispensed with the cuirass, citing issues of weight and problems of manoeuvring in the saddle. By 1809 the Austrians had begun to place a demi-cuirass on their cuirassiers, which covered only the front part of the torso, leaving the flanks and back exposed. While this lightened the cuirassiers' load and made it easier on their horses on campaign, it also made them more vulnerable in mêlée combat with French heavy cavalry.

For example, at the battle of Eckmühl in 1809, French cuirassiers dealt a stinging defeat to their Austrian counterparts. During the course of the engagement, the French inflicted nearly five times the number of casualties on their opponents, and much credit for this accomplishment was given to the superior armour of the French horsemen.

Curassier Equipment

French horsemen found the extra weight of the full cuirass negligible, and while certainly more encumbered than an unarmoured opponent, they believed the defensive benefits of the armour far outweighed any inconvenience. The cuirass could easily turn aside an enemy blade and could even stop the low-velocity lead balls that were the standard firearms projectiles of the age. Thus, as these ironclad cavalrymen spurred their horses into a headlong charge, they felt a certain comfort in their perceived invulnerability. Other heavy cavalry, such as dragoons and the famous *Grenadier à Cheval* of Napoleon's Imperial Guard, lacked body armour. Therefore, it was common practice for dragoons to take their cloaks and roll them into a crossbelt of heavy cloth that they wore diagonally across their torsos. This improvised 'armour' actually provided some protection from enemy blades.

'Any Hussar who is not dead by the time he is thirty is a blackguard.'

– General Antoine Lasalle, French cavalry commander

Besides body armour, all types of heavy cavalry in every nation's army wore some kind of helmet. A horseman charged into battle bent forward over his saddle, and thus his head was thrust forward and vulnerable. Some helmets were made of thick leather, such as British dragoon helmets, which were both stylish and functional. Although light, they were capable of deflecting sword blows or lance thrusts and offered a modicum of protection from spent musket balls.

Russian, Austrian and some French dragoons also wore leather helmets, though in widely different styles. French cuirassiers and carabiniers wore iron helmets. Although ornate by modern standards, with their distinctive high brass combs and horsehair plumes, they provided real protection to their wearer from enemy blades and bullets, and were the best helmets worn by any horsemen.

Heavy cavalry attacks were an awe-inspiring sight. Drawn up in great masses of squadrons, these horsemen charged with tremendous fury, forming a mounted fist of steel that could smash through a weak point in the enemy line. They could also be used as an effective counterattack force against an enemy advance. If they could catch infantry in column or line formation and strike their flank or rear, heavy cavalry could wreak havoc, ramming right through such formations and cutting down the foot soldiers or trampling them under the flailing hooves of their powerful steeds.

A heavy cavalry charge would begin with the horsemen advancing at a walk, then increase the tempo to a trot. The idea was to maintain their tight-packed formation as long as possible to maximize striking power when they collided with the enemy. As they closed on their objective, the pace would be stepped up, reaching a thundering gallop in the last 100m (110 yards) until the cavalry crashed headlong into their target, slashing with sabre to right and left as they sliced through the enemy. The sheer mass of these armoured men on their mighty steeds provided a strike force unlike any other on the battlefield.

Dragoons

Dragoons were used by all armies, although in most forces their original role as mounted infantry had been all but abandoned by 1805. Dragoons were often used as heavy cavalry, especially in the Peninsula. The harsh, arid landscape that dominated much of Spain led to an inordinately high attrition rate among French heavy cavalry. The big men and their large horses broke down in a land where water and forage were often scarce. As a consequence, only a single cuirassier regiment served in the Peninsula, and it was strictly limited to operations in the more moderate climate of Catalonia. French commanders were forced to utilize dragoons, hussars, *Chasseurs à Cheval* and lancers in the heavy cavalry role, and thus operated at a handicap in comparison with other French forces in Europe.

British cavalry in the Peninsula was divided into heavy and light horse, although British heavy cavalry did not wear the armour and helmets used by similar formations in France or in the armies of the Allies. Dragoons made up the bulk of the British heavy cavalry and tended to be better than their French dragoon counterparts. This disparity came

Austrian Dragoon

The multi-ethnic army of the Austrian Empire went through more radical changes during the Napoleonic age than perhaps any other. Austrian dragoon regiments were composed primarily of Czechs and Austrians and were originally used as heavy cavalry in the 1790s. However, their generally poor performance caused them to be relegated to the role of light cavalry by the turn of the century. They were average in combat, but performed poorly in the vital reconnaissance role of the light cavalry. As a consequence, they were converted back to a heavy cavalry role by the time of the 1809 campaign, but again fared poorly against French heavy cavalry in the major engagements of the campaign. When the Austrians reentered the Napoleonic Wars in the summer of 1813, they were pitted against the depleted ranks of a French cavalry arm still suffering from the disaster in Russia, and they acquitted themselves well in the campaign. Throughout the wars of the Napoleonic Age, the Austrian cavalry suffered from poor leadership and lacked the tactical finesse to conduct successfully massed charges on the battlefield.

about mainly because the French cavalry in Spain had to contend for recruits and mounts with cuirassier and carabinier regiments serving elsewhere in Europe, who tended to get their pick of the best.

British cavalry was noted for its bravery but also for its impetuosity, causing the Duke of Wellington (1769-1852) to quip: 'They gallop hard at everything and come galloping back as fast.' Nevertheless, at Waterloo they successfully held their own in their first major encounter with the famed French cuirassiers.

Despite the fact that dragoons had virtually lost their mounted infantry function in Europe, the United States Army employed mounted riflemen in their wars against the Native Americans of the Ohio Valley as well as in the War of 1812. A charge by mounted American riflemen destroyed the Miami Confederation at the battle of Fallen Timbers in 1794 and mounted Kentucky riflemen made a dramatic charge that decided the day at the battle of the Thames in 1813.

Since shock tactics were emphasized in both light and heavy cavalry, firearms were secondary weapons to the sabre or lance. Nevertheless, most cavalrymen carried a pistol, and some also carried a carbine or musketoon. Heavy cavalry would often use their pistols when attacking an enemy square, but the pistol was a weapon of frustration more than an arm of decision. Cavalry on the attack were in a constant state of motion and it was nigh impossible for a galloping trooper to reload his pistol once he had discharged it. Pistols could also be used in a cavalry mêlée, but in close action the sword was always preferable to an inaccurate single-shot pistol with a high instance of misfire.

Light cavalry, operating as they did on the fringe of the army and constantly brushing up against enemy infantry as well as cavalry, were far more likely to employ their carbines or musketoons in action, but usually dismounted to do so. Carabinier and dragoon squadrons would often unleash a volley of fire before moving to

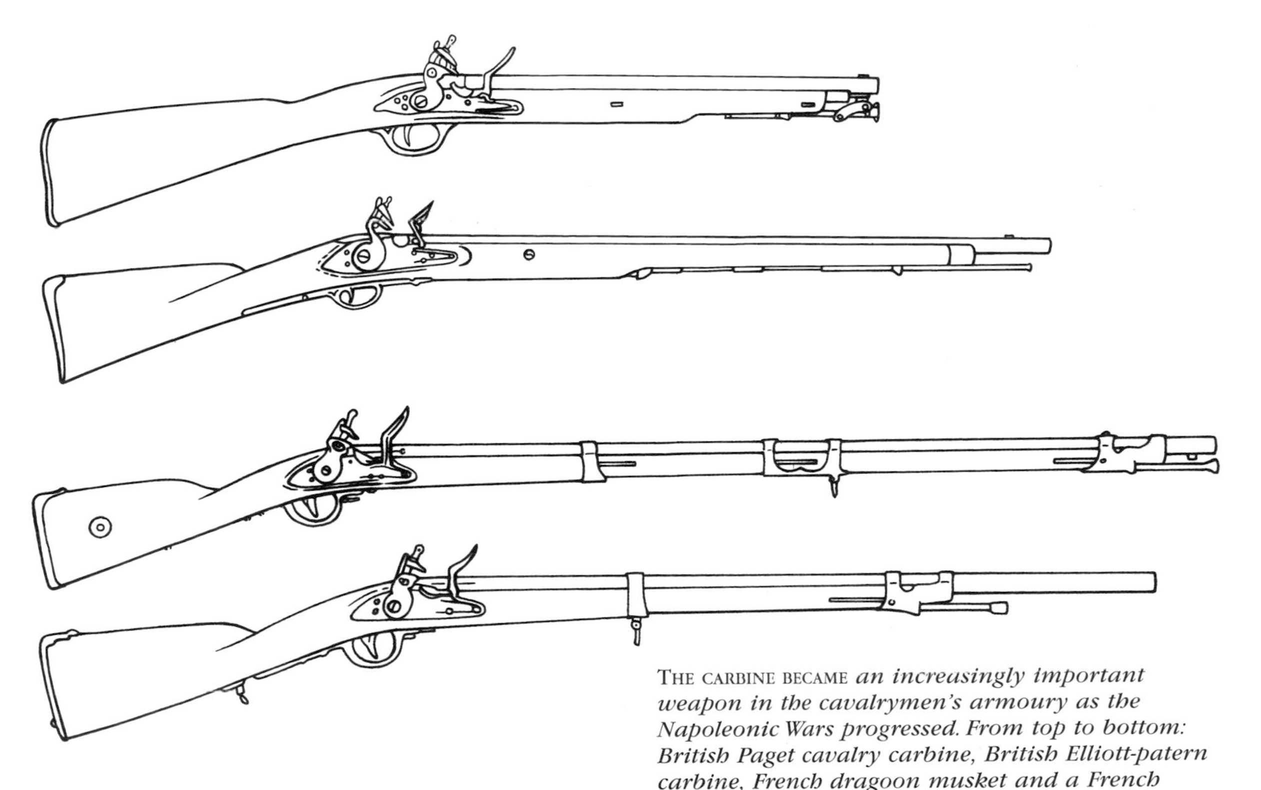

THE CARBINE BECAME *an increasingly important weapon in the cavalrymen's armoury as the Napoleonic Wars progressed. From top to bottom: British Paget cavalry carbine, British Elliott-patern carbine, French dragoon musket and a French IX-XIII Pattern carbine.*

Lancer, French Chevau-Léger

When Napoleon prepared to invade Russia, he converted six dragoon regiments into lancer regiments. This was done to help counter the lance-armed Cossacks and to provide scouts for the heavy cavalry divisions that would enable him to keep his cuirassiers and carabiniers fresh for battle. For the Russian Campaign, the Napoleonic Chevau-Léger Lanciers *contained mostly raw recruits and newly commissioned officers, mounted on barely trained horses, but led by exceptional senior officers.*

The lancer depicted here wears a green tunic, a holdover from his regiment's initial designation as dragoons, and is also armed with a dragoon musket in addition to his sword and lance. The French lance was slightly shorter and heavier than those carried by the Poles. The French Chevau-Leger Lancier *regiments established a superb reputation during the final campaigns of the Napoleonic Wars.*

hand-to-hand combat with an enemy, but it was rare that they reloaded their weapons and engaged in extended firefights.

Light cavalry and heavy cavalry of all nations developed rivalries that were sometimes none too healthy. In the French Army, insults flying between hussars and cuirassiers in a local tavern often escalated into fights, while duels between officers of the rival branches of horsemen were commonplace. Nevertheless, cavalry was capable of prodigious feats and could even take on entrenched infantry and artillery, as would be proved in 1812 during the Russian campaign.

The Battle of Borodino: 7 September 1812

In June 1812, Napoleon led the largest army in European history, over 500,000 strong, against Russia in a campaign that he believed would bring the long series of wars that had shaken Europe since the revolution to a conclusion in total victory for France. Napoleon's objective was the Russian Army itself, which he hoped to destroy in a major battle just inside Russia. It is significant to note that at no point in his plans did he contemplate a deep advance into Russia and could foresee nothing that would take him further east than Smolensk. The Russian commander, General Mikhail Barclay de Tolly (1761–1818), knew that it would be impossible to defeat Napoleon's massive host at the border. He therefore initiated a strategic withdrawal to the east in order to pull the French and their allies deep into Russia and thus thin their numbers through attrition before facing them on the battlefield.

The French cavalry faced numerous hardships from the beginning. Desperate to find and engage the retreating enemy, Murat wore out his troopers and their mounts chasing the elusive yet omnipresent Cossacks, who hovered around the army just beyond his reach. Used to campaigning in the fertile regions of central and western Europe, the French cavalry and their mounts found the sparse landscape of Russia a severe challenge. Forage was scarce, as was water, especially when the Russians repeatedly poisoned their wells and set fire to their own fields in order to deny sustenance to the French. Although such practices made it hard on everyone, the French cavalry and their allied horsemen felt it the most keenly. Two months into the campaign, Napoleon thought he had his first major encounter at last at Smolensk, where the Russians were drawn up for battle. Yet hardly had the manoeuvring started, than Barclay changed his mind and ordered a full-scale retreat, leaving a surprised Napoleon to strike only glancing blows against an enemy force in flight. Napoleon, however, was not the only one frustrated by Smolensk. Tsar Alexander I (1777–1825), tired of watching Napoleon's uncontested advance and his country laid waste by Barclay's scorched-earth policy, replaced his commander with Field Marshal Mikhail Kutusov (1745–1813).

Eager for battle, Kutusov halted the army and established his forces in a strong defensive position 30km (19 miles) west of Moscow, on a series of low fortified hills along the Moskva River, near the village of Borodino. Needing a battle to bring the campaign to an end, and fearful that any attempt at complicated manoeuvring would only prompt the Russians to retreat, Napoleon dismissed a proposal by Marshal Davout for a flanking attack. Instead, he determined to hit the Russians head on.

At dawn on 7 September 1812, 400 French cannon roared to life, marking the opening of the battle of Borodino. Prince Eugène de Beauharnais' (1781–1824) IV Corps held the left flank and opened the French assault by attacking the Russians at the village of Borodino, while Marshal Ney's III Corps and Marshal Davout's I Corps awaited their orders to move against the Russian centre. Marshal Murat's Cavalry Reserve was initially held out of the fighting. It was deployed on the centre right of the French position, with the cavalry corps (from north to south) of Grouchy, Marie-Victor Latour-Maubourg (1768–1850), Louis-Pierre Montbrun (1770–1812) and Nansouty forming a chain to connect with Prince Josef Poniatowski's (1763–1813) V Corps, which had commenced a desultory attack on the far flank.

The initial phase of the battle was thus an infantry and artillery affair, but the Cavalry Reserve was by necessity deployed within range of the Russian artillery in order to maintain the integrity of the line. Thus, though not formally engaged in the early hours of the fight, they were exposed to the frightful cannonade that was a hallmark of this battle, and they suffered significant losses from gunfire.

As the fighting developed, Davout's I Corps battered its way forward in an attack on a series of three *flèches* that formed the linchpin in the centre of the Russian line. Davout succeeded in taking the southernmost *flèche* but only after a desperate fight. The Russians promptly counterattacked with a powerful reserve force, driving Davout's divisions from their prize. As they fell back in disorder, Russian heavy cavalry swarmed to the attack and destroyed several battalions of infantry before the light cavalry of Davout's corps launched a skilful counterattack in turn, which hit the Russian horsemen on both flanks and threw them into disarray. Davout rallied his infantry and moved them forward once more, reaching the foot of the south *flèche* before an artillery shell burst next to Davout, killing his horse and sending him hurtling senseless to the ground.

> *'Our horses have no patriotism. The men will fight without bread, but the horses won't fight without oats.'*
>
> — *Cavalry General Nansouty, during the 1812 campaign*

Murat Goes Forward

With the attack stalled, Napoleon ordered Murat to move Latour-Maubourg's cavalry corps forward to assist Ney's III Corps and the remnants of I Corps in taking all of the *flèches* and opening the Russian centre. Ney led his corps from the front of his assault columns like 'a captain of grenadiers', while Murat, resplendently conspicuous as usual in a green velvet tunic and yellow boots, placed himself at the head of his horsemen as they spurred their mounts into the battle. The fight was once more a desperate one, but within an hour the French had captured all three *flèches* at bayonet and sabre point. Once more the Russians began to organize a counterattack to reestablish their line.

With his customary panache, Murat rode ahead of his horsemen to reconnoitre the enemy positions for a new assault. He was in this vulnerable forward spot when the Russian counterattack began. Within moments he was engulfed in a sea of Russian cavalry, who sought to capture the rider they assumed must be someone important from his gaudy attire. Murat put spurs to his horse and fought clear of his would-be captors, then headed at a gallop for the northern *flèche*. The defensive work was held by a battalion of Württemberg infantry, who had begun to waver as they saw the immensity of the Russian assault coming directly at them.

Just as they were about to break, Murat appeared. As Russian horsemen closed in on him, he eluded their grasp by leaping from his galloping mount into the defensive work. He seized a musket and cartridge box from a dead soldier and then called out to the wavering infantry, defying them to abandon their position while a marshal of France still stood and fought. The Württembergers rallied to their posts. The king of Naples, and the greatest cavalry commander in Europe, became a foot soldier and led the battalion as it hurled back repeated Russian assaults in furious hand-to-hand fighting.

The two southern *flèches* were overrun and recaptured by the Russians during their counterattack. Ney's leading infantry divisions were struck particularly hard by a mass of Russian cuirassiers. In desperation, Ney threw his III Corps cavalry, a light division of hussars, in the path of the onrushing Russian heavy horse, but the fierce enemy cavalry made short work of them. However, the hussars' sacrifice did slow the momentum of the Russian attack, and as the enemy cuirassiers continued forward, General Nansouty unleashed regiments of Polish lancers against both flanks of the exhausted Russian heavy cavalry. He dealt them a serious blow before they could extricate their shattered squadrons from the trap and retreat to Russian lines.

General Lautour-Maubourg committed his cavalry corps to the fight in support of Ney, whose

Trooper, 1st Hussar Regiment (1812–14)

Hussars could be a colourful lot, though this French hussar of the line is dressed more functionally than most. He dates from the latter years of the age and wears the traditional queue (pigtail) and side locks of a hussar. He is well armed with a carbine and light sabre. Hussars were used primarily for scouting and moved freely in unknown country, probing for the enemy and engaging in small-scale skirmishes where necessary. They were not a welcome sight to civilians as they enjoyed a reputation as looters. The infamous arrogance of hussars was insufferable to their counterparts in the heavy cavalry, who generally held them in low regard. Duels between the two were common.

men surged forward once more, retaking the central and southern *flèches*, linking up with Murat and firmly establishing control over these important defensive positions, never to yield them again.

Ney and Murat, with the help of Davout's early attack, had blown open the centre of the Russian line. Meanwhile, on the left flank, Prince Eugène's IV Corps had captured Borodino, crossed the Moskva River and begun a seesaw struggle for control of a large earthen fort soon to be dubbed 'the Great Redoubt', or 'Raevskii Redoubt' in honour of the Russian general whose VII Corps defended this critical fortification. After a brief consultation with one another, Ney and Murat concluded that the Russian Army was in disarray and the moment of decision had arrived. They hurriedly sent General Augustin-Daniel Belliard (1769–1832) to the emperor's headquarters with an urgent request for the Imperial Guard Corps to be thrown into the fight to seal the victory.

Napoleon had spent the opening hours of the battle sitting or slowly pacing at his headquarters near the Schevardino Redoubt, a small Russian fort captured the previous day and chosen by Napoleon because it occupied a high piece of ground in a central location on the battlefield. The emperor had moved little from this spot because he was suffering with a high fever and the effects of a severe cold. Napoleon was greatly frustrated that, with the outcome of this critical campaign hanging in the balance, he was in worse health than he had ever been at any previous engagement in his career. Belliard was shocked when he saw how lethargic Napoleon was when he received the news of the breakthrough in the centre. In order to emphasize his point, Belliard reported the Russians in full retreat and unable to regain their footing. Napoleon paced, hesitated and then ordered the Guard forward. Yet, just as the divisions began to move, Napoleon abruptly countermanded the order. He stated that the battle was still young and patience was needed. Belliard rode back to the front and informed Ney and Murat that there was no possibility that the Guard would be released at this time.

Ney was furious at the news and flew into a dark rage as he realized that his efforts in taking the fortified line were about to count for naught. 'Are we then to come so far to be satisfied with a field of battle?' Ney raged. 'What business has the Emperor in the rear of the army? Since he will no longer make war himself; since he is no longer the general, as he wishes to be emperor everywhere, let him return to the Tuileries and leave us to be generals for him!'

'In the pursuit of glory you win many things: the gout and medals, a pension and rheumatism. Also frozen feet, one limb missing, a musketball lodged between two bones where the surgeon cannot extract it. All those bivouacs in the rain and snow, all those privations endured when you are young, you pay for when you are old.'

– Captain Elzéar Blaze

While contemplating his next move, Napoleon received news that a powerful force of Russian cavalry had turned his left flank and was threatening to descend upon the army supply wagons and even his own headquarters. Startled by this report, he ordered General Grouchy to send his cavalry corps northwards to investigate. When further news arrived confirming the reports and that several regiments of French hussars screening the left flank of the army had been hit hard, Napoleon believed a major Russian counteroffensive was under way. He then shifted forces away from the vulnerable centre of the Russian line in order to refuse his endangered left flank, and ordered Grouchy to engage the enemy horsemen as best he could.

FRENCH HUSSARS CHARGE *at Friedland, 14 June 1807. Light cavalry was mainly used for reconnaissance before a battle and for pursuit after a victory (or rearguard action after a defeat). On occasion, however, they would be thrown into a charge during the battle itself, as shown here.*

The reports of the situation, though basically true, turned out to be greatly exaggerated. The enemy horsemen were a mass of Cossacks, led by their formidable chieftain General Matvei Platov (1751–1818), and a large number of Russian light cavalry under the command of General Fedor Uvarov (1769–1824). Held out of the fighting, as was normal with light cavalry, Uvarov had become anxious to get involved in the battle.

Sensing that Eugène's IV Corps, the left wing of Napoleon's army, had its northernmost flank 'in the air', Uvarov convinced Field Marshal Kutusov to unleash the light cavalry and Cossacks on a large-scale raid. Their mission was to exploit any weakness they found and wreak as much havoc as they could in the French rear area. For a while they caused a general uproar, but Grouchy's horsemen met them, and with the use of dragoons and carabiniers made short work of the Russian light horse and sent them scurrying back to their lines having caused very little real damage. At the time, the raid was judged a defeat on the Russian side. Kutusov was furious that Platov and Uvarov had accomplished nothing more than getting a lot of light horsemen killed. His wrath spill ed over into his otherwise glowing report to the tsar about the battle, in which the names of Uvarov and Platov were conspicuously absent.

Yet, the raid had unforeseen consequences, as it shook Napoleon more than Kutusov realized, and caused a large number of French troops to be sent north to contain it at a time when they could have been better utilized exploiting Ney's and Murat's success in the centre of the line. The episode also reinforced Napoleon's determination to keep the Guard in reserve as insurance against any more such surprises.

The Great Redoubt

With the cavalry raid settled, Napoleon refocused on the centre of the Russian line, which had been hastily reconstituted after a three-hour delay. The emperor readied a massive assault to pierce the Russian centre by seizing the Great Redoubt. He ordered Prince Eugène's IV (Italian) Corps to make one more assault on the objective that had defied them all day. The exhausted men gathered in the gullies near the foot of the hill upon which the Russian fort sat, and braced for one more effort. To support Eugène, Napoleon massed 170 cannon and then ordered General Auguste de Caulaincourt (1777–1812) to take the heavy cavalry division of the fallen General Montbrun, assault the Russian line just south of the redoubt and then swing around and into the fort from its relatively open rear area. As the French artillery began to pound the Russian position, General Caulaincourt arrived at his new command to find the troopers in the regiments shaken and the officers positively distraught over the death of their beloved leader Montbrun. Caulaincourt pulled his sabre and galloped among the troopers crying out: 'Do not mourn him, follow me and avenge him instead!' The heavy cavalry division formed up for the attack. Marshal Murat,

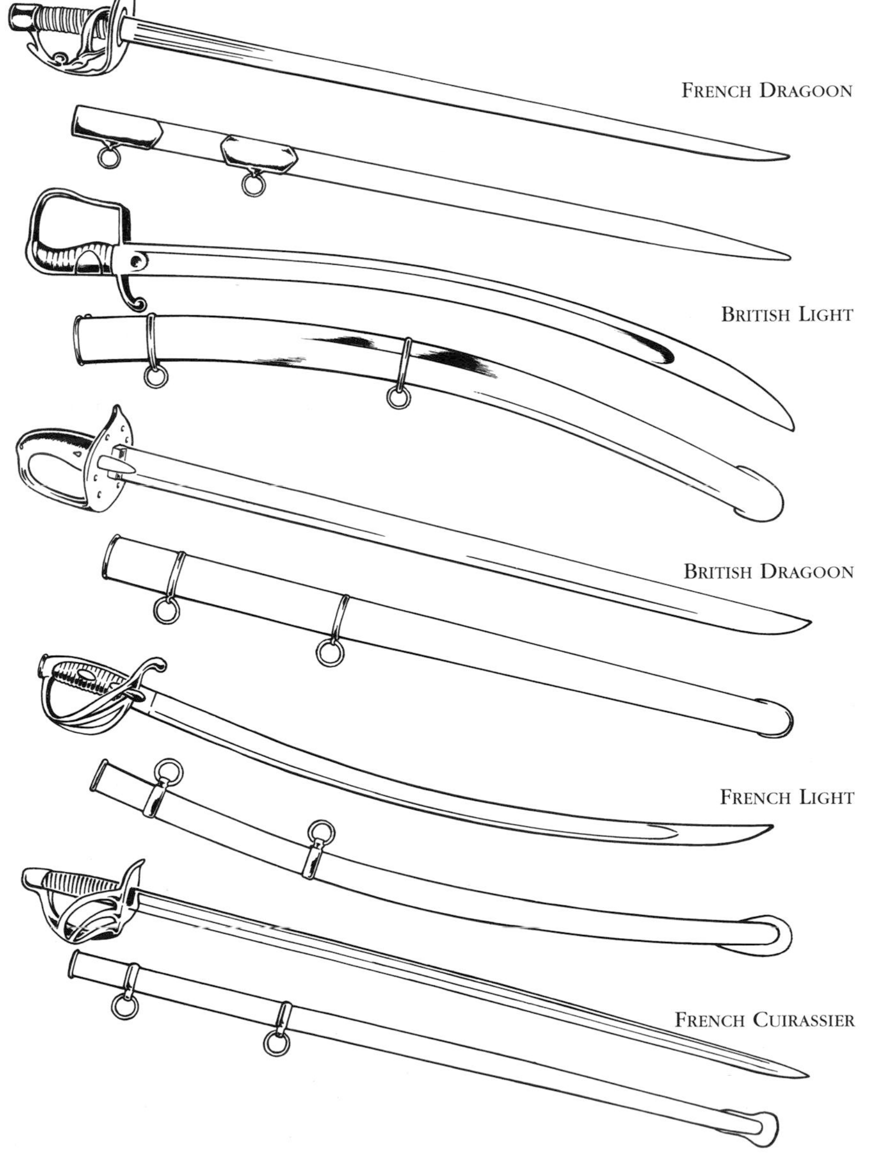

Cavalry sabres *of the Napoleonic era. The sabre was the main weapon of a horseman and the style varied depending on the branch of service. Heavy cavalry used a long, heavy, straight-edged sabre, while light cavalry preferred a lighter weapon with a short, curved blade.*

RUSSIAN INFANTRY AND ARTILLERY *at Borodino. The Russian Army was deployed in a series of field fortifications (*flèches*) and a large earthen fort that came to be known as the Great Redoubt. Cavalry was considered impotent against fortified infantry and guns, yet at Borodino French and Allied cuirassiers would perform the impossible by storming the Great Redoubt.*

his gaudy uniform discoloured by powder smoke and blood, galloped over to Caulaincourt. With Davout essentially out of action, Murat was in command of I Corps as well as his own and thus could not lead the cavalry attack as he would have wished. Therefore, he swiftly outlined the general plan of the assault to Caulaincourt and explained how he believed the heavy cavalry could flank the redoubt and storm it from the rear. 'Break their lines and take the Redoubt!' Murat commanded. 'You shall soon see me there, dead or alive,' Caulaincourt replied sternly, saluting the marshal.

At 2 p.m., the 170 French cannon opened fire on the Great Redoubt. Eugène's 14th Infantry Division and the 1st and 3rd Infantry Divisions of I Corps formed into assault columns in the ravine below the hill upon which the Great Redoubt sat and prepared to make yet one more assault. The cannon fire was effective and caused serious damage to defensive works that had already taken a pounding; in places it even breached the redoubt's earthen walls. After some minutes of this preparatory bombardment, the infantry began to surge forward towards their objective. As they moved, the shrill bleat of cavalry trumpets sounding the charge pierced the crashing din of the cannonade and six cavalry divisions moved to the attack as well. At the point of the massive charge was General Caulaincourt, who had placed himself with the French 5th Cuirassier Regiment, which, along with the 8th Cuirassier Regiment, led the attack.

The French cavalry crested the plateau before them and then broke into a wild gallop that swiftly outpaced the supporting infantry. The pounding hooves of this blue-and-silver mass of horsemen carried all before them, overrunning a Russian artillery battery before slamming into swarms of Russian infantry hurrying to reinforce

Battle of Borodino

7 September 1812

Napoleon's plan for 1812 was to crush the Russian Army near the border, but the Russians withdrew into the vast hinterland of their empire. Napoleon pursued them deep into Russia until, finally, Field Marshal Kutusov made a stand near the village of Borodino. Marshal Davout argued for a turning movement against the Russian left flank, but on 7 September, Napoleon hit them head on in one of the fiercest battles of the Napoleonic Wars. The focal point became the *flèches* and a large earthen fort known as the Great Redoubt in the Russian centre. In a series of attacks the corps of Ney, Murat and Davout wrested the *flèches* away from the Russians while Prince Eugène's corps wrestled for control of the Great Redoubt which changed hands many times. Determined to take and hold the Great Redoubt, Napoleon ordered his heavy cavalry regiments to storm it. Incredibly, the redoubt fell, tearing open the Russian centre. Napoleon refused to release his Imperial Guard to exploit the breakthrough, believing there would be more battles to fight. Kutusov's army limped off, battered but intact. Napoleon captured Moscow one week later.

Borodino is a village along the Moskowa River astride the main highway to Moscow, which is roughly 80km (50 miles) east of the village.

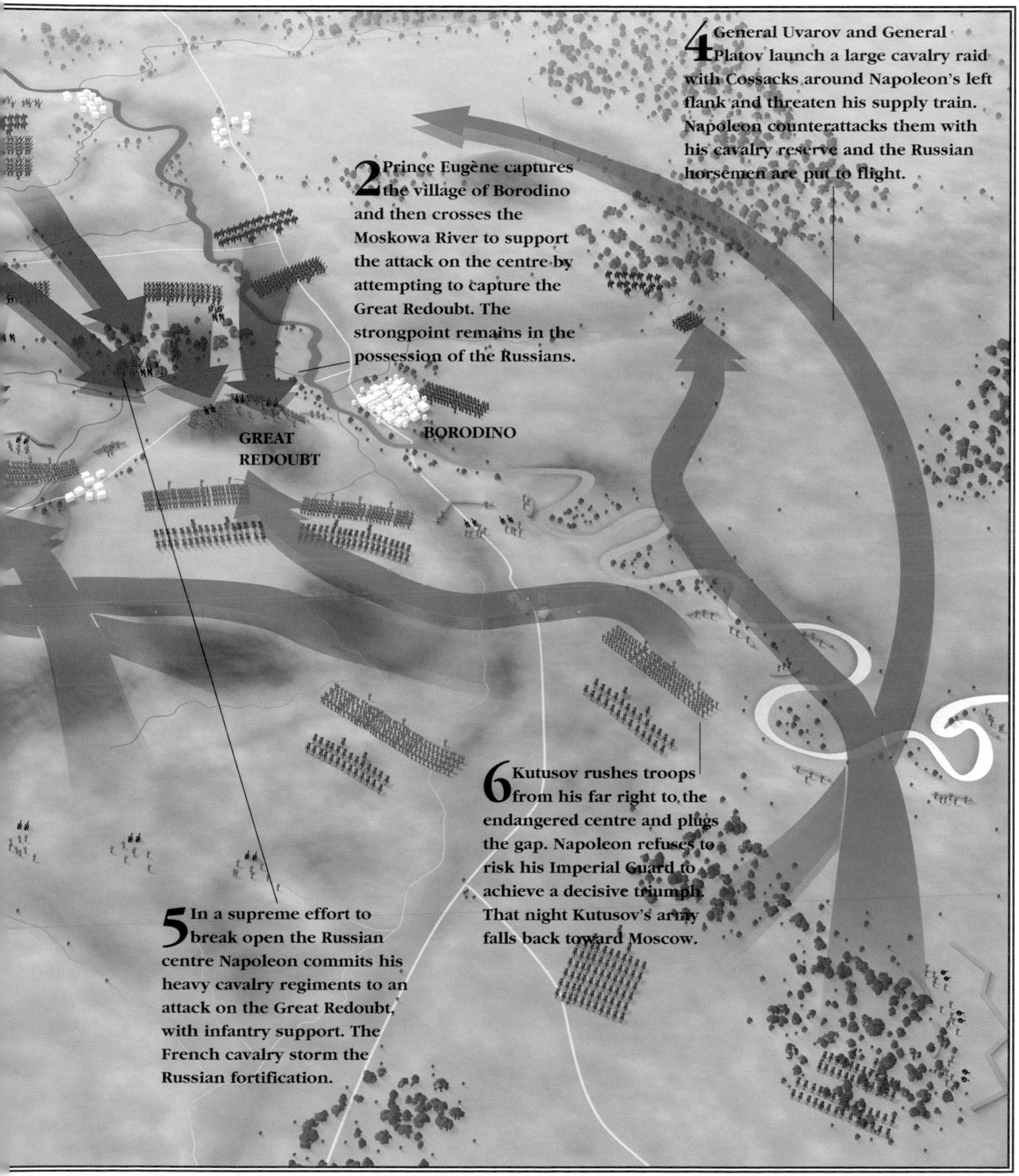

4 General Uvarov and General Platov launch a large cavalry raid with Cossacks around Napoleon's left flank and threaten his supply train. Napoleon counterattacks them with his cavalry reserve and the Russian horsemen are put to flight.

2 Prince Eugène captures the village of Borodino and then crosses the Moskowa River to support the attack on the centre by attempting to capture the Great Redoubt. The strongpoint remains in the possession of the Russians.

GREAT REDOUBT

BORODINO

6 Kutusov rushes troops from his far right to the endangered centre and plugs the gap. Napoleon refuses to risk his Imperial Guard to achieve a decisive triumph. That night Kutusov's army falls back toward Moscow.

5 In a supreme effort to break open the Russian centre Napoleon commits his heavy cavalry regiments to an attack on the Great Redoubt, with infantry support. The French cavalry storm the Russian fortification.

the Great Redoubt. Caulaincourt led his armoured horsemen straight into the mass of green-clad foot soldiers, running the Russian infantry through and cutting a bloody swathe through their disorganized ranks. The French cavalry pounded around the southern flank of the Great Redoubt, and then Caulaincourt wheeled his horsemen to the left, swooping down upon yet more Russian infantry who were ill deployed to receive a cavalry attack. The shaken Russian soldiers scattered under the impact of the French cavalry, and Caulaincourt brought his brilliant charge to a stunning climax by leading his thundering troopers through the back opening of the Great Redoubt and straight in amongst its hard-pressed garrison of artillerymen and infantry.

The Russian infantry formed squares inside the fort and fired volleys of musketry at the attacking horsemen. Many troopers went down, including the intrepid Caulaincourt, who received a ball in the chest and died before he hit the ground. By this time, however, the charge had assumed a life of its own, and the French heavy cavalry were not to be denied their prize. They urged their mounts in amongst the Russian infantry and gunners, cutting

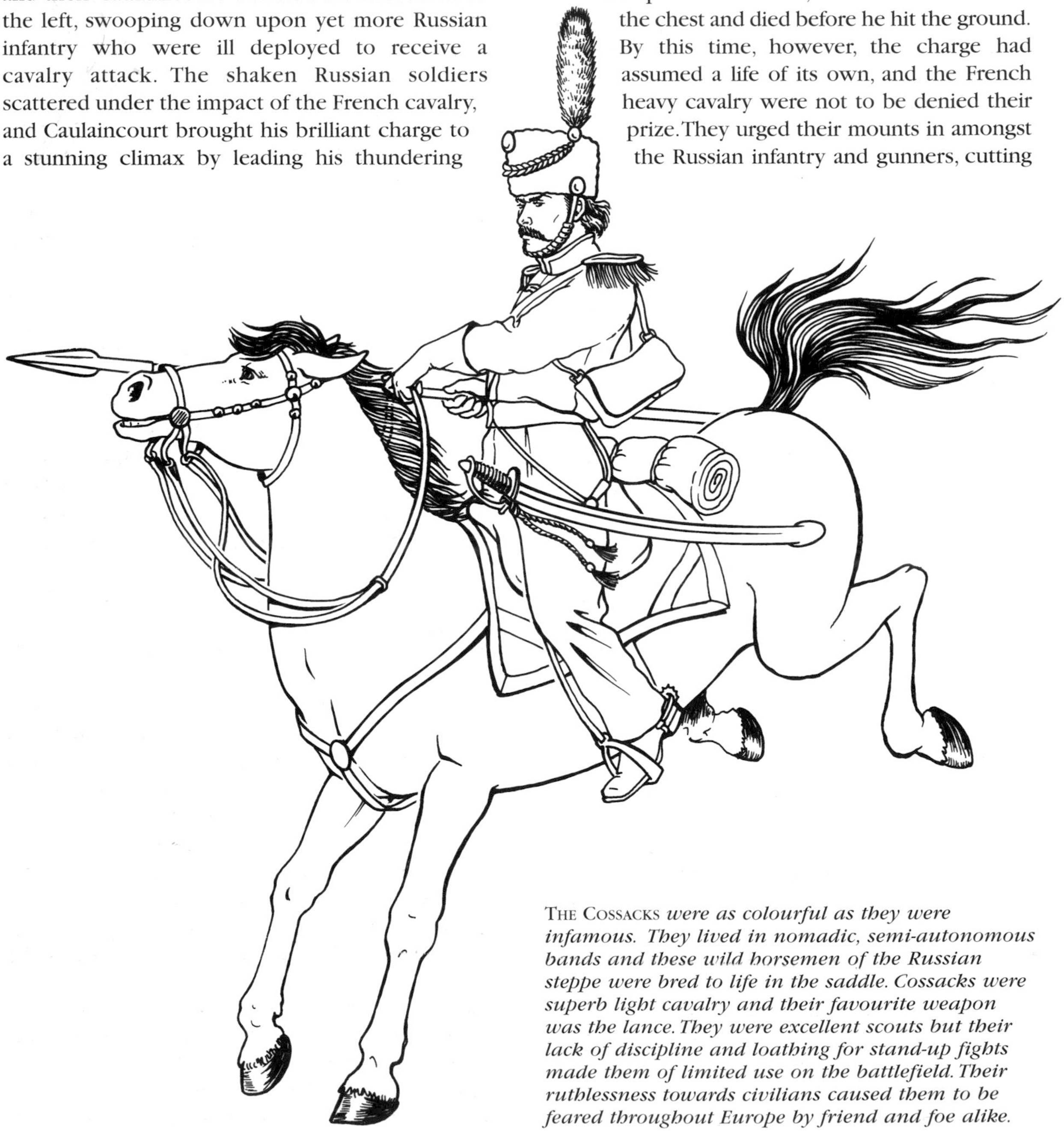

THE COSSACKS *were as colourful as they were infamous. They lived in nomadic, semi-autonomous bands and these wild horsemen of the Russian steppe were bred to life in the saddle. Cossacks were superb light cavalry and their favourite weapon was the lance. They were excellent scouts but their lack of discipline and loathing for stand-up fights made them of limited use on the battlefield. Their ruthlessness towards civilians caused them to be feared throughout Europe by friend and foe alike.*

the enemy down ruthlessly and offering no quarter. The 5th and 8th Cuirassiers battled within the redoubt but were beginning to recoil when more horsemen, including Saxon and Polish cuirassiers, charged forward fearlessly into the fray. The Saxon troopers of the Garde du Corps Regiment jumped their horses over the battered walls of the redoubt and plunged into the swirling melee raging inside. Meanwhile, the Saxon 'von Zastrow' Cuirassier Regiment, the Polish 14th Cuirassier Regiment, and the French 10th Cuirassier Regiment followed Caulaincourt's path to the rear of the redoubt and then stormed in from behind.

The Redoubt is Taken

Simultaneously, the three infantry divisions from IV Corps and I Corps rushed the daunting defences of the Great Redoubt from the front. They bayoneted their way across the earthworks, climbed the parapets and then hurled themselves into the fight inside the fortification. After half an hour of furious slaughter it was all over, the four Russian regiments inside annihilated. Anxious eyes from both sides were transfixed by the spectacle played out in and around the redoubt, awaiting the outcome. Suddenly tricolours sprouted upon the walls of the fort, and over the din of battle a great shout rent the air as cheers spread through the French lines.

The scene at the massive Russian redoubt was appalling. The bitter fighting had turned the earthwork into a charnel house. Dead men and horses covered the outer ditches and the earthen walls of the fort, while inside, where the battle had raged hottest, the ground was thickly covered with a grisly carpet of mangled bodies lying as many as eight deep. Even hardened veterans were aghast at the sight. General Caulaincourt's men retrieved their slain commander from amidst the carnage and bore him to the rear on a white cuirassier cloak deeply stained with his blood. Caulaincourt was one of 47 French generals killed or wounded on this sanguinary day of battle.

'Cossacks are the best light troops among all that exist. If I had them in my army, I would go through all the world with them.'

— Napoleon

A messenger carried official tidings of the capture of the Great Redoubt to Napoleon's headquarters and also relayed to General Armand de Caulaincourt (1773–1827), Napoleon's chief of horse, news of the death of his brother. Caulaincourt was for a moment overcome, then he steeled himself and betrayed no further emotion, although tears streamed down his face. Napoleon turned to him and brusquely demanded: 'You have heard the news, do you wish to retire from the field?' Caulaincourt, unable to speak, bowed slightly and touched his cap in deference but remained at his post. Napoleon's tone then softened as he offered words of condolence: 'He has died as a brave man should, and that is in deciding a battle.'

The capture of the Great Redoubt had caused the battle's momentum to swing back in Napoleon's favour, and the Russian centre seemed once more ripe for a decisive blow. Back at the redoubt, Prince Eugène assumed tactical control of the situation. He managed to scrape together some cavalry reinforcements from nearby forces, including two regiments of carabiniers, and deployed them east of the captured fort. The cavalry of the French and their allies were to assault the retreating Russians and make the most of the enemy's confusion in order to broaden the gap in their lines and prepare for the death blow that the emperor was surely now preparing.

Eugène sent a rider pounding off to the Emperor's headquarters with news of the victory and an urgent request that Napoleon commit the Imperial Guard to the battle and seal the triumph. However, the Russians retired in good order and soon regained their footing. The exhausted French and allied horsemen struck at them, only to find two fresh corps of Russian cavalry moving forward at the gallop to seal off the breach. A desperate fight ensued, but the combination of the superior numbers of the Russians, and their own fatigue after the heavy fighting for the redoubt, forced the

French horsemen to retire to the environs of the Great Redoubt. Here, they could recover their strength amidst the protective infantry of Eugène's IV Corps and the large number of artillery batteries that had moved forward at Napoleon's command in order to solidify his hold on the redoubt and prepare the ground for a new attack.

Dense columns of Russian infantry began to lumber forward, but as they came in range, the French guns let fly with round shot. The iron balls smashed great swathes through the densely packed columns; yet the Russian reputation for stoic courage was never better exemplified than in their troops' dogged march into this storm of fire. At length, the tattered battalions reached grapeshot range, and the French guns raked the Russian infantry, finally bringing their advance to a halt. Russian artillery was brought into action, and a massive artillery duel erupted.

Uncharacteristic Caution

All this was reported back to Napoleon's headquarters, the news arriving almost simultaneously with further urgent requests from Eugène and Ney to commit the Imperial Guard infantry to the battle and seal the victory. Napoleon refused, stating that the battle was still raging and the time was not right. His advisor Comte Daru (1767–1829) cautiously offered that all sides were now calling for the Guard to enter the battle. Napoleon again refused, declaring that the Guard was his last reserve and arguing: 'And if there should be another battle tomorrow, where is my army to fight it with?'

Many were astounded to hear such unheard of caution from their great leader. Marshal Bessières, commander of the Guard Cavalry, urged prudence by reminding Napoleon that 'All of Europe lies between us and France. We are 700 leagues from Paris.' Berthier also advised caution, and even Murat, so eager to send the Guard forward earlier in the battle, admitted that such an action now could result in great bloodshed for little further gain. Such sentiments reinforced Napoleon's own view, and the emperor kept the Guard in reserve. The French and Russian guns hammered at one another until nightfall brought the bombardment to a halt. Kutusov sent a bombastic message back to the tsar, announcing that he had won a great victory. His army then limped off to the east, abandoning 50,000 casualties and leaving the French, who had lost 30,000 men, masters of the battlefield. In contrast with other engagements, the French pursuit of the retreating Russians in the days that followed Borodino lacked the usual dash and verve.

The French cavalry had suffered terrible casualties in the battle, including a large number of senior officers. These casualties were in addition to the men and horses already lost through attrition over the past three months of campaigning. Because of this heavy toll, the Cavalry Reserve Corps was a shadow of its former self and was incapable of effectively pursuing the defeated enemy.

Napoleon won the battle of Borodino (*La Bataille de la Moskowa* to the French) in large part because of Caulaincourt's magnificent charge with the heavy cavalry regiments, which accomplished its mission of storming a major fortification, an unheard of feat of arms for horsemen. Napoleon recognized this in the official bulletin announcing his victory, in which he wrote: 'General Caulaincourt advanced at the head of the 5th Regiment of Cuirassiers, overthrew everything, and entered the redoubt on the left by its gorge. From this moment there was no longer any uncertainty. The battle was won.' Napoleon neglected to mention the role of the Saxons, Poles and other French cuirassier regiments in the charge, but chose instead to single out a fallen hero for the special attention he deserved.

POLISH LANCERS *(left) engage with General Duka's 2nd Cuirassier Division in front of the Great Redoubt in this panoramic painting by artist Franz Roubaud (1856–1928). The charge by just 100 or so Polish lancers saved the Great Redoubt from being recaptured by the Russian cavalry at a crucial point in the battle.*

The victory at Borodino brought Napoleon the prize of Moscow, which was taken without further struggle one week later. Yet his hopes for complete victory were dashed when the Russians fired their ancient capital to deny the emperor its use as a base and Tsar Alexander I refused to discuss peace terms. The retreat from Moscow that ensued turned into a nightmarish disaster. The brutal winter weather combined with a complete breakdown of the French supply network

PRINCE MIKHAIL KUTUSOV *was an iconic figure in the Russian Army. His first experience in war came fighting against the Poles and the Turks, and he lost an eye in battle. Kutusov led the Russian Army in the 1805 campaign and, along with the Austrians, was annihilated by Napoleon at the Battle of Austerlitz. He won back his reputation through his successful prosecution of the Russo-Turkish War (1806–1812). Summoned by Tsar Alexander I to stop Napoleon's invasion of Russia, he fought a stubborn defensive battle at Borodino, where he lost half his army. He avoided a repetition of Austerlitz, but had to abandon Moscow.*

destroyed the *Grande Armée* and revealed Napoleon's triumph at Borodino to have been a tactical victory in an otherwise calamitous campaign. Napoleon's final pronouncement on the desperate fight was: 'Of all my battles, the most terrible was the one I fought before Moscow. The greatest valour was displayed, and the least result gained of any of my victories.'

Cavalry Tactics

Trained infantry with steady nerves could shift into square formation to receive a cavalry charge. If organized properly, these infantry squares presented the charging horsemen with a series of battalion-sized hedgehogs bristling with bayonets and virtually impervious to cavalry attack. This was why a cavalry attack, like any successful tactical manoeuvre on a Napoleonic battlefield, required the careful coordination of all the combat arms of infantry, cavalry and artillery working in combination.

Napoleon stated that it was imperative that cavalry assaults be supported by artillery, since the horsemen, armed exclusively with melee weapons, could not generate firepower on their own. Consequently, artillery batteries were attached directly to cavalry divisions. Known as horse artillery, these units had mounted gun crews that enabled them to keep up with the cavalry. Horse artillery was assigned as an integral part of every cavalry division in the French Army. These batteries were equipped with light guns that fired a 4lb (1.8kg) or 6lb (2.7kg) ball, and they provided the main fire support to a cavalry attack. Although the projectiles their guns fired were small in comparison with those of the foot artillery, the horse artillery were usually presented with vulnerable targets, since infantry would form into their tight-packed squares to resist a cavalry attack.

Such formations multiplied the effectiveness of the guns, which could send their shot bounding through these tight clumps of soldiers. The ability of the horse artillery to move more rapidly than their foot artillery counterparts also allowed for the lighter guns to be rapidly deployed at quite short ranges. Should they come under attack, horse artillery batteries could also limber up and manoeuvre away from their attackers far faster than foot artillery.

As previously mentioned, cavalrymen, especially light cavalry, occasionally carried pistols, musketoons or carbines. Nevertheless, their main weapon remained the sabre. Heavy cavalry wielded a long, heavy, straight-bladed sword designed for thrusting. Light cavalry used a smaller weapon, with a slightly curved blade, designed for slashing at an opponent. Debate raged throughout the era over the most efficient way to use a blade on horseback, but most agreed with the French that the thrust was by far the more lethal of the two types of blows.

When fighting enemy horsemen, as a charge mounted in intensity and approached its target, cavalrymen would turn their blades so that they were horizontal rather than vertical in section, thus allowing the sword to slip more easily between an adversary's ribs, lessening the chance of the weapon becoming stuck in his body. The impact of a charging horseman was enough to drive the blade home, so cavalrymen were trained to begin withdrawing their weapon as soon as the blade penetrated, in order to deliver a second thrust to finish off their opponent or engage a new adversary if the first man was down or had surrendered. When slashing, a cavalryman was trained to aim his swing low, so that even if his opponent ducked down in the saddle - a common reflexive defensive manoeuvre, the blade would still strike some part of his body.

'It is the business of cavalry to follow up the victory, and to prevent the beaten army from rallying.'

– NAPOLEON

The Lance Returns

While the sabre remained the main weapon employed by the cavalry of all the major combatants, the lance enjoyed a renaissance as a cavalry weapon during the Napoleonic Wars. The lance was the traditional weapon of the horseman for centuries, but it had largely fallen into disuse by the end of the eighteenth century. In the 1805 campaign, the Austrian cavalry contained some lancer regiments, and the Cossacks of the Russian Army also utilized the weapon. On the eve of the Russian campaign, Napoleon converted a number of Chevaux-Légers (light cavalry) regiments into lancers, and also assigned regiments of lancers to his heavy cavalry divisions to provide them with a scouting force. This measure allowed the heavy cavalry regiments to stay rested and ready for battle.

French lancers carried two types of lance. The original was the model 1809 *lance polonaise,* which was carried by the original Polish lancer regiments, and was 2.8m (9.2ft) long, with a 38.3cm (15in) iron spear tip. When French lancer regiments were formed on the eve of the Russian campaign, they were issued with the model 1811 *lance française,* which was slightly shorter at 2.75m (9ft), had a smaller (21.6cm/8.5in) spear tip and was of lighter construction. Though the Poles shunned the shorter, lighter weapon, the French found it an easier weapon on which to train new horsemen and also found it easier to carry when on extended rides. Frenchman and Pole alike complained about the regulation of attaching a pennant to the lance. Though it added to the aesthetic appearance of the lancers, the flapping pennant created drag while riding, making it a nuisance on campaign.

The effectiveness of lancers on the battlefield is evidenced by the widespread adoption of the lance as a weapon by Prussian, Austrian and Russian cavalry from 1812 onwards. In the Austrian and Prussian armies, the lancers were called uhlans, and their weapons tended to be roughly the same length as those of their French adversaries. Russian Cossacks favoured the lance, and their weapons could reach more than 4m (13ft) in length.

Allied lancer regiments were increasingly more numerous from 1813 onwards, but their training was far less thorough than that of the French lancers. Even against the green French cavalry of 1813, the uhlans rarely performed well, although there were some notable exceptions to this general rule. British cavalry theorists were initially more

sceptical of the weapon but Britain would eventually form lancer regiments after the Napoleonic Wars. The lance gave the cavalryman tremendous reach, although it was found that in its traditional arena of mounted combat, the weapon proved unwieldy at close quarters. In fact, when lancers were engaged with enemy cavalry it was not uncommon for them to drop their lances and draw sabres, which were more effective in the close-packed mêlée of a cavalry battle.

Conversely, when fighting against infantry, the lance was indispensable. A lancer could impale his foot soldier opponent with ease, and the lance was the only *arme blanche* (the French equivalent of 'cold steel') weapon that could be used effectively against infantry in square formation. A famous example of this was at the battle of Dresden on 26 August 1813. Napoleon launched a powerful cavalry attack in the late afternoon during a driving rainstorm. Although the foul weather conditions made it almost impossible for the horses to get up speed for a proper charge across the muddy fields, the rain also rendered muskets useless since it saturated the powder and flints of the infantry.

French lancers picked apart Austrian and Russian squares during the battle by trotting round the impotent foot soldiers and skewering them at their leisure. When used against broken infantry formations, retreating enemy columns or when

FRENCH CUIRASSIERS *versus British heavy cavalry (Life Guards) at Waterloo. The Battle of Waterloo marked the first major clash between French cuirassiers and British heavy cavalry because, generally speaking, the French did not use their elite heavy cavalry in the Peninsula. The British heavy cavalry held its own at Waterloo and, though suffering grievous casualties, gave the famed cuirassiers a tough fight.*

amongst an enemy supply train during a pursuit, lancers were without peer and could wreak havoc. Perhaps no engagement better exemplifies the use of the lance, and also the effectiveness of infantry in square formation than the battle of Quatre Bras, fought in central Belgium in the summer of 1815.

The Battle of Quatre Bras: 16 June 1815

Napoleon, exiled to Elba in May 1814, escaped from his island prison less than one year later, and returned to power in the spring of 1815. His latest ascension to the throne reignited the Napoleonic Wars as all of Europe declared against him and began to mobilize their armies once more to secure his downfall. As powerful enemy forces began to gather on the frontiers of France, Napoleon made the first move, electing to take the offensive rather than allow the combined weight of the Allied forces to crush him. Napoleon placed a small screening force along his eastern frontier to face the Austrians and Russians, who were gathering there, while he personally led the newly formed *Armée du Nord* north into Belgium to confront the Anglo-Allied and Prussian armies.

The *Armée du Nord* possessed the finest cavalry force Napoleon had fielded since the Russian campaign three years earlier. It included a large number of the famed cuirassier regiments, as well as the Polish lancers of the Imperial Guard, which comprised the only foreign contingent in the army. Most of the troopers were splendidly mounted, courtesy of horses imported over the course of the previous year by the late Bourbon regime. Veteran cuirassier General Emmanuel Grouchy was promoted to the rank of marshal on the eve of the campaign and named commander of the right wing of the army. Many of the great cavalry commanders of the wars had rallied to the cause of their returned emperor, including Piré, Kellermann and a host of veteran regimental and squadron commanders. Yet for all this talent, there was a massive void, for the greatest cavalry commander of them all, Marshal Joachim Murat, was not with them.

Murat had abandoned the emperor after the defeat at Leipzig in 1813 and entered into treasonous negotiations with the Allies in the hope of securing his own throne in Naples in exchange for his cooperation. After Napoleon's abdication, however, the victorious Allies turned cold towards him and at the Congress of Vienna sought to usurp Murat's rule over the kingdom of Naples. Murat consequently spent the duration of Napoleon's first exile lamenting his decision to abandon the emperor. Realizing that he had made a horrible mistake, Murat was therefore overjoyed when he learned of Napoleon's escape from Elba and had immediately voiced his kingdom's support for the restored French Empire by rashly declaring war on the Allies, even though formal hostilities had not yet begun. Napoleon had been angered by the rash Gascon's decision, even though there was really little hope of the Allies quietly acquiescing in Napoleon's resumption of the throne.

Murat travelled to Paris and sought an audience with Napoleon, but the emperor refused to see him. Crestfallen, Murat returned to Italy to fight his own private war in support of the empire, while Napoleon's decision not to forgive Murat for his actions cost him the services of the greatest cavalry commander in Europe. Given the critical role that the French cavalry would play in the 1815 campaign, and the numerous times it was misused at Quatre Bras and later at Waterloo, the impact of Napoleon's decision to deny Murat a command is one of the great 'what ifs?' of the Waterloo campaign.

'The Cuirassiers, in their sparkling steel breastplates and helmets, mounted on strong black horses...were galloping towards me, tearing up the earth as they went, the trumpets blowing wild notes in the midst of the discharges of grape and canister shot from the heights. Around me there was one continuous noise of clashing arms, shouting of men, neighing of horses.'

– Sgt-Major John Dickson, Scots Greys, Battle of Waterloo

As the *Armée du Nord* moved north into Belgium, Napoleon divided his forces, sending Marshal Michel Ney, commander of the left wing, with 24,000 men to engage the Duke of Wellington's Anglo-Allied army and prevent them from coming to the aid of Field Marshal Gebhard von Blücher's (1742–1819) Prussians. The latter were deeply ensconced in the hills near the village of Ligny and would be the main objective. Napoleon took the bulk of the army eastwards to attack the Prussians, maintaining the Comte d'Erlon's (1765–1844) 20,000-strong I Corps, which was technically assigned to Ney's left wing, as a general reserve. Napoleon's orders to Ney were to capture the crossroads of Quatre Bras, keeping the Anglo-Allied and Prussian armies separate, and then, if possible, to fall upon the left rear of the Prussians.

With two infantry divisions and one cavalry division, Ney decided to advance cautiously, since scouts reported Wellington's Anglo-Allied army to be in close proximity. In reality, only 8000 troops held the crossroads when Ney first arrived. Having fought Wellington in the Peninsula, Ney was aware of the duke's skill in concealing his main force and therefore believed that what he saw was just a false front to entice him into a rash attack. It was, therefore, not until 2 p.m. that Ney began to move cautiously forward.

Wellington Reacts

As the sounds of fighting erupted to his front, Wellington realized the importance of Quatre Bras and ordered his powerful Anglo-Allied army to converge on the crossroads as quickly as possible. British reinforcements began arriving in short order and what began as a skirmish escalated into a full-scale engagement, with both Ney and Wellington feeding more forces into the fight.

As he slowly gained the upper hand, Ney ordered a powerful cavalry attack by General Piré's lancers of the Imperial Guard. The French cavalry force formed into a solid mass and began to move up the Brussels road towards the crossroads, increasing their tempo as they went. Partially obscured by the wheat, which stood tall in the fields in high summer, the advance of the

British Light Dragoon

He wears the distinctive high fur cap of the British light dragoons and is armed with a light sabre. Dragoons also carried a carbine and were trained to fight as dismounted infantry. The British Army divided their dragoons into light and heavy to differentiate between the role of certain regiments for reconnaissance and others for shock action on the battlefield. In spite of this distinction, the formal lines became blurred on active service and light dragoons took part in numerous battles during the course of the Peninsular War. In the Peninsula, British light cavalry did not enjoy a good reputation as a scouting force but fought bravely, if often undisciplined, on the field of battle.

Battle of Quatre Bras

16 June 1815

On 16 June 1815, Napoleon ordered Marshal Ney, commanding the left wing of the *Armée du Nord*, to take possession of the crossroads of Quatre Bras. Ney moved cautiously forward, fearful of encountering the Duke of Wellington's main Anglo-Allied Army. Ney's attack was methodical and, initially, successful. However, Wellington's army rushed to the scene of action, offering stubborn resistance. Weighing the odds, Ney ordered Comte d'Erlon's I Corps to support him, only to have Napoleon direct d'Erlon to support the main French army engaged against the Prussians at Ligny. Napoleon also ordered Ney to speed his capture of Quatre Bras in order to fall upon the Prussian rear. A furious Ney hurled his cavalry forward in a desperate attempt to smash the Anglo-Allied forces. With reinforcements arriving steadily, Wellington repulsed Ney's attack and, by early evening, the French were outnumbered. Wellington counterattacked, driving Ney's forces back to their original starting positions, though the battle ended in a draw. Wellington withdrew from the field the next day, retreating to fight the decisive Battle of Waterloo.

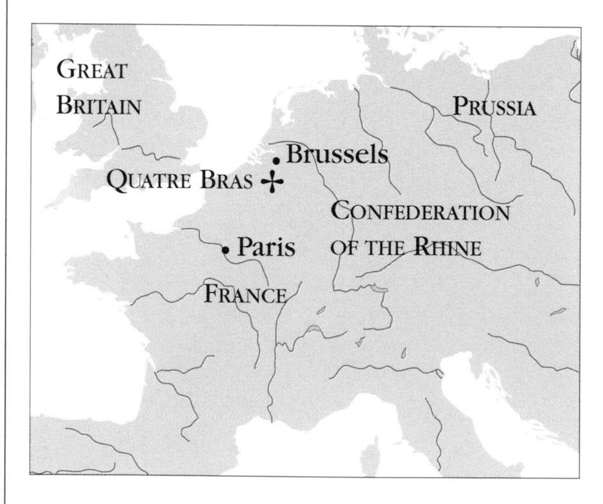

Quatre Bras was a tiny hamlet in southern Belgium located at a vital crossroads of the main highway to Brussels some 40km (25 miles) to the north.

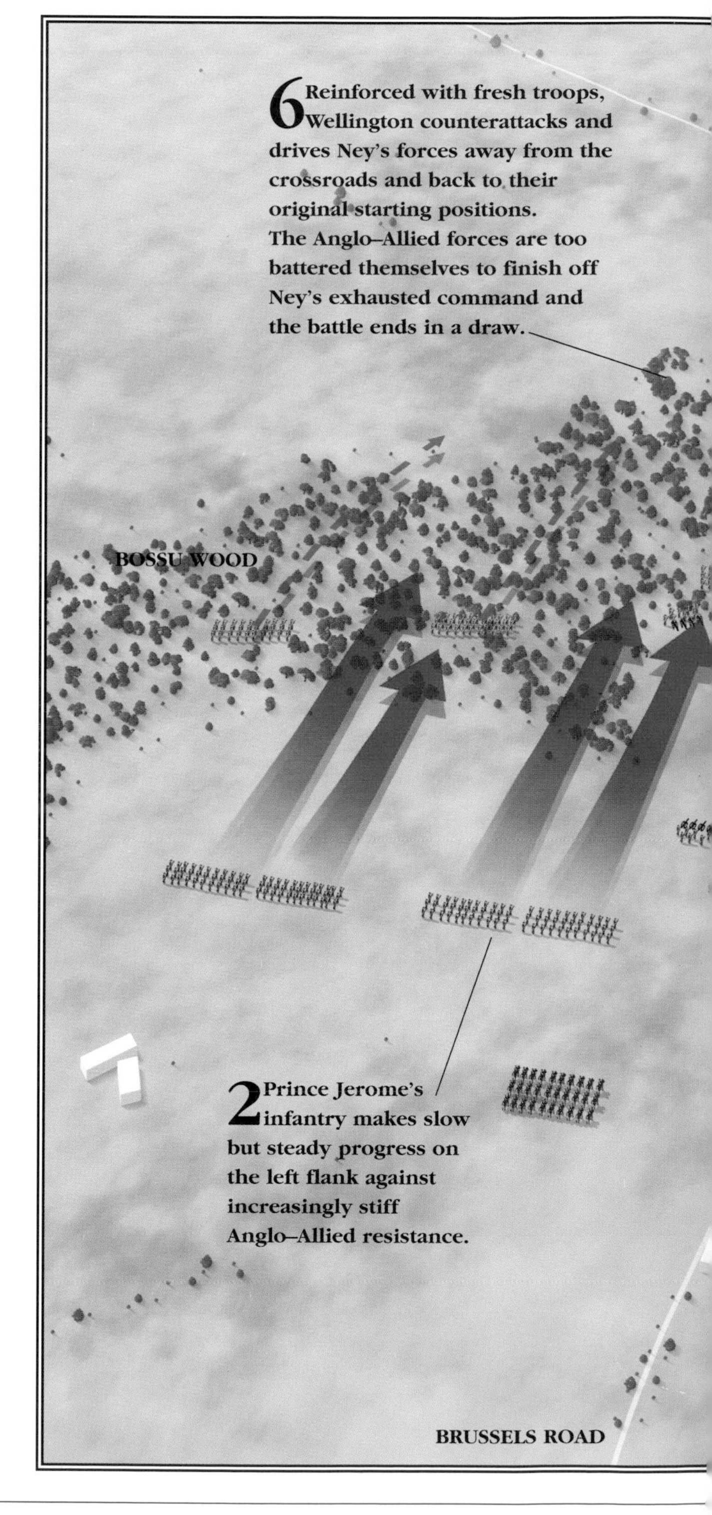

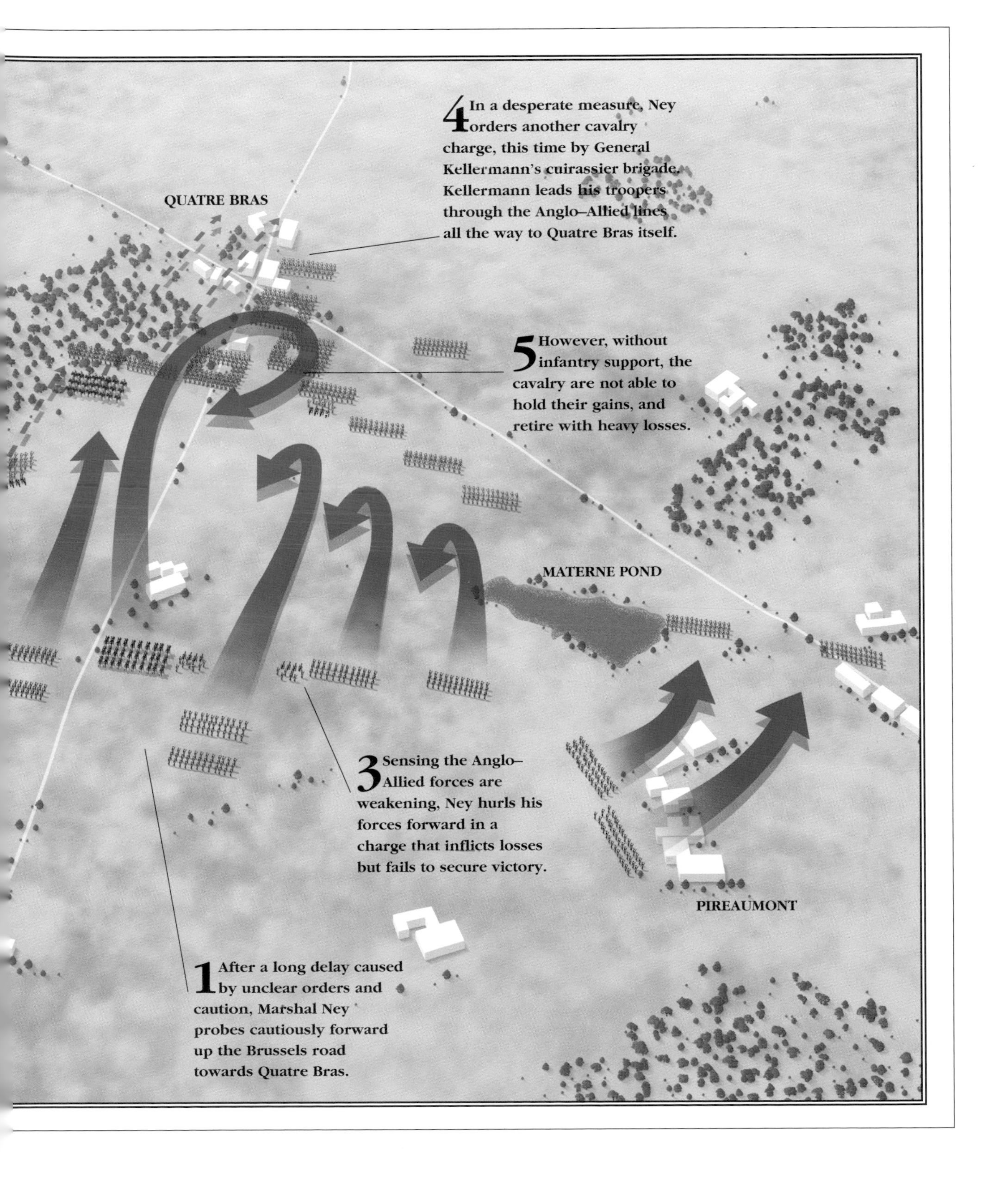

4 In a desperate measure, Ney orders another cavalry charge, this time by General Kellermann's cuirassier brigade. Kellermann leads his troopers through the Anglo–Allied lines all the way to Quatre Bras itself.
QUATRE BRAS
5 However, without infantry support, the cavalry are not able to hold their gains, and retire with heavy losses.
MATERNE POND
3 Sensing the Anglo–Allied forces are weakening, Ney hurls his forces forward in a charge that inflicts losses but fails to secure victory.
PIREAUMONT
1 After a long delay caused by unclear orders and caution, Marshal Ney probes cautiously forward up the Brussels road towards Quatre Bras.

horsemen - and their objective - was initially screened from the Anglo-Allied forces. A Dutch battalion was caught completely unawares by the thundering cavalry, who smashed it to pieces and scattered it from the field.

At this point the Coldstream Guards and the Black Watch, who had been rushing towards the battle all that morning, abruptly emerged from the Bossu Woods. The French horsemen deftly manoeuvred to meet them, and the exhausted British infantry attempted to form square to meet the advancing enemy. The flanks and rear of the British regiments came under attack from the French lancers, who caused heavy casualties. At one stage, lancers even penetrated the incompletely formed square of the Black Watch, wreaking utter havoc until the square closed about them and the lancers were wiped out to a man.

The 44th Regiment received a bad mauling when its commander refused to form square and instead received the lancers in line formation, unleashing a volley of musketry into their faces at point-blank range. Although casualties were inflicted, the volley was far too weak to halt the charging mass of horsemen, who swiftly fell upon the ill-deployed British infantry, slashing through their lines and inflicting grievous losses.

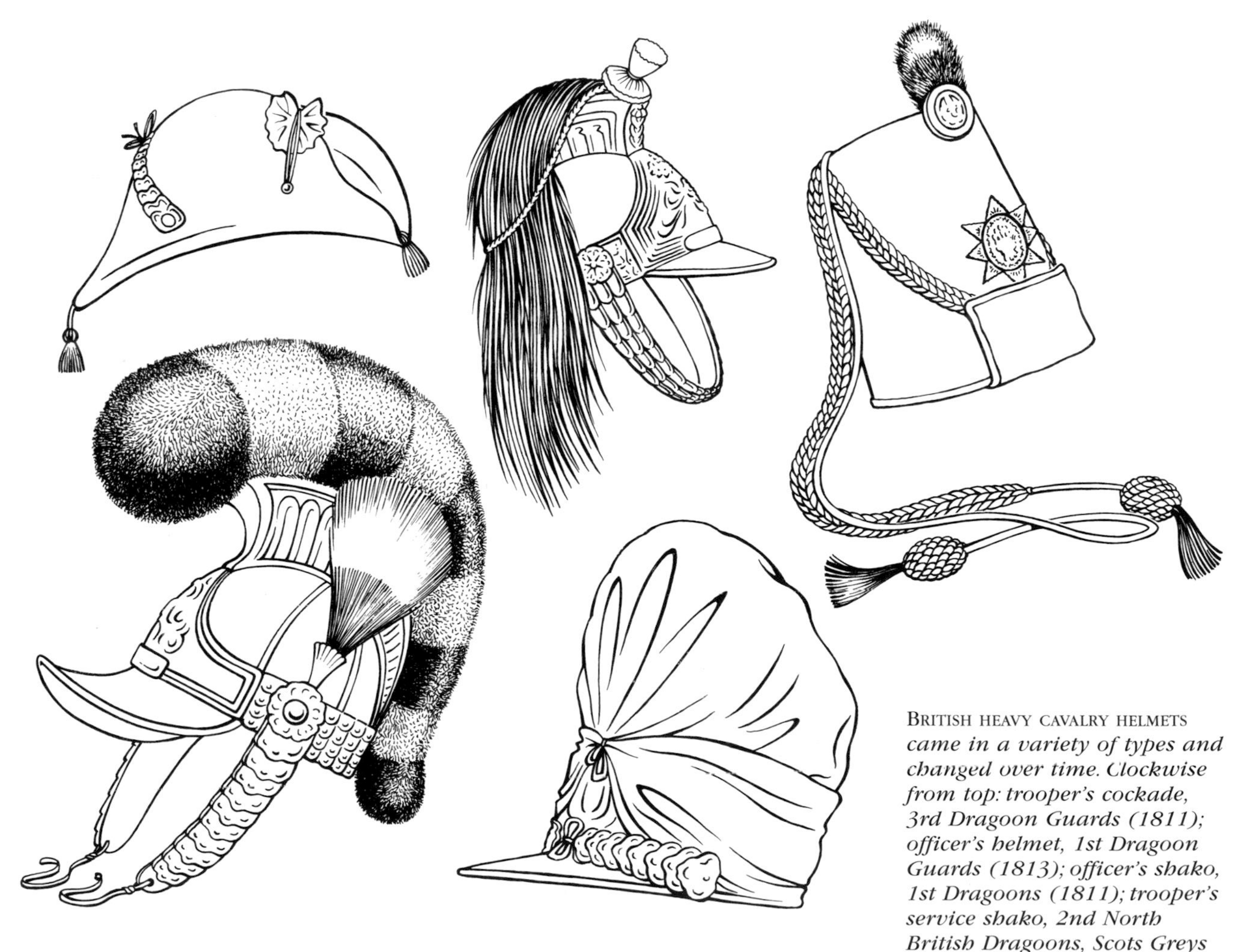

BRITISH HEAVY CAVALRY HELMETS *came in a variety of types and changed over time. Clockwise from top: trooper's cockade, 3rd Dragoon Guards (1811); officer's helmet, 1st Dragoon Guards (1813); officer's shako, 1st Dragoons (1811); trooper's service shako, 2nd North British Dragoons, Scots Greys (1815); troopers helmet, 3rd King's Own Dragoons (1812).*

The French cavalry had caused mayhem in the British lines. Now, the opportunity to shatter Wellington's position beckoned, but Ney lacked a force to exploit the situation. He had ordered General d'Erlon's I Corps to move at the double-quick to the battle, and could not understand why he had still not arrived. Then a messenger arrived informing Ney that the emperor had ordered d'Erlon's corps to the battle of Ligny in order to fall upon the right flank of the Prussians and complete his victory there.

A furious Ney sent a courier to imperial headquarters with a request to countermand that order as d'Erlon's men were desperately needed at Quatre Bras. Napoleon's reply was terse, telling Ney that it was out of the question, while simultaneously ordering him to seize the crossroads at all costs, since 'the fate of France depends upon it'. All of this wasted valuable time, and Wellington's force at Quatre Bras was increasing in size by the minute. At this critical point General Kellermann arrived at Ney's command post with a brigade of cuirassiers from his III Cavalry Corps. Desperate for any reinforcement that could yet turn the tables in his favour, Ney ordered Kellermann to attack and seize the crossroads. 'A supreme effort is necessary,' Ney told Kellermann. 'That mass of hostile infantry must be overthrown.'

From the vantage point of Ney's command post Kellermann looked with his spyglass at the mass of more than 20,000 enemy troops covering the landscape. Kellermann expressed astonishment at Ney's order, and informed the marshal that he did not even have his entire corps at hand as they were still strung out on the road making their way towards the battlefield. If the marshal insisted on the attack, Kellermann argued, at least allow him to bring up his remaining three brigades before launching it. 'Charge with whatever you have got,' demanded Ney. 'Crush them, ride them down.' Kellermann began to protest again and Ney harshly cut him off, commanding: 'Go! Go now!'

Kellermann's Charge

Kellermann was stunned by the rebuke, not to mention the seeming impossibility of the assignment, so he angrily spurred his horse over to his single cavalry brigade. Then, the general and his two cuirassier regiments galloped forward without support onto the plateau and began pounding towards the British positions. Knowing that his horsemen would baulk once they saw the size of the force they were to attack, Kellermann deliberately took his men into a full trot as they crested the plateau, so that their momentum would carry them forward in spite of whatever fear seized them. The cuirassiers charged north astride the Brussels road and slammed into the 69th Regiment, which was caught off guard by the sudden onslaught and was destroyed, losing its regimental colours. The 33rd Regiment met a similar fate as the seemingly unstoppable armoured horsemen incredibly carried all before them in their mad dash towards Quatre Bras.

The French cuirassiers hurtled through the centre of Wellington's line and with Kellermann at their head burst onto the crossroads at Quatre Bras. For one shining moment they had achieved the long-sought objective. However, while cavalry was superb at capturing ground, it was not the arm of choice to hold it, and Kellermann's cuirassiers mounted on blown horses were vulnerable to a counterstroke. Ney knew this and hoped against hope that d'Erlon's long-delayed I Corps would emerge at this critical juncture with fresh troops to deliver the final blow to Wellington's forces. D'Erlon, though, was nowhere to be seen, and so Ney attempted to move his already bloodied infantry and artillery forward to exploit the opening Kellermann had made.

The progress of these reinforcements was slowed by steady British resistance, and minutes ticked by while Kellermann and his cuirassiers waited desperately for support to arrive that would solidify their hold on the hard-won ground. None was forthcoming, however, and British forces began to close in on the isolated horsemen. An artillery battery from the King's German Legion began pouring grapeshot into the cuirassiers, and Kellermann's own horse went down, blown through by grapeshot. Musketry seemed to come at them from every direction in ever increasing volume; men and horses were dropped at a frightful rate.

British Life Guard Trooper

The 1st and 2nd Regiments of Life Guards, along with most of the British heavy cavalry, remained in Britain during the Peninsular War. Kept away from the rigours of the war in Spain, these regiments were superbly mounted and at full strength when they joined Wellington's Anglo-Allied Army for the Waterloo campaign in 1815. They were assigned to the Household Brigade and were, along with the Union Brigade, the most elite cavalry force in the British Army. At the critical moment when the French threatened to break the British centre, Wellington flung his heavy cavalry brigades into a massive charge that shattered the French attack. The Life Guards smashed a disorganized force of cuirassiers and swept into the French lines, with one regiment mingling with the Union Brigade and briefly overrunning Napoleon's gun line. Ignoring repeated calls to reform, they became dangerously exposed and were struck by a French countercharge that inflicted heavy casualties on them.

Now threatened with encirclement and annihilation, the cuirassiers faced their mounts about and began to hack their way out of the predicament they had so boldly ridden into. As British skirmishers rushed forward to pick off survivors, Kellermann escaped by seizing the bridles of two passing cuirassiers and dashing off with them as he clung on for dear life. Almost half his command lay dead or wounded on the battlefield behind him. The British were awed by the courage of the French cavalry, and Colonel Sir Augustus Frazer (1776–1835) wrote: 'The enemy's lancers and cuirassiers are the finest fellows I ever saw. They made several bold charges and advanced in the very teeth of our infantry.'

BATTLE OF QUATRE BRAS. *The Duke of Wellington confronted Marshal Michel Ney in a bitterly contested fight that ended in a draw. The French cavalry were opposed almost exclusively by infantry but Ney's attacks were poorly coordinated.*

Ney spurred his horse into the ranks of the retreating horsemen, rallying their broken squadrons and re-forming them, while he simultaneously moved artillery batteries forward in order to blow apart the stubborn British squares. The 42nd and 44th Regiments were singled out and solid shot was sent tearing through their compact ranks.

Believing they had been softened up enough, Ney again sent his cavalry forward, reinforced with General Piré's tired lancers, whose momentary break after their initial battle now ended as they were hurled back into the fray. Despite casualties mounting by the minute, the British stood firm against this renewed attack.

The French cuirassiers and lancers sought in vain to break the redoubtable British squares, and the cavalry attack spent itself in sweat and blood under a blazing summer sun. Ney's determination to break through up the Brussels road remained

unshaken and he ordered his cannon to be brought up within case-shot range of the British battalions. The French guns roared and the British battalions were torn apart by a hail of shot while simultaneously being peppered with fire from French skirmishers moving through the tall wheat, plying their deadly trade.

Charging the Squares

Ney now readied a third cavalry charge. For this new attack, Ney reinforced Piré's and Kellermann's weary troopers with a fresh regiment of Imperial Guard lancers. This time he sent his horsemen against Wellington's left flank east of the Brussels road. A Hanoverian battalion was caught unprepared by this new attack and virtually wiped out, but the obstinate British squares held their ground as islands of red in a sea of swirling blue horsemen, and the exhausted French cavalry were once more forced to retire. With them went any hope of victory.

'The only thing that [the British cavalry] can be relied upon to do is to gallop too far and too fast.'

– Sir Arthur Wellesley, Duke of Wellington

By 18:30 Wellington had gained the upper hand in the battle. Unlike Ney, Wellington had been receiving reinforcements at a rapid pace and by early evening he had more than 36,000 men on the field, which gave him a substantial numerical superiority over his French adversary. Turning the tables, Wellington went over to the attack. He drove the French away from Quatre Bras, retaking the ground the enemy had fought so hard all afternoon to capture and pushing the French back to their original positions. Yet Ney, who had two horses killed beneath him that day, rallied his battered regiments and put up ferocious resistance to the Anglo-Allied advance. Wellington's push was halted. By 9:30 p.m. darkness had fallen and put an end to the fighting.

A Bloody Draw

Wellington lost some 4800 men from his Anglo-Allied army at Quatre Bras, while Ney's force suffered approximately 4000 casualties. The battle was a draw, since neither side had truly accomplished its mission.

The following day, under cover of a driving rainstorm, Wellington withdrew his army from its exposed position and established his forces near the village of Waterloo for the decisive engagement of the campaign. Napoleon was sharply critical of Ney's performance at Quatre Bras, believing that had he accomplished his mission and fallen upon the flank of the Prussians, their whole army would have been destroyed. While there is certainly room to criticize Ney's handling of the battle, he had prevented the British from joining the Prussians at Ligny and kept the Allied armies separated. Had Marshal Grouchy achieved the same result two days later at Wavre, the destiny of the world would have been changed.

Quatre Bras offered vivid evidence of both the strengths and weaknesses of cavalry. However, it is important to note that the image of the resilient British squares at Quatre Bras, and later at Waterloo, fending off the French cuirassiers has offered the false impression that all an infantry battalion had to do was form a square and it would become impervious to attack by horsemen. This is a patently false notion. One cannot take the squares formed by the British regiments at Quatre Bras as the norm for the period. The British infantry of the Napoleonic Wars was among the finest of the era. Their morale and training were superb, and their reputation for being able to doggedly defend a position was amply demonstrated by their remarkable stand at Quatre Bras.

Indeed, over the course of the Napoleonic Wars, French cavalry as well as Allied horsemen did break infantry squares; there was more to repelling a cavalry attack than merely assuming a certain formation. It took steady nerves, superb training and icy courage for an infantry square to stand firm against a thundering heavy cavalry charge. Even then, a unit could be overwhelmed. Thus, the accomplishment of the British infantry at Quatre Bras, and later at Waterloo, should be recognized for the tremendous military performance that it was.

Conclusion

By the end of the Napoleonic Wars, cavalry was still an indispensable branch of every major nation's army, and it would remain so throughout the nineteenth century. The constant improvements in firearms, especially in the mid- to late nineteenth century, did, however, diminish the power of cavalry on the battlefield itself. Battles became prolonged firefights in which attaining fire supremacy – rather than delivering the decisive shock action with cold steel at which cavalry had so excelled in the Napoleonic Wars – was the key to victory.

Yet the other traditional roles of cavalry as a scouting and screening force remained vital and would continue to be so into the twentieth century. Even in World War II, cavalry were still used for scouting, especially on the Eastern Front. Still, there can be no question that the Napoleonic Wars marked the apex of the mounted warrior. Although cavalry remained, its role diminished over time, leaving cavalrymen to think nostalgically of the Napoleonic Wars, when thundering horsemen in shining armour decided the fate of empires on the field of battle.

TROOPER OF THE 2ND ROYAL SCOTS GREYS. *The Scots Greys spent most of the Napoleonic Wars in Great Britain, but were deployed to the continent with Wellington's forces for the 1815 campaign. Assigned to Ponsonby's Union Brigade of heavy dragoons, they were deployed with the main Anglo-Allied army at Waterloo. When French General D'Erlon's II Corps attacked the British centre, Wellington responded with a powerful cavalry attack, with the Scots Greys in the van. They scattered D'Erlon's corps, captured an eagle and then pushed on to penetrate Napoleon's Grand Battery. However, as often occurred in British cavalry charges, they overextended themselves and were counterattacked by French cavalry, who drove them back. The Union Brigade lost almost half its number in the charge, including their commander Ponsonby, and was* hors de combat *for the remainder of the battle.*

CHAPTER 3

COMMAND AND CONTROL

The French Revolutionary and Napoleonic Wars (1792–1815) ushered in a revolution in military affairs with the introduction of national conscription, which necessitated alteration of military organizations' command and control. The dramatic expansion of armed forces required a more logical and efficient means of controlling armies on campaign and in battle.

An effective military bureaucracy, a competent staff system and the establishment of permanent army corps and divisions facilitated the conduct of armies at the strategic, operational and tactical level. Furthermore, the earlier snail-paced military reforms in France became the order of the day under the revolution. The changing nature of French armies and French warfare compelled European states either to introduce or speed up their own reforms to meet the challenges of a

NAPOLEON AND HIS MARSHALS *on the march in France in 1814. His energetic leadership, which had eluded him for several years, returned for this short but dynamic campaign, albeit too late to save his empire from collapse.*

general European war that lasted 23 years. Karl Freiherr Mack von Leiberich (1752–1828) received the Order of Maria Theresa for storming the breach at Belgrade in 1789. He began his career as a junior officer in the Habsburg army, in a cavalry squadron commanded by his uncle. Mack's award, the highest military honour in the Austrian Empire, brought reputation and promotion to the bold young man but, most importantly, it meant ennoblement. Although a commoner, Mack could legally proclaim himself a member of the Habsburg nobility. The Habsburg monarchy, unlike France or Prussia, had not developed a large standing army until the time of the War of the Austrian Succession (1740–48). That crisis, which challenged the very existence of the empire, compelled the young Maria Theresa (1717–80) to create an army capable of defending the monarchy and its disparate territories.

'Review repeatedly the campaigns of Alexander, Hannibal, Caesar, Gustavus Adolphus, Turenne, Eugene and Frederick. Model yourself upon them. This is the only means of … acquiring the secret of the art of war.'

— Napoleon

Unfortunately Austrian nobility generally shunned military service, so the empress turned to foreign and domestic professional officers from military families or to commoners who sought glory as a means of social and economic elevation. The participation of the nobility, however, was eagerly pursued, as they – by virtue of their historic origins as the 'warrior class' of Europe – would enhance the quality and character of the army. Mack, thus, was a product of the Habsburg system that emerged in the eighteenth century, and his superiors in 1789, Field Marshals Freiherr von Loudon (1717–90) and Count Lacy (1725–1801), were cut from similar cloth.

The same year that Mack received his decoration, a young artillery lieutenant by the name of Napoleon Bonaparte (1769–1821) completed his training at the premier French artillery school at Auxonne. The French and the Habsburgs reformed their officer corps in the wake of the Seven Years War (1756–63). While their Austrian counterparts desired to increase the military participation of their nobility, the French introduced non-nobles into their officer corps. The result was the creation of military academies to train adolescents from middle class families and from the lesser nobility who could not afford to purchase a commission.

Furthermore, significant failings in the technical branches – artillery and engineering – compelled the French war ministry to emphasize mathematics and engineering both in the junior academies and at the prestigious royal military academy, the *École militaire*. Napoleon was a product of these reforms. His family hailed from Corsica, and after France took possession of the island in 1768, his father secured patents of nobility from Florence. As a descendant of Florentine nobility and through the intercession of the French military governor in Corsica, Napoleon – aged nine – received a scholarship to attend the military academy at Brienne. At 15 he was accepted at the *École militaire*, and a year later he received a commission as a second lieutenant in the artillery.

Despite the attempt to reform the officer corps, the French nobility tempered the extent of the changes, and those who were unable to purchase commissions or came from obscure origins were limited to the technical branches. The cavalry and infantry cost too much, because an officer was required to pay for his horse, kit and valet. Officers were similarly expected to subsidize the cost of maintaining their company. The artillery and engineering corps were not attractive to wealthy and powerful nobles. These branches of the military required too much cerebral activity, and there was little glory to be had in firing a cannon or digging a parallel trench.

Swiss Voltigeur Officer, 3rd Swiss Regiment

*Switzerland came under French influence during the War of the Second Coalition (1798–1802). General Andre Massena's brilliant campaign in 1799 denied the Archduke Charles a victory before Zurich. In 1803, Napoleon imposed a political settlement, the Act of Mediation, on the contentious cantons, which became the foundation of the Swiss political system. According to the treaty of alliance, Switzerland provided 16,000 troops, including four infantry regiments, to the French Imperial armies. The officer here was posted to one of the light infantry (*voltigeur*) companies of the 3rd regiment. The distinctive Swiss red was often criticized as being to similar to the colour of British uniforms. The Swiss wore bicorns, prior to 1805, which were gradually replaced with the shako.*

THE BATTLE OF FLEURUS *destroyed Austria's hope of regaining Belgium from the French Republic. This painting illustrates the desperate fighting on the French right during the day. Note the grenadiers on the right wearing bearskins, compared to the bicorn of the line infantry in the foreground.*

The 1789 French Revolution, however, would illustrate the critical importance of the technical branches to French arms, since the two greatest military leaders of the revolution - Napoleon and Lazare Carnot (1753-1823) - received their training in these branches. Carnot was a captain of engineers who rose to prominence in the Jacobin Party, becoming Minister of War in 1794. Known as the 'organizer of victory', Carnot shaped the revolutionary armies and established a coherent strategy and cogent leadership in the midst of political radicalism.

The Officer Corps

Promotion in eighteenth-century armies came very slowly and at great cost. Officers were expected to subsidize the maintenance of their respective commands. Colonels purchased their regiments along with their commissions and shouldered a significant financial burden, keeping their soldiers clothed, fed and trained. Although standing armies were largely paid by the state, governments often cut corners, making these financial requirements part of the contract. In most European states, the regimental designation became the property of the colonel; hence in Austria and Prussia, a colonel, or *Inhaber,* gave his name to the regiment, and when the *Inhaber* changed, so did the name. Thus, a regiment under one colonel one year might be renamed under another if the colonel were killed or resigned his command. The personal expense of command, then, limited further opportunities for promotion, even during a campaign.

Karl Mack attained the rank of colonel in 1789 after 16 years of service. This was rapid promotion in the Habsburg army, particularly for a commoner, and his participation in the War of the Bavarian Succession (1778-79) and the Turkish War (1788-91) provided the opportunity for such promotion. Most officers throughout Europe spent decades as captains, because their circumstances did not permit them to rise through the ranks. It was therefore commonplace to find 'soldiers of fortune' travelling Europe, looking for opportunity and promotion in foreign armies. The Russian and Austrian officer corps were filled with foreign officers, and tsars and tsarinas from Catherine the Great (1729-96) to Alexander I (1777-1825) were pleased to employ men of talent and martial prowess in their armies.

Frederick the Great (1712-86) purged his officers corps of non-nobles after the Seven Years War. Membership of the officer corps in Prussia became largely confined to the Junkers - landed Prussian nobility - supplemented by 'foreign' officers. 'Foreign', however, meant German from outside of Prussia; rarely were non-Germans employed as officers in the Prussian Army. Charles William Ferdinand (1735-1806), Duke of Brunswick, led the Prussian Army from 1792 to 1806, but was an independent prince, ruling a neighbouring German territory. William IX (1743-1821), Landgrave of Hesse-Cassel, too, held rank as a general in the Prussian Army through 1806. Generals Gerhard Johann von Scharnhorst (1755-1813) and August von Gneisenau (1760-1831), responsible for the critically important reform of the Prussian Army after the debacle of 1806, were originally from Hanover and Anspach-Bayreuth.

They entered Prussian service prior to the French Revolution and rose through the ranks. The French officer corps prior to 1789 was similar to the European standard, with the exception of the emphasis on military education and the opportunity for lesser nobles and wealthy non-noble families to attain junior rank, but promotion remained dreadfully slow. Even Napoleon Bonaparte, commissioned a second lieutenant in 1785, was only a captain in 1793, before his exploits at the siege of Toulon late that year. His leap from captain to general could have only occurred during the French Revolution and with two very powerful members of the National Convention - Augustin Robespierre (1763-94) and Paul Barras (1755-1829) - observing his operations. The former was the brother of the infamous Revolutionary leader Maximilien Robespierre (1758-94), and the latter was soon to be a director of France.

The French Revolution, however, created enormous opportunity for promotion. The long-standing service nobility, who monopolized the officer corps, abandoned their posts or resigned their commissions in great number throughout 1793. The expansion of the French Army from 120,000 in 1789 to 750,000 in 1793 necessitated the exponential growth of the officer corps. Promotion would be dictated by campaign and battle performance during the decade of war after 1792. Continual warfare also guaranteed vacancies in the officer corps because of high casualty rates. These factors applied to professional officers as well and were not limited to those of the former National Guard battalions.

Royal Army and National Guard

After 1790 the royal army found its position as defender of the state challenged by the more patriotic National Guard, established in 1789. National Guard battalions comprised two-thirds of the French Army by 1792 and eventually eclipsed the professional army with the *amalgame* of 1793 and 1795, which combined one professional battalion with two National Guard battalions in forming *demi-brigades* (regiments). The National Guard and the former royal army had merged by 1793, and the officer corps reflected both the radicalism of Revolutionary politics and the integration of the two armies.

Prior to the amalgamation, serious tension existed between the two branches and their officers. National Guardsmen initially elected their officers. Democratic principles outweighed military necessity, and the first year of combat illustrated clearly the problem of electing popular men versus electing men of experience. By the beginning of 1793, election was eliminated in favour of a more traditional method of appointment. The changing political climate of the revolution also created opportunities for professional officers who had been purged from the ranks early on. Louis Davout (1770-1823), future marshal of France, was a lieutenant in the Royal Champagne Cavalry Regiment. He was dismissed from duty in August 1790, due to suspicion of his nobility. He joined a National Guard battalion from his *département* in 1791 and was immediately elected lieutenant-colonel because of his earlier military experience. Another future Napoleonic marshal, Jean-Baptiste Jourdan (1762–1833), served in the *Régiment d'Auxerrois* of the French colonial infantry during the American Revolution. He left the royal army in 1784 but joined the National Guard at Limoges in 1789 and was elected captain. By late 1793, Davout held the rank of general of brigade, and Jourdan was commander-in-chief of an army.

The Battle of Fleurus: 26 June 1794

The campaign in Belgium, which culminated in the battle of Fleurus, occurred at the moment when the radical revolution in France, the Reign of Terror, achieved its domestic goals of purging its enemies from the National Convention. The Committee of Public Safety, the executive committee of the National Convention, composed of 12 represent-atives, was responsible for safeguarding the security of the revolution against its domestic and foreign enemies. Lazare Carnot, one of the 12, presided over the war ministry and established a sense of order and centralized direction to French war efforts. It was commonplace for the Convention to dispatch representatives to the various armies on the frontiers to ensure their patriotic fervour and keep a watchful eye on the generals. The Committee had made a habit of calling generals to Paris to answer for their failures or lack of determination to press the campaign as demanded by the Convention. Victorious commanders such as the Comte de Custine (1740–93) and Jean Houchard (1739–93) were denounced before the republican government in 1793 and executed. Jourdan had commanded the Army of the North in Belgium in 1793 when Carnot was the *représentative en mission*. Jourdan's victory at Wattignies was won with Carnot's direct interference, and shortly thereafter Jourdan was dismissed from command. In June 1794, Carnot restored him to the army as commander of the 'Sambre and Meuse'. It was a new army composed of the right wing of the Army of the North, the Army of the Ardennes and most of the 'Rhine and Moselle'. With the Sambre and Meuse were six future Napoleonic marshals: Jourdan (its commander), François Lefebvre (1755–1820), Jean-Baptiste Bernadotte (1763–1844), Edouard Mortier (1768–1835), Nicolas Soult (1769–1851) and Michel Ney (1769–1815). At the time, the last two were junior officers; the first three were generals.

The Anglo-Imperial armies in Belgium were divided between an Anglo-Austrian army under Frederick (1763–1827), Duke of York, and the Count of Clerfayt (1733–98) and the main Habsburg army under the Prince of Sachsen-Coburg (1737–1815). The coalition forces in Belgium outnumbered the French. However, the Duke of York drew his army ever closer to the Channel coast, as General Charles Pichegru's (1761–1804) Army of the North pressed towards the city of Tournai. Although it is possible to believe that Pichegru's move was a deliberate plan to draw the Allied armies apart, only the British left wing was within operational distance of Coburg's army. Coburg detached forces under General Jean-Pierre Beaulieu (1725–1819) to protect Namur from a French advance along the Meuse, while he concentrated his forces around Quatre Bras to the west, covering the strategic city of Charleroi.

The French had consistently failed to cross the Sambre and take Charleroi. The city's defences were considerable, and the proximity of Coburg's army prevented the French from carrying out a formal siege before they had defeated it. Carnot

FRENCH INFANTRY RANKS, *as with all European armies, were denoted on the uniform sleeve. The chevrons were limited to the rank and file and non-commissioned officers. Officer ranks were identified by their epaulettes, and collars.*

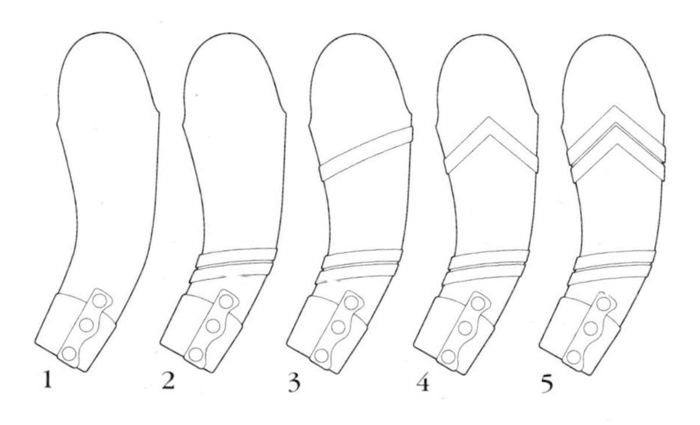

1 PRIVATE, 2 CORPORAL, 3 FOURRIER (SUPPLIES)
4 SERGEANT 5 SERGEANT-MAJOR

considered Charleroi a principal objective, since it would enable further French forces to move unmolested along a parallel axis with the Army of the North. Indeed, in 1815, during the first days of the Waterloo campaign Napoleon saw Charleroi as his gateway to Belgium and seized it quickly, before the British or Prussian armies could take it. The Revolutionary authorities therefore created Jourdan's Army of the Sambre and Meuse in order to concentrate sufficient force to take the city and press into Belgium. The presence of Louis de Saint-Just (1767–94) with the army was a clear indication of the critical importance the Committee collectively placed upon the city's capture and the subsequent defeat of Allied forces. Jourdan crossed the Sambre on 18 June. He bombarded Charleroi and tasked General Jacques-Maurice Hatry's (1742–1802) division with the siege. He deployed the remainder of the army, six divisions, in a semi-circle 1.6–3.2km (1–2 miles) from Charleroi. Saint-Just busied himself providing motivation and oversight for the siege, while Jourdan prepared for the imminent arrival of Coburg's relief army.

'An army's effectiveness depends on its size, training, experience, and morale, and morale is worth more than any of the other factors combined.'

– Napoleon

The Austrian columns were divided, however, with Beaulieu covering Namur to the east, while the preponderance of Coburg's forces lay to the northwest towards Brussels. The Duke of York refused to bring his force further inland and leave Ostend, his lifeline to England, unprotected against Pichegru's army. The Prince of Orange (1748–1806), commanding Austrian and Dutch troops, however, moved east to unite with Coburg. All told, the Allied army had 45,700 men and 98 artillery pieces. Jourdan's strength was greater, some 72,000 men.

Coburg Arrives

The battle of Fleurus illustrates the flexibility of the French divisional system compared with the eighteenth-century ad hoc column, and its benefit to the command and control of armies. On 25 June, Coburg's army approached Charleroi. Coburg intended to assail Jourdan's position, pressing him front and flank with five separate columns. The Prince of Orange with 13,000 men on the right, General Peter Quasdanovich (1738–1802) with 6400 men in the centre and, towards Coburg's left, two columns (15,500 men) under the command of the Archduke Charles (1771–1847) would advance through Fleurus towards Charleroi. On Coburg's far left was Beaulieu's column of 10,300 men, brushing the Sambre.

Jourdan arrayed his divisions 4.8km (3 miles) from the city. General Jean-Baptiste Kléber's (1753–1800) *corps d'armée* of two divisions were in front of Courcelles, facing the Prince of Orange. A brigade defended the Sambre at Landelies, south of Kléber's position. To the east, along the Sambre, General François Marceau's (1769–96) weak division held the woods beyond Lambusart. Jourdan personally directed the centre with two divisions, between Gosselies and Heppignies, which he fortified with a redoubt and heavy guns. Lefebvre's division took up an entrenched position between Wagnée and Fleurus. Although Jourdan outnumbered Coburg, his position was extended, with a besieged city to his rear. Fortunately the garrison of Charleroi had surrendered the city the previous day, allowing Jourdan to deploy Hatry's division in reserve, with the cavalry around the town of Ransart.

The Prince of Orange led the Allied attack, moving his battalions and squadrons across the Piéton stream in three smaller columns; one advancing on Fontaine l'Evêque, and the other two towards Courcelles. General Anne Charles Basset de Montaigu's (1751–1821) division, holding the French flank, came under immense pressure, and under heavy fire withdrew upon Courcelles. General Charles Daurier's (1761–1833) brigade at Landelies advanced against Orange's columns, only to be assailed by cavalry, artillery fire and infantry. They too withdrew. By 10 a.m. Orange was

Battle of Fleurus

26 June 1794

The Austrian and Anglo-Allied armies successfully threatened the French occupation of Belgium and Holland in the spring of 1794, with a counteroffensive forcing them to withdraw their armies to the French frontiers. The Committee of Public Safety dispatched the bloodthirsty deputy St Just to ensure the armies and their commanders understood the severity of the situation. General Jean-Baptiste Jourdan, temporarily removed from command in 1793, was appointed general-in-chief of the new Army of the Sambre et Meuse. Jourdan crossed the Sambre at the end of June, besieged Charleroi and deployed his army in a semicircle to prevent the Austrian relief army from reaching the city. On 26 June, the Prince of Sachsen-Coburg attacked Jourdan around Fleurus. After a desperate battle in which Jourdan's flanks broke, his ability to rapidly deploy his reserves, combined with the steadfastness of his centre, forced the allies to withdraw from the field with heavy casualties.

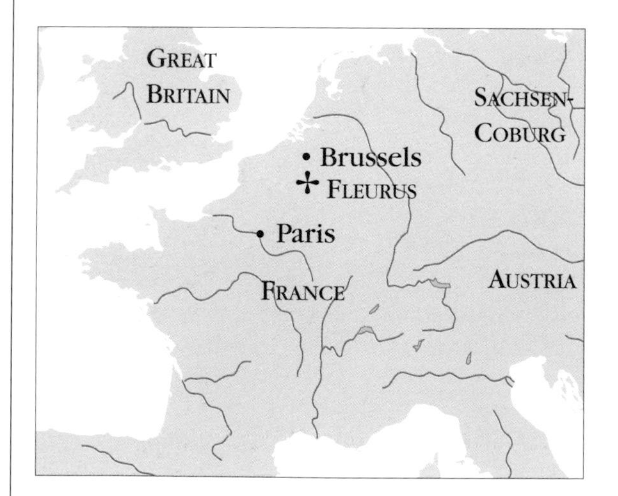

After several failed attempts to cross the Sambre River and capture Charleroi, the French finally succeeded in June 1794, defeating the relief army under the Prince of Sachsen-Coburg.

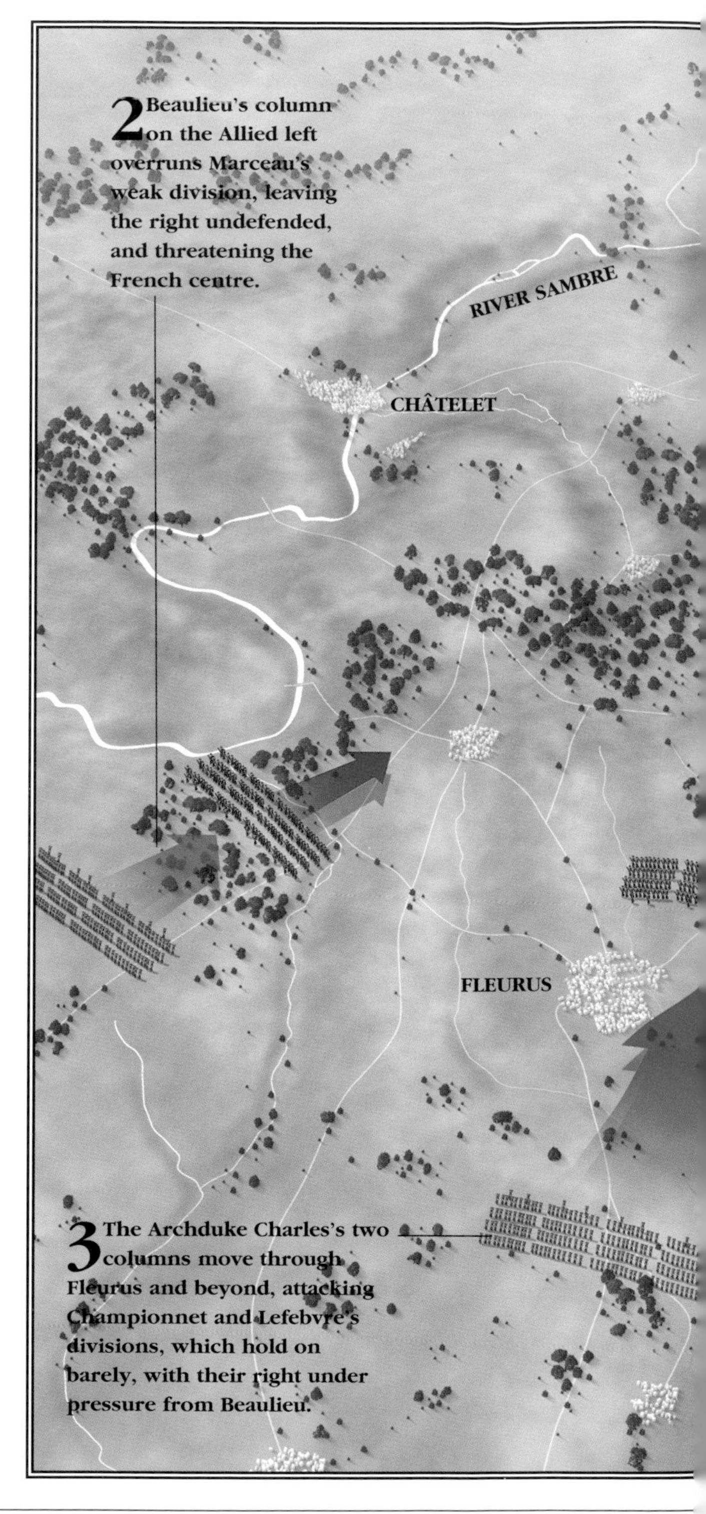

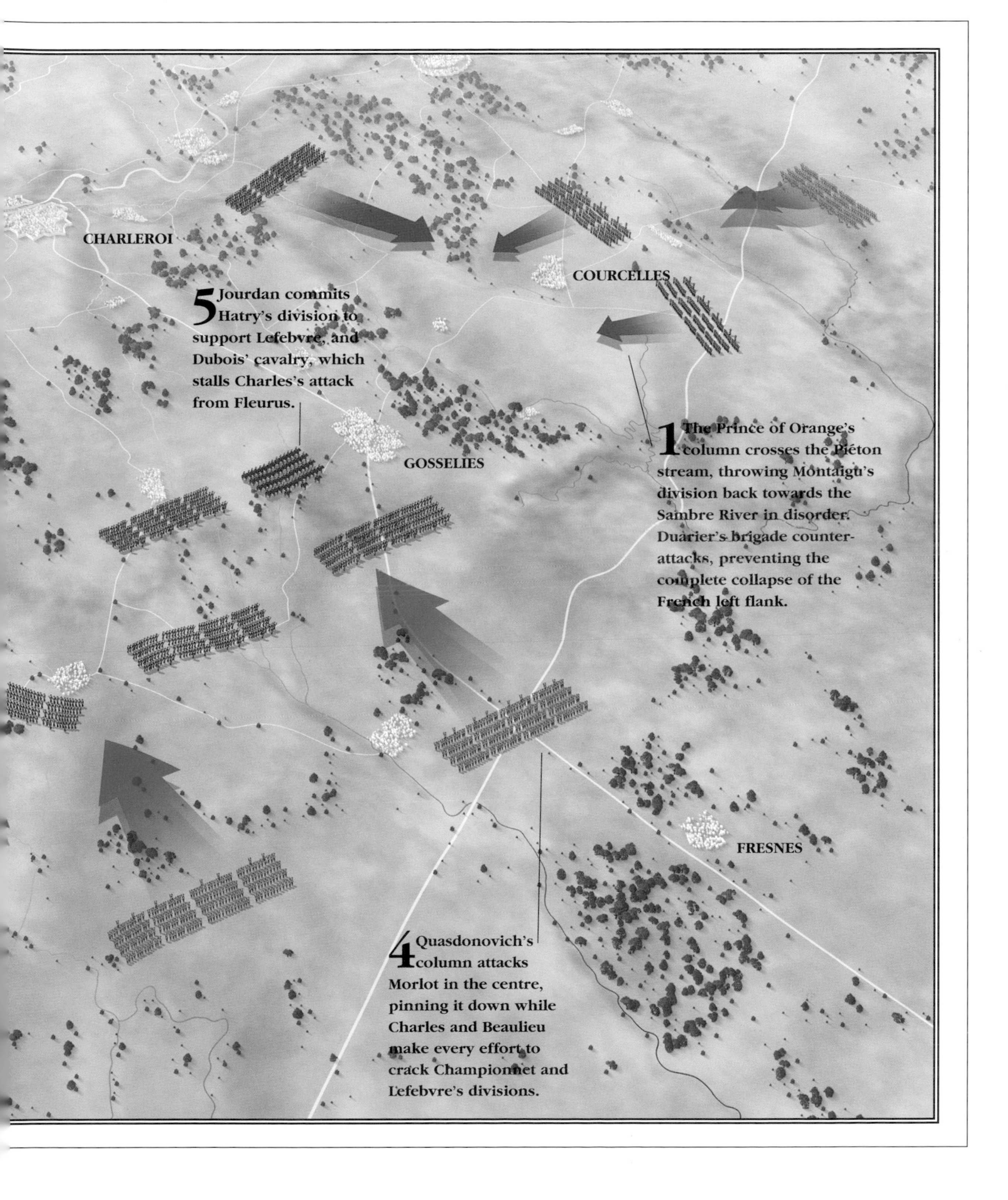
CHARLEROI
COURCELLES
GOSSELIES
FRESNES
5 Jourdan commits Hatry's division to support Lefebvre, and Dubois' cavalry, which stalls Charles's attack from Fleurus.
1 The Prince of Orange's column crosses the Piéton stream, throwing Montaigu's division back towards the Sambre River in disorder. Duarier's brigade counter-attacks, preventing the complete collapse of the French left flank.
4 Quasdonovich's column attacks Morlot in the centre, pinning it down while Charles and Beaulieu make every effort to crack Championnet and Lefebvre's divisions.

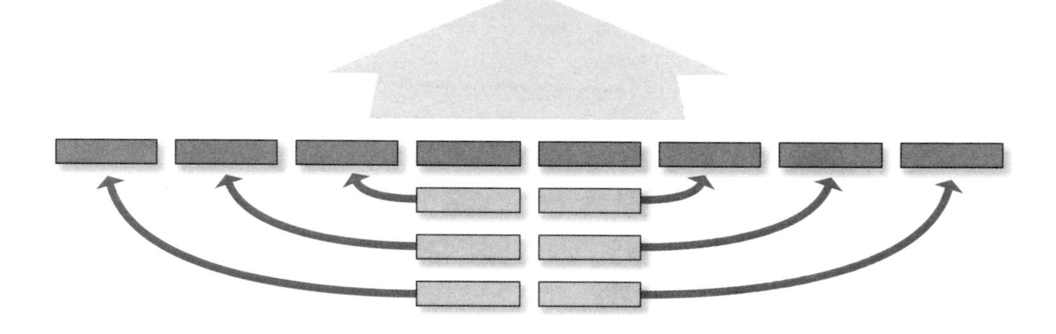

A PRUSSIAN BATTALION *of four companies deploying from column to line. Prussian infantry were highly trained and disciplined. They were a formidable force even during the disastrous 1806 campaign.*

threatening to roll up the left flank. Montaigu and Daurier, south of Courcelles, re-formed and counterattacked, halting the Austrians. Kléber, with General Guillaume Duhesme's (1766–1815) division northeast of Courcelles, detached a brigade and rushed it to the flank. Fighting raged for the next two hours. Kléber fed Bernadotte's brigade into the battle and, by 2 p.m., he had compromised Orange's position and forced the prince to order a general withdrawal back across the Piéton.

While Kléber fought to hold the left flank, Jourdan faced a greater crisis on his right. Quasdanovich's column moved forward from Frasnes on the French centre. General Antoine Morlot's (1766–1809) division bore the brunt of the attack. After heavy fighting for much of the day, Morlot was forced back towards Gosselies. Quasdanovich occupied Jourdan's front as the Archduke Charles and Beaulieu threw their weight against the divisions of Lefebvre, Marceau and General Jean Etienne Championnet (1762–1800). The Archduke Charles's columns vigorously assailed the French entrenchments between Fleurus and Heppignies. A redoubt with 18 heavy guns supported Championnet's position. The Austrian column attacking there floundered in the face of artillery fire and musketry.

Lefebvre, too, held his own against Charles's other column. A crisis, however, soon threatened the entire right flank, as Beaulieu's column broke Marceau's division, which fled through Lambusart, leaving Lefebvre's right in the wind. Shortly thereafter Charles renewed his attack, supported by concentrated artillery fire plus cavalry. Championnet lost the redoubt and fell back beyond Heppignies. Lefebvre was in a desperate situation. He detached Colonel Soult with three battalions and some cavalry, refusing the flank and occupying entrenchments at Campinaire. Beaulieu's column ran headlong into Soult's troops, now supported by the remnants of Marceau's division.

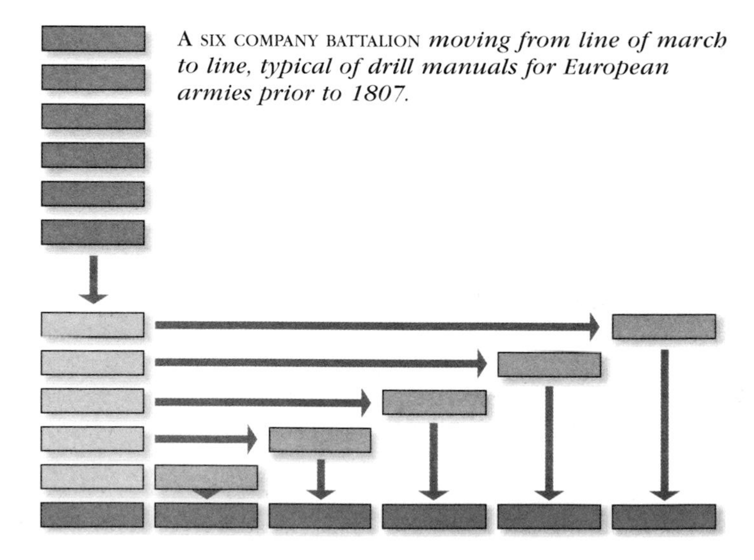

A SIX COMPANY BATTALION *moving from line of march to line, typical of drill manuals for European armies prior to 1807.*

Jourdan observed his centre press back, and Austrian battalions in two lines advance from Heppignies towards Ransart. He immediately directed General Paul-Alexis Dubois' (1754–96) Cavalry Reserve against their serried ranks. The Austrian first line broke against the charge, while the second formed square. Championnet advanced to support and the Austrians withdrew, leaving all their light artillery. Lefebvre was still barely holding his position against Charles and Beaulieu. With the centre stable, Jourdan ordered Hatry's division to the flank. Reinforced, Lefebvre repelled Charles's column and advanced upon Lambusart, retaking it from Beaulieu. By evening, with no sign of a decisive outcome, Coburg withdrew his army, having suffered heavily.

Jourdan nearly lost at Fleurus. If Coburg had been his equal in numbers, it is likely the result would have been different. As it was, Coburg's concentric attack by columns did not permit him to control the battle adequately, let alone coordinate his forces with those of the Prince of Orange. Jourdan's victory can be attributed to the impressive skill of his divisional generals and their ability to manipulate their divisions and brigades on the battlefield in quick order when faced with rapidly changing situations. Jourdan's position in the centre allowed him to feed Hatry and the Cavalry Reserve under Dubois to support Championnet and Lefebvre, preventing the Allies from breaking those divisions. Coburg's column commanders, however, had no larger organization than the battalion, severely restricting their ability to react to circumstances.

'To the one who unites and employs the greatest force in the shortest time at the decisive point belongs victory in war as well as in every other physical or moral contest.'

– Archduke Charles

The Evolution of Army Organization

One of the most significant developments in command and control during the Revolutionary and Napoleonic Wars was the introduction of the combat division and army corps. The increasing size of armies during the eighteenth century as well as multiple theatres of war required administrative reorganization of European armies. Generally, the standard military unit was the infantry regiment, composed of one or two combat battalions and a depot battalion. Cavalry regiments also remained the standard, although their squadrons could be divided among armies in different theatres.

The army commander therefore contended with controlling numerous battalions and squadrons on the strategic, operational and tactical level. This created an enormous burden for army staffs, who had the responsibility for keeping track of the units within an army, keeping them supplied and ensuring that orders were properly disseminated in a timely fashion. This was no easy task. The coordination of tens of thousands of men on campaign often led to confusion and inefficiency. To reduce the difficulty, European armies were often organized into ad hoc wings, columns (*Abteilungen*), divisions and brigades whose composition depended entirely on the mission at hand. There was no standardization of army organization above the regiment.

In 1759, during the Seven Years War, the Duc de Broglie (1718–1804) established combat divisions within French Army, but these were temporary formations. Also during the mid-eighteenth century, the French army introduced the administrative military division. France was divided into military regions and each general of a division was responsible for the regiments garrisoned within his region. This organization, however, did not translate into the standing combat division that emerged during the French Revolutionary Wars (1792–1802), but it provided the foundation for that development.

Pierre de Bourcet (1700–80), a staff officer, advocated the introduction of the division as a standard formation in his *Principes de la Guerre des Montagnes,* written in the 1760s–1770s. Divisions would enable an army to advance along parallel routes and unite rapidly for battle. The formation would facilitate greater efficiency on campaign and provide for the rapid movement of larger numbers of troops over great distances, as opposed to an army using a single road, moving slowly and encumbered by supply trains. To that end, another French military theorist, the Comte de Guibert (1743–90), argued in his *Essai général de tactique* of the early 1770s that armies should dispense with their supply trains in order to increase their flexibility and mobility.

'March Divided, Fight United'

The division began to develop in the mid-eighteenth century as a means of improving an army's strategic mobility and its ease of command. A general commanding an army did not have to keep track of each battalion and squadron but merely of his divisions. Meanwhile, the divisional generals were responsible for controlling their respective regiments. Indeed, while the French explored divisional organization they also introduced the infantry brigade – a unit formed of two infantry regiments. Prussia, too, organized its army into brigades but did not adopt the combat division. What made the French division unique was the integration of artillery and cavalry into the table of organization. Typically, artillery and cavalry were under the direct control of the army commander, who apportioned it to his subordinates as needed. By integrating artillery and cavalry into the divisional structure, the French possessed greater firepower and reconnaissance at a lower level. Divisions could march divided, engage the enemy and have adequate support for a short period until reinforced by other divisions. The principle is often cited as 'march divided, fight united'.

During the French Revolutionary Wars, the increased size of campaign armies compelled the Revolutionaries to introduce the combat division as a permanent entity within army organization. Each division comprised two infantry brigades, a cavalry detachment – a squadron or regiment – and an artillery battery. At times, generals gave command of multiple divisions to a single subordinate, dependent upon the plan of operations. General André Masséna (1758–1817), for example, led two divisions of Napoleon's Army of Italy in 1796; General Kléber also led two divisions in Belgium in 1794.

Napoleon built upon the divisional foundation to expand the organizational system, introducing the *corps d'armée.* These bodies existed during the revolution but in a temporary state. Each corps comprised two or three infantry divisions, a cavalry brigade (later division), divisional artillery and a corps artillery reserve. Engineer companies and a corps staff were included to make the organization a self-contained fighting unit of 20,000–30,000 men.

A marshal of France, and occasionally a general of division (*général de division*), commanded a French corps after 1804. Each divisional commander, his brigadiers and the regiments comprising the corps remained part of the corps from campaign to campaign. A French corps also, like a Roman Legion, generally remained in a specific European theatre. Thus Marshal Louis Davout's vaunted III Corps of the *Grande Armée* retained its composition from its establishment in 1803 through to 1812 and was based in Germany.

Ideally, French corps operated on independent axes of advance but within mutual support of another. This allowed Napoleon to coordinate the *Grande Armée* on campaign with greater ease than his opponents could control their armies; the latter rejected the corps system, preferring the traditional column, or *Abteilung.* During the 1806 campaign against Prussia, Napoleon deployed his army into essentially three columns of three corps, the *bataillon carré.* Each corps was a half-day march from the supporting corps and a full day from all corps in any direction.

Prussia and Austria adopted the divisional system by the early nineteenth century, but their divisions remained largely administrative, and no standing combat divisions came into being until 1809 and thereafter. The Russians did develop military divisions and combat divisions by 1805, but they were incredibly cumbersome and lacked the appropriate staff to manage the brigades and regiments adequately. In Britain, brigade and divisional organization were ad hoc, with formations established for specific expeditions.

Battle of Austerlitz: 2 December 1805

Napoleon's victory over the Russians and Austrians at Austerlitz was perhaps his most decisive and dramatic victory. The French emperor and his army of 60,000 men stood 65km (40 miles) north of Vienna, facing a numerically superior enemy of 89,000. To the southeast, in Hungary, the Archduke Charles commanded 90,000 men and was within striking distance of the Austrian capital. To the northwest, in Bohemia, the Archduke Ferdinand (1754–1806) held Prague but pushed his weak divisions south. The Prussian Army, however, was Napoleon's greatest concern. Although his country was not officially at war with France, the Prussian monarch, Frederick William III (1770–1840), dispatched his foreign minister, Count von Haugwitz (1752–1832), to Vienna to present Napoleon with an ultimatum: cease hostilities or Prussia would join the Allied coalition. The emperor met briefly with the Prussian minister, not allowing him to tender the threat. The Prussian ultimatum would have to wait until the battle was decided.

Napoleon, like Frederick the Great before him, was both the military and political leader of his state. Power was personalized and embodied in the individual, and thus the personal ambitions of the ruler translated into the dedication of the state to achieve those ends. Napoleon therefore fought in a strategically disadvantageous position and in a tactically inferior position at Austerlitz but nonetheless achieved a decisive victory over his enemies. The result was not merely a military victory but the consolidation of French conquests in Italy and Germany, which had begun in 1792.

The battle is a brilliant example of the organizational superiority of the French Army, veteran leadership and elan. One must not, however, assume that the Russians and Austrians fought poorly, but it is abundantly clear that Russian and Austrian leadership was severely lacking that day. In fact, the Third Coalition poorly directed the entire campaign, which had commenced the previous August.

Austria, Russia and Britain formed the backbone of the Third Coalition, but the majority of Continental forces were supplied by Habsburg Austria. Indeed, the greatest difficulty facing the anti-French coalitions from 1792 was that they allowed their individual territorial and dynastic interests to interfere in the conduct of the war. Austrian, British and Russian competition for influence in Germany and Italy plagued Allied strategy for a decade. Unfortunately, in 1805, the situation remained relatively similar.

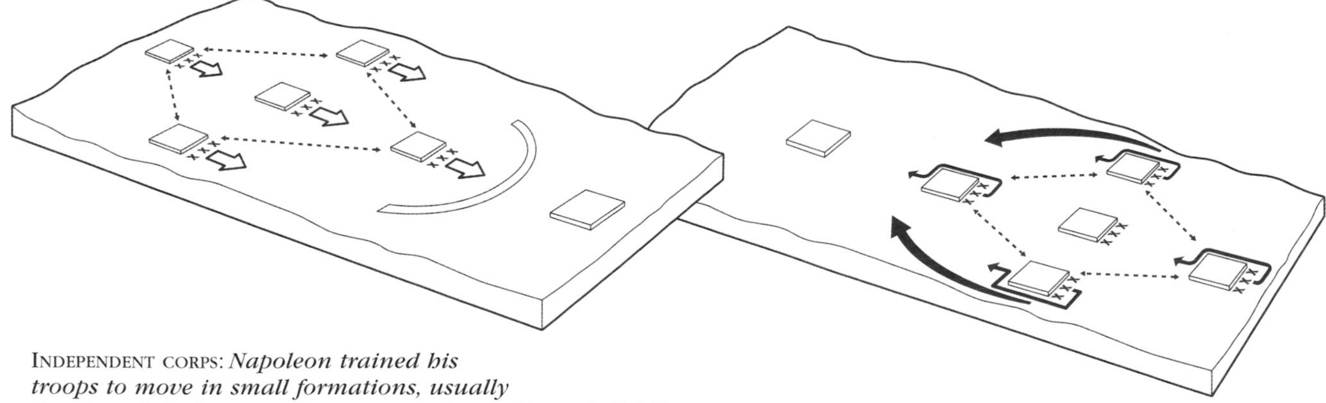

INDEPENDENT CORPS: *Napoleon trained his troops to move in small formations, usually the size of single corps. He overcame the problem of dividing an army by ensuring that they were no further apart than a day's march. Since all corps were of the same strength, whichever first made contact with the enemy was able to make a feint attack or contain them for several hours. The other corps could then carry out an outflanking manoeuvre, using a cavalry screen.*

Karl Mack, now quartermaster-general of the Habsburg army, had achieved substantial power and influence over the Emperor Francis I (1768–1835), advising the monarch to strike in Italy and Germany before his Russian allies arrived in mid-October. Thus the Archduke Charles, brother of Francis I, took command of the large army allocated to Italy, while Mack and the Archduke Ferdinand invaded Bavaria, a French ally, and took up positions around Ulm a full month before the arrival of the Russian Army. Napoleon's Grande Armée was on the Channel coast, waiting for a Franco-Spanish fleet that would never arrive.

As a Continental war loomed in August, Napoleon dispensed with the illusion of a Channel crossing to England and redeployed his corps to the Rhine. The rapid movement of 120,000 men divided into five *corps d'armée* from the Pas-de-Calais and Holland to the German frontier – more than 800km (500 miles) in 30 days – was a tremendous feat.

Mack Miscalculates

Mack anticipated French redeployment would take no less than two months; more than enough time for his allies to arrive. He did not count on the flexibility of the French corps d'armée and their ability to move quickly along parallel routes without substantial logistical support. Napoleon, however, benefited from his army's capacity to endure forced marches and resupplied from the fortress cities on the Rhine. Furthermore, he established military agreements with the princes in Bavaria, Württemberg and Baden to provide food and fodder for his army once they crossed into Germany.

Although surprised by the speed of the French advance, Mack prepared to receive a French offensive head on. Within 10 days of the French Army's crossing into Germany, however, it was all too clear to Mack and the Archduke Ferdinand that Napoleon had caught them in trap. The French corps to Mack's west diverted his attention while the majority of the army moved north and then east to arrive on the Danube and his right flank. Mack quickly concentrated his outlying divisions on Ulm as the French noose tightened. Two French corps moved to the Bavarian border to prevent the Russians, who were fast approaching the frontier, from reaching the beleaguered Austrians. The remaining four corps enveloped Mack's army. Several attempts to break out of the encirclement failed, and Archduke Ferdinand succeeded in reaching Bohemia with fewer than 2000 cavalry. By 18 October Mack had surrendered the remnants of his army – 20,000 men. The remainder had been scattered or captured during the preceding weeks.

The destruction of the Austrian Army in Germany struck the Archduke Charles like a thunderbolt. The young and able Austrian general still led the larger of the field armies, and from his position in Venetia he withdrew the empire's last army to Vienna. Pursued by Marshal Masséna's French Army in Italy and cut off by Marshal Ney's VI Corps, which blocked the passes to Vienna, Charles turned east to Hungary. The Archduke Ferdinand in the meantime pulled together various contingents in Prague.

The Russians committed their army to the conflict in stages. General Mikhail Kutusov (1745–1813) led the first army of 50,000 to the Bavarian frontier. When news of Ulm's capitulation reached him, the wily general fought a tenacious rearguard to Vienna and then north to join with the other two Russian armies arriving from Poland. By mid-November, Vienna was in French hands, and Tsar Alexander I's (r. 1801–1825) armies were concentrated in Moravia, and with 20,000 Austrians, mostly conscripts, prepared to renew the offensive.

Napoleon moved north into Moravia to engage the Russo-Austrian armies before Prussia joined the war. He took with him three corps (I, IV, V), the Imperial Guard and a cavalry corps, led by his brother-in-law, Marshal Joachim Murat (1767–1815). He left Marshal Davout's III Corps in Vienna to observe Archduke Charles in Hungary. His Bavarian allies under General Karl-Philipp von Wrede (1767–1838) advanced against Archduke Ferdinand, whose position might threaten Napoleon's communications to Vienna.

The collapse of the Austrian Army at Ulm reflected the clear failings in Habsburg political and military leadership surrounding the emperor. Francis I fled with his entourage to the safety of

FRANÇOIS GÉRARD'S *famous painting of Napoleon at Austerlitz, commissioned in 1810. General Rapp presents Napoleon with captured cavalry standards after the battle. Rapp was one of the emperor's aide-de-camps.*

Tsar Alexander's army, and there his advisors continued to encourage the continuation of the war. The Archduke Charles remarked that his brother was surrounded by 'idiots and fools'.

Nonetheless, the Russian Army had done rather well against the French. Kutusov had bloodied the French advance guard at Amstetten a month earlier, and General Peter Bagration (1765–1812) kept superior French forces at bay at Hollabrun during the retreat into Moravia. The Russian generals did not lack sangfroid, but they disagreed on the course of action. Kutusov advised caution. He preferred the tsar to wait for the Prussians to move into Bohemia. Alexander and Generals Franz von Weyrother (1755–1806), Count von Buxhowden (1750–1811) and Bagration argued that the situation afforded the offensive. There was little reason to wait. Napoleon was clearly outnumbered, and if his strategic flank could be turned away from Vienna, he would be trapped. Mack's fate could very well also befall the French.

Weyrother's Plan

On 1 December, the Allied army took up positions on the Pratzen Heights, overlooking the French army below. North of the heights was the main road west to Olmütz, Napoleon's headquarters. To the south, frozen lakes protected the flank, and to the west ran the Goldbach stream. From the heights, the Allies observed Napoleon's deployment and confidently determined its apparent weakness. The French army was arrayed along a 6.5km (4-mile) front, with Marshal Nicolas Soult's IV Corps defending two-thirds of the line.

Of Soult's three divisions, that of General Claude Legrand (1762–1815) held the Goldbach from Telnitz to Kobelnitz, some 3.2km (2 miles) of front, broken only by Sokolnitz Castle and two ponds. The bulk of the French army, some 45,000 men, was concentrated on the left flank, astride and south of the Olmütz road. There Napoleon placed the intrepid Marshal Jean Lannes' (1769–1809) V Corps in the first line, with Marshal Bernadotte's I Corps, General Nicolas Oudinot's (1767–1847) grenadier division, the Imperial Guard and the Cavalry Reserve squeezed into a box no larger than 4km2 (1.5 square miles).

General Weyrother, Alexander's chief of staff, concluded that Napoleon's seemingly faulty deployment left his army vulnerable to a flank attack along the Goldbach stream. The Allied army, divided into five columns, would advance along

Battle of Austerlitz

2 December 1805

Napoleon's strategic victory in Germany in October 1805 over the Austrian Army at Ulm led to a rapid march down the Danube to Vienna. Shortly thereafter he faced a strategic dilemma, with the Archduke Charles's substantial army to the southeast in Hungary, the Russo-Austrian armies to the northeast in Moravia and the Prussian Army to his northwest in central Germany. He determined to attack and destroy the Russo-Austrian army under Tsar Alexander I before the Prussians advanced into Bohemia, and Archduke Charles marched on Vienna, thus knocking out his various opponents one-by-one. The Tsar ignored General Kutusov's advice to avoid battle and wait for the Prussians, to provide a greater advantage. Confident that his superiority in numbers and Napoleon's supposed 'faulty' deployment would give him victory, the predominantly Russian army attacked and was promptly crushed at Austerlitz by Napoleon's knock-out blow on the Pratzen Heights.

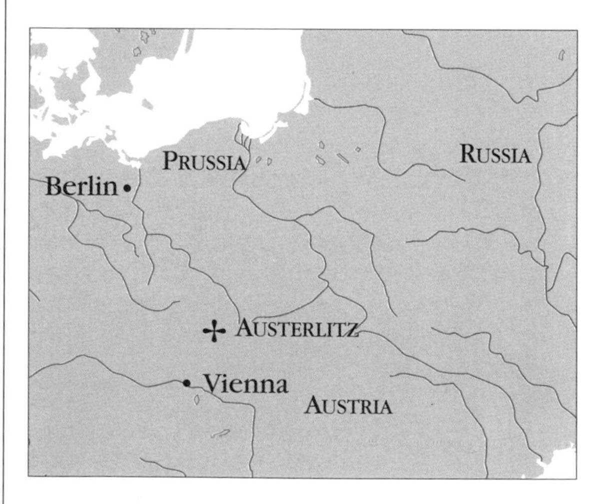

Outnumbered and deep in the heart of Moravia, Napoleon faced a Russo-Austrian Coalition army. His victory at Austerlitz was his most decisive and greatest achievement.

3 Napoleon orders Marshals Soult and Bernadotte, along with Oudinot's grenadiers, and part of the cavalry reserve onto the Pratzen, now largely devoid of Allied forces, excluding the Russian Imperial Guard.

2 Elements of Davout's corps arrive to reinforce the French right, preventing an Allied breakthrough.

SOKOLNITZ

TELNITZ

GOLBACH STREAM

1 Allied columns advance from the Pratzen against the supposedly weak French right, between Telnitz and Sokolnitz. A single French division under Legrand held a 3km (2-mile) front.

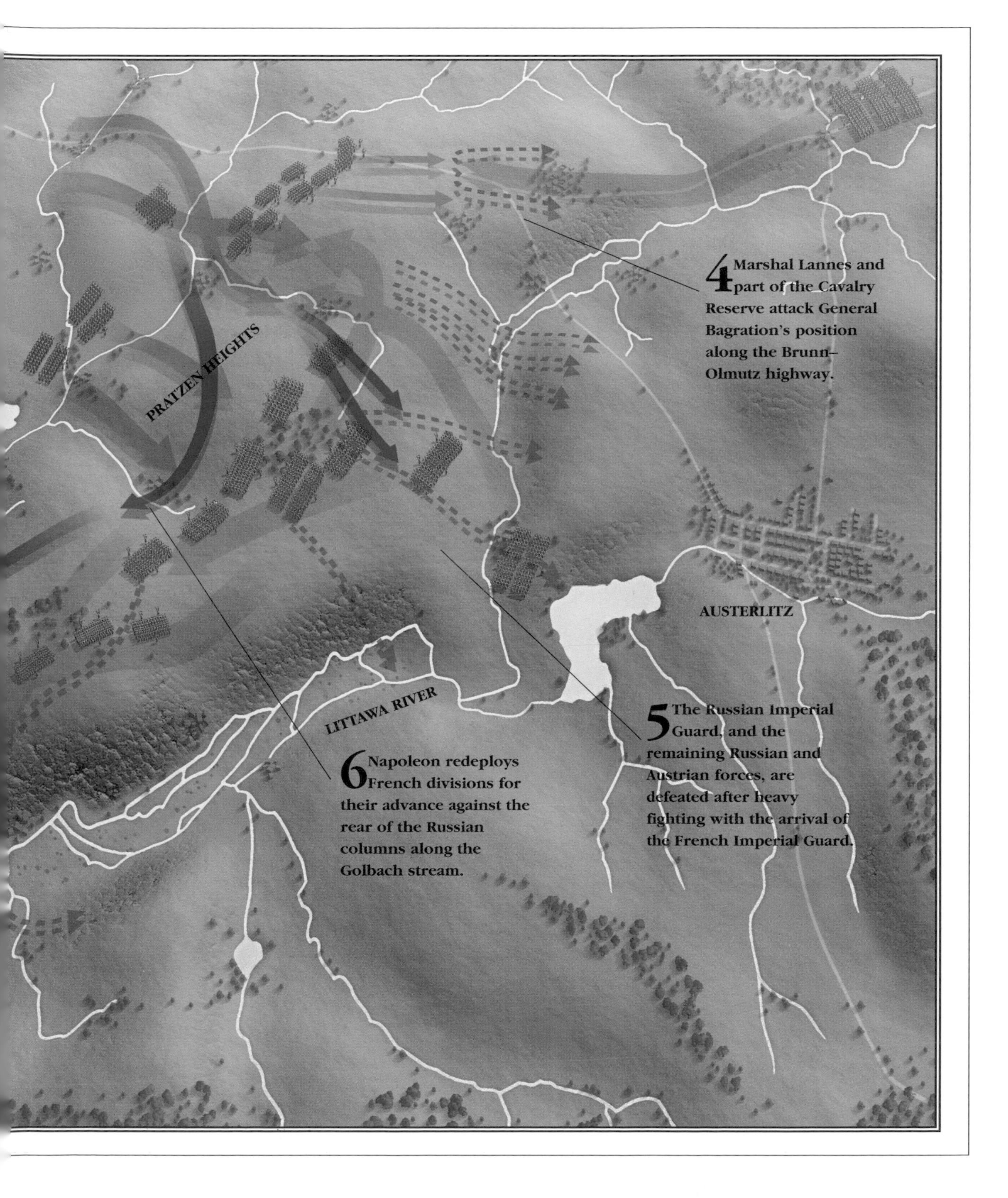
PRATZEN HEIGHTS
LITTAWA RIVER
AUSTERLITZ
4 Marshal Lannes and part of the Cavalry Reserve attack General Bagration's position along the Brunn–Olmutz highway.
5 The Russian Imperial Guard, and the remaining Russian and Austrian forces, are defeated after heavy fighting with the arrival of the French Imperial Guard.
6 Napoleon redeploys French divisions for their advance against the rear of the Russian columns along the Golbach stream.

the front, with three columns falling upon the French right between Telnitz and Sokolnitz. In short, 40,000 Russians would advance on fewer than 10,000 French. The collapse of Napoleon's right would compel the emperor to refuse his flank away from Vienna and further isolate his army, pushing it back to Olmütz.

Weyrother is often very harshly criticized for foolhardy behaviour. Yet, it should be pointed out that his observations were correct and that, under the circumstances, the plan was an appropriate one. What Weyrother and the Russians did not know was that Napoleon had ordered Marshal Davout to conduct a forced march from Vienna with all or part of his corps to reach the battlefield before 2 December. By the evening of 1 December, Davout was within 8km (5 miles) of Telnitz, having covered 65km (40 miles) with 10,000 men in a single day. It was truly an extraordinary achievement. For all, however, that is written about the battle of Austerlitz, the odds, the position and the plan were in the Allies' favour.

'My soldiers are as brave as it is possible to be, but they argue too much. If they had the impassible firmness and the docility of the Russians the world not be great enough for me.'

– Napoleon

A fog preceded the 'Sun of Austerlitz', covering the low ground for several hours. From the Pratzen, Tsar Alexander and his staff could barely see the Goldbach below. The weather favoured the French. Davout woke his men early, wanting to reach Telnitz before the Russian attack. Although fog did not disrupt the Allied columns on the heights, the ad hoc nature of the columns, and the oblique manoeuvres required to move 40,000 men to the southwest, led to confusion as regiments and commands intertwined.

Perhaps the greatest failing of the Allied armies on that fateful day was the lack of centralized leadership. Each column had a commander and specific orders, but no single general directed the battle after the orders were disseminated. General Weyrother, who proposed the plan, was a staff officer, and Tsar Alexander had marginalized General Kutusov, the senior Russian general, on the day of battle. The Emperor Francis I of Austria was merely an observer, and in any case was not a soldier. If plans had gone accordingly, this would not have been a problem, but the changing face of battle required an appropriate command structure.

The Allies Attack

The confusion on the Pratzen was finally sorted out after a delay of two hours. When the columns descended on the Golbach stream, the attack came in waves, allowing the French to address the crises as they appeared and not in a single overwhelming onslaught. Although Russian numbers weighed heavily as three of the five columns crashed into French positions at Telnitz and Sokolnitz, at 9.30 a.m. the timely arrival of Marshal Davout's reinforcements was enough to keep the line from breaking. Two Allied columns remained, but as circumstance would have it, neither was committed to breaking the Goldbach.

General Buxhowden had nominal control of the assault on the French right, and while the majority of his command was embroiled in heated combat at Telnitz and Sokolnitz, he held the fourth column under General Dmitry Dokhturov (1756–1816) in reserve. Once Davout's division had shored up the French defences, Buxowden failed to commit these forces. The fighting was desperate, and the weight of another column could clearly have turned the French flank, but it was not sent and the tsar's staff could not observe the combat on the Golbach from their position on the heights. In any case, they could not alter the situation, as Napoleon, watching the Allied columns move off the Pratzen, ordered an attack on the heights by two infantry corps, his Cavalry Reserve and the grenadier division.

The advancing French corps caught the Allies by surprise. By 10 a.m., only the Russian Imperial Guard and two Austro-Russian divisions remained on the heights. Marshal Soult's two divisions advanced to the crest, where they engaged the Austro-Russian regiments, who fought fiercely but unsuccessfully to halt the French attack. Marshal Bernadotte's I Corps moved directly upon the Staré Vinohrady (Old Vineyards), the Allied headquarters. Tsar Alexander and Emperor Francis I had to flee their vantage point as Grand Duke Constantine (1779–1831) led the Russian Imperial Guard in a counterattack. The fighting for control of the Pratzen was fierce. Although Soult's divisions finally forced the Austrians and Russians from the heights, and Bernadotte blunted the Russian Guard, Napoleon dispatched his reserves, including his own Imperial Guard, to secure the area. Shortly after 1 p.m., the Allied army was cut in two, separating the columns on the Goldbach and the Russians north of the Pratzen under General Bagration. The Russian centre regrouped desperately and organized a fighting withdrawal. The tenacious Bagration held Marshal Lannes' V Corps along the Olmütz road for much of the morning. Napoleon's victory on the heights, however, permitted the commitment of Marshal Murat's cavalry corps by early afternoon. The attack promptly turned the Russian flank. Along the Goldbach, the French successfully ejected the Russians from Telnitz and Sokolnitz but were exhausted. Buxhowden had yet to commit his reserves, but by lunchtime the situation on the Pratzen had become clear and the Russian general prepared to face an attack by Soult's corps from the north. Trapped between two French corps and the frozen ponds to his rear, Buxhowden extricated his columns as Soult descended from the heights.

Napoleon's victory was decisive and complete. The Allied army, now cut into three – Bagration, the tsar and Buxhowden – tried desperately to retreat in some order and rejoin their comrades somewhere to the east, towards Austerlitz. The French pursued cautiously as Russian and Austrian cavalry ably conducted a rearguard. Four days later, Prince John Liechtenstein (1760–1836), emissary of Francis I, signed an armistice, effectively ending the War of the Third Coalition.

Command and Staff Systems

Napoleon's victories from 1805 to 1807 made him master of Europe. The French military system succeeded to such a degree that even if it did not revolutionize the nature of military organization

RUSSIAN INFANTRY *in great coats, at Austerlitz. The Russian Army was relatively new to warfare, having fought only during the War of the Second Coalition, where it achieved substantial success in Italy under the legendary General Alexandre Suvarov.*

and command structures, it certainly was the catalyst for significant change. All major European powers pursued reforms of their military bureaucracy and command structures prior to and during the French Revolutionary Wars. Yet after 1807, every European state defeated by Napoleon instituted further substantial changes to their military systems. The results varied, and no other system reached the level of flexibility of that of the French. Nonetheless, the changes did enhance Allied strategic and operational abilities throughout the subsequent campaigns of the Napoleonic Wars of 1805–15.

The French war ministry had had more than 150 years to evolve since the establishment of a standing army in the seventeenth century. The French Revolutionaries may have rejected the old order, but they benefited tremendously from the monarchy's military administration. The most difficult period of adjustment followed the call for volunteers in 1791 that created a National Guard alongside the long-term professionals of the former royal army.

Similarly, the advent of war and the economic and military demands placed upon the administration brought immense difficulties in managing large numbers of men. The French army swelled to more than half a million men in 1793 following the levée en masse, and the sheer size of the army made everything, from logistics to armaments to pay, incredibly difficult to direct. Lazare Carnot took the reins of military administration that year and with the powers of the Revolutionary dictatorship, brought order to the war ministry. There was, however, a significant difference between the war ministry and the staff that served the commander-in-chief of an army.

The French army slowly developed a competent staff system over the course of the eighteenth century. The Marquis de Ségur (1724–1801), Minister of War, created a staff corps, building upon the recommendations made by Pierre de Bourcet. The creation of the combat division and later the *corps d'armée* meant the further development of a military staff capable of translating orders into action while on campaign as well as handling all the mundane issues that had to be dealt with to keep an army in the field.

'Strategy is the art of making use of time and space. I am less concerned about the latter than the former. Space we can recover, lost time never.'

– Napoleon

As First Consul, then as Emperor of the French, Napoleon had a dual role as ruler of France and commander-in-chief of its armies. To ensure he could attend to his duties while on campaign, he established the *Grand Quartier-Général* (GQG). This organization comprised his military staff, his household staff (*Maison*) and his imperial administration. Napoleon directed the affairs of state and war from the field. The GQG included handpicked and experienced officers with initiative. Napoleon always maintained a cadre of aides-de-camp, generals attached to the *Maison,* who would carry the emperor's orders on the field of battle and take personal command of divisions of corps. It extended Napoleon's reach beyond the simple and inefficient use of couriers during a battle.

Allied Reforms

The Habsburgs did not establish a centralized staff until the 1720s and then it was placed under the war ministry. However, the *Hofkriegsrat* – Imperial War Council – was outside the war ministry's control. It combined civilian and military responsibilities, advising the Habsburg emperors, managing the disparate military bureaucratic offices and administrating the armed forces throughout the empire. Military professionals and members of the royal family vied for control of this body.

After 1801, the Archduke Charles held offices as both president of the *Hofkriegsrat* and minister of war. Although he was temporarily eclipsed in 1805, he did return to his duties thereafter as *Generalissimus*, Supreme Commander of Habsburg armies. Charles set about completing

TSAR ALEXANDER I *took a decidedly anti-French stance in 1803, although he became Napoleon's ally after 1807. His leadership during the invasion of Russia 1812, and his determination to pursue Napoleon into central Europe afterwards, provided the encouragement for Prussia's defection from the French Empire.*

reforms he had begun in 1802, including the subordination of the *Hofkriegsrat* to the war ministry. This move antagonized the traditionalists at court, who saw the institution as a fundamental part of the emperor's authority. Charles, an Austrian hero, having defeated the French in 1796 and 1799 in Germany, wrote extensively on the changing nature of the art of war. In 1806 he produced *Fundamentals on the Higher Art of War for the Generals of the Austrian army,* which addressed the strategic and tactical observations of a decade of commanding armies. He recognized the social factors that enabled the French to field large armies but equally understood that this was incompatible with, and not desirable for, the monarchy. He did, however, believe that the French *corps d'armée* were clearly superior to the ad hoc *Abteilungen,* or columns, used by most European armies. He adopted the French organizational system against immense opposition from the Habsburg army, which feared revolutionary contagion in anything 'French'.

As *Generalissimus,* Charles pursued his reforms without regard for the opposition. During the Austrian War of 1809, he divided the Habsburg field armies into nine corps and two reserve corps. Each corps comprised two cumbersome divisions that were not easily handled in battle. After Austria's defeat and Charles's dismissal, the army dispensed with corps and returned to *Abteilungen* (columns). Only in 1813 did Field Marshal Karl Schwarzenberg (1771–1820), commander of the Austrian Army, reintroduce the concept of corps. In both 1809 and 1813, however, the army had little time to become comfortable with the new organization before it was tested in battle.

The Russian Army proved itself against the French in Italy in 1799, and again in Poland at Eylau in 1807. Their defeats at Austerlitz (1805) and Friedland (1807) perhaps dampened their earlier successes and clearly necessitated reform. Although the Russian army maintained divisions prior to 1807, they were large and included substantial cavalry and artillery components. The Russian divisions were not formed of brigades, so their flexibility in battle was limited. General Mikhail Barclay de Tolly (1761–1818) became Minister of War in 1808 and streamlined the Russian division, establishing administrative divisions (inspections), as in France, and introducing the brigade and corps. When war came in 1812, Russia fielded 11 corps, including the Imperial Guard, and four cavalry corps. Each corps was composed of two divisions of three brigades, plus a cavalry regiment and artillery. The performance of the Russian Army in 1812 illustrated its greater ease of direction and manoeuvre on the battlefield.

The Russian Army lacked adequate staff officers, particularly after Barclay's reforms. Foreign officers had always been welcome in the ranks of the Russian Army, and Tsar Alexander I followed the trend, employing French *émigrés* and 'German' officers, including Prussians who had left for Russia in the years following its subjugation by Napoleon. Carl von Clausewitz (1780–1831), a Prussian general, entered Russian service in 1812. Antoine-Henri Jomini (1779–1869), a French staff officer for Marshal Ney, defected to the Russians in 1813. Interestingly enough, both Clausewitz and Jomini became the voices of military theory and military science in the years following the Napoleonic Wars.

The British Army lacked a higher organization beyond the regiment. Its size and employment did not necessitate permanent brigades or divisions.

CARL VON CLAUSEWITZ, *colonel, later general in the Prussian Army, became one of the best-known military theorists in the nineteenth century. His book,* On War, *is standard reading on the relationship of war and politics.*

During the Peninsular War (1808–14), however, Arthur Wellesley (1769–1852), later Duke of Wellington, organized his army into divisions that became standard for the period of the conflict. Further, he needed properly to integrate the Portuguese Army into his own. Initially, in 1809, Portuguese battalions were assigned to British brigades; later, each British division included a Portuguese brigade. The Spanish never amalgamated their army into the British command system, although Spanish divisions often fought alongside the Anglo-Portuguese army from Talavera (1809) to Vittoria (1813).

Nowhere did Napoleon's military victory elicit a reaction more than in Prussia. The confidence and hubris with which the Prussian Army marched to war in 1806 dissipated rapidly after the humiliating defeats at Jena and Auerstädt on 14 October of that year. An era of social, political and military reform followed from 1808 to 1813. Generals Gerhard von Scharnhorst and August von Gneisenau spearheaded the military programme facilitated by the death or retirement of the octogenarians who had led the army to defeat in 1806. They established a Prussian War Academy in 1810 to educate officers, and emphasized the advantages of initiative and intellect. Scharnhorst also pressed for the creation of a Prussian General Staff and for a subordinate staff system under which staff officers would in future share command with their presiding generals.

He also reorganized the Prussian army for the 1813 campaign. A Prussian corps consisted of three large brigades of infantry, with cavalry and artillery attached. He integrated the *Landwehr* – a kind of militia or national guard – into the military hierarchy, establishing one brigade of regular infantry alongside two of the *Landwehr.* The staff system and new organization worked extremely well and was a fundamental reason for Prussia's much-improved performance from 1813 to 1815.

The Battle of Wagram: 5–6 July 1809

The battle of Wagram was the largest European battle in scope and numbers to date. The fighting took place over a 16km (10-mile) front on the north bank of the Danube. The outcome decided the Austrian War of 1809 and illustrated the coherence and military effectiveness of Napoleon's Grand Empire. Although Napoleon suffered his first defeat at the hands of the Archduke Charles at Aspern-Essling in May, the war and the battle well illustrate the ability of both commanders to direct hundreds of thousands of men at the strategic, operational and tactical level. Archduke Charles's organizational reforms prior to 1809 yielded a certain level of success, as he more adeptly handled a rather cumbersome army filled with generals and officers either jealous of his power or opposed to the 'French system'.

'The commander must trust his judgment and stand like a rock on which the waves break in vain.'

– CARL VON CLAUSEWITZ

The Habsburgs chafed at their defeat in 1805. Napoleon stripped them of their lands in the Tyrol and Dalmatia and presided over the abolition of the Holy Roman Empire, the medieval administration of Germany established in AD 800 and ruled by the Habsburgs since the thirteenth century. In its place the French emperor created the Confederation of the Rhine (*Rheinbund*), a new Germany of 37 states, whose lands were enlarged and their princes elevated by Napoleon's grace. The War of the Third Coalition in 1805 was supposed to restore the pre-1792 status quo to Europe but instead led to the dissolution of the old order. The conquest of Prussia in 1806 and Tsar Alexander I's alliance with the French at Tilsit in 1807 assured Napoleon of his mastery of Europe.

Victory over England, however, eluded him and in 1808 Napoleon betrayed his Spanish allies by taking direct control of the Iberian kingdom and placing his brother Joseph Bonaparte (1768–1844) on the throne. The conquest of Spain led to popular insurrection, guerrilla war and a Continental theatre for Britain. By December 1808, Napoleon sat in Madrid with a quarter of a million men in Spain; his diplomats and spies in Austria warned him of plans for a war while his attention was in the west.

The Archduke Charles's organizational and tactical reforms of the Austrian Army ruffled many feathers in Vienna. Francis I, however, remained confident in his brother's ability to wage war. Charles, nevertheless, had been terribly reluctant to pursue war with France in 1809. He wanted more time to raise and train a larger army; there were no more than 300,000 first-line troops available. Nonetheless, the strategic situation favoured the Habsburgs. Napoleon had no more than 60,000 French troops in south Germany. True, the Confederation of the Rhine collectively possessed 100,000 men, but the Austrians hoped they would not support Napoleon. Furthermore, the Austrians hoped to garner Russian support. Prussia, under French military occupation, could offer no assistance, and its ruler, Frederick William III, feared for the security of his kingdom.

Austrian Preparations

Charles determined to lead the main army of 200,000 men, divided into eight corps, in a pre-emptive strike into Bavaria. A second army of 60,000 men under his brother, the Archduke John (1782–1859), would invade the Napoleonic kingdom of Italy, and the Archduke Ferdinand with 30,000 would attack the Grand Duchy of Warsaw. A small division of 10,000 was earmarked for Dalmatia. In all, Charles hoped speed and numbers would compel the quiescence of the German princes, enabling the archduke to destroy the French Army piecemeal. Unfortunately for Charles, Napoleon acted swiftly, mobilizing his forces in Germany and redeploying troops from Spain. When the Austrians finally attacked in April, they had numerical superiority, but Napoleon's allies held to their agreements. The Austrian invasion of Bavaria was stalled by a determined rearguard and the stubborn action of Marshal Davout's III Corps before Abensberg. Charles's advance bogged down south of the Danube, with his corps strung out between the Danube and Isar Rivers. Napoleon arrived in Germany with three corps under Masséna, Lannes and Oudinot. While Davout and the Bavarians under Marshal Lefebvre held

Charles's front, Masséna and Oudinot conducted a *manœuvre sur la derrière* at Landshut, cutting Charles off from his direct line of supply and communication to Austria. Napoleon then ordered the three corps to roll up Charles's flank at Eckmühl. Charles extricated his army to Bohemia by staged withdrawal across the Danube at Regensberg. By the end of April, three weeks into the war, the only thing that stood between Napoleon and Vienna was the Austrian VI Corps under General Johann von Hiller (1754–1819). Napoleon entered Vienna shortly after 12 May. Five days later, the Archduke Charles, with his entire army, arrived on the north bank of the Danube opposite his capital city, having conducted a forced march from Bohemia.

On 21 May 1809, Napoleon threw his army across the Danube, straight into the face of the Archduke Charles. The battle of Aspern–Essling was an extremely hard fought one. Overconfident, Napoleon managed to establish a tenuous bridgehead using Marshal Lannes' and Marshal Masséna's corps, in addition to Marshal Jean-Baptiste Bessières (1768–1813) cavalry corps. In total, there were no more than 62,000 men against Charles's army of 100,000. A single, hastily constructed bridge connected the Danube's banks, and the Austrians floated debris down the river, breaking the structure several times. By nightfall, the French clung tenaciously between the villages of Aspern and Essling.

On the morning of 22 May, Napoleon was on the north bank with some of his Imperial Guard as Marshal Davout's III Corps were preparing to cross the river. The Austrians, however, sent a granary barge down the river, causing significant damage to the bridge, and Charles launched a counterattack. The French repelled the Austrian assaults, but Napoleon ordered a general withdrawal. The battle of Aspern–Essling was Napoleon's first defeat.

'The best means of organizing the command of an army is first to give command to a man of tried bravery, bold in the fight...second to assign as his chief of staff a man of high ability...'

– Antoine-Henri Jomini

The French emperor did not take defeat lightly and immediately called much of his army to Vienna. By the end of June the ranks of the *Grande Armée* had swollen with the arrival of the Bavarians, Saxons and Württembergers. Prince Eugène de Beauharnais (1781–1824), Napoleon's stepson, brought his Army of Italy, containing Italian and French divisions fresh from their victory in Hungary. Napoleon truly commanded an imperial army. Charles, however, had not been able to increase his army significantly enough to match Napoleon's numbers. However, to reinforce his position on the north bank, he built earthworks running from Aspern to Essling to Gross Enzerdorf and beyond.

French Defences

In the six weeks following the battle of Aspern–Essling, the French constructed a number of massive artillery emplacements on Lobau Island on the Danube, in preparation for a methodical attack across the river, with the island as the central crossing point. A total of 129 heavy guns were dug in opposite the Austrian defence works, and French engineers drove wood pylons into the river upstream to prevent the Austrians from floating down barges and debris. Three separate bridges were constructed from the south bank to Lobau Island, and Napoleon's engineers prepared at least 12 pontoon bridges, which would eventually connect Lobau to the north bank. Napoleon determined to pound the Austrian positions, while he pushed his corps across the Danube with great speed, preventing another disaster like Aspern–Essling.

Napoleon assumed Charles remained in strength along the north bank. The Archduke posted General Joseph-Armand von Nordmann's (1759–1809) advance guard and General Johann von Klenau's (1758–1819) VI Corps along the line to screen his position and delay a French crossing. Charles, however, withdrew the main army from the Danube to the Russbach plateau, some

A COLONEL OF A RHEINBUND *regiment encourages his men immediately prior to battle. Such a performance, in the spirit of Shakespeare's* Henry V, *was commonplace and expected.*

8–10km (5–6 miles) across the Marchfeld, the flat ground leading from the Danube to the plateau. On 4 July, the guns of Lobau began bombarding the Austrian works on the north bank. Napoleon with seven corps, the Imperial Guard and the reserve cavalry corps – some 134,000 infantry, 27,000 cavalry and 433 cannon – faced the Archduke Charles, with six corps plus the advance guard – 121,500 infantry, 14,700 cavalry and 414 guns.

The crossing began at 8 p.m. on the night of 4 July. Unlike in his previous attempt, when he had charged straight into Charles's army, this time Napoleon pinned the Austrians to their defence works with a massive bombardment as the crossing was made from the east side of Lobau Island to the north bank, southeast of the Austrian position. Elite companies rowed across the river, overwhelming Austrian detachments observing the island. Engineers swung prefabricated pontoon bridges from Lobau to the north bank under the protection of the elite companies and small gunboats sailed from Vienna. By 2 a.m. Marshal Oudinot's II Corps was across and expanding the bridgehead against minimal resistance. At 5 a.m. Marshal Masséna's IV Corps reached the north bank, followed rapidly by Marshal Davout's III Corps. Twelve hours after Napoleon had given the order, three corps comprising 72,000 infantry, 9200 cavalry and 280 cannon were safely across the Danube and swinging north to widen the bridgehead.

Charles observed the fighting from his position near the village of Wagram. Nordmann's and Klenau's troops fought stubbornly but were overwhelmed by Oudinot and Masséna's divisions. Davout's corps covered the right flank, and the three corps in line pushed the Austrians back across the Marchfeld. Oudinot and Davout pursued Nordmann north towards the Russbach plateau as Masséna advanced against Klenau, who withdrew to the west. Prince Eugène's Army of Italy filled the gap between the French II and IV Corps that developed by midday. His divisions moved toward Raasdorf, which became Napoleon's headquarters.

Officer, Royal Horse Artillery

Horse artillery was introduced in the eighteenth century as a means of providing artillery support rapidly on the fluid battlefield. All major armies possessed horse batteries, allocating some to cavalry divisions, but those held in reserve, or attached to corps or columns, could be deployed effectively by a general during the course of battle. The British horse artillery proved incredibly effective during the battle of Waterloo. Wellington possessed six troops (batteries) for the campaign in Belgium in 1815. Although they were attached to the cavalry corps, Wellington disposed of them as needed on the field. Generally consisting of lighter guns and a full complement of horses for the artillerists, the troop could move tactically with much greater speed than the heavier foot batteries.

Marshal Bernadotte's Saxon IX Corps, the Imperial Guard and the Cavalry Reserve were all across and moving out onto the plain by 2 p.m. General Marmont's XI Corps, the Bavarian VII Corps and two more divisions from Eugène's army prepared to cross in the late afternoon to early evening. Within 24 hours of the signal to move, Napoleon had transported his entire army to the Marchfeld. It was a truly impressive feat.

Charles Faces the Onslaught

Klenau and Nordmann had broken contact with the French by late afternoon, the latter commander being killed during the day's combat. Charles arrayed his army along the plateau in preparation for receiving a French attack. He held a strong, elevated position behind the Russbach stream. The Austrian left was anchored by the town of Markgrafneuseidl, the centre stiffened by the village of Baumersdorf and the right strengthened by Wagram.

Three Austrian corps - I, II and IV - were deployed on the heights, with the cavalry from the Reserve Corps held back. To the west, the grenadier divisions of the Reserve Corps were posted at Gerasdorf, with III and V Corps 4.8km (3 miles) upstream. Charles did not think Napoleon would chance an assault at dusk. He was wrong.

Napoleon remained uncertain whether the Austrians along the heights were a rearguard or Charles's entire army. At 5 p.m. he ordered Eugène, Oudinot and Davout to storm the Austrian positions. However, the orders were not received simultaneously, and instead of mounting a coordinated attack by three corps, the French moved piecemeal against the Austrians. Charles, stunned by Napoleon's boldness, tried to reinforce his line as the French scaled the heights. Oudinot managed to seize Baumersdorf after fierce fighting, but the town caught fire and he was obliged to withdraw lest his men be burned to death. Eugène had better luck on the left between Baumersdorf and Wagram.

His divisions pressed the Austrian I Corps, and the timely if late arrival of Bernadotte's reinforcements created a crisis on Charles's right. The archduke, however, personally orchestrated a counterattack, throwing Eugène's divisions off the plateau with heavy losses. Fighting continued along the line until 11 p.m. as the fires at Baumersdorf illuminated the sky. Napoleon now knew Charles and his army were present in force. If the evening attack had failed, the emperor was confident he would do better come morning.

Charles wanted Napoleon to array his army on the Marchfeld, so he could destroy it with its back to the Danube. His confidence was bolstered by his victory at Aspern and the knowledge that his brother, the Archduke John, had rallied his army in Hungary and was merely 16km (10 miles) to the east. Charles believed John could arrive by early afternoon to turn Napoleon's right as his own army held the centre and pressed from the west. The archduke did not remain passive during the night, but wrote to his brother again; he then conceived of a rather 'Napoleonic' manoeuvre to cut the French from their bridges.

Charles shifted his army on the Russbach plateau to the west, with part of I Corps deployed between Wagram and Aderklaa. The entire Reserve Corps was united to the north and west of the latter town, held by Bernadotte's Saxons. Charles directed Klenau's battered VI Corps and General Johann Kollowrath's (1748–1816) uncommitted III Corps to make a night march attacking Napoleon's left flank along a 6.5km (4-mile) stretch between the Danube and Sussenbrunn. The emperor had only a single division to cover Aspern, since he anticipated a battle to his front. If Charles's generals were not able to move accordingly, they would roll up the French along the riverbank and cut the bridges, isolating the French Army and its emperor on the north bank.

Napoleon obliged Charles by redeploying his army in a line from Aderklaa to Markgrafneuseidl. Bernadotte, Eugène, Oudinot and Davout stood in the first line. Masséna held the left flank north of Sussenbrunn. The emperor kept XI Corps, the Bavarians, the Imperial Guard and Bessières' cavalry corps in reserve. Oudinot and two of Eugène's divisions were ordered to attack the Russbach plateau, while Bernadotte's Saxons pinned the Austrians west of Wagram. Marshal Davout's III Corps would sweep around the Austrian left at Markgrafneuseidl and turn Charles's flank. Eugène's two remaining divisions

Battle of Wagram

5-6 July 1809

After Aspern-Essling, Napoleon, undeterred, called most of his corps to Vienna in the month following his first defeat. Learning the lessons of his previously hasty river crossing, the French Army constructed gun emplacements, deployed heavy batteries and built numerous pontoon bridges for a second crossing of the Danube. The Archduke Charles abandoned his forward deployment on the north bank, withdrawing much of his army to the Russbach plateau to receive the French attack. The details of the crossing on the night of 4-5 July resembled an early nineteenth-century special forces operation rather than a traditional conventional battle. The Austrian divisions guarding the bank were overwhelmed and within four hours Napoleon had three full corps across the river. The French emperor's ability to move more than 150,000 men to the north bank in less than a day is a tribute to his organizational skills, and the performance of the *Grande Armée*.

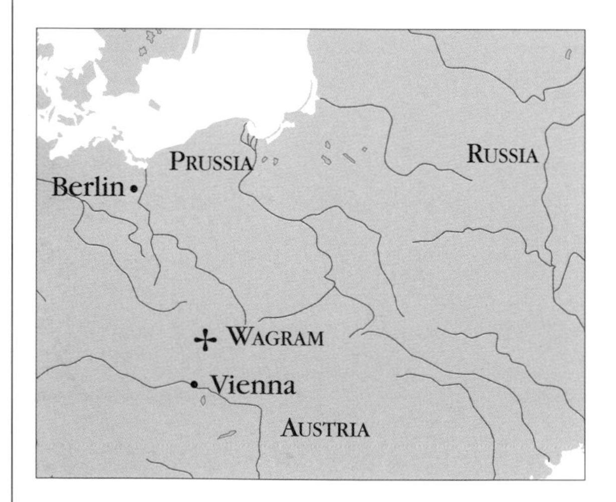

The Archduke Charles met Napoleon for a second time on the north bank of the Danube, across from French-occupied Vienna. The battle would decide the campaign, and the future of the House of Habsburg.

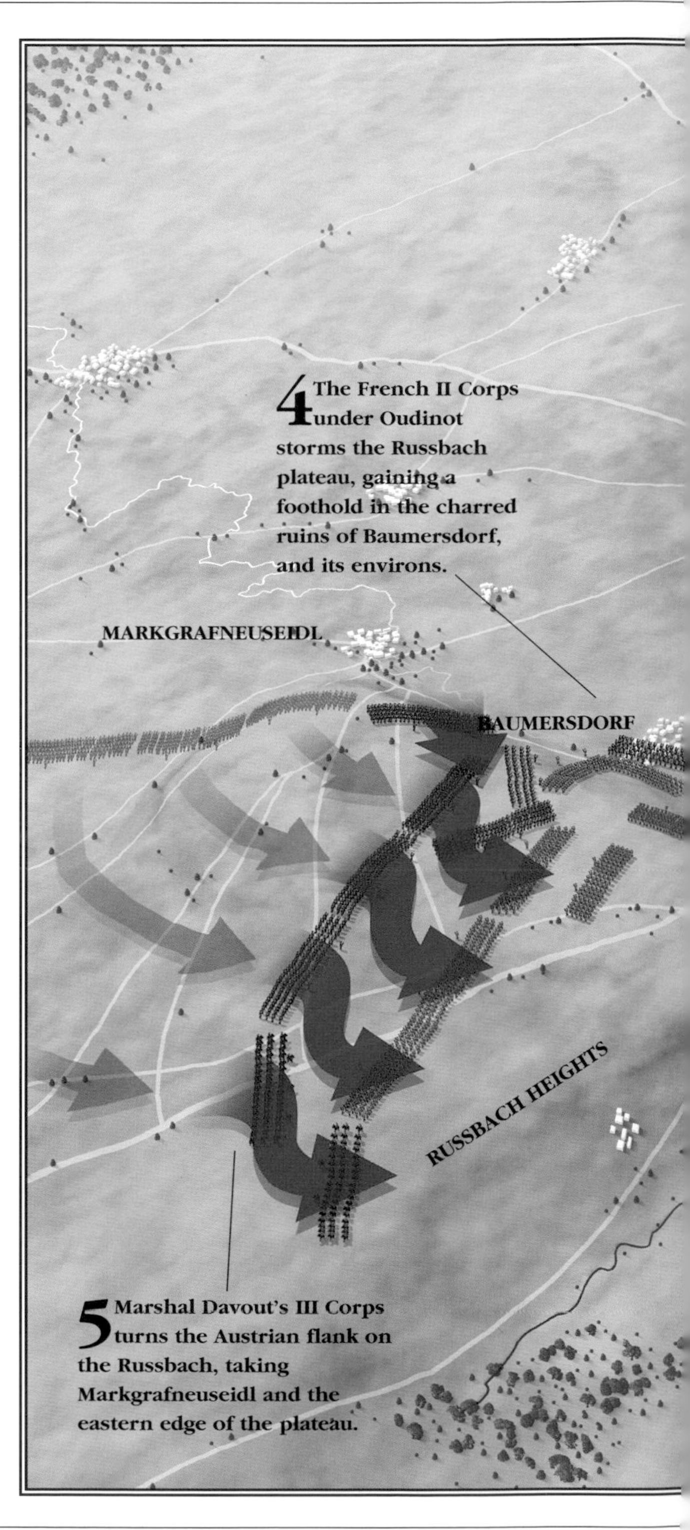

6 Napoleon still retains the IX Corps, the Saxon IX Corps and much of the Imperial Guard in reserve. The Archduke Charles committed all his forces, and was compelled to withdraw once his morning attack failed, and the French gained the Russbach.

2 After stabilizing the centre at Aderklaa, Marshal Massena's IV Corps rapidly redeploys via an impressive flank march to contain the Austrian VI Corps along the Danube.

VIENNA

RAASDORF

LEOPOLDAU

ADERKLAA

WAGRAM

GERASDORF

1 The Austrian III and VI Corps threaten the entire French left flank and bridgeheads. Due to a delay in orders, the Austrian corps did not arrive until late morning, after the French crisis at Aderklaa had passed.

3 Napoleon orders the Army of Italy to hold the centre at Aderklaa, while Macdonald's corps in hollow square attacks the Austrian III Corps. The counterattack is reinforced by a 100-gun grand battery – the Young Guard and the Bavarians.

under General Etienne Macdonald (1765–1840) would then storm the Russbach east of Wagram and break the Austrian right.

Day Two

At 4 a.m. the Austrians opened their attack with a bombardment. The French responded in kind and the artillery duel ushered in a most bloody day of combat. The Austrian IV Corps on the heights moved to the attack as the French began their advance across the Russbach stream. As the two armies collided, the French gained the upper hand and repelled the Austrian assault after two hours of fighting. Napoleon reinforced Davout with another heavy cavalry division to spur on the flanking movement. Although the right flank stabilized, Napoleon received shocking news that Bernadotte's Saxons had abandoned Aderklaa to the Austrians without a shot. Indeed, without informing the emperor, the French marshal had withdrawn and redeployed his corps beyond the town, believing it could not be held. Napoleon relieved Bernadotte of his command later that morning.

By 6 a.m., the Austrian I Corps, supported by the grenadier division of the Reserve Corps, took the town and advanced against the Saxons. Napoleon looked to Masséna to retake it. The French IV Corps shifted north, and fighting raged for most of the morning, with Aderklaa changing hands several times.

At noon, the Austrians finally recaptured it. Then, to make his morning worse, Napoleon had to contend with the appearance of Klenau's and Kollowrath's corps, whose advance had begun at 4 a.m. and brought them within artillery range by 8 a.m. Klenau moved along the bank of the Danube and into Aspern, which was held by a single division. The French gave way under weight of numbers and by mid-morning sought shelter among the earthworks between Aspern and Essling. Kollowrath moved towards Breitenlee but did not take advantage of the open ground and the absence of French troops to his front. Instead, he unlimbered his artillery and bombarded the French flank. Napoleon sent a rider to Marshal Masséna, whose corps had recently been ejected from Aderklaa, ordering him to countermarch to the Danube. Within the hour, his divisions turned about and advanced against Klenau, supported by the Cavalry Reserve. Masséna coordinated the attack from his carriage, being unable to walk after suffering wounds during the battle for Aspern-Essling in May. Between 11 a.m. and 2 p.m., Klenau faced repeated assaults that forced him from Aspern and its environs.

'The whole art of war consists in getting at what is on the other side of the hill.'

– Duke of Wellington

Napoleon, meanwhile, still had to contend with Kollowrath's corps and the Austrians in Aderklaa. He ordered Prince Eugène to shift his divisions to the left to contain Aderklaa, while General Macdonald's corps – the reserve of the Army of Italy – redeployed to attack Kollowrath. The general formed his 10,000 men into a hollow square, with cavalry on his flanks and artillery batteries to his front. From the Austrian position, the French counterattack appeared as a solid mass of men. Kollowrath concentrated his artillery on Macdonald's corps, which suffered awful losses.

Napoleon dispatched a division of his Young Guard, the XI Corps and the Bavarians to stiffen the attack. He reinforced the artillery, creating a grand battery of 100 heavy guns. The firepower and numbers forced Kollowrath to withdraw, under increasing pressure though still in good order. Charles committed his Cavalry Reserve to stabilize the line. By 3 p.m., the Austrian threat had abated; the fighting on the French left continued but with no result.

As the day wore on, and casualties mounted, Charles and Napoleon kept watch for Archduke John. Although he had only 16km (10 miles) to march to reach the battlefield, there was no sign of him by late afternoon. Oudinot and Davout renewed their attacks on the Russbach. Davout's corps swung around the plateau and assaulted Markgrafneuseidl from two sides. Attacked in front and flank, the position fell, and Davout's divisions

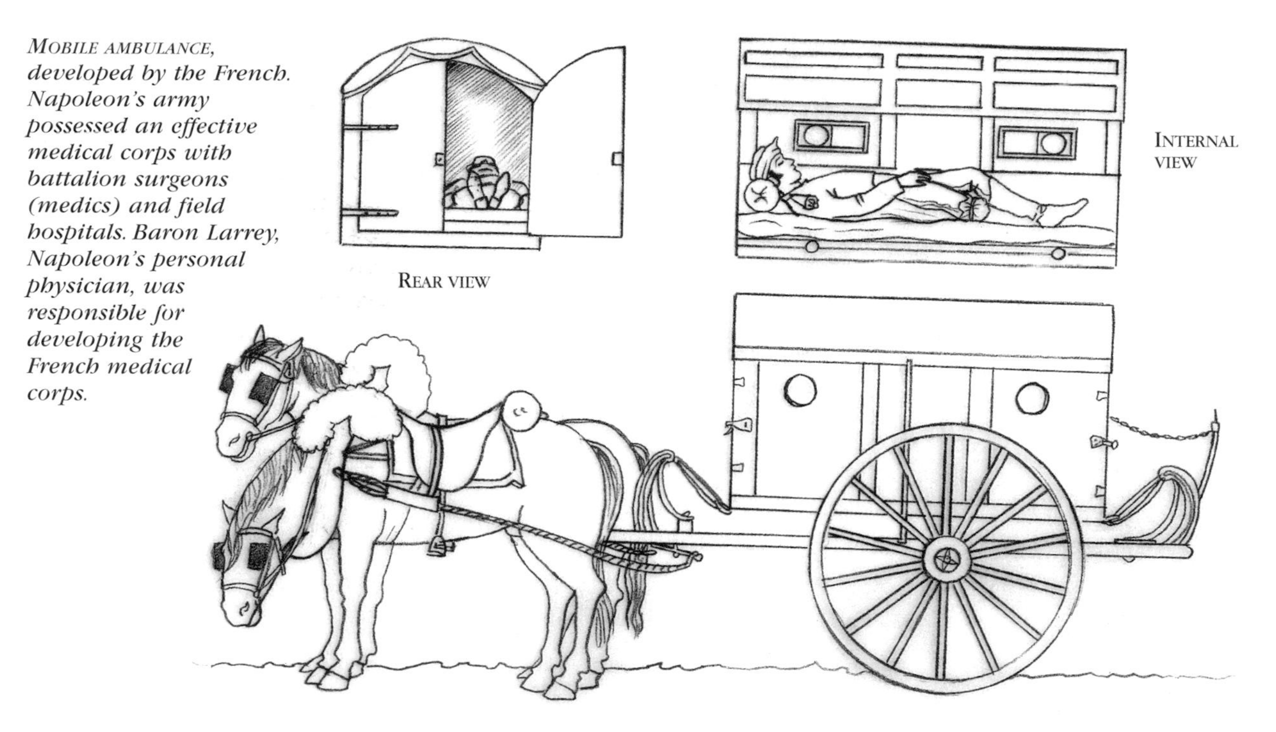

MOBILE AMBULANCE, developed by the French. Napoleon's army possessed an effective medical corps with battalion surgeons (medics) and field hospitals. Baron Larrey, Napoleon's personal physician, was responsible for developing the French medical corps.

gained a foothold on the Russbach. Charles observed his position deteriorating and Davout's advance turning his left. With John nowhere to be found, and Klenau and Kollowrath in retreat, but his centre holding, Charles decided to cut his losses and abandon the field to the enemy. At 6 p.m. the archduke issued orders for a phased withdrawal to the northwest, and two hours later the guns fell silent. John's light cavalry finally appeared to the east, but it was too little, too late. Napoleon's army was exhausted. He had defeated the Archduke Charles but at a heavy cost. Charles was able to extricate his army with little difficulty and in very good order, but the two days of hard fighting led him to conclude that the War of the Fifth Coalition (1809) was over.

Coalition Warfare

Austria's grand strategic failure in 1809 was largely due to its inability to gather allies. Prussia remained neutral and Tsar Alexander abided by his French alliance, to the extent that Russian troops occupied Austrian Poland. The German princes of the *Rheinbund* held to their agreements and provided a great many men for Napoleon's army. The French emperor clearly had much of Europe as satellites, clients or allies, and their troops marched off to war under French command. Napoleon's imperial armies were less a coalition than European armies under centralized direction. The secret of Napoleon's success through to 1813 can be found in his ability to play upon the rivalries of the emperors, kings and princes of Europe, keeping them divided. Fewer than half of the 500,000 men who invaded Russia in 1812 were French. The Austrians committed 40,000 to the endeavour and Prussia contributed 22,000 men. As long as Napoleon could prevent the major powers from making common cause, his empire would hold.

None of the previous anti-French coalitions had possessed a unitary command structure, while even during the revolution, French armies were coordinated after 1793 by Carnot. While the First Coalition established a general strategic outline, it did not synchronize its movements effectively. Coalition armies generally operated independently, in different theatres of war. In the Austrian Netherlands (Belgium) during the revolution, Austrian and Anglo-Allied armies operated separately or in conjunction but directed

BATTLE OF LEIPZIG: *the Allied leaders confer on the third day of the battle, 18 October 1813. The Allies combined their forces for the campaign, allowing for greater coordination of armies.*

separately. This is precisely what happened prior to Fleurus. During the War of the Second Coalition in 1799, the Austrians subordinated their larger army in Italy to the Russians under General Alexander Suvarov (1729–1800).

Although the aggressive Russian general succeeded in sweeping the French from northern Italy, the Austrians complained it was done with their blood. Discontent and distrust among Austrian and Russian commanders led to the dissolution of the Continental coalition. Animosity among the former allies continued into 1805, when the political decision to establish a new coalition with the Russians was met with severe opposition from the Archduke Charles and members of the imperial court. Mack's ill-fated campaign in Germany was conducted prior to the arrival of the Russians instead of in concert with them. The Prussian Army marched to war in 1806, long before their Russian allies were prepared for campaign.

Competition and hubris dictated the character of European coalitions, but a decade of Napoleonic hegemony, followed by the debacle in Russia in 1812, provided another opportunity for a European coalition to face Napoleon. The question remained whether the European powers would act in concert or their endeavour suffer the fate of previous coalitions. What was unique about the Sixth Coalition in 1813 was the willingness of the European powers to set aside their differences in order to achieve total victory over Napoleon. Furthermore, they ensured their coalition forces would operate effectively by combining their armies, establishing a joint command and appointing a supreme Allied commander.

The spring campaign of 1813 may have introduced a unitary Allied command, but it failed to achieve an Allied victory. Prussia joined Russia in March 1813, but both states fielded fewer than 100,000 men combined. The Russo-Prussian army faced a reconstituted imperial army of almost 180,000 men and was defeated at Lützen and Bautzen during May and June of that year. Napoleon and the coalition agreed to a two-month armistice. During this time Tsar Alexander worked assiduously to bring the Austrians into the alliance. Francis I and Prince Karl zu Schwarzenberg, Archduke Charles's successor as Austria's commander-in-chief, mobilized the Habsburg army for war. The Duke of Wellington's operations in Spain yielded strategic victory with the defeat of the French Army at Vittoria in June. In August 1813, Napoleon faced a central European coalition of Austria, Russia, Prussia and Sweden as an Anglo-Spanish Army prepared to cross the Pyrenees into France. Europe had indeed united against Napoleon, and his empire would soon crumble.

The Battle of the Nations (Leipzig): 16–18 October 1813

The Allied sovereigns established combined armies for the fall campaign. A Russo-Swedish army under Jean-Baptiste Bernadotte, now crown prince of Sweden, operated in northern Germany. A Prusso-Russian army under General Gebhard von Blücher (1742–1819) formed in Silesia, and a third army, Austro-Russian and Prussian in make-up, under Schwarzenberg, prepared to cross the Bohemian mountains into Saxony. The Austrians were the key to the coalition. Austria possessed an army of 300,000 men, greater than the Russians, Swedes and Prussians combined. Napoleon faced a coalition of 500,000 in central Europe. Against this, he could bring no more than 450,000 men. The coordination of coalition armies was of the utmost importance, and a coherent Allied strategy was critical to victory. Throughout the fall campaign, the Allies often bickered about operations but in the end kept the alliance together and cooperated more often than not.

During a meeting in July 1813 at Grand Allied Headquarters, the coalition established a clearly defined and sound strategy known as the Trachenberg Plan. Napoleon occupied the central position in Saxony, with the three coalition armies opposing him to the north, east and south. Allied forces would withdraw in the face of Napoleon but attack his subordinates, all the while closing the ring. In short, the Trachenberg Plan was a concentric advance of Allied armies towards a central point, and they would finally unite on the battlefield. The sizes of Napoleon's imperial army and of the armies of the coalition illustrate the expanding scope of war. Whereas in 1805 the French corps system revolutionized the operations of armies on campaign, seven years later the coordination of armies in a single theatre of war would result in decisive victory. While the French Army could boast of a highly efficient command and control system, Napoleon's marshals did not excel as army commanders. The Allies were no better but certainly no worse, and on a level playing field, numbers matter.

Napoleon wanted to strike at the Prussians before Schwarzenberg's army could cross the mountains. He marched east against Blücher's Army of Silesia, leaving Marshal Laurent Gouvion St Cyr (1764–1830) with a small corps at Dresden. Marshals Oudinot in Saxony and Davout in Hamburg would drive on Berlin with the aim of defeating Bernadotte's Army of the North. Napoleon was confident that with Bernadotte and Blücher defeated and Berlin under occupation Frederick William III, king of Prussia, would leave the coalition, seeking to save his realm. It was a simple plan but never came to fruition. The Allied strategy, on the other hand, did. Blücher quickly withdrew into Silesia to avoid a confrontation with Napoleon. Schwarzenberg took his army over the mountains and advanced upon Dresden. The emperor dispatched Macdonald to pursue Blücher while he himself countermarched rapidly, arriving at Dresden on 26 August. Napoleon defeated Schwarzenberg's Austrians, who withdrew back into Bohemia, pursued by General Dominique Vandamme's (1770–1830) corps.

Once in Bohemia, Schwarzenberg turned on Vandamme, trapping the French general at Kulm and forcing him to surrender with half his command. Oudinot did not fare much better. He attacked Bernadotte's army at Grossbeeren, only to be repulsed with heavy losses. Napoleon gave Ney command of Oudinot's army, but the vaunted marshal suffered a similar fate at Dennewitz. Davout's advance on the Prussian capital did not materialize due to logistical difficulties. However, the worst news came from Silesia, where Blücher's army attacked Macdonald on the Katzbach River, defeating him soundly. For the month of September, Blücher eluded Napoleon, while Schwarzenberg reorganized his army and marched across the mountains once again.

Leipzig

By October, the French emperor found the Allied armies closing in from the north, and Schwarzenberg advancing from the south.

Napoleon withdrew his army to Leipzig, closer to his Rhenish allies. The coalition armies followed cautiously. On 13 October, the emperor took up position at Leipzig, awaiting the allied attack. Napoleon assembled 200,000 men, divided into nine *corps d'armée,* five cavalry corps and two Imperial Guard corps. He arrayed his army in a semicircle running from the Elster River in the north to the Pleisse River south of the city. Blücher and Schwarzenberg arrived first with 200,000 men. Another 110,000 under Bernadotte and General Levin August Bennigsen (1745-1826) were a day behind.

Leipzig differed from previous Napoleonic battles in that the emperor's enemies coordinated their operations and cooperated effectively. The battle of Leipzig, also known as the 'battle of the Nations', was the largest battle fought in Europe until the wars of German unification of 1866 and 1870-71. Almost half a million soldiers from more than a dozen European states were engaged during the three days of fighting. In the end, Napoleon lost a large part of his army, and all of Germany. To make matters worse, his most stalwart German ally, Bavaria, defected to the coalition, thereby threatening his line of communication to the Rhine.

Napoleon intended to attack Schwarzenberg while keeping Blücher at bay. He knew that Bernadotte's army was not far behind, and he had relative numerical parity with the coalition's forces until Bernadotte's arrival. Napoleon deployed three corps to the north, under Marshal Marmont and Generals Henri Gatien Bertrand (1773-1844) and Joseph Souham (1760-1837), and the remainder of his army - eight corps and the cavalry - to the south around Waschau. A single division under General Pierre Margaron (1765-1824) defended the western approaches to the city at Lindenau.

Schwarzenberg wanted to approach Leipzig from both banks of the Pleisse River. Tsar Alexander objected, not wanting to divide the army with a river in between. He thought it a recipe for certain disaster and told Schwarzenberg that he could send his army west of the Pleisse, but the Russians would not follow. The Austrian general deferred to the tsar on this point, leaving only Count Maximilian von Merveldt's (1770-1815) corps on the left bank. It was a sound decision, for if Schwarzenberg had had his way, Napoleon would certainly have destroyed the Army of Bohemia. Schwarzenberg and Blücher did not intend to pass the initiative to Napoleon. The Austrian field marshal was well aware that he faced the bulk of Napoleon's army. Confident that he could bring greater numbers to bear, Schwarzenberg ordered a general advance, hoping to turn Napoleon's flank to the east while he pinned the larger part of the French Army south of the city. Blücher, reinforced by an Austrian corps, was to vigorously attack Leipzig from the north, preventing the French corps in that vicinity from moving to support Napoleon later in the day. To complete the destruction of the French imperial army, Schwarzenberg dispatched Count Ignaz Gyulai's (1763-1831) Austrian corps west of the Elster, with Lindenau and Napoleon's line of retreat as its objective.

At 9 a.m., the Russian and Prussian corps under General Ludwig Wittgenstein (1769-1843) advanced

A DIAGRAM OF *a six-company battalion moving from line into square. The ability of infantry to manoeuvre swiftly into square was the difference between life and death when facing a cavalry charge.*

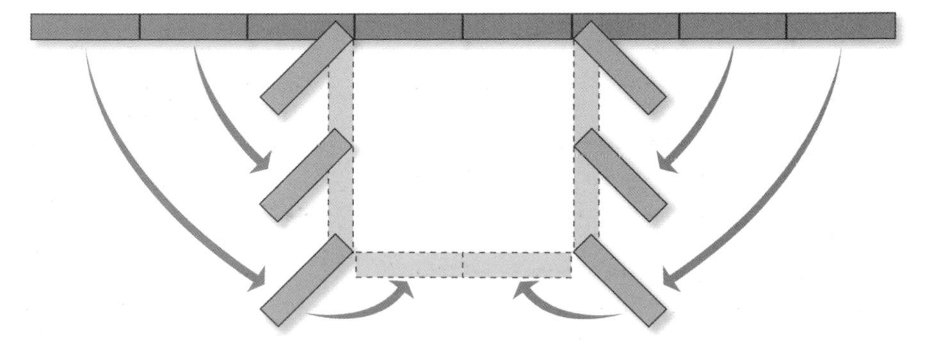

into the face of Napoleon's corps, hoping to press them back towards the city. Napoleon observed the Allied dispositions and the development of the attack. He decided to maintain the defensive until the impetus of the coalition offensive died out. He held back substantial reserves, including much of the cavalry, the Imperial Guard and Marshal Pierre Augereau's (1757-1816) corps. Macdonald's corps and General Horace Sébastiani's (1772-1851) cavalry were posted east of the city, but Napoleon called them south to press the Russian flank.

The Allied attack suffered from a lack of coordination and the critical fact that their corps were separated by gaps large enough for Napoleon to exploit. Tsar Alexander observed this immediately and ordered the Russian and Prussian Guard Corps up to fill the space between General Friedrich Kleist's (1762-1823) Prussians and Eugen of Württemberg's (1788-1857) Russians.

'An army ought to only have one line of operation. This should be preserved with care, and never abandoned but in the last extremity.'

– Napoleon

The Russians seized Waschau in the centre, but Napoleon massed heavy batteries to prevent them from exploiting their position. The artillery fire was so intense that Eugen's corps withdrew with heavy losses and the town was easily retaken by a concerted French counterattack. To the west, Kleist's advance along the right bank of the Pleisse made headway, as Merveldt on the left bank tried to cross the river and turn the French right. Prince Josef Poniatowski's (1763-1813) Polish corps threw the Austrians back across the river after difficult fighting.

Kleist could not continue his advance in the face of artillery fire and the arrival of Augereau's corps from the French reserve. On the Allied right, a Russian corps under the command of Duke Gortschakov (1768-1855) moved on Liebertwolkwitz without waiting for Klenau's flanking columns. His corps was savaged as well by French artillery fire.

By the time the Austrian corps appeared before the town, Napoleon had dispatched a reinforced corps from his Imperial Guard, which stalled Klenau's flanking attack, threatening to isolate it from the rest of Schwarzenberg's army. Soon after, Macdonald's corps arrived, ending any hope of an Allied flanking manoeuvre. By 11 a.m., two hours after the Allies began their offensive, the initiative had passed to the French emperor.

Napoleon Counterattacks

Napoleon's army, holding interior lines of operation, had the ability to redeploy by moving through Leipzig. The Allies, however, occupying exterior lines, required greater time to move from one part of the field to another.

Aware of an advantage, Napoleon ordered Marmont and Souham to redeploy south, leaving only a reinforced corps to observe Blücher's army as he believed the Prussian general would not risk an attack. As the fighting in the south developed, however, Blücher's army fell on Marmont's position at Mockern with great alacrity. Through midday, Marmont fought tenaciously, but Blücher ejected the French infantry from the town and forced three French corps back towards Leipzig. Marmont and Souham therefore were unable to carry out the emperor's orders.

Napoleon's counterattack began shortly before midday. Advancing through Waschau, two French corps drove back the Allied centre. Macdonald then moved against Klenau, while Poniatowski and Augereau drove their corps on Kleist's Prussians. Napoleon anticipated Marmont and Souham's arrival, planning to reinforce Macdonald's attack. Their failure to arrive, however, reduced the strength of the French onslaught. Although the assault was supported by the Imperial Guard and cavalry, Klenau managed to extricate his command without losing the flank. As the fighting on the Allied right raged, Napoleon organized an attack on the Allied centre. He formed a grand battery of 84 cannon supported by a heavy cavalry corps and directed fire on the remnants of Eugen's divisions. The Russians cracked under artillery fire and the

Battle of Nations (Leipzig)

16–18 October 1813

'The Battle of Nations', as Leipzig is often called, illustrated that the Allies had finally adopted a successful strategy for confronting Napoleon. The Trachenberg Plan called for avoiding battle with the French emperor, while engaging his subordinates. Although their spring campaign ended in failure, a rejuvenated coalition, with the addition of Austria, led to triumphant victory in the autumn. The Allied armies advanced in an ever-shrinking concentric semicircle towards the epicentre of Napoleon's armies in Saxony. On the field of Leipzig, a titanic battle lasting three days, and involving more than half a million men, decided the fate of Europe. Napoleon's German allies abandoned him, including the defection of Saxon troops on the battlefield. By the night of the first day, Napoleon knew he had lost the battle, but decided to stand and fight, hoping to weaken the Allies sufficiently, prior to his withdrawal from the field. However, none of this worked out as planned.

An empire that took seven years to build collapsed in central Germany in a climactic three-day battle, which remained the largest engagement in Europe until 1866.

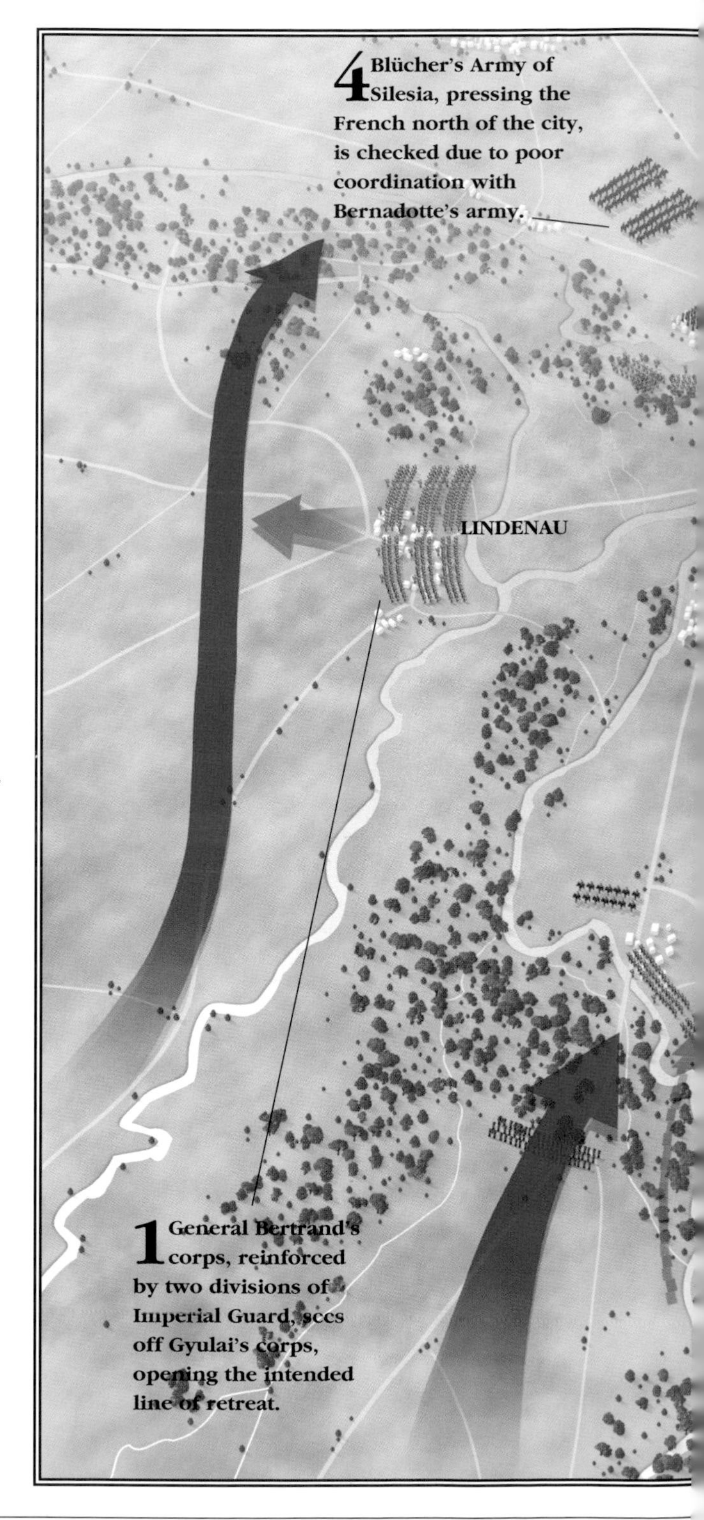

5 Bernadotte's Army of the North moves slowly, only assailing Ney's corps late in the afternoon, instead of supporting Blucher's attacks.

LEIPZIG

6 The defection of the Saxon VII Corps to the Allies at 4 p.m. compromises Ney's position facing Bernadotte. He quickly stabilized the line using his few reserves.

3 Arriving on 17 October, Bennigsen attacks Macdonald's corps east of the city, preventing them from reinforcing Napoleon's position, as they had two days earlier.

2 Barclay de Tolly's corps of the Army of Bohemia attack Napoleon's corps south of the city, with little effect.

THE CHARGE OF *the Brandenburg Hussar Regiment at Leipzig. Their attack at Mockern late on 16 October broke the French counterattack, giving the Prussians a tactical victory.*

subsequent cavalry charge. The attack carried the French and Saxon regiments within metres of the Allied headquarters, sending Tsar Alexander I and King Frederick William III searching for cover. A counterattack by Allied cavalry and the appearance of Russian grenadiers prevented the collapse of the Allied centre, but the flanks were in dire difficulty. Nightfall and exhaustion saved the Army of Bohemia. Napoleon's decisive victory eluded him, and Blücher's success at Mockern was critical for the Allies. Despite severe losses, Schwarzenberg had no intention of withdrawing. The imminent arrival of Bernadotte's Army of the North would more than compensate for the tens of thousands of casualties on the first day. Napoleon could not count on similar reinforcements.

Both armies spent 17 October recuperating. Napoleon's position was precarious. Bernadotte's arrival bolstered Allied ranks, and Blücher had pushed the French back towards the city. Gyulai's Austrian corps in front of Lindenau temporarily blocked Napoleon's line of retreat. More problematic was the information received from Merveldt, who had been captured on 16 October, that the Bavarians had defected a week earlier and were moving on Frankfurt and Mainz to Napoleon's strategic rear. Napoleon, however, understood that withdrawal would provide the Allies with a tremendous victory and no doubt lead to the collapse of his empire in Germany. He therefore decided to fight on 18 October, despite the likelihood that he would not fare well.

Napoleon drew closer to Leipzig and divided his army into three wings: Ney on the left, facing Blücher and Bernadotte; Macdonald to the east; and Murat on the right. The latter two wings were to contend with the enlarged ranks of the Army of Bohemia, now divided into armies under Barclay de Tolly (formerly Wittgenstein) and Bennigsen. Napoleon sent Bertrand's corps to clear Lindenau of Gyulai's Austrians, reinforcing Bertrand with two divisions of Imperial Guard. The Allied generals were confident that their numbers – almost 300,000 after deducting the casualties of 16 October – gave them the advantage over Napoleon, who possessed no more than 150,000 men. Their plan was to simply press on Leipzig in six converging columns.

For much of the morning and early afternoon, the Allied columns advanced towards the new French positions around Leipzig. Despite their overwhelming superiority in cavalry, the Allies' scouts failed to detect the redeployment of the *Grand Armée*. Intense fighting began in the early afternoon, with the Allied columns making difficult progress against stubborn French resistance. At Lindenau, Bertrand's attack scattered Gyulai's regiments and opened the road west. Napoleon could now prepare a general retreat, hoping his army would wound the Allies before escaping towards the Rhine. Unfortunately, Blücher once again proved an intractable foe.

'In this age, in past ages, in any age, Napoleon.'

– Wellington, when asked who he thought was the greatest general

The Prussian corps pressed from the north and northeast, then the entire French wing was compromised when the Saxon infantry regiments of General Jean-Louis Reynier's (1771–1814) VII Corps defected to the Allies at 4 p.m. As Reynier protected Ney's right, this completely undid the French position north of the city and created further opportunity for the Allies against Macdonald's left and rear in the centre. Ney acted quickly, committing what regiments he could into the gap left by the Saxons. By 6 p.m., he managed to stabilize the line, although at a heavy cost. Responsibility for the Allies' inability to take full advantage of this opportunity falls upon Bernadotte, who was reluctant to commit his Russians and Swedes to the battle, although he was nominally in command in that sector.

After more than six hours of combat, night fell without the Allies having reached the city. Napoleon's luck held, but the emperor knew it would not do so for another day. That night, he ordered a phased withdrawal of corps through the city and across the Elster. Engineers placed charges on the bridge, and were given orders to blow it once the army was across. On 18 October, the imperial army began to move to the west bank of the Elster. The Allies launched attacks into the city's suburbs, reaching the walls by late morning. Hard fighting around the city gates continued until 1 p.m., prematurely destroying the bridge over the Elster. More than 30,000 French and imperial troops were trapped in Leipzig. With Napoleon leading his army away to the west, the defenders surrendered.

Leipzig was a tremendous coalition victory at a heavy price. Napoleon suffered 70,000 killed, wounded or taken prisoner. The Allies lost 54,000 men. The Trachenberg Plan produced a strategic victory in Germany. Although the Allies coordinated their battle plans, their expertise in synchronizing the movements of their armies and corps simply did not compare to that of the French. Napoleon's capacity, and that of his subordinates, to manoeuvre corps on the battlefield saved the French on 16 and 18 October. Despite this, the Allies succeeded in bringing their armies together in overwhelming numbers, producing a strategic victory.

Towards the Nineteenth Century

Perhaps the Prussians came away with the most acute observations of Allied strategy and its culmination at Leipzig. Helmuth von Moltke (the elder; 1800–91), future chief of the Prussian – later German – General Staff, drew much from the autumn campaign of 1813. He attended the Prussian War College in 1823, and his reform of the General Staff system and his strategic thought suggest that he was profoundly influenced by the Napoleonic Wars. The General Staff became the central institution for military planning, and Moltke achieved Scharnhorst's goal of placing the staff on a level equal to or higher than the army commander. Finally, Moltke's planning and conduct of the Austro-Prussian War (1866) clearly recalls the Sixth Coalition's successful campaign in Germany.

– L'arrivée de Blücher.

CHAPTER 4

ARTILLERY AND SIEGE WARFARE

From meagre origins in the fourteenth century to the development of the artillery systems that were employed during the Napoleonic period, there was a quantum leap in how gunpowder artillery was designed, constructed, supported and employed on the battlefield. It is very interesting to look into the different artillery developments among the main belligerents who fought each other during the French Revolutionary and Napoleonic Wars (1792–1815).

Mobile artillery development actually started with Gustavus Adolphus (1594-1632) in the Thirty Years War (1618-48). He is also credited with being the first commander to organize his light artillery into batteries. In the wars between the Thirty Years War and the start of the French Revolutionary Wars in 1792, competent

PRUSSIAN FOOT ARTILLERY *going into position. Prussia had the worst artillery arm of the period, largely thanks to the interference of Frederick the Great, who knew nothing of artillery and treated his gunners as second-class soldiers. Prussian artillery performed poorly in 1806, even with more guns on the field.*

generals and commanders had always sought to mass their guns for more devastating effect on the enemy. There are myriad examples to choose from: Gustavus Adolphus himself at Breitenfeld (1631) and Lützen (1632); British artilleryman Captain (later Major-General) William Phillips (d. 1781) at Minden in 1759; George Washington (1732–99) and Henry Knox (1750–1806) atMonmouth in 1778. The Prussians in the War of the Austrian Succession (1740–48) surprised and outclassed the Austrian artillery, and the Austrians reversed the tables on the Prussians in the Seven Years War (1756–63) with their reorganized and excellently trained light artillery arm. In the early Revolutionary Wars, Austrian artilleryman Josef Smola employed his reinforced cavalry battery in support of the Austrian infantry to smash the attacking French column, suffering heavy losses in an action that was reminiscent of Phillips' action at Minden.

FRENCH FOOT ARTILLERYMAN *in the new 1812 regulation uniform that probably was not issued until 1813. Clothed in the usual dark blue, French artillerymen were considered elite troops and received* haute *pay. They were chosen for intelligence and strength, and were the best artillery arm of the period. This is a line artilleryman.*

In the development of European artillery systems, there was much cross-fertilization of ideas.The French developed a light artillery system as early as 1679, introduced by the Spaniard Antonio Gonzales and employed by General François de la Frézelière (1624–1702), but by 1720 it was abolished in favour of heavier guns that could be used in both siege and field, but would later cause the French much trouble. The Swedes were consistent artillery innovators, much of what they did being a great influence on the Prussians, French and Austrians.

The first artillery system is generally recognized to have been that of the French artilleryman Vallière in 1732. He standardized the French artillery to the calibres of 4-, 8-, 12-, 16- and 24-pounders, which were to be employed for both field and siege work, though the emphasis was to be on siege artillery. There was, however, no standardization of artillery vehicles, and they were built differently in each of the French arsenals, allowing no capability for the interchangeability of parts, which was a very definite handicap.

Development of Field Artillery

Field artillery had come into its own by the middle of the eighteenth century. Field artillery, often referred to as light artillery, during the Napoleonic period consisted of foot artillery, with the gunners expected to walk beside their piece; horse artillery, in which the gunners either rode individual mounts or were mounted on vehicles; and mountain artillery, whose very light guns could be broken down into mule loads for

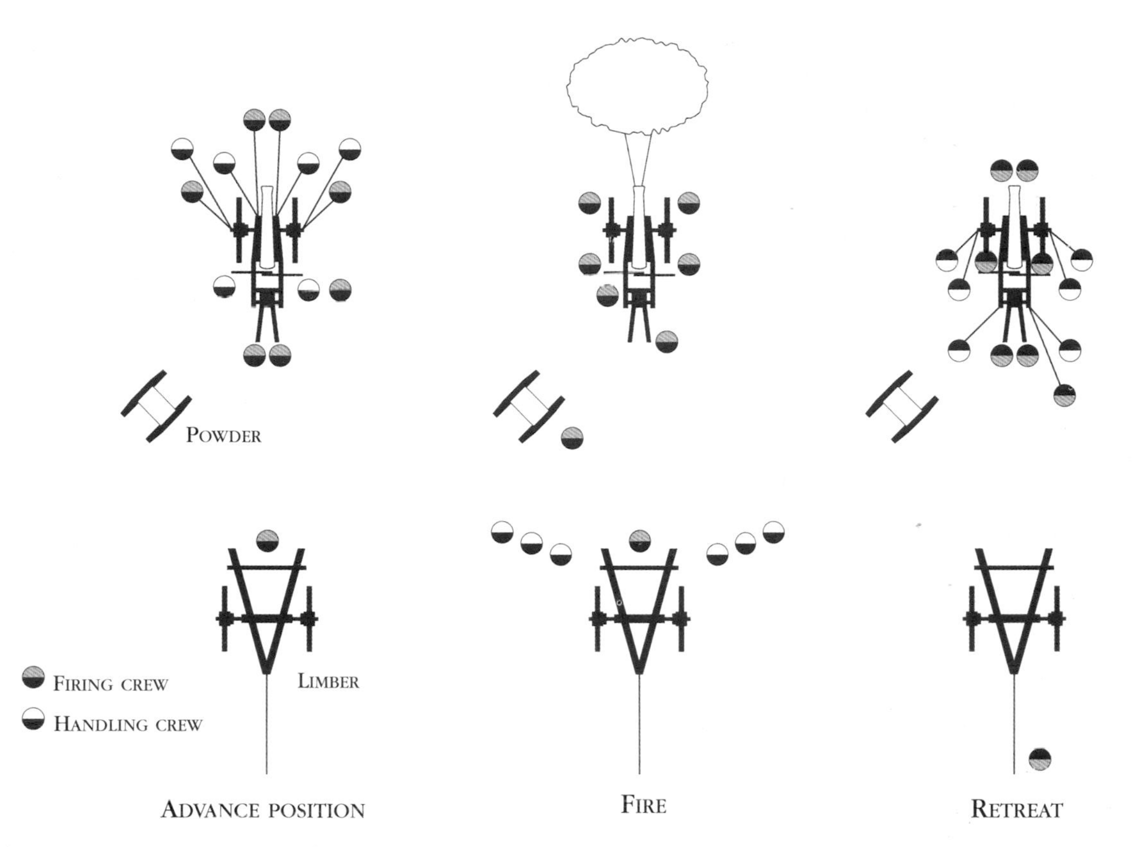

A DEPICTION OF THE DRILL *for a 'man team', which would manoeuvre their field pieces on the battlefield with the* bricole *or man harness. The* bricole *was a leather shoulder strap with a steel ring that held a length of rope with a hook on the end. The gun crew would attach the hooks to eye bolts on the gun carriage and manoeuvre the gun close to the enemy in order to save the horse teams.*

transportation, then reassembled before going into action. Further, light artillery and artillery *volante* can be additional terms for horse artillery, depending on their use. Usually, the largest calibre used for field artillery was the 12-pounder.

The development of field artillery was not accomplished by any one man or nation. It was a development whose time had come by the 1740s, as both artillerymen and commanders saw the need for guns that could go with the infantry and cavalry on campaign and keep up with them on the battlefield. No longer would artillery merely be emplaced on the battlefield and left there. Now artillery batteries would emplace and displace based on the tactical situation and the needs of the troops who were being supported.

In the 1740s, the practical Prussian artilleryman von Holtzman developed the screw quoin (which would later be copied by both the Austrians and Russians for their field artillery) as well as the limber with an attached ammunition chest. The screw quoin now allowed the piece to be elevated and depressed with accuracy and did away with the simple quoin, which was merely a wooden wedge placed under the gun tube's breech. This new development not only allowed the gunners to elevate and depress the piece quickly, but also greatly increased the gun's accuracy. The caisson limber gave the gunners a ready supply of ammunition as soon as they went into action.

During the same period, the French general Brocard developed the artillery cartridge. Prior to that, and sometimes after if necessary, loose powder had been loaded into the gun tube from powder barrels with a long-handled tool called a ladle. The ladle was still used in an emergency, but the loading of loose powder into the gun tube was a dangerous proposition even on a good day. One spark, and the loose powder in the gun tube could ignite and kill or maim the gun crew and also take the piece out of action.

The development of fixed ammunition (in which the cartridge and round were bound together in one piece to facilitate loading) probably had several grandfathers from different countries. The inclusion of a wooden sabot instead of the traditional wadding was probably the most important development since it helped cut down the windage (the distance between the round and the inside of the bore), thus giving the piece more inherent accuracy.

'Artillery, like the other arms, must be collected in mass if one wants to attain a decisive result.'

– Napoleon

Various materials were used for cartridges. The French preferred flannel because it burned cleaner, and they did not have varnished/painted rounds in their inventory by the time of the French Revolution. The cloth of the cartridge had to be impenetrable so that the powder would not leak through the material, which is why serge, which was used at one time, was no longer a preferred material - it was too thick and caused difficulties in loading.

The first cartridges were made of linen and were painted. These caused excessive fouling and also clogged up the vent, which made firing difficult. The vent was a hole pierced in the top of the breech into which the primer, or fuse, was inserted. First a picker, or pricker, which was a long iron needle, was inserted into the vent to pierce the cartridge. Then the primer was inserted into the vent and this was fired with the use of a portfire, basically a short metal pole with a slow match burning from it, which ignited the powder train and fired the round.

Between rounds a cannoneer would 'thumb the vent', closing the vent with his thumb, which was covered with a leather thumbstall, while the gun tube was swabbed and the new round loaded. Not swabbing the gun tube regularly brings a very real danger of premature detonation of the round in the tube, which can be catastrophic for that part of the gun crew at the business end. That is also the reason for 'thumbing the vent' when loading. In an emergency, swabbing can be foregone, but failing to swab for more than a few rounds at a time is not smart.

No matter what material is being used for the cartridge - even if it is paper - there is going to be fouling in the gun tube. That is the reason pieces had to be thoroughly cleaned and washed out after an action. It should be noted that the sustained rate of fire for a 12-pounder field piece was one round per minute; for smaller calibers (3-, 4-, 6-, 8 and 9-pounders), it was two rounds per minute. The guns could be fired faster, but this was usually only undertaken in emergencies. It was also prudent in combat in order to conserve ammunition.

Also during that same period, the French mathematician Bernard Forest de Belidor (1698–1761), an instructor at the French artillery schools, discovered that the powder charge per round could be greatly reduced and still achieve the same range and effect on the target. This discovery greatly facilitated the development of light field pieces, because guns could now be cast much lighter, which also reduced recoil and allowed gun carriages to be reduced in weight.

New Principles of Gunnery, written by Benjamin Robins (1707–51) and published in 1742, challenged the current understanding of ballistics and was an outstanding volume. Robins worked with the ballistics pendulum on musket rounds to measure muzzle velocity; he did not work with artillery.

However, another Englishman, Charles Hutton (1737–1823), did so in 1775; he used 6-pounders in his experiments. The German mathematical physicist Leonhard Euler (1707–83) translated Robins' text into German and also further

PRUSSIAN TROOPS *retreating from the Battle of Ligny on 16 June 1815. Here, Napoleon, outnumbered, outfought the Prussians under Field Marshal Blücher. The French artillery was massed against the Prussian centre in the evening and blew it out, paving the way for the decisive French infantry assault that broke the Prussians.*

developed the mathematical analysis of the trajectory of a ball travelling through air. Robins and Euler share the credit in this field, since Euler continued what Robins had begun and corrected some of his theoretical errors.

The Lichtenstein System

During the early to mid-eighteenth century the Prussian artillery clearly was better organized, better trained and had much more manoeuvrable field artillery than had the Austrians, whose artillery arm was still a guild in the 1740s. Based on the lessons learned from the War of the Austrian Succession - in which the Austrian artillery was outmanoeuvred and outshot by the Prussians - Prince Lichtenstein (1696-1772) developed a new artillery system, the first integrated artillery system in history. Lichtenstein, originally an *Inhaber* (colonel) of an Austrian dragoon regiment, assembled a team of artillery specialists to produce his new system. Undaunted by initial failure, Lichtenstein financed his reforms from his own considerable fortune and produced a first-rate artillery system by 1753.

He based his new system on the Prussian field calibres of 3-, 6- and 12-pounders, copied such innovations as the Prussian screw quoin for Austrian use and simplified carriage and limber design, as well as standardizing parts so that they could be easily changed between carriages and ancillary vehicles.

The Austrian Lichtenstein System was developed to counter the Prussian light field artillery that had taken the field in the War of the Austrian Succession. Lichtenstein copied the elevating system, and the gun carriages are very similar. Lichtenstein was also influenced by the standardization of gun tubes in the French Vallière System. Lichtenstein also established an excellent school system based on the French model, which produced technically proficient artillerymen and made the Austrian artillery pre-eminent in Europe. The Austrians surpassed the Prussians and surprised them in the next confrontation, the Seven Years War of 1756–63. This excellent system lasted until the mid-nineteenth century, by which time it was becoming somewhat long in the tooth. Lichtenstein's reforms were thorough and far-reaching, but he was to be outdone by a French 'competitor'.

That competitor was Jean-Baptiste Vaquette de Gribeauval (1715–89), who would design the most complete artillery system of the period, surpassing all that had come before him, and have immense influence over not only artillery material, but also organization, tactics, uniforms and schooling. Not only did he completely revamp the French artillery (through long and hard argument with Vallière's son, who wished to retain his father's

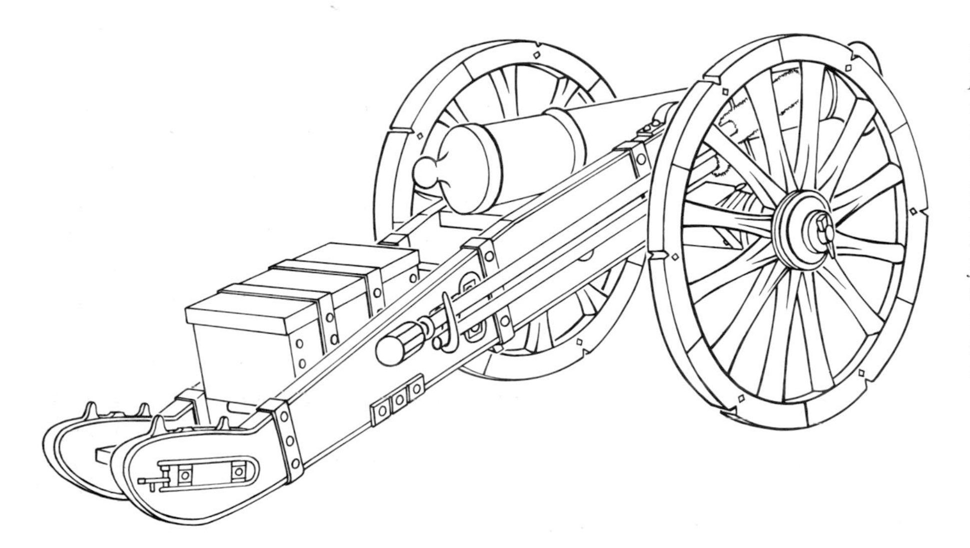

PRUSSIAN 6-POUNDER *field piece. This was a standard calibre in the Prussian service. The box resting on the trail of the piece is the ready ammunition box. The gun carriage is the older, straight type, which forced most of the gun's recoil to the rear and did not absorb any downward as did the better-designed Gribeauval gun carriages.*

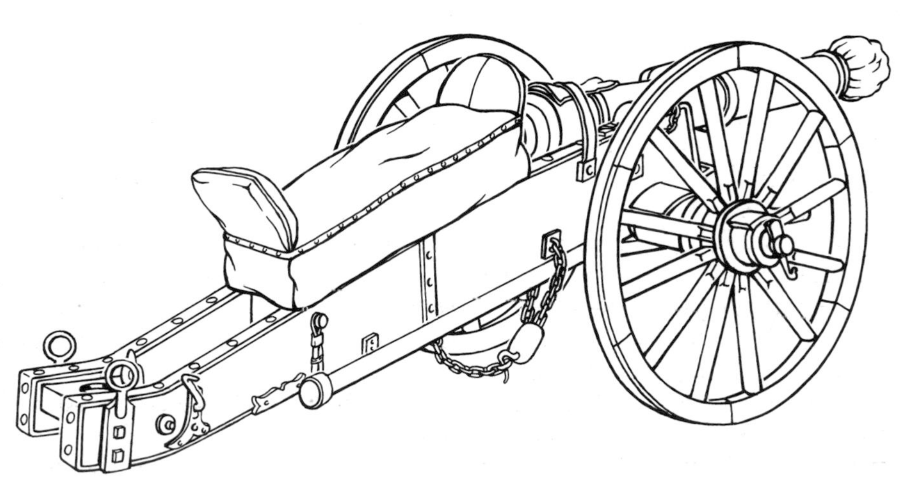

AUSTRIAN 6-POUNDER *field piece. This is the cavalry battery model that was developed in 1780. The gun carriage was modified to be able to seat most of the gun crew on the trail of the piece on a seat referred to as a* wurst. *Ammunition for this mobile battery was carried on pack horses. These units were not true horse artillery, merely mobile field artillery that had to be supported by mounted units.*

older, obsolete system), he also produced a system whose tenets would be employed by other makers of systems and would be admired by his adversary. Gribeauval was a harbinger of things to come and produced the most thorough overhaul of a nation's artillery to date, remarked upon by Captain Ralph Adye, the author of *Bombardier and Pocket Gunner*, published at the beginning of the nineteenth century.

> *'Leave the artillerymen alone. They are an obstinate lot.'*
>
> – Napoleon at Friedland

The best-designed gun tubes and gun carriages, however, belonged to the British. Beginning in the early 1790s, a new gun carriage using a block trail was being designed for use with field pieces. The block-trail carriage gave the guns a better balance and shortened the turning radius and would be the basis for the French Valée System, introduced in 1827. The elvvevating screw was attached directly to the cascabel at the breech, making it much easier and quicker to use than any other elevation system then in use.

Gribeauval

Gribeauval was born into a recently ennobled family that tended to produce magistrates and soldiers. He entered the army in 1732 and was commissioned as an artillery officer into the La Fère Regiment, where his competence and inventiveness gained him a reputation for ordnance construction early in his career. His development of a new gun carriage for fortress guns in 1748 was a major advance that was copied by other European powers. In 1752, because of the Prussian ascendancy in light artillery during the War of the Austrian Succession (in which Gribeauval had served both in Flanders and Germany), Gribeauval took a trip to Prussia to study the country's artillery. He got hold of the Prussian artillery designs and upon his return to France built copies of the guns and tested them in live firing.

From 1757 to 1762, Gribeauval was seconded to Austria, giving him the opportunity to view Austrian light pieces, which he also later copied and tested. Gribeauval served with the Austrian artillery against the Prussians in the Seven Years War, being promoted to *feldmarschall-leutnant* by Maria Theresa (1717–80) and named 'commandant in chief of the engineers, artillery, and miners' for faithful and valuable service. While in Austria, there is strong evidence that Gribeauval was working on a new system of artillery for France, and when recalled to France in 1762 he wrote to the French Minister of War, the Duc de Choiseul (1719–85), explaining that he wanted to work on a system of light artillery to replace the outmoded Vallière System of artillery that the French still used.

Gribeauval completely reorganized the French artillery 'from muzzle to buttplate'. His gun carriages and gun tubes were of a more modern design than the Austrian and Prussian equivalents, and his designs were very specific and a great improvement in simplicity, mobility and accuracy. Besides having his own ideas on artillery, Gribeauval was influcnced by Vallière, the Prussians, the Swedes and the Lichtenstein System, with which he had become familiar while in Austria.

Gun tube design was set at 18 calibres in length (compared with 16 calibres for the Austrian gun tubes and 14 for the Prussian design). Gribeauval was not satisfied with the weight of metal to weight of shot of the Prussian and Austrian guns. He believed that these pieces were not strong enough and would last only a few campaigns or a maximum of three years. Gribeauval set his tube design weights at 150lb (68kg) per pound (0.45kg) of the round fired by the piece; the Austrians had set theirs at 120lb (54kg) and the Prussians at 100lb (45kg). The effect of Gribeauval's decision was to prolong the life of French gun tubes and set them apart as better constructed and designed than their Austrian and Prussian equivalents.

Instead of the 3-, 6- and 12-pounders that both the Austrians and Prussians used, Gribeauval stayed with the standards set by Vallière: 4-, 8- and 12-pounders. To begin with, Gribeauval retained the older Vallière pieces as siege guns, but he later simplified siege-gun design, producing lighter,

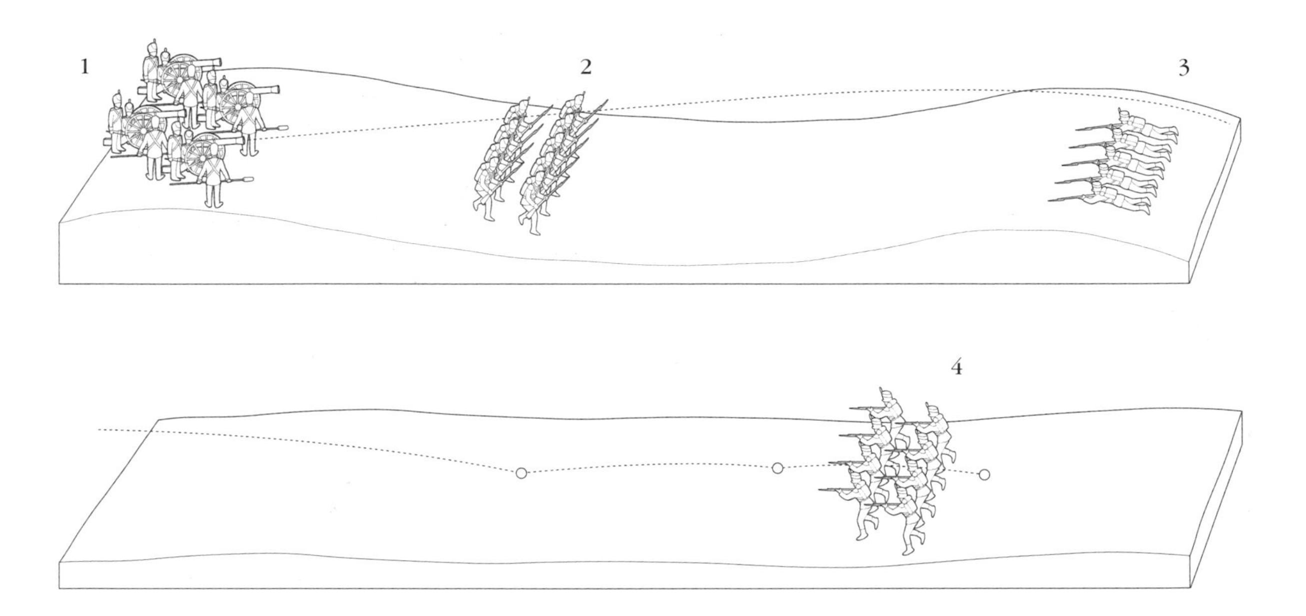

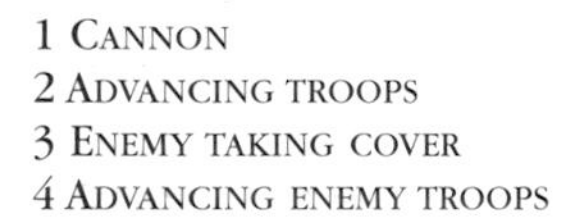

When firing round *shot, the correct position for forward troops was critical, since a gun's elevation had to be such that its shot fired over the advancing troops' heads but would still reach the enemy. Roundshot was fired almost parallel to the ground to devastate the enemy's ranks.*

more accurate weapons. For the first time, a howitzer was used for field artillery by the French, a 6in (152mm) model being employed, initially with the Prussian/Austrian screw quoin and later fitted with a Gribeauval elevating screw.

Ranges and Rounds

The Chevalier du Teil (1738–1820) remarked that field artillery should never fire at a range greater than 960m (1050 yards), which would equate to the modern term of 'maximum effective range'. Maximum effective range for a 12-pounder was 915m (1000 yards) for solid shot and 595m (650 yards) for canister; for a 6- or 8-pounder gun it was 820m (900 yards) and 550m (600 yards) respectively; for a 4-pounder, 730m (800 yards) and 410m (450 yards); and for a 6-inch (152mm) howitzer firing shell, 1190m (1300 yards) and 500m (550 yards). On appropriate ground, however, field artillery could double its effective range by using ricochet fire. Originally used for sieges, this technique involved firing the rounds so that they hit the ground and then began to bounce or bound towards the target. Roundshot had immense kinetic energy, and even when moving slowly could cause damage, wounds and death. This method of firing was very effective in both battle and siege, and was terrifying, since the recipient could see it coming and generally had to stand and take it.

It should be noted that the term 'pound' in the context of gun calibre constituted a different weight in different countries. For example, a French 8-pounder was almost the equivalent of the English 9-pounder, and the pound used by the Austrians was less than that used by the French. So, the calibres employed by the different armies are somewhat difficult to compare. As another point of interest, every army bar the French determined calibre by the diameter of the bore; the French determined it by the diameter of the round.

An Innovative System

Gribeauval designed new gun carriages for each calibre and for the new 6-inch (152mm) field howitzer, the carriages being specifically constructed with the use of the new prolonge (see below) in mind. Gribeauval's gun carriages were built to take in both axes of recoil - backward and downward - hence the characteristic bend in the carriage that is more pronounced than on any other Continental model; the Austrian and Prussian gun carriages, for example, were long and straight. Recoil had been one of the problems of the French light artillery system of 1679–1720; it had never been resolved and was one of the reasons for the system being abolished.

The Gribeauval System stressed interchangeability of parts and also incorporated some innovations introduced under the Lichtenstein System, such as the double trunnion plates on the 8- and 12-pounder gun carriages. However, Gribeauval also introduced many innovations of his own and they revolutionized artillery development. Among them were the *prolonge*, a length of rope 9–12m (30–40ft) in length that was attached to the trail of the piece and the limber. It was used to displace the gun without limbering up and was more than useful for crossing ditches and other rough terrain. Gribeauval brought in the *bricole*, a leather strap or shoulder belt with a length of rope attached for manhandling the piece.

Other innovations included the iron axle, a screw-in vent that could be easily replaced when it wore out, brass wheel hubs that made guns easier to move, a fixed front sight as well as a new rear sight that was adjustable and did not have to be removed when the piece was fired, and a new elevating screw that elevated or depressed the gun tube, which now had the breech resting on a wooden plate over the mechanism.

Furthermore, Gribeauval invented the *étoile mobile,* a new, much-improved searcher for checking flaws inside the gun tube. This was a great technological advance, and pictures of it show a very modern tool that consigned the traditional searcher, or 'cat', to the old guild days of artillery. Also under the Gribeauval System, a double trail handspike was introduced, which, combined with the excellent balance of the gun carriages, enabled one man to traverse a piece.

The Gribeauval System was designed for mobile warfare, and the new field pieces were as mobile as the older Prussian and Russian guns. Gribeauval designed his field guns to be drawn by horse teams in tandem: four horses for the 4- and 8-pounder guns, and six for the 12-pounder. The guns were also designed to be moved easily by 'man teams' using *bricoles*. Nor did it take long to transfer either an 8-pounder or a 12-pounder gun tube from the travelling to the firing position. In fact, it took just the amount of time necessary to unlimber (lift the trail from the limber and put it on the ground).

The mobility of the Gribeauval System contributed greatly to France's outstanding proficiency in artillery from 1792 to 1815 and to the success of an outstanding crop of French artillery generals, such as Jean Baptiste Eblé (1758–1812), Alexandre de Sénarmont (1769–1810), Antoine Drouot (1774–1847) and

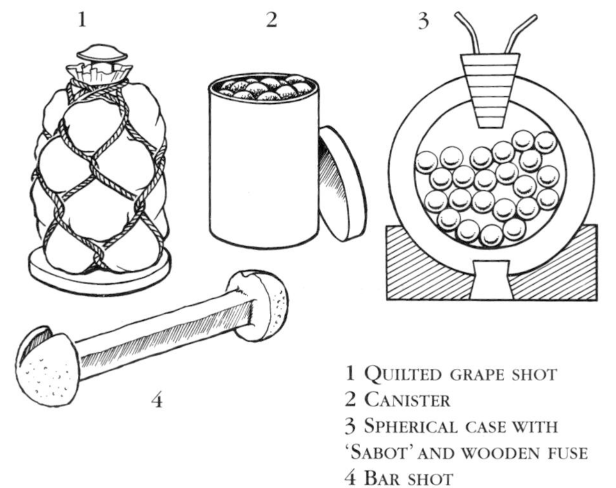

1 Quilted grape shot
2 Canister
3 Spherical case with 'Sabot' and wooden fuse
4 Bar shot

Cannon could be charged *with a number of different types of shot, depending on the intended effect. Grape shot (1) and canister (2) both consisted of lots of tightly packed objects or musket balls, which, when fired, would cause devastating casualties on infantry and cavalry formations. A rudimentary high explosive (3) was often used when assaulting fixed fortifications. Bar shot (4) was more often used in naval warfare, although it might also be used on land against fixed defences and buildings.*

Jean Ambroise de Lariboisière (1759-1812). Infantry/artillery cooperation was French doctrine, and was taught in the French artillery schools from 1764 onwards.

Tightening Tolerances

Tolerances in the manufacturing of artillery pieces grew tighter as artillery progressed. Gribeauval stressed very small tolerances in the production both of his new pieces and of the ammunition. Windage, the space between the round and the inside walls of the gun tube, was very small in the Gribeauval pieces, tighter than in any other European guns with the possible exception of British weapons.

For the 'three calibres' of French field pieces of the Gribeauval System, it was 3.3mm (0.13in), half the tolerance of the Vallière System and half that accepted by the Austrians for their 12-pounder gun. Meanwhile, the tolerance allowed in the construction of gun carriages and ancillary vehicles was 0.5mm (0.02in).

In the case of ammunition, the production of roundshot was strictly overseen, and three types of gauges were used either to accept or reject newly cast rounds. For years European artillerymen had a gauge that ensured that rounds would fit in the gun tubes. Gribeauval had another gauge introduced that checked a minimum tolerance for the rounds so that the windage tolerances would be maintained (in today's military parlance these would be referred to as 'go' and 'no go' gauges). Further, all roundshot had to pass through a tube to ensure that there were no external faults in the rounds that would interfere with their clear passage down the gun tube. This was the strictest set of tolerances for artillery ammunition in Europe up to that time and helped increase both range and accuracy of the rounds by keeping them within the windage requirements for all calibres. Tolerances and processes were highly regulated and specifically spelled out. Rounds too large or too small were discarded by the quality control officers. This care over tolerances contributed to the Gribeauval pieces being inherently more accurate than the Austrian Lichtenstein pieces, for example. The reduction of windage also prevented caroming - the round bouncing off the sides of the gun tube when fired - which, in turn, prevented further weakening of the barrel and lengthening the service life of the piece.

Gribeauval took full advantage of the new casting process that had been developed by the Swiss gunmaker Jean Maritz, whose family was employed by the French. The new guns were cast solid, and then bored out along the centre of the gun tube, a process that made for a more accurate piece. Previously artillery had been cast around a central core, which may or may not have been through the centre of the gun tube. The tube was then bored out to the proper calibre. The Austrians had been manufacturing Lichtenstein gun tubes in this traditional way, and had also used scrap in the metal mix for casting, thus causing the finished gun tubes to be less strong than they were originally designed to be.

Artillery pieces could be cast from either iron or bronze (sometimes referred to as brass). Bronze was preferred to iron as it was sturdier, lasted longer and was not as brittle. However, it was also heavier, so siege guns and naval guns were often constructed of iron. The usual alloy mix for bronze was 100 parts of copper to 10 parts of tin, Austrian method; and 90 parts of copper to 10 of tin, French method.

The new gun tubes and carriages were tested at Strasbourg in 1764 in a series of firing tests in which the lighter Gribeauval tubes were seen to have the same ranges and hitting power as the heavier, longer Vallière gun tubes. Based on the tests, the Gribeauval System was officially adopted by the French on 17 August 1765, though from 1772 to 1774 the Vallière System was readopted because of political infighting. Then, in 1774, a committee made up of four marshals proposed the official reinstatement of the Gribeauval System, which was codified with the 3 October 1774 ordinance. After Vallière the Younger's death in 1776, Gribeauval was finally named inspector-general of artillery and his system was permanently in service until replaced by the Valée System in 1829.

The Gribeauval System of artillery was the most comprehensive developed up to that time and was marked by simplicity, manoeuvrability and accuracy. Two aspects of artillery reform, however, were not addressed by Gribeauval: horse artillery and the militarization of the artillery train. When asked by a subordinate why he had not introduced horse artillery into the French service, Gribeauval replied that they had asked for enough, and horse artillery would have to wait for another day. The artillery train, the people who hauled the guns and caissons on campaign, were not militarized in the French Army until 1800, by Napoleon Bonaparte (1769-1821).

Horse Artillery

Frederick the Great (1712-86) usually gets the credit for the development of horse artillery. The Prussians had a horse artillery arm, but it suffered the same problems as the rest of the artillery under Frederick. The king did not understand either the artillery or the engineers, and both arms were neglected and only started to recover after Frederick's death. It is probable that the first to employ horse artillery in combat were the Austrians. Whatever the case, horse artillery was an outstanding innovation, which gave guns the ability to keep up with cavalry on the battlefield.

The Austrian artillery developed what they termed 'cavalry batteries' in the 1780s. The gun carriages for the 6-pounder and the howitzer were modified, becoming longer so a *wurst* seat could be placed on the trail to allow the gun crew to ride it into combat. Ammunition was carried in caissons and later by pack horse, but these batteries were not true horse artillery.

Doctrine for employment was neglected or overlooked, and these artillery units had to be supported by the cavalry, instead of the other way round as was the case in armies fielding true horse artillery. Cavalry batteries were certainly more mobile than foot artillery, but they were definitely not 'state of the art'.

> *'In most battles the Guard artillery is the deciding factor since having it always at hand, I can take it wherever it is needed.'*
>
> *Napoleon writing to Clarke, US Minister of War, in 1813*

The French and British both developed their horse artillery arms in the 1790s - the French in 1792 and the British in 1794. The French horse artillery originally had some of the gunners individually mounted and some mounted on *wursts*. This practice, borrowed from the Austrians, was found to be inefficient. The wursts soon disappeared for mounted gunners and all French horse artillerymen became individually mounted. This system allowed the companies to displace quicker than they had with the *wurst* caissons, and though the gun crews needed horse holders (one for each three or four horses) such units still

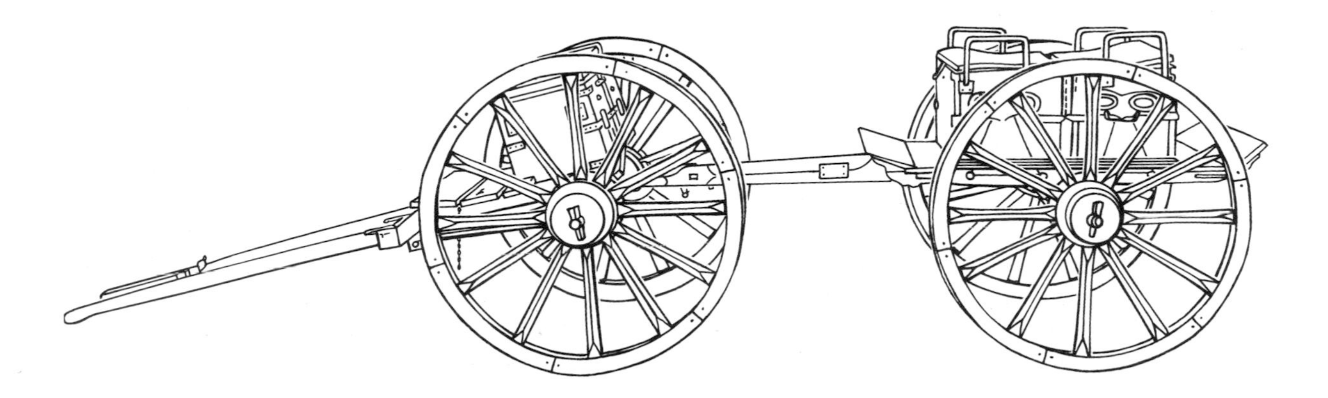

THE NEW PATTERN *British gun limber and caisson. This was the best-designed system of artillery vehicles employed during the period. They had a shorter turning radius than comparable vehicles of the other belligerents, and the gun crews could be seated on both the limber and caisson.*

Napoleon at the Battle of La Rothiere *in 1814. Napoleon was first and foremost a gunner, and he would not hesitate to jump in and 'assist' a gun crew when needed in action, to the point where the imperial boot was applied to hesitant gunners' rumps.*

had the advantage over vehicle-mounted horse artillery.

Not having the gunners individually mounted restricted speed and manoeuvrability; it also increased the weight the gun team had to pull. Besides the French and British, the Württembergers, the Dutch and others had horse artillery that was much more mobile than the Austrian cavalry batteries. Marshal Michel Ney (1769-1815) praised his Württemberger horse artillery in Russia as the equal or superior to his comparable French units. The British thought the French horse artillery superior to their own.

The French initially preferred 8-pounders and 6in (152mm) howitzers for their horse artillery companies, though once it was introduced into service, the Système AN XI 6-pounder was also used and gradually replaced the 8-pounder, while the AN XI 5.5in (140mm) howitzer largely took the place of the 6in (152mm) weapon. All French horse artillery pieces were pulled by six-horse teams to increase speed and mobility.

The 8-pounder gun tube had to be changed when the company was emplacing. Moving from travelling to firing trunnion plates took no time at all. The crew used handspikes to lift the gun tube, put another underneath on which to roll the tube forwards or backwards and slipped the tube into place. Prior to emplacement, gun guides would have been sent forwards to find the spot where their piece would be set up. The gun teams would then be guided into position, sometimes at speed. Limbers were used in action, and the French attached the *prolonge* to the limber and gun trail after unlimbering the piece. The caissons were normally kept under cover. Even in uneven terrain, it did not take long to unlimber an artillery piece. Crew drill became automatic since it was performed over and over again - it was almost a type of ballet. Crew members were also cross-trained on each other's jobs because of the frequency of casualties.

Système AN XI

The Système AN XI was designed to replace the Gribeauval System. An entire range of vehicles, gun carriages and, of course, guns were recommended and designed. The system was to consist of a 6-pounder, a 5.5in (140mm) howitzer, a 12-pounder, three pieces of mountain artillery (a 3-pounder, a light 5.5in/140mm howitzer and a light 6-pounder) designed to be broken down into mule loads, and a new 24-pounder siege gun.

However, the Gribeauval System pieces, particularly the 8-pounder, were very well liked by the French artillery community, and although the adoption of the Systeme AN XI was approved, there was still much dispute over its merits among the artillery generals. Among the officers on the 1801 artillery committee who opposed the new ordnance was General Jean-Jacques-Basilien Gassendi (1748–1828), who thought that the Gribeauval 8-pounder a better piece than the AN XI 6-pounder. This opposition doomed the complete adoption of the new system.

In the event, the only pieces of the new system produced in any quantity were the 6-pounder gun and the 5.5in (140mm) howitzer – sometimes referred to as the 24-pounder howitzer. The new 6-pounder did not look anything like its Austrian equivalent, being a much more modern gun tube; the reinforcing bands had been abolished as redundant, giving the gun tube much cleaner lines.

Nevertheless, the new carriage for the 6-pounder was found to be unsuitable, and the older, sturdier Gribeauval models, which stood up to campaigning much better than the new vehicle, were used for the 6-pounder tube.

The 6-pounder was probably a compromise between the 4- and 8-pounder, designed to replace them both. It was also a popular calibre among the Allies, since the Austrians, Prussians and British all had adopted that calibre as standard and the French had captured many Allied artillery pieces, some of them being employed in the field armies. The old 4- and 8-pounders were either put into the arsenals or continued to be used in the field, especially in Spain, where in many cases 8-pounders, which were not obsolete, merely replaced, took over from the heavier 12-pounders, which were unsuitable because of the terrain and the lack of remounts available for their larger gun teams. There was also a huge quantity of captured ordnance, which was also used. Additionally, it took time to 'tool up' for the new ordnance, which may be one of the reasons only two of the gun tubes were produced in any numbers.

Napoleon set up a new commission in 1810 headed by General Nicholas Songis (1761–1810) that finally decided that the Systeme AN XI was neither practical nor suitable for adoption and the decision was made to keep the Gribeauval System but augment it with the new 6-pounder and howitzer. In 1815, after Waterloo, on the recommendation of a study by General Charles-Etienne-François Ruty (1774–1828), the 6-pounder was taken out of service and the older 4- and 8-pounders were brought back in. When the new Valée System was adopted in 1827–29, the two calibres chosen were the 8- and 12-pounder.

Age of the Artillery Battle

The Napoleonic Wars constituted the age of the artillery battle. During the period, field artillery grew from a supporting arm to one that was the equal of the infantry and cavalry on the battlefield. At the beginning of the French Revolutionary Wars in 1792 artillery systems were in place in European armies that would allow artillerymen to

GRIBEAUVAL'S NEW FIELD ARTILLERY *pieces were the 4-, 8- and 12-pounder, all with newly designed gun carriages. The 8-pounder (below) became a favourite with French artillerymen and was employed both by foot and horse artillery. It was an excellent field piece, and although it was partially replaced in 1805-09 by the Systeme AN XI 6-pounder, it was continually used by the French and their allies throughout the period. After Waterloo, it was brought back into service, the newer 6-pounder being retired, until the Gribeauval System itself was replaced by the new Valée System in 1829.*

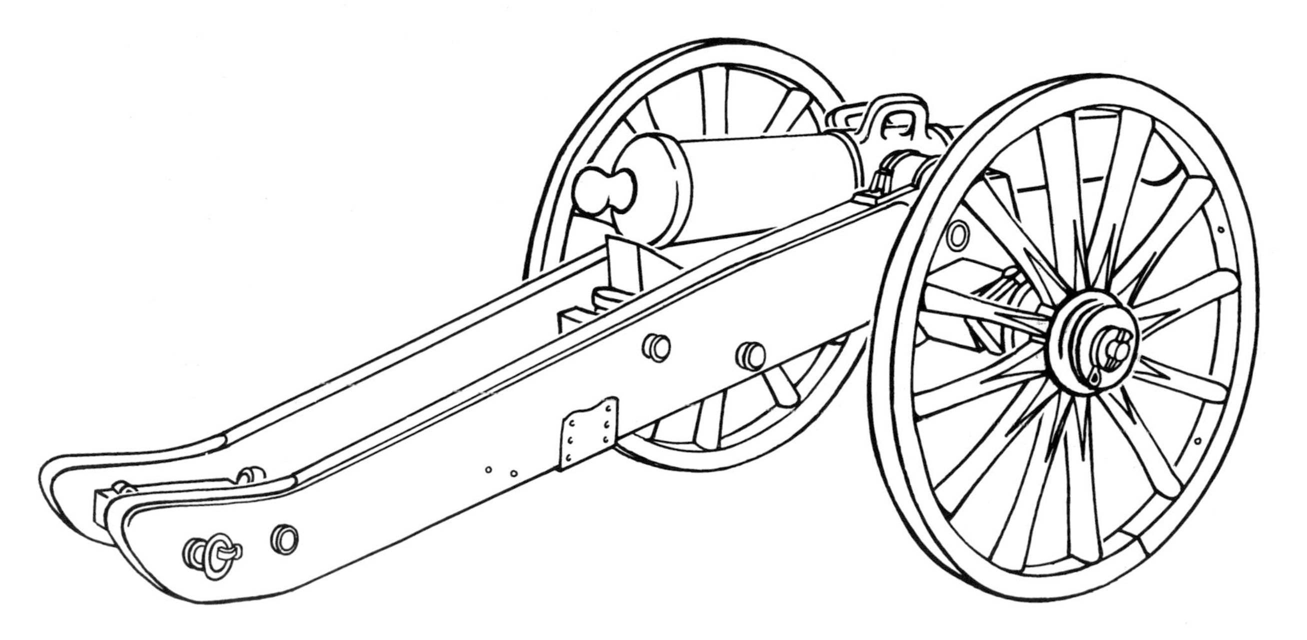

make their mark on how battles were fought and how wars were won.

The basic tactical element for the artillery was the company, which was made up of 6–8 pieces. If losses were heavy enough during a campaign and there were no replacements readily available, gun companies would man fewer pieces. In 1805 Marshal Louis Davout (1770–1823) had to leave some of his pieces at Mainz, because of a shortage of horses, as he continued on into Germany. The companies still operated as companies, though some at reduced strength in guns.

Artillery is best employed in mass; massing artillery means employing more than one company, or even a multitude of companies, together. The companies do not necessarily have to be in physical proximity to one another to be massed; they merely need to be used for one purpose or against one target.

Napoleon, or his subordinates, massed artillery notably at Lodi in 1796 (30 guns), Jena in 1806 (25 guns) and Wagram in 1809 (102 guns). At Friedland in 1807, Sénarmont's 30-gun battery destroyed the Russian centre in 20 minutes, leaving 4000 Russians on the ground; and at Lützen in 1813, Drouot's 80 guns blew out the Allied centre to prepare the way for the decisive assault by the Guard against the Allies. There were also notable artillery concentrations at Hanau (1813), where massed Guard artillery destroy an Allied cavalry attack and pounded General Karl Philipp von Wrede's (1767–1838) Allied infantry, and at Ocaña (1809), Raab (1809) and Waterloo (1815). Occasionally, the French detached their howitzers to be used en masse against a specific target. Three instances in which this happened during the wars were at Borodino (1812), Dresden (1813) and Waterloo. However, the largest concentration of the period was probably by Austrian colonel Josef Smola in 1809 at Essling, where he massed almost 200 guns against the French centre, inflicting heavy casualties on the French II Corps and Old Guard infantry, silencing the French artillery and effectively ending the battle against an outnumbered foe.

Artillery was a killer of large numbers, and after Friedland in 1807 was a decisive arm on the battlefield. French artillery doctrine, for example,

THIS IS THE EXCELLENT *British block trail design that went with the new pattern limber and caisson. It was the best-designed gun carriage of the period and was much admired by the French. Note the elevating screw under the breech. The French Valée System of 1829 was greatly influenced by this design.*

was to dispense with counterbattery fire and concentrate on the enemy infantry, something that the Russians and Prussians learned the hard way. The British, though their artillery was less numerous, also scorned counterbattery fire – it took too long and used up a lot of ammunition. The rule of thumb was that if the enemy artillery was hurting your infantry more than you were hurting theirs, only then would you engage in counterbattery fire. That was usually undertaken with lighter guns with a higher rate of fire, concentrating fire on one gun or battery at a time, silencing it, then moving to the next target.

Allied Artillery

The belligerents' artillery arms varied in quality and effectiveness. The Austrian artillery was well trained and well equipped; its material was also

excellent and when captured by the French was employed by their gun companies when necessary. However, its employment and higher-level command and control were not as sophisticated as they could have been. The Austrian artillery had few commanders of the calibre of Smola (see above); Archduke Charles (1771–1847) complained that the Austrian artillery commanders were competent but too old.

Prussian artillery was hamstrung in 1806, Frederick the Great having nearly ruined the arm by tending to interfere in an area he did not understand. Further, he gave his artillery little credit and no prestige in the army. In 1813, while individual batteries could undoubtedly be good or bad depending on the battery commander, higher-level command and control were lacking, and mass employment, with a doctrine to go with it, was not understood and usually not well coordinated. The Prussians had the worst artillery arm of the major belligerents. The artillery arms of Württemberg, Baden, Hesse-Darmstadt and Bavaria were more proficient than that of Prussia.

Russian artillery officers were poorly educated, thus hurting the efficiency of the arm, though they were hard-working, and their gun teams and drivers were excellent. Russian artillery material and field pieces were brought up to date by the Arakcheev reforms that resulted in the System of 1805. However, the Russians used much more artillery per unit than did the other belligerents – for example, a Russian division would have as much artillery supporting it as a French corps did – and undoubtedly substituted quantity for quality. Their sights were poor, their technical proficiency suffered and they probably needed that number of guns to get the results they wanted. Nevertheless, the Russian artillery continuously improved throughout the wars and was probably the most improved of all the belligerents' artillery arms.

The British artillery was excellent, although it had two major problems: the corps of drivers and the fact that there just was not that much of it. Its guns and equipment were the best of the period, and both the foot and horse artillery arms were excellent in terms of both officers and other ranks. Outstanding senior officers such as Sir Augustus Frazer (1776–1835) and Alexander Dickson (1777–1840) went a long way to making up for numeric deficiencies.

The Portuguese and KGL (King's German Legion) artillery arms were also outstanding. The

THE BATTLE OF LODI *in 1796 during Napoleon's first Italian campaigns. Napoleon is pictured here in general's uniform 'pointing' or aiming a field piece in support of the French attack across the bridge in the background.*

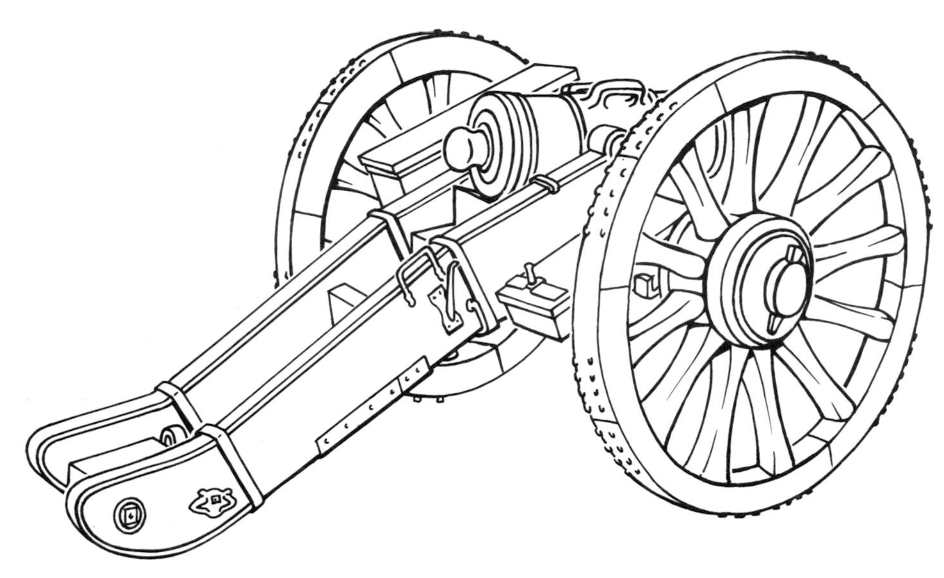

THE BRITISH 6-INCH (152MM) HOWITZER *retained the split or bracket trail carriage during the period because of elevation problems with the block trail carriage.*

Portuguese should be considered part of the British artillery arm at least for the Spanish campaign, while the KGL actually was part of the British Army.

French Command and Control

The French had the best artillery command and control system of the major belligerents. The artillery chief at corps level was almost without exception a general officer, and the army artillery reserve was handled particularly well. The French learned their artillery lessons from the Seven Years War. Their organization was excellent, resupply outstanding and the artillery commanders more than competent. They also had written artillery doctrine that was practised, as well as an aggressive group of generals who would risk guns to gain an advantage. 'Get up close and shoot fast' was not just a saying.

No other army's artillery arm influenced battles as the French did. French artillery, especially after 1807, usually dominated the battlefield, and French gunners were at home serving field, siege and garrison pieces; some French artillerymen served afloat with the navy. Drouot was one of the few people in any service of the period who fought at both Trafalgar (1805) and Waterloo.

In combat, artillery positions were fought to the last and the guns saved if at all possible, so although French commanders would hazard their guns to win an advantage and continually put their guns as close to the enemy as practicable in support of their own infantry, they would fight to the bitter end in their weapons' defence. At Hanau in 1813 Allied cavalry actually reached Drouot's large battery of Guard 12-pounders, where the gunners fought them with musket and bayonet, rammer and handspike until the *Grenadiers à Cheval* arrived to drive the Allied remnants off the gun line.

As Waterloo drew to its conclusion, one Guard company commander, his battery out of ammunition, ordered his gunners to load and prepare to fire at the oncoming British cavalry. His bluff worked, gaining the retreating French a brief respite.

The organization of French artillery was second to none. Each French corps had an artillery chief – a general officer, who worked for the corps commander. This artillery general had his own staff, headed by a chief of staff who was also an artilleryman (Sénarmont's chief of staff was killed in action at Friedland in 1807, commanding half of the guns in the attack). It is just plain common sense to have an artillery general as a corps or army artillery chief. One general talking to another is quite different from a senior field-grade officer trying to convince a sceptical infantry general on the best use of his artillery. Common doctrine was taught in the French artillery schools, especially infantry/artillery cooperation.

In the Allied camps, however, it was an altogether different story. The Austrians did not have corps artillery chiefs until 1809, and even then they were not artillery generals. The Prussians did not have an army artillery reserve, which really hurt their artillery employment, and their corps artillery chiefs were not usually general officers. This led to coordination problems at every level, and massing artillery, which most generals knew was essential, was more difficult to achieve in the Prussian, Austrian and Russian service.

> *'Where a goat can go, a man can go. Where a man can go, he can drag a gun.'*
>
> – William Phillips, Peninsula Campaign

Russian senior officers were well aware of this. Both General Mikhail Barclay de Tolly (1761–1818) and outstanding artillery commander Alexander Kutusaiv laboured mightily to improve higher-level artillery support and coordination with the other arms. The education of other senior officers took time.

The French artillery companies themselves were 'brigaded' with a train company that hauled the vehicles and guns. Horses and harness belonged to the train company, and the guns and vehicles to the artillery company. Long service together hammered the two organizations into one homogeneous outfit. The train company commander was subordinate to the artillery company commander, which is why the former was usually a lieutenant. When the companies were initially formed in 1800, the commanders were senior NCOs, but that was changed by experience. The train battalion commanders were captains.

The French kept their artillery supplied on the battlefield by means of a shuttle service forward from the parcs. In the case of an 8-pounder artillery company, for example, each 8-pounder had three caissons for ammunition, and the two howitzers had five each.

One caisson belonging to each weapon was with what would now be called the 'firing battery' in the field. The remaining caissons were running the shuttle service to and from the company, probably under the command of the train company commander. So, at any one time 20 caissons would be on the road to and from the gun company - empty going to the rear, full coming forward - or at the parc, being replenished. If the gun company were with an infantry division, there would be four more caissons assigned to it that carried infantry

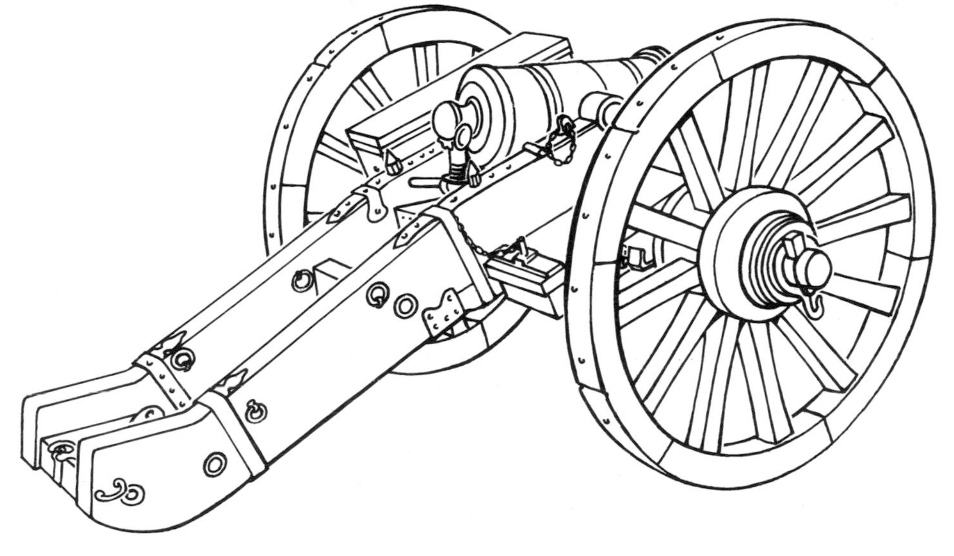

A French 5.5-inch (140mm) howitzer *of the System AN XI, which was designed to replace the Gribeauval System in 1803. However, the only two field pieces that were put into production were this howitzer and the 6-inch (15cm) gun.*

ammunition for the regiments. It was an efficient and effective service, and the only time that Napoleon even came close to running out of ammunition was at Leipzig in 1813, because his trains had been cut off at Eilenberg to the north of the city.

Napoleon insisted on a 'double issue' of artillery ammunition for each piece with the *Grande Armée.* The divisional artillery companies and parcs had 170 rounds per gun; the corps parcs had a further 85 rounds per gun. The mobile section of the army parc had an additional 85 rounds, and the forward depot had 250 rounds per gun. This is a total of 590 rounds per gun, 340 of which were 'on wheels' at any one time. The other belligerents learned from bitter, bloody experience and disaster on the field of battle; and although their artillery arms were not as proficient, especially at the higher levels, they took the lessons on board and attempted to apply them.

The Battle of Friedland: 14 June 1807

In June 1807, field artillery came into its own as a combat arm, becoming the equal of the infantry and cavalry. No longer would artillery be a mere supporting service; it would now be a supported arm in that it could be employed as the main force with the support of infantry. It could not only lead attacks but, in certain circumstances, could be the main attack. This development was the work of French General Sénarmont, who on 14 June 1807, acting as the I Corps artillery chief under General Claude Victor (1764–1841), organized and led, on his own initiative, an artillery attack against the Russian centre, annihilating it through close-range rapid artillery fire and opening the way for a decisive victory.

Friedland (modern-day Pravdinsk in Russia) is on a loop in the Alle River in what was formerly East Prussia. The commander of the main Russian Army, General Levin August Bennigsen (1745–1826), discovered that Marshal Jean Lannes' (1769–1809) corps of the *Grande Armée* was on the western bank of the river overlooking the town. Lannes apparently being unsupported, Bennigsen decided to cross the river and destroy his force. By deciding on this course of action, Bennigsen committed himself to fight with a river at his back. Further, he had his *pontonniers* construct three bridges leading into Friedland and nowhere else, though he also had the civilian bridge over the river at his disposal. This plan of action limited Bennigsen's ability to withdraw quickly if necessary. Lannes immediately sent couriers galloping off to find Napoleon and the main French Army and proceeded to fight an expert delaying action against the Russians. The French general never had more than 26,000 men at his disposal to face 60,000 Russians. Not only did Bennigsen fail to destroy Lannes' corps, he deployed almost his entire force against it, so when Napoleon arrived at about 5 p.m. on the afternoon of 14 June, he could not believe the opportunity with which the Russian commander had presented him.

Napoleon's plan was to fight an economy-of-force battle on his left flank and to attack the Russian left flank with Ney's VI Corps. Ney formed under cover in the forest of Sortlack, and when the prearranged signal was given (three salvoes from the artillery behind the French centre), he debouched from the woods and attacked without deploying.

THIS FRENCH HORSE ARTILLERY OFFICER *wears an early uniform dating from 1806. The unwritten rule for all horse artillery personnel was that they should adopt a hussar style of dress to emphasize their dash and alacrity.*

Almost immediately he was hit hard by Russian artillery batteries on the eastern bank of the river, and almost his entire corps was routed by a Russian counterattack. The initial French effort was a costly failure.

Sénarmont's Advance

In the French centre, General Pierre Dupont (1765-1840), commanding an infantry division in Victor's I Corps, advanced on his own initiative. He was supported by 12 guns of the corps artillery. Sénarmont, the corps chief of artillery, successfully requested the use of the entire corps artillery contingent, 36 guns, to advance with Dupont. Sénarmont initially formed the artillery into two 15-gun batteries on the flanks of Dupont's division. The other six guns were kept in reserve along with the ammunition caissons. The artillery batteries soon outpaced Dupont, and Sénarmont took the responsibility of ordering them forward against the Russian centre. They advanced by bounds, opening fire on the Russians at approximately 410m (450 yards) from the centre of the enemy line. The Russian infantry stood firm. After firing five or six salvoes, Sénarmont ordered his companies forward, stopping at a range of 230m (250 yards) to open fire once again.

Ordering his guns to cease firing, Sénarmont again ordered the companies forward, stopping once again to open fire, this time at 135m (150 yards). Some sources state that Sénarmont closed the range to less than 90m (100 yards), but he probably stopped somewhere between 90m and 135m (100 and 150 yards) from the Russian positions. Whatever the case, the French artillery companies went to rapid fire. Just over 20 minutes later, more than 4000 Russians littered the field and the Russian centre was destroyed. This was the decisive action of the battle.

Ney by this time had reorganized his corps and counterattacked, supporting Sénarmont's manoeuvre. Dupont had also brought his division forward in support and defeated the Russian

THIS COLOUR ILLUSTRATION of the *battle of Friedland from the Rue des Archives shows Napoleon prominent on horseback on left. In the background can be seen his* Grenadier á Cheval *elite cavalry.*

Guard infantry in close combat. Sénarmont was counterattacked by the cavalry of the Russian Guard, and his artillery companies changed front and gave the Russian horsemen two canister volleys, shattering their charge.

The remainder of the battle was almost anticlimactic. The Russian left was crushed and there was a rush for the bridges. Ney and Dupont continued to advance and now Sénarmont supported the French advance on Friedland, their combined efforts nearly destroying the Russian Army. The Treaties of Tilsit followed in July, and the Fourth Coalition was over.

Friedland was one of the outstanding victories of the empire and dramatically marks a decisive change in artillery tactics and employment. Sénarmont initiated a new school of artillery tactics, which were repeated on other battlefields, including Ocaña (again by Sénarmont), Raab, Lützen, Wagram, Hanau and at Ligny and Waterloo in 1815. In so doing, he fulfilled the horse artillery dictum of Maximilien Sebastien Foy (1775–1825): 'Get up close and shoot fast.'

Independent Artillery

Sénarmont's artillery attack at Friedland was the first time artillery had been used as an independent manoeuvre element on the battlefield in an offensive role. The guns, essentially unsupported, operated independently of any other manoeuvre arm or force. They also provided the impetus (and casualties) that turned the fight in favour of the French. It should be noted that at Friedland the infantry supported Sénarmont's guns, which was a reversal in roles. No longer would field artillery, at least in the French service, be a mere supporting arm. It had now established itself as an equal partner on the battlefield with the infantry and cavalry, as well as as a manoeuvre element that could take and hold ground. Sénarmont's battery inflicted some 4000 casualties and gutted the Russian centre, virtually destroying entire units – for example, the 3rd Battalion of the Izmailovsk Regiment lost 400 out of 520 on the field. According to Sénarmont's after-action report of 15 June, his guns expended 368

NAPOLEON AT THE BATTLE OF FRIEDLAND *on 14 June 1807. General Oudinot, bareheaded, is on the emperor's left, and Russian prisoners are on the emperor's right. Captured Russian standards are in the background. This battle was noteworthy in that French artillery General Sénarmont employed innovative artillery tactics.*

canister rounds and 2516 roundshot. Casualties for the French were 11 dead and 45 wounded plus 53 horses lost. Sénarmont's mount was badly wounded. A fitting footnote was provided by the reaction of a Russian artillery officer who witnessed the action. He referred to Sénarmont's artillery as that 'ghastly battery'.

At the conclusion of the 1807 campaign, some interesting observations were made by Russian artillery general Sievers. He believed that there

Battle of Friedland

14 June 1807

After the indecisive bloodbath at Eylau in February between the main French and Russian armies, both went into winter quarters. Napoleon worked tirelessly to restore the *Grande Armée* to fighting trim, and when spring came he took the field, his objective being the destruction of the Russian Army. Napoleon, thanks to the expert delaying action by Marshal Lannes outside the village of Friedland, caught General Bennigsen's army on the wrong side of the River Alle. While holding with his left in an economy of force effort against the numerically superior Russian right, he attacked on the left. The main effort under Marshal Ney initially failed, but General Senarmont, who commanded the artillery of General Victor's corps, attacked the Russian centre on his own initiative, shattering it with close-range artillery fire. Ney's second attack supported this effort, and the Russians were thrown into the river at their backs. Russian losses were very heavy, and this battle, as decisive as Austerlitz in 1805, led Tsar Alexander to sue for peace.

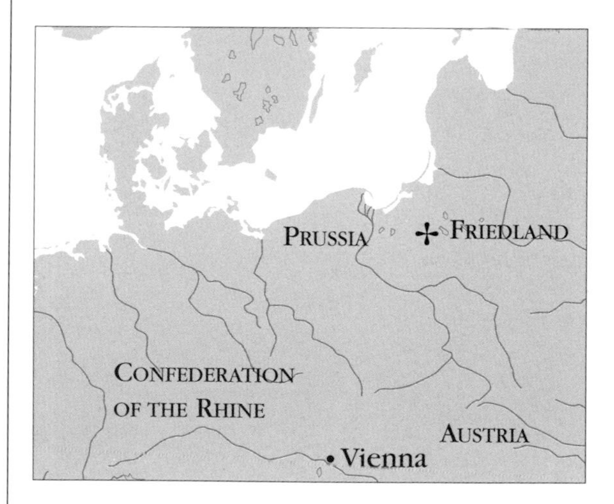

Friedland brought to a conclusive end to the campaigns that started in September 1806. With both Prussia and Russia defeated, and Austria still trying to recover from the disasters of 1805, Napoleon was master of central Europe.

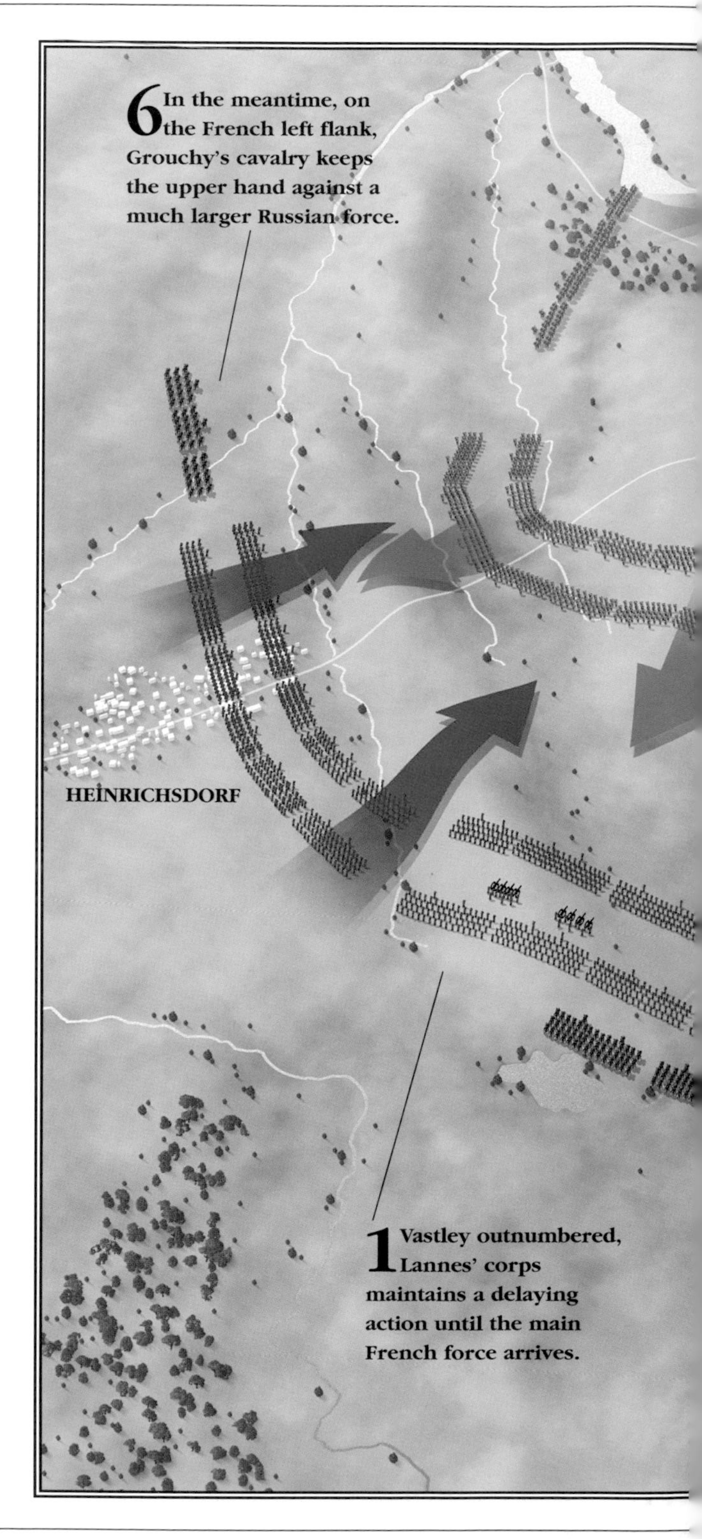

4 After 20 minutes of rapid artillery fire, more than 4000 Russian infantry lay dead in the centre of the Russian line.
FRIEDLAND
ALLE RIVER
5 Ney's forces renew their attack in support of Dupont's division, and rout the Russians.
3 On their own initiative, Dupont's infantry division in Victor's I Corp advances towards the Russian centre. They are supported by 12 guns.
POSTHENEN
2 Ney's forces soon arrive on the scene. Advancing from the forest of Sortlack, Ney attacks but his forces are initially repulsed.

was little difference in the quality of French and Russian field pieces and ancillary equipment. What set the French artillery apart was their command-and-control structure and the way they employed their weapons. He also admired the manner in which the French massed and deployed their howitzers, usually out of sight in a depression where they could fire on the Russians with near impunity. Sievers noted that the French artillery seldom engaged in counterbattery fire, instead concentrating on the enemy infantry. He soberly remarked that his own army's artillery did not do that. He also believed that while the French appeared to enjoy long-range firing, it wasn't too effective. Perhaps that was why Sénarmont liked to get as close as possible.

'The fate of a nation may depend sometimes upon the position of a fortress.'

– NAPOLEON

The Battle of Lützen: 2 May 1813

From an artillery point of view, the battle of Lützen is noteworthy for a large assault that paved the way for the decisive infantry attack against the Allied centre that won the battle for the French. Napoleon, having organized a new army from the survivors of the Russian campaign, was marching into Germany by April 1813 to face the Russians and Prussians.

Joining forces with Prince Eugène de Beauharnais' (1781–1824) Army of the Elbe, the newly rechristened *Grande Armée* was advancing on Leipzig in Saxony when, at around 12 noon on 2 May, Ney's III Corps, on Napoleon's right flank, was surprised in their positions by the advance of a corps commanded by General Gebhard von Blücher (1742–1819). What ensued was a vicious, confused battle that achieved little except for more than 20,000 casualties on each side and the reestablishment of Napoleon's military reputation.

The Allied army was commanded by Russian General Ludwig Wittgenstein (1769–1843), who had taken over when Field Marshal Mikhail Kutusov (1745–1813) had died earlier in the year. Wittgenstein had planned sloppily for the initial phase of the campaign, and Allied execution was even worse; they may have been even more surprised than Ney's troops were when they collided with Blücher. In the action that followed, the Allies and the French both hustled troops forward into the growing crescendo of fire and smoke, the fighting going back and forth throughout the afternoon.

As the French gradually gained a numbers advantage over the Allies – Napoleon having ordered all units within marching distance to the battlefield – the latter were beginning to be enveloped on both flanks. Seeing an opportunity, Napoleon wanted to attack through the Allied centre. General Drouot, the able artilleryman who had formed the Guard foot artillery regiment in 1808 and who had led them into their first fight at Wagram in 1809, massed between 70 and 80 guns from the Guard artillery and other uncommitted artillery into a huge battery and led them straight into action.

Advancing into canister range, as close as possible to the Allied line, the French artillery opened a rapid fire that devastated the Allied centre. The deadly canister rounds ploughed furrows through the Allied ranks, whole regiments disappearing in the blood and smoke of what had to be an unspeakable inferno. Volley after volley of close-range artillery fire ripped through the position until nothing was moving.

As the guns continued to fire, with Drouot personally directing, the Guard infantry advanced on the left of the grand battery and marched against the Allied centre, or what was left of it. Return fire against the Guard was minimal, if any. As the Guard reached the Allied position, the bodies were packed so close together in death that even the horses of the mounted field officers did not touch the ground. Attacking through the carnage, the Guard infantry penetrated the Allied centre and were finally met by sporadic musket fire from surviving Allied infantry. As the Guard pressed forward, the enemy survivors broke and fled, leaving the field to the victorious French.

Drouot's action was a spectacular iteration of Sénarmont's pioneering tactic of six years before. Again, the artillery action was short: Drouot fired for approximately 20–30 minutes, ruining the Allied centre and allowing an infantry assault to carry the position relatively unharmed.

The Siege

For all the sweep of the campaigns fought from 1792 to 1815, there was not the emphasis on siege warfare that there had been in previous European wars. Although sieges were conducted and fortresses and cities defended and taken, the accent during this period was on manoeuvre and battle involving increasingly large armies that decided the fate of nations and empires.

In earlier European wars, sieges were common, and siege artillery formed a significant portion of an army's artillery train. Siege and garrison artillery were usually of larger calibre than field artillery and mounted on larger carriages. Siege carriages were usually bigger versions of field artillery carriages. Garrison carriages were used in fortresses and along the coast; they could be simple, such as those employed on warships, or more complex, like Gribeauval's very effective garrison carriage developed in 1748.

Sieges did have a significant place in the war on the Spanish peninsula. The campaign of the French commander Louis Gabriel Suchet (1770–1826) in eastern Spain was noted for them, and the successful reduction of cities during the Spanish war definitely helped to pacify the regions conquered by the French.

In western Spain and Portugal, the French were usually successful in their siege operations, although the first siege of Saragossa in 1808 was a notable exception. Siege operations were both an art and a

NAPOLEON AT THE BATTLE OF LÜTZEN *2 May 1813. Although the French were initially surprised by the Allied army under Russian General Wittgenstein, it ended as a French victory, highlighted by a repeat on a much larger scale of Senarmont's artillery charge at Friedland. The French artillery commander who led the manoeuvre at Lützen was General Antoine Drouot.*

Battle of Lützen

2 May 1813

After the disastrous Russian campaign, Napoleon rebuilt the shattered *Grande Armée* and by April 1813 was advancing into Germany to link up with Prince Eugène's Army of the Elbe. The new *Grande Armée* was numerically superior to its Allied antagonists, but except for the Imperial Guard, the army was in large part made up of new conscripts with less than a year's service. The battle for Lützen is noteworthy for the spectacular artillery action led by General Drouot. With the battle 'ripening', Drouot organized and led forward 80 artillery pieces from the Imperial Guard and line artillery that, massed within canister range of the Allied centre, literally blew a hole in the Allied line and paved the way for the decisive infantry assault by the Guard infantry, spearheaded by the two fusilier regiments of the Middle Guard. Whole Allied infantry regiments were destroyed in the Allied centre, covering the ground with dead and wounded.

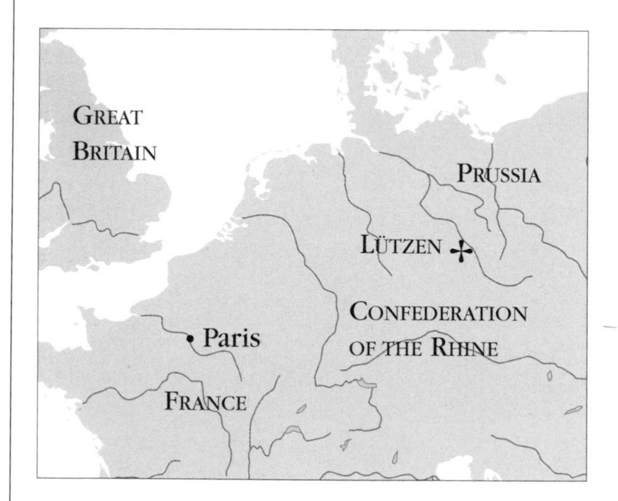

Lützen, near Leipzig in Saxony, was the site of the first large battle of the 1813 campaign. The Allies, though achieving surprise, were thoroughly beaten. Napoleon, lacking large numbers of reliable cavalry, failed to follow up his victory with a vigorous pursuit.

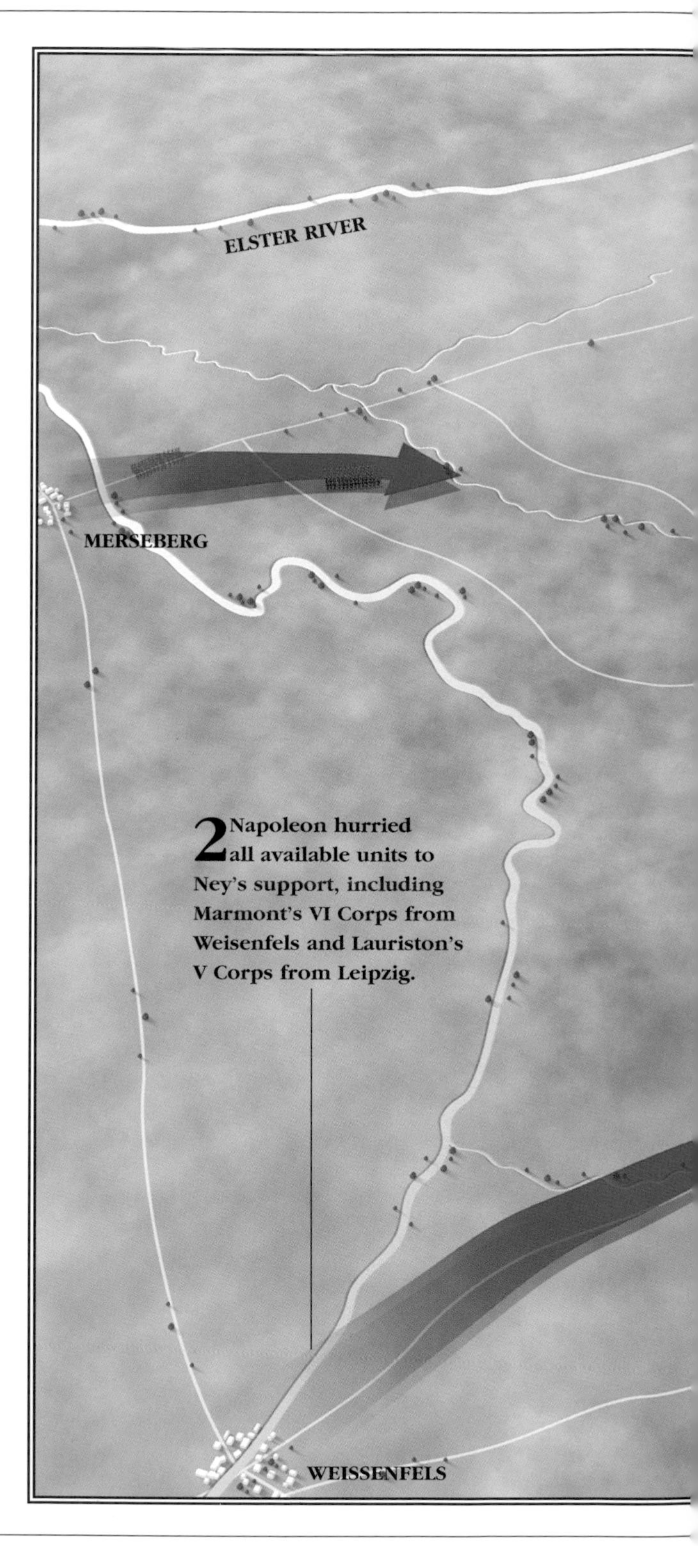

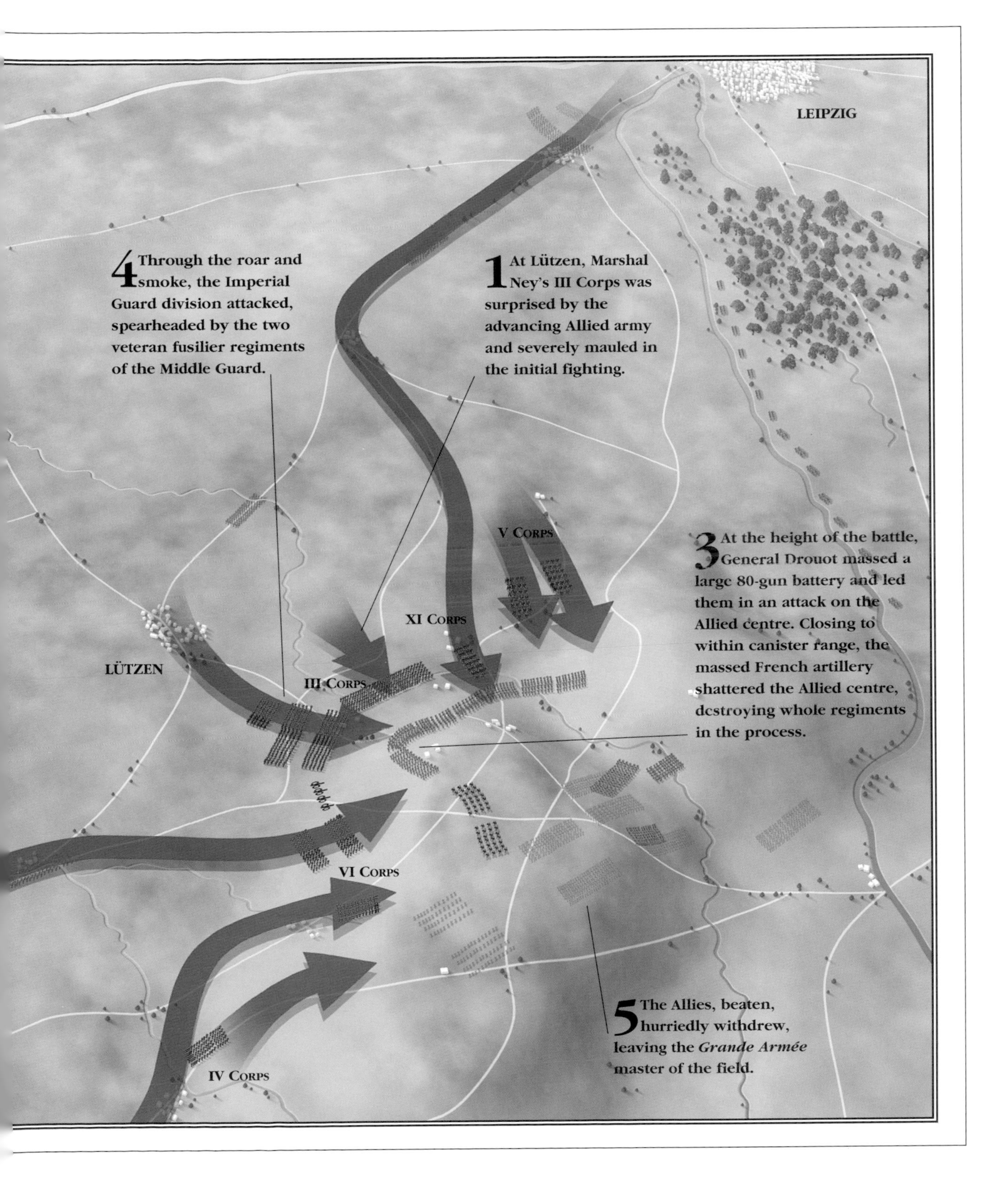
LEIPZIG
4 Through the roar and smoke, the Imperial Guard division attacked, spearheaded by the two veteran fusilier regiments of the Middle Guard.
1 At Lützen, Marshal Ney's III Corps was surprised by the advancing Allied army and severely mauled in the initial fighting.
V Corps
3 At the height of the battle, General Drouot massed a large 80-gun battery and led them in an attack on the Allied centre. Closing to within canister range, the massed French artillery shattered the Allied centre, destroying whole regiments in the process.
XI Corps
LÜTZEN
III Corps
VI Corps
5 The Allies, beaten, hurriedly withdrew, leaving the *Grande Armée* master of the field.
IV Corps

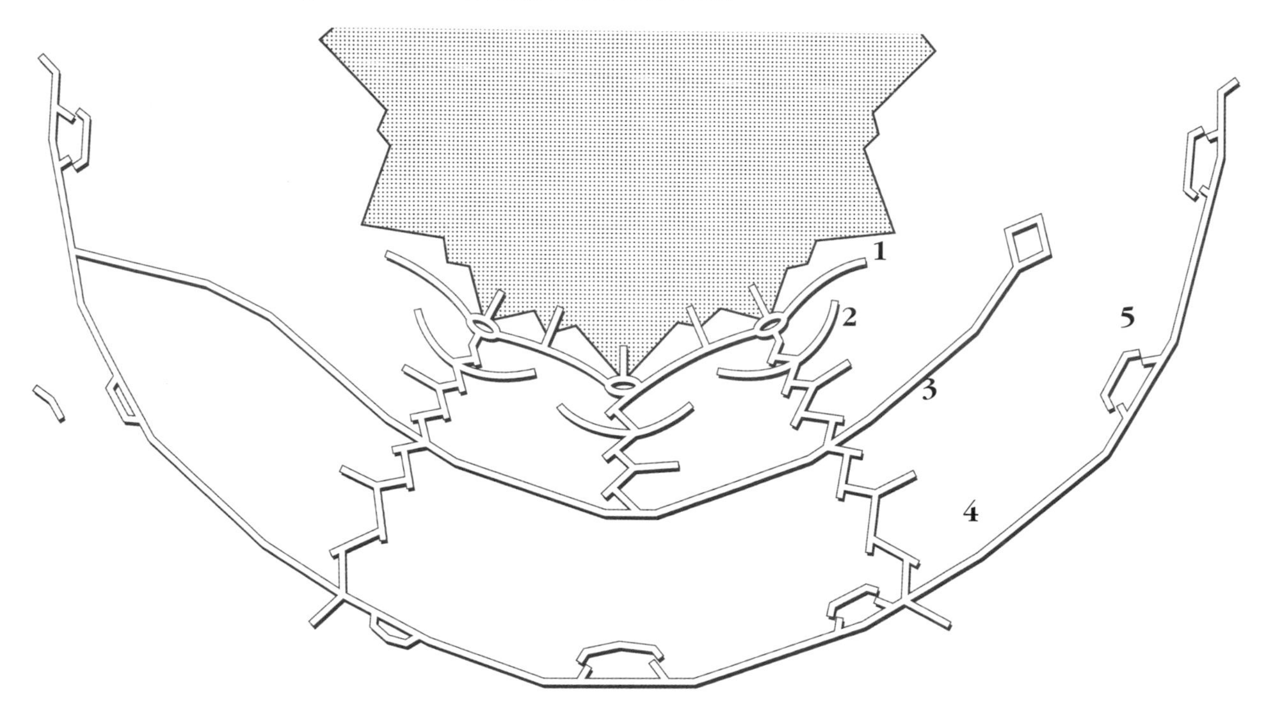

THIS AERIAL DIAGRAM *demonstrates the principles of siege work in the Napoleonic era: 1) third parallel; 2) demi-parallel; 3) second parallel; 4) first parallel; 5) siege batteries. The principles of siege operations developed by Marshal Vauban in the seventeenth century were still applied in the Napoleonic period.*

science, and the principles of fortifications, siege operations and the investment of a city or fortress that were hammered out by the outstanding eighteenth-century engineers the Marquis de Vauban (1633–1707) and Baron van Coehorn (1641–1704) were as valid during the Napoleonic period as they had been 100 years earlier.

The Engineer Arm

Military engineering and the formation of engineer units in armies of the various belligerents of 1792–1815 had come a very long way since Vauban's time. Then, there had been no military engineer arm. French infantry officers were detailed as apprentices to senior engineer officers and thereby learned their trade. It was not until 1715 that the term *génie* first came into standard use.

Initially, the French Royal Corps of Engineers was an officers-only organization, whereas the skilled miners, organized in companies, were part of the artillery and were usually commanded by hand-picked artillery officers.

The engineers became a separate arm in 1758 and to join, an officer had to be a graduate of the engineer school at Mezières, which had been established in 1749. It was not until 1793 that the engineers became a combat arm, with 12 battalions of *sapeurs du génie* (combat engineers) being formed and the miners transferred from the artillery. Napoleon added an engineer train to haul their tools and equipment in 1806, and two years later the miner companies were given a definite battalion organization. In 1811, a company of *sapeurs-ouvriers* (engineer-artificers) was raised for work in the depots. The engineer arms of the other belligerents lagged behind the French in expertise. The Russian and Prussian services were barely adequate.

The Russians, as in the case of their artillery, were niggardly in the education of their technical arms, while the Prussian engineer branch still suffered from the neglect of Frederick the Great. The Austrian engineer arm was poor and disorganized up to the period of the Seven Years War. At the beginning of that conflict, Empress

BRITISH INFANTRY SERGEANT *charges the fortifications at Badajoz. This British infantry NCO is armed with a sword and spontoon, which could be a handy weapon in close combat. It was also a sign of rank in the British Army. Sergeants would use the spontoon to defend the colours of their battalion.*

Maria Theresa requested experienced and qualified French artillery officers be seconded to the Austrian service. Among those sent was Gribeauval, and he helped to reorganize and train the Austrian engineer arm, which did excellent service during the war.

The British Royal Engineers at the beginning of the period consisted solely of officers, as had previously been the case in France. Well educated and hard working, the British engineer arm had little or no practical knowledge of or training in siege operations and had no qualified engineer troops until after the siege of Badajoz, when the Duke of Wellington (1769–1852) complained about this shortcoming in a letter to the secretary of war, Lord Liverpool (1770–1828). The Royal Corps of Sappers and Miners was activated shortly thereafter. In a large sense it was too little and too late, but in the long run it was a great improvement on what had gone before.

The Siege of Badajoz: March–April 1812

There were four sieges of Badajoz during the Peninsular War, all taking place in 1811–12. The initial siege was undertaken by the French and was a success; it was followed by two failed British attempts. The fourth and last of these operations was also undertaken by the British. This time they carried the day, but it was a very bloody episode and the superb performance of the British infantry was marred by their disgraceful conduct afterwards. They indulged in a three-day orgy of rapine, drunkenness and plunder against an allied and friendly population that had not opposed the British siege operations in any way.

Wellington's sieges in Portugal and Spain are not noted for the skill and thoroughness with which they were conducted. Many of them were failures, and those that succeeded were usually marked by heavy casualties incurred by the besiegers because the cities had to be taken by storm. Badajoz was one of the keys to Spain; it had to be taken so that the Allied army could continue into the interior and eventually into southern France. It stood on the Guadiana River and water formed a natural obstacle on two sides. The city was strongly fortified and had formidable outworks called the Pardaleras and the Picurina. Across the

Siege of Badajoz

March–April 1812

The last siege of Badajoz conducted by Wellington's army was typified by a failed main assault on the breech and a successful secondary assault on the castle. The Allies had failed to take Badajoz before, and the lack of an adequate British siege train, along with qualified engineer officers and engineer troops, would make infantry assaults the major instrument in the siege. The gallantry of the British infantry is legendary, and Wellington undoubtedly felt grief over the horrific losses. The skilled defence of Badajoz by General Phillipon and his garrison is contrasted with the amaterish way in which the British engineering arm conducted the siege. The heavy losses prompted the British to create the Royal Corps of Sappers and Miners.

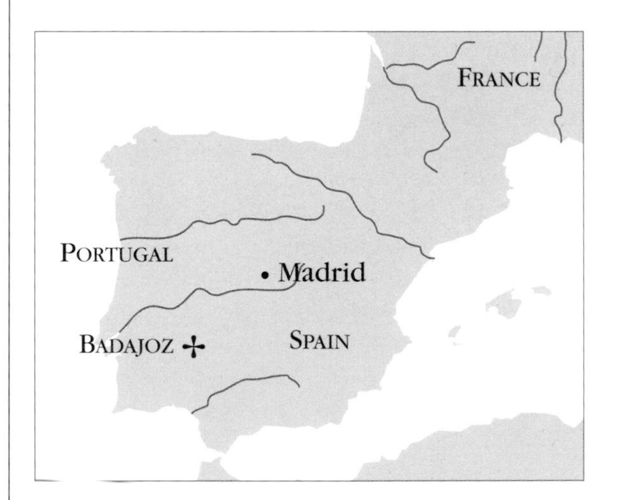

More sieges were conducted in Spain and Portugal, 1808–14, than in any other theatre of war during the period. French sieges were usually conducted expertly, and the bloody assaults at Badajoz prompted the British to form the Corps of Sappers and Miners.

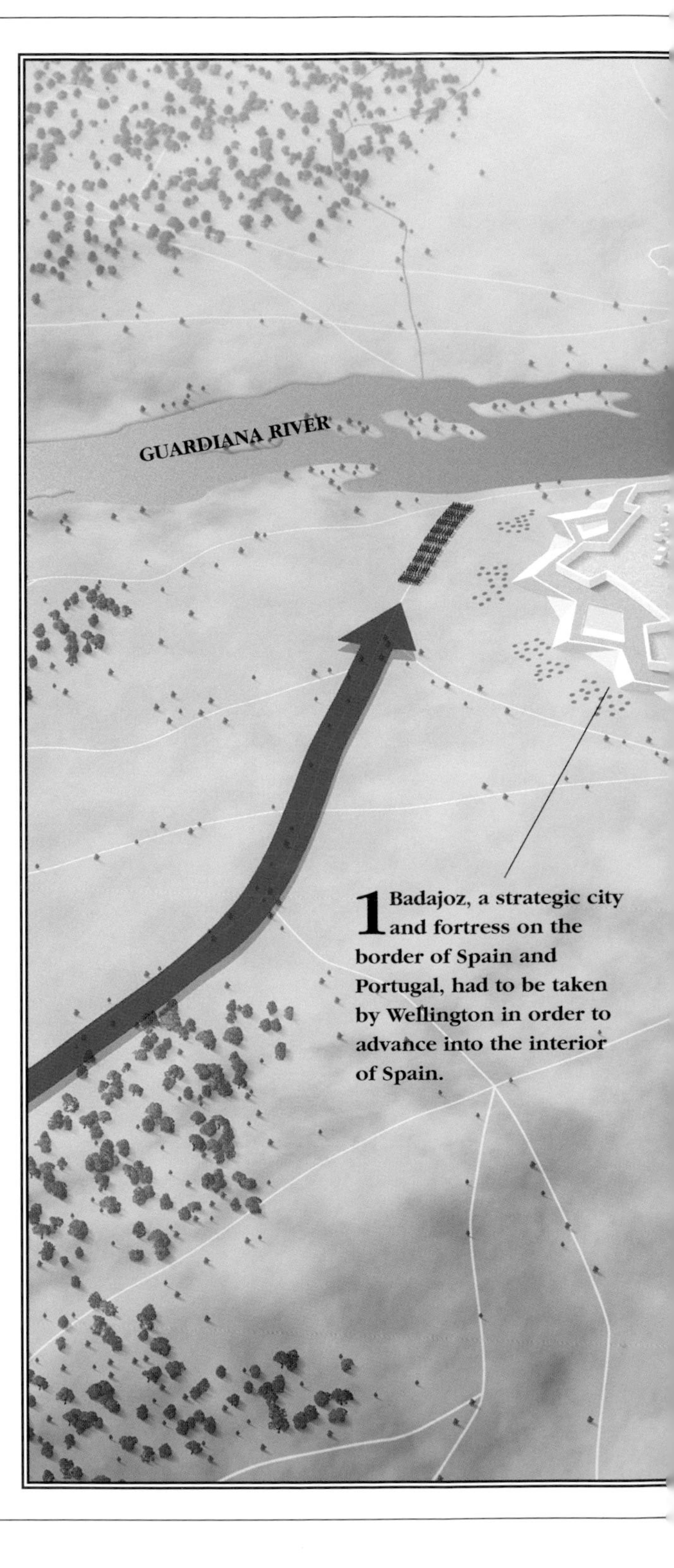

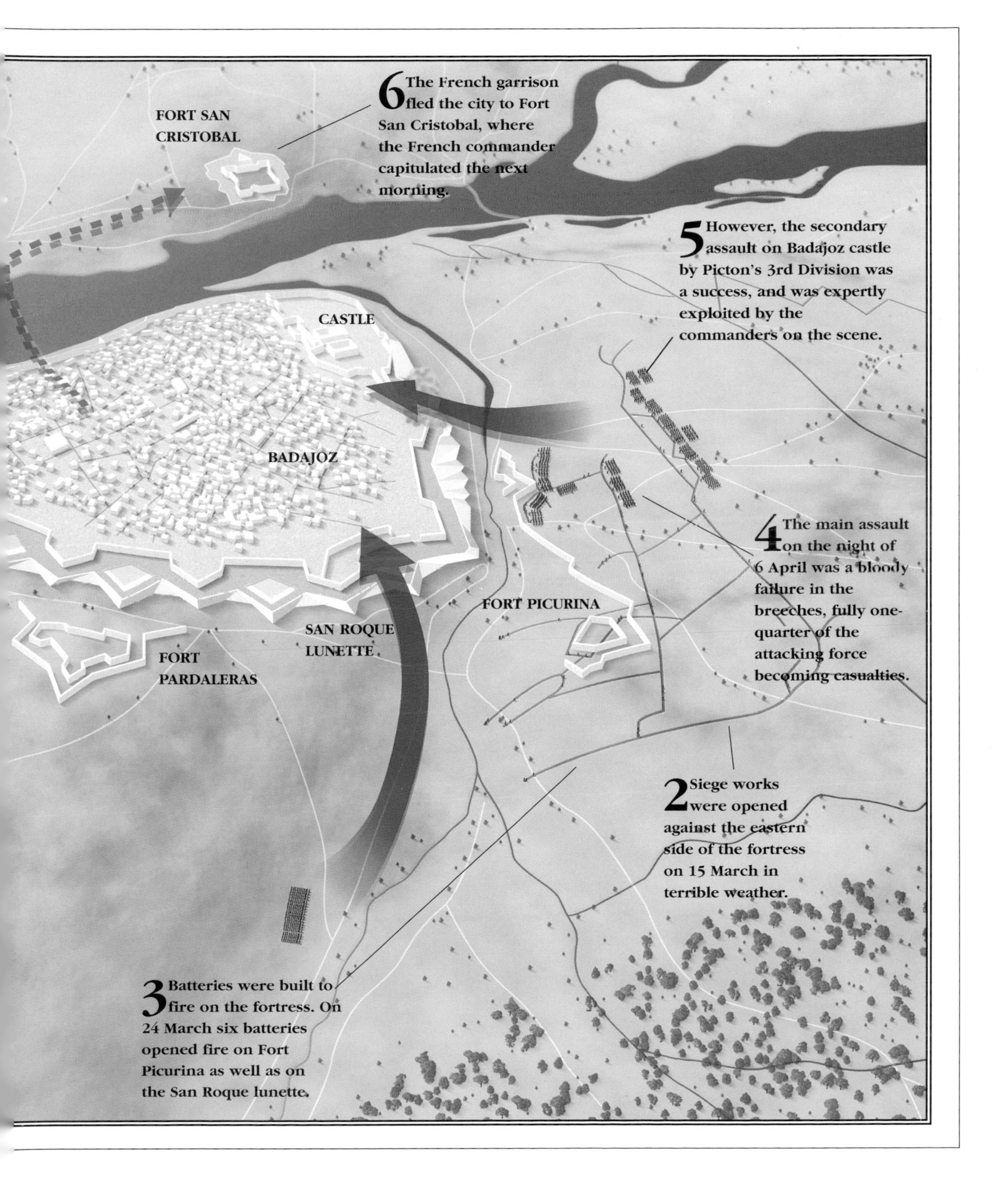
6 The French garrison fled the city to Fort San Cristobal, where the French commander capitulated the next morning.
FORT SAN CRISTOBAL
5 However, the secondary assault on Badajoz castle by Picton's 3rd Division was a success, and was expertly exploited by the commanders on the scene.
CASTLE
BADAJOZ
4 The main assault on the night of 6 April was a bloody failure in the breeches, fully one-quarter of the attacking force becoming casualties.
FORT PICURINA
SAN ROQUE LUNETTE
FORT PARDALERAS
2 Siege works were opened against the eastern side of the fortress on 15 March in terrible weather.
3 Batteries were built to fire on the fortress. On 24 March six batteries opened fire on Fort Picurina as well as on the San Roque lunette.

THE BRITISH 88TH FOOT *scaling the castle walls at Badajoz. This was the secondary attack, which became the decisive effort when the main attack on the breaches became a bloody failure.*

Guadiana was San Cristobal and the fortified bridgehead for the bridge over the river. The works were garrisoned by about 5000 men ably commanded by General Armand Philippon (1761–1836), who proved a redoubtable adversary.

Siege works were then opened against the eastern side of the fortress on 15 March 1812 amidst terrible weather that made construction difficult at best. The troops that worked on the first siege parallel laboured in water up to their waists and were under heavy French fire from the outset. The French sortied from the fortress on 19 March but were repulsed, and work continued.

Batteries were built to fire on the fortress and on 24 March six batteries opened fire on the Picurina as well as on the San Roque lunette. Additionally, artillery bombarded the main walls, or curtain, of Badajoz between the bastions of Trinidad and San Pedro.

Stolid Defence

Major-General Thomas Picton's (1758–1815) division assaulted the Picurina on the night of 25 March and took it after a desperate fight; Picton's casualties were heavy. The next day the British siege guns opened fire on Badajoz once more, this time bombarding the curtain between the Trinidad and Santa Maria bastions. The city wall was formidable however, and it was not until 5 April that two breeches were opened that were believed to be passable by an assault force. Still, Wellington ordered that another breech to be opened before an assault could take place.

Wellington underestimated the lengths to which the defenders had gone to make an assault upon Badajoz if not impossible, then at least as expensive as possible for any attacker. Obstacles had been built in the ditch to render it unusable as a customary rallying place. Although the walls had been breeched, the defenders had erected more obstacles within them and had shored up the defences behind the breeches to stop any penetration of the fortress.

Wellington had planned a main attack by two columns, consisting of the Light Division and the 4th Division, which would go for the breeches. A supporting attack against the fortress's castle across the Roillas, which was flooded and could only be crossed by a dyke that was 60cm (2ft) under water, was to be made by Picton's 3rd Division. Other, smaller supporting attacks were to be made on the Pardaleras, the San Vicente bastion and the San Roque lunette.

The attacks jumped off at 8 p.m. on 6 April. The assaults on the breeches were expensive failures, the defenders not only causing the attacking columns horrendous casualties but also taunting the attackers throughout the fighting. The performance and sacrifice of the British officers and men was exemplary, but the defence was too professional and savage, and the breeches were choked with British killed and wounded.

Picton's attack on the castle at first failed, and Picton himself was wounded. He rallied his men, however, and they gained a foothold on the lower walls. Scaling ladders were raised and the British poured over the parapet. Again, resistance was savage, but the British fought through adversity, taking the castle but with heavy casualties. The San Vicente bastion was also taken, and the heart went out of the defenders.

General Philippon and the garrison withdrew into San Cristobal, where they surrendered the next day. Badajoz thereby fell, and the British troops who had behaved so well in the mayhem of

WELLINGTON'S SIEGES IN THE PENINSULA *were inexpertly handled by the British engineer arm, primarily for the lack of trained engineer troops and the lack of siege training for the British engineer officers. Consequently, the Corps of Sappers and Miners was finally formed in 1813 and hastily sent to Spain.*

the breeches now went wild and sacked the city. The orgy continued until it finally burned itself out and order was restored. The same would happen when San Sebastian was taken the following year.

The Siege of Hamburg: December 1813 – May 1814

The best defence of a fortified position during the period was undoubtedly Marshal Davout's stand in the city of Hamburg in 1813–14. The area to be defended and held was large and there was a sizeable civilian population. The besieging force was between two and three times the size of the defending army, and the episode was notable for there being virtually no excesses committed by the French garrison against the populace. Davout gave up the city only after Napoleon's abdication and when he had received affirmation from competent French authority that this was so. It was a model defence and an epic stand.

The strategic situation for the French at the beginning of 1813 was grim. The remnants of the *Grande Armée* were limping out of Russia after a disastrous campaign and were being slowly rallied by Prince Eugène and Marshal Louis-Alexandre Berthier (1753–1815), the *Grande Armée* chief of staff. Napoleon had left the army and hastened back to France to solidify the government after an abortive coup and to raise a new army.

The Russian spearheads, which had also suffered terribly in that epic campaign, were slowly venturing into central Europe, and Prussia had, meanwhile, turned against the French. French garrisons stubbornly held out in the major fortresses, but there were few troops - and fewer veterans - available to fight off all the incursions by Cossacks and hastily raised Allied 'free corps'; and there was either apathy or resistance from some of the Confederation of the Rhine contingents and their governments.

General Claude Carra St Cyr (1760–1834) panicked and was hustled out of Hamburg by rumours, bad intelligence and an exaggeration of the enemy strength actually facing him in that strategically important area. Marshal Davout was ordered to take command of the situation, so he dispatched General Dominique Vandamme (1770–1830) to seize Hamburg from any hostile forces and reestablish French dominance in the city and the outlying districts. This Vandamme did efficiently with his own infantry division and the help of a Danish contingent.

Davout's Command

Davout's new command was christened the XIII Corps and was composed of three French infantry divisions, plus assorted cavalrymen, many of them Polish. With the addition of the Danish contingent that supported him, Davout had a total of 43,000 men available.

Being a former cavalryman, and far from official eyes, Davout also had a cadre of cuirassiers from the 1st Cuirassier Regiment. He ordered the horsemen to form a new cuirassier unit from the material available, and dutiful to their marshal's wishes they scrounged the necessary saddles, harness and armour to form a ramshackle regiment. Named, unofficially, the 15th Cuirassiers, it started out almost as a comic opera outfit, but by the time the siege was over and the unit was on its

THIS IS A TYPE OF SIEGE MORTAR *used in the Napoleonic period. All of the belligerents had their own pattern of mortars and of different calibres. They were capable of lobbing large calibre shells into a fortress or city and causing considerable damage.*

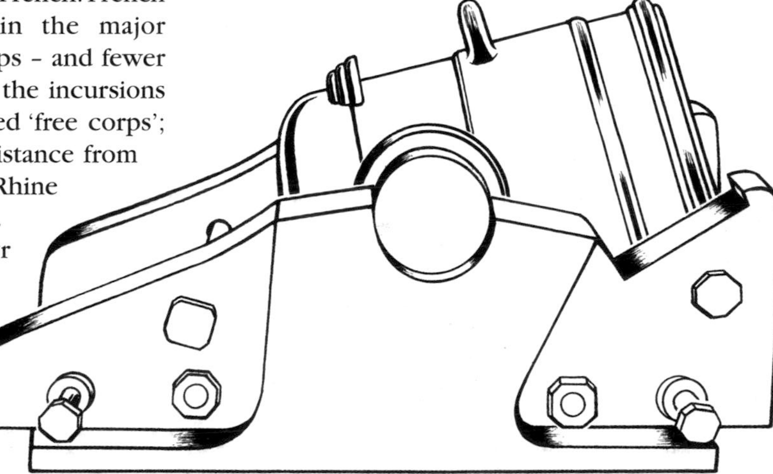

way back to France, the 15th was a seasoned and well-respected regiment.

Under Siege

The siege began in December 1813. By that time, Davout had been in command of Hamburg and the outlying military district since May and had been conducting field operations against the Allies. However, from May until December, he had become increasingly isolated, with no news from the main army or from France, and could only assume he was on his own. Davout had taken every precaution to defend the city to the last.The neglected defences had been improved, the civilian inhabitants had been warned to start storing food for a siege, and even some of the suburbs had been razed to provide adequate fields of fire for his artillery. Still, many of the inhabitants had turned a deaf ear to French proclamations, and because of the food situation at the beginning of the siege, 25,000 civilians had to be expelled from the city.

Davout, as was his practice, kept his troops under strict discipline - in fact, for the siege, they were sometimes maintained under severe discipline. Consequently, the troops were well trained, well ordered and ready for the siege when it came. Such a regime also kept excesses against the civilian population to a minimum. Davout being Davout, he was strict but just.

On 2 December, Davout withdrew into Hamburg, and the Allies soon invested the city. However, Russian General Bennigsen, the commander of the Russians and assorted Germans in the surrounding force, failed to begin actual siege operations against Davout until January. Bennigsen was joined briefly by Crown Prince Bernadotte of Sweden (1763-1844), who was in command of a Swedish-German force. His arrival swelled the besiegers to a strength of more than 120,000 men, but Bernadotte was not anxious to cross swords with Davout, whom he had left on his own to face the Prussian main army at Auerstädt in 1806. He soon departed in search of glory elsewhere and cheated Davout of the satisfaction of defeating his former 'comrade-in-arms'.

'Fortified towns are hard nuts to crack, and your teeth are not accustomed to it. Taking strong places is a particular trade, which you have taken up without serving an apprenticeship to it. Armies and veterans need skilful engineers to direct them in their attack. Have you any? But some seem to think that forts are as easy taken as snuff.'

– Benjamin Franklin

Following Bernadotte's hasty departure eastwards, Bennigsen still outnumbered Davout by more than two to one. He launched three major attacks on the Hamburg defences in February - on 7, 17 and 27 of the month. All were defeated with heavy losses, Davout having organized an effective defence in depth that was triggered by a clever alarm system. Further, Davout had established mobile reserves, picked troops supported by horse artillery, which could be rushed to any area threatened with attack to reinforce the garrison.

After three costly failures, Bennigsen settled down to starve his opponent into submission - or perhaps just to wait for the end of the war. Napoleon had been defeated at Leipzig and the Allies had invaded France, but in February the issue was still very much in doubt. Behind his defences, Davout and his garrison grimly held out. The troops were well cared for, well disciplined and more than ready for a fight.

Honourable Exit

One more attack took place towards the end of the siege. Under cover of white flags of truce, the Russians launched an assault on the French

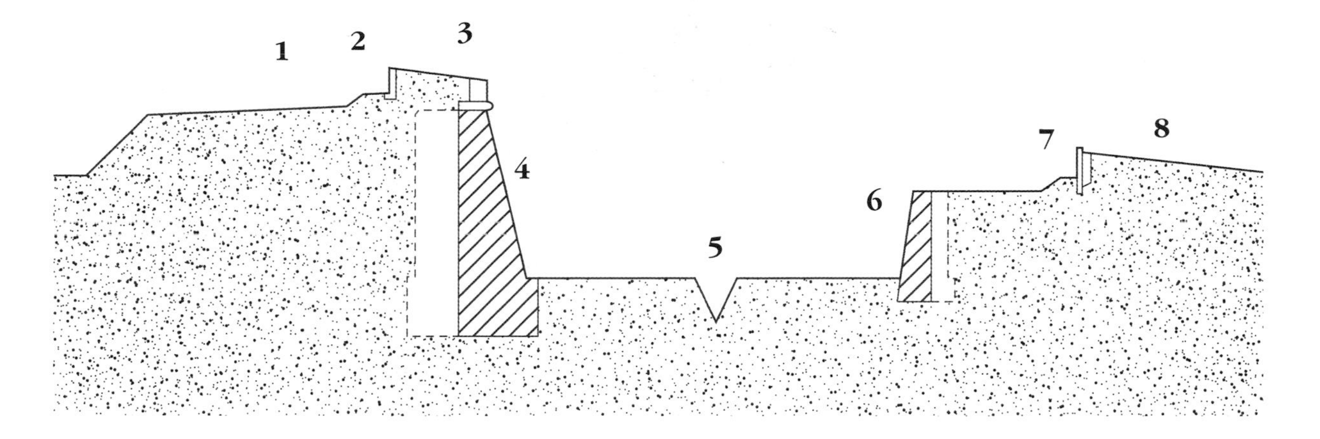

ABOVE: A CROSS-SECTION of a typical fortification of the Napoleonic period. 1) terreplein; 2) banquette; 3) parapet; 4) scarp revetment; 5) cuvette; 6) counter-scarp revetment; 7) pallisade; 8) glacis.

BELOW: THIS ILLUSTRATION SHOWS *a plan and elevation of part of defensive battery. The gun would be positioned on a downward-sloping wooden platform for stability.*

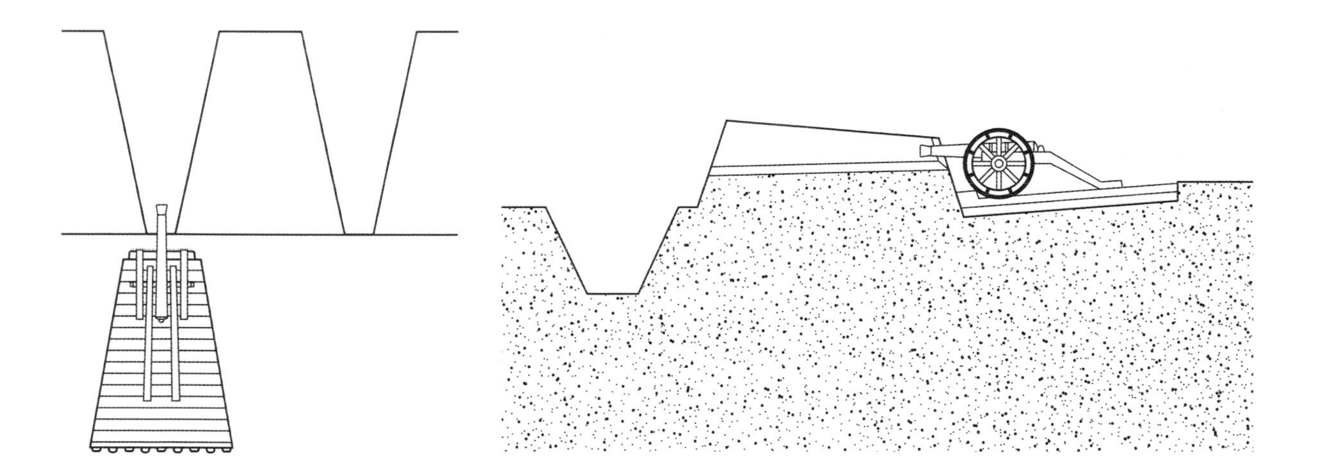

outpost line. The French, however, were ready and neatly repelled the Russians, sending them back to their lines with heavy losses.

Nevertheless, the end was near. Word came that Napoleon had abdicated in April, but Davout refused to surrender until he was ordered to by competent French authority. That word came by General Etienne Gérard (1773–1852), who was to assume command of XIII Corps from Davout. Both men took a hard line with the Russians, and the French left Hamburg under arms with their colours, artillery and baggage. The evacuation started on 27 May and was completed by the end of the month, except for those too sick or wounded to march. They would return to France as soldiers as soon as they could travel.

Davout could add this successful defence of a fortified city to his battle laurels of Auerstädt, Eylau (1807), Eckmühl (1809) and Moghilev (1812). It was the most successful defence of a fortified position during the period and would be studied by professional soldiers for years to come.

Siege of Hamburg

December 1813 - May 1814

In accordance with Davout's considerable military reputation, the defence of Hamburg against a numerical superior enemy for over six months is the most successful defence of a fortified place during the Revolutionary and Napoleonic periods. Davout held the city against all comers, successfully repelled any and all Allied assaults and kept perfect discipline inside the city during the occupation and siege. In line with his reputation as an incorruptible administrator, the troops calling him 'The Just', and there were few, if any, incidents against the civilian population during the siege by the French troops. The defence of the city was skillfully handled, Davout forming a mobile force of infantry and artillery ready to march to any threatened part of the city's defences. Davout even organized and trained a cuirassier regiment, unofficially numbered the 15th, during the siege. Successfully holding the city, Davout only surrendered when he was presented with evidence that Napoleon had abdicated and that the war was over.

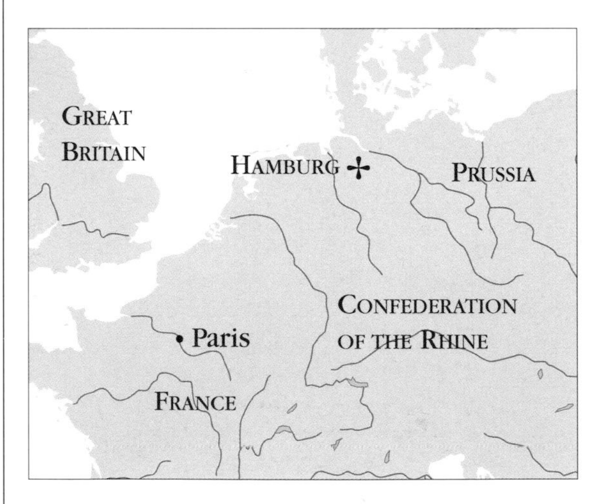

Hamburg is a strategic port city on the lower Elbe, which Napoleon considered vital to hold. Consequently, Marshal Davout commanding the XIII Corps was tasked with its defence after the Russian campaign of 1812.

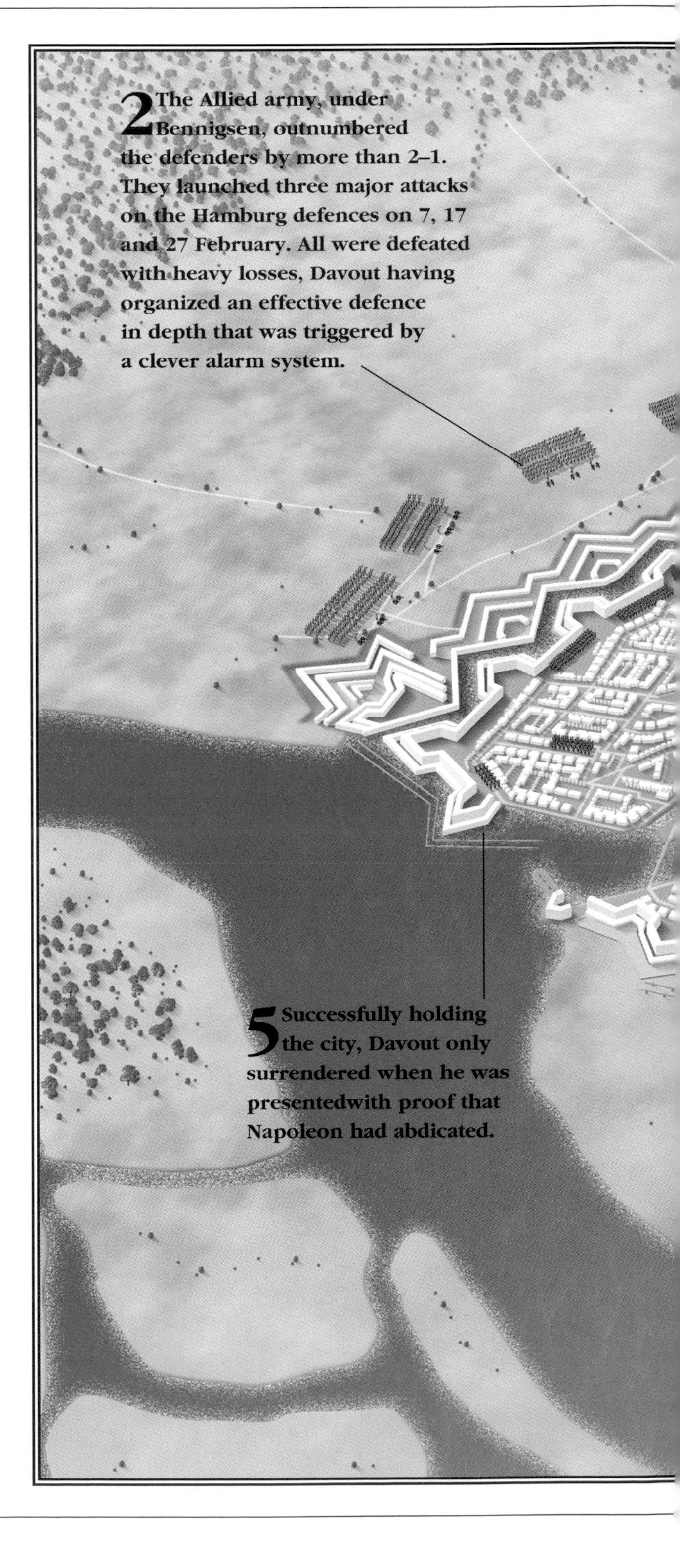

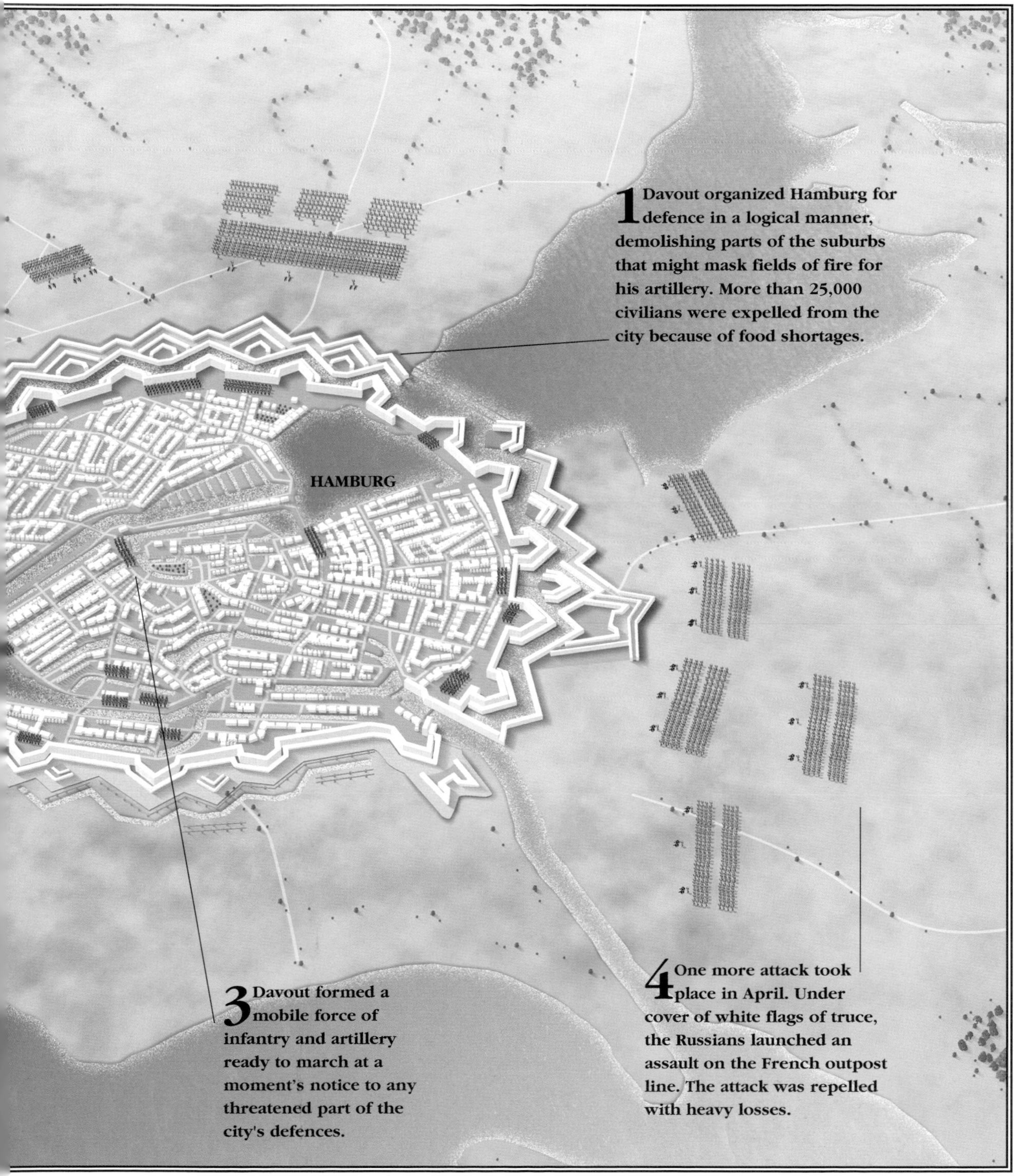

1 Davout organized Hamburg for defence in a logical manner, demolishing parts of the suburbs that might mask fields of fire for his artillery. More than 25,000 civilians were expelled from the city because of food shortages.

HAMBURG

3 Davout formed a mobile force of infantry and artillery ready to march at a moment's notice to any threatened part of the city's defences.

4 One more attack took place in April. Under cover of white flags of truce, the Russians launched an assault on the French outpost line. The attack was repelled with heavy losses.

CHAPTER 5

NAVAL WARFARE

Several factors dictated the tactical options available to a naval commander in this period. The motive power of a sailing ship was harnessed by a vast array of rope, wood and canvas. The only alternative to this was oar power, which added the complication that the oars were just where you wanted to put your huge, cumbersome guns. Further, they flapped about at the sides of your ship, where they were most vulnerable to enemy action.

Both sail and oar power required large numbers of at least semi-skilled and fit seamen to operate them efficiently. The definition of a 'ship' lay in its rigging: three masts, each setting square sails. Each of the three masts would normally set three square sails linked vertically, so that the sails on a single mast were controlled by two ropes or sheets. A ship would also have up to three 'fore-and-aft' sails, each controlled by a single sheet. The bowsprit would

THIS PAINTING OF THE BATTLE OF TRAFALGAR *shows the enormous damage ships could suffer. Falling masts and spars litter the upper deck, while cannon balls smash and splinter the wooden sides.*

have perhaps two more square sails, and a further large fore-and-aft sail could be set on the aftermost mast. In fair weather, eight studding sails could be added outboard of the lower square sails.

Putting up or taking down sails was necessary when the wind strength changed or you needed to alter speed, and the operation required time, sea-room and a lot of manpower. Tacking – turning towards and through the wind to sail in a new direction – was especially tricky. In order to control the crew who heaved on this multitude of outhauls, downhauls, haliyards and sheets, an officer corps of considerable skill and experience was required.

Square sails meant that ships could adequately sail across the wind or downwind but were poor at sailing, even obliquely, into the wind. Consequently, battles were usually fought under 'easy sail'. The largest of the square sails at the bottom of each of the three masts was furled up. The huge cumbersome studding sails were dispensed with altogether, and the fore-and-aft sails between the masts reduced to, perhaps, just two. Although this reduced the speed of the ship, it also reduced the number of men running about the deck whilst others were trying to fire the guns. It also freed a reserve of manpower to augment the gun crews and maintain, among other duties, the flow of ammunition from the lower deck.

Oar power traded all-round manoeuvrability for hull strength – the ships had to be lightly built to give the oarsmen a chance. Also, the sizeable guns carried by these ships, more properly known as galleys, could only be mounted to fire forwards, since the recoil of a full broadside might tip the vessel over; also there would be chaos as gun crew and oarsmen tried to carry out their respective tasks. In this period galleys were often rowed by slaves or convicts, and frequently carried masts

ALL THESE SMALL ARMS *operate using the same flintlock mechanism: flint strikes steel, makes spark and ignites powder. However, the flint needs to be adjusted exactly right and degrades as pieces are chipped off by the steel, and the wind can carry off the sparks before they reach the powder. They are not as reliable as popular myth would have us believe.*

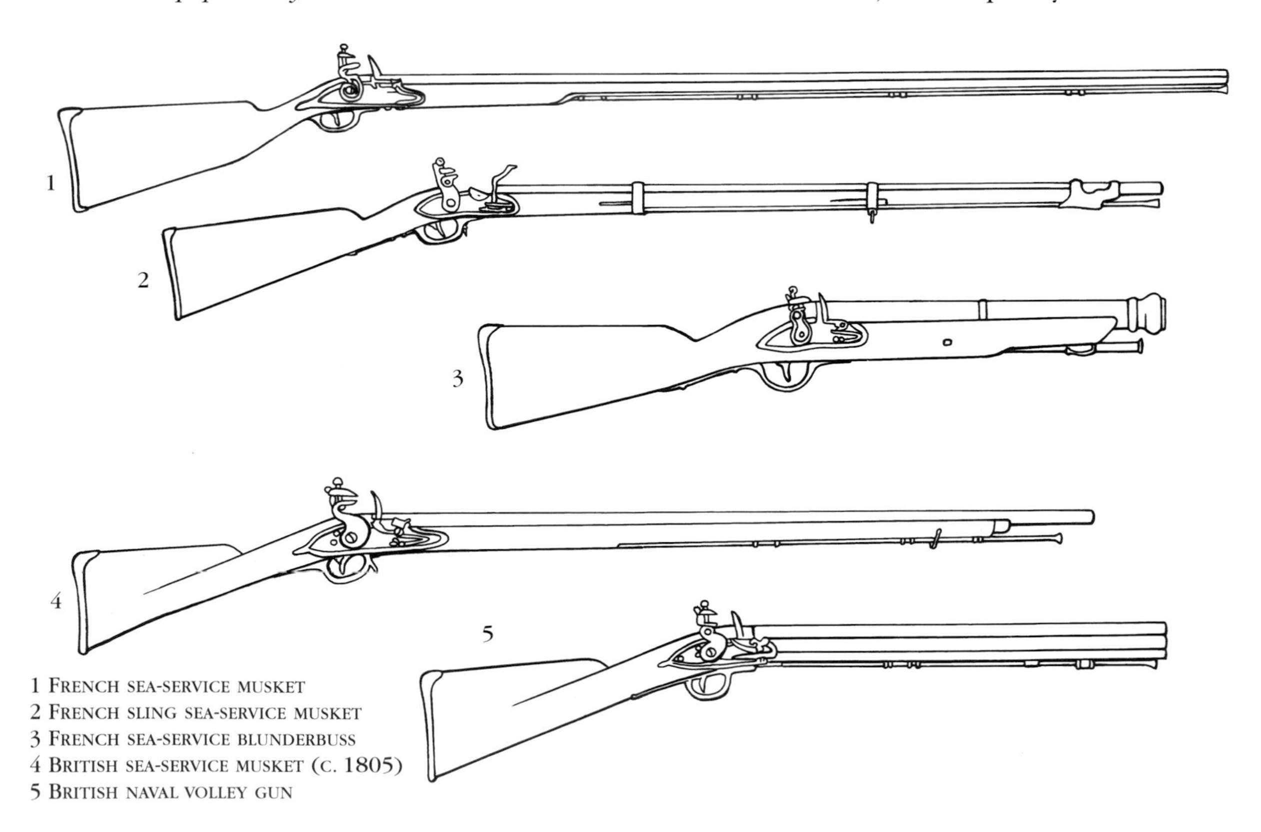

1 FRENCH SEA-SERVICE MUSKET
2 FRENCH SLING SEA-SERVICE MUSKET
3 FRENCH SEA-SERVICE BLUNDERBUSS
4 BRITISH SEA-SERVICE MUSKET (C. 1805)
5 BRITISH NAVAL VOLLEY GUN

and sails for when the wind was favourable. They guarded large ports and operated in rivers and lakes and in the Mediterranean. In a flat calm, galleys could be a real problem to the larger ships by manoeuvring to fire into their vulnerable sterns, where there were few guns mounted to return the fire.

THIS FRENCH GUNNER (C.1805) *wears the typical bicorne and revolutionary cockade. He carries a linstock - a stick with some lighted match cord impregnated with powder to make it burn slowly, wrapped around the end. To fire his cannon, he blows on the lighted end to make it glow and thrusts it into the touch hole on the barrel. With all the loose gunpowder there was around, this was highly dangerous. It was replaced in the British Royal Navy with a flintlock firing mechanism.*

Offensive Power

The commander had three forms of offensive power. First, he had naval artillery capable of firing a variety of shot. His guns could strike at an impressively long range with solid balls to turn the very fabric of an enemy's ship into thousands of lethal splinters. From closer range, guns could fire chain shot (two heavy objects linked with a short length of chain), aiming high in the hope of wrapping the chain around the enemy masts and rigging, cutting them through and so reducing the vessel's speed and ability to manoeuvre. At even closer range, short-barrelled carronades, a British speciality, might sweep the crowded enemy decks with small balls, rendering the enemy crew a bloody pulp.

Unfortunately, none of these unrifled, muzzle-loaded cannon was very accurate. The iron balls attracted rust like flies round an open wound. This had to be chipped off and the balls painted, a process that inevitably impaired their spherical shape. Irregular shape combined with the difference between gun bore and ball diameter, the windage, meant that cannonballs did not fly very straight. Additionally, both target and firing ship were moving to the rhythm of the sea. All in all, to achieve a decisive result, close range was preferred - less than 450m (500 yards).

The second form of offensive power available was the crew itself. A commander could bring his ship alongside the enemy and unleash a savage and confused mêlée across each of his, perhaps six, decks to swamp the crew completely through fierce hand-to hand-fighting. Such a fast-moving scrum meant that firearms - muskets or pistols - were one-shot weapons. Swords, short pikes and axes could injure more enemy more quickly than a pistol, which needed reloading.

However, get the timing right with a carronade mounted on your own top works, and your crew could be jumping onto a bloody deck against an already beaten foe.

Third, you could turn a smallish ship into a floating fireball or bomb and attempt to sail it into the midst of an enemy fleet. This tactic was normally used when the target was at anchor. It sounds a bit hit and miss, but the effect on the enemy was startling. Imagine being trapped in a wooden box clutching a bag of gunpowder and watching a bonfire on wheels roll slowly in your direction …

The Royal Navy's Captain Thomas Cochrane (1775–1860) used 20 fire-ships to stunning effect in 1809 at the Basque Roads. He attacked at night when the tide was right and the ships would be at their most terrifying. He illuminated the narrow channel with two fire-ships. He then blew up the boom protecting the entrance with two bomb ships, each loaded with 500 barrels of gunpowder, allowing the rest of the fire-ships to waft in amongst four frigates and eleven ships of the line, all at anchor. The French ships cut their anchors and drifted aground. The next morning the French had only two ships of the line and a frigate under command. Cochrane attacked with his reserve frigates. Two enemy ships and a frigate were burned and two ships struck their colours – surrendered.

'the Able Seamen can not only hand, reef and steer but are likewise capable of heaving the lead in the darkest night, as well as the daytime… use the palm and needle of the sailmaker… versed in every part of the ship's rigging…'

– CAPTAIN BASIL HALL

Fleet Tactics

By the time of the Napoleonic Wars (1805–1815), naval tactics had evolved over more than 200 years into a simple formula: bring your fleet into a single line following a lead ship, then bring that line alongside the enemy's and blast away. The side that fired fastest for longest usually won. Individual ships would rig nets above the upper gun deck to reduce the debris falling from above. The crew's hammocks would be packed around the sides of the ships to reduce splinters. To preserve the ship's boats, another source of splinters, they would be towed astern or released, hopefully to be collected later. The splinters we talk of here are not those that would have you reaching for a needle. These are huge jagged lumps of wood that could sever a limb or impale a body. It also became normal to post marines or seaman-snipers in the rigging to pick off the officers. Since the small arms of the time could barely manage to hit anything even at 200m (220 yards), this was a truly intimate assault.

The British developed the tactic of 'crossing the tee': sailing their line across the leading or rearmost enemy ship and firing along its length rather than into its side. This was known as a raking shot. In turn, each British ship would concentrate overwhelming force at a single vulnerable point. The tactic required the British commanders to hold their nerve, taking fire from the enemy before they could return it. More crucially, perhaps, it required British crews to handle all those sails efficiently while under increasingly accurate enemy fire. This technique was refined by turning each ship into the enemy line as Lord Howe (1726–99) did on the Glorious First of June in 1794. That rather pell-mell battle did not end as gloriously as proclaimed. The French lost just six ships and escaped with 19.

The most effective refinement came through cutting the line. One or two columns of ships would sail straight through a midpoint of the enemy's line. The downwind enemy ships would struggle to make it back to aid their fellows, and the British would concentrate a succession of their ships at just two points of the enemy's line. Trafalgar (1805) is the prime example of this ploy.

Prior to the French Revolutionary and Napoleonic Wars (1792–1815), the most recent major war had been the American War of Independence (1775–83). Britain had lost, principally through the intervention of France and Spain and the subsequent naval defeat at Chesapeake Bay in 1781. The French taxes levied to pay for that war contributed to the upswell of unrest that led to the Revolution. When Britain entered the French Revolutionary Wars in 1793, there had already been three British fleet mobilizations in the 10 years since the end of the American Revolutionary War. The first was in support of William of Orange, the second against Spain over a trading dispute in the Pacific and the third against Russia over Turkey. None had come to blows, but they were useful rehearsals. This time Britain had something to prove and knew it had to maintain naval supremacy over France and its allies. Traditional British naval strategy was three-pronged:

i) Bottle up enemy ships in harbour where they could do no damage but consumed enemy resources.
ii) Bring to battle any ships that might venture forth and destroy or capture them.
iii) Deliver to, and maintain the army at, any destination King George's government saw fit.

Overseas Challenge

To maintain and supply the fleet, additional overseas bases would be required. Although British strategy dominated the wars, Britain did not have everything its own way. France, which had successfully challenged the British less than 20 years previously, had undergone a revolution. As is typical in these events, the Revolutionary government was more draconian than its predecessor. It had both to consolidate its own position within France and fend off successive assaults from allies of the deposed monarchy. Purges of political opponents and potential nuclei of counter-revolutionary movements followed like waves on the beach.

Getting rid of army officers was relatively inconsequential, as they could be replaced from the ranks of experienced NCOs. However, the French navy lost an enormous number of experienced and skilled officers. In 1790, more than half of the officers on leave 'failed to return' to duty. By 1791, this had increased to more than 80 per cent absenteeism.

Inevitably the French navy, except in some occasional incidents, struggled to recover its professionalism. Nevertheless, it mounted two raids against Ireland and one against Wales. These gained minimal or no local revolutionary support and the supporting fleets were hounded down by the Royal Navy. A strong raiding force attacked the Newfoundland trade, and the Royal Navy managed to provide escorts for incoming and outgoing convoys. One such convoy, returning from the US

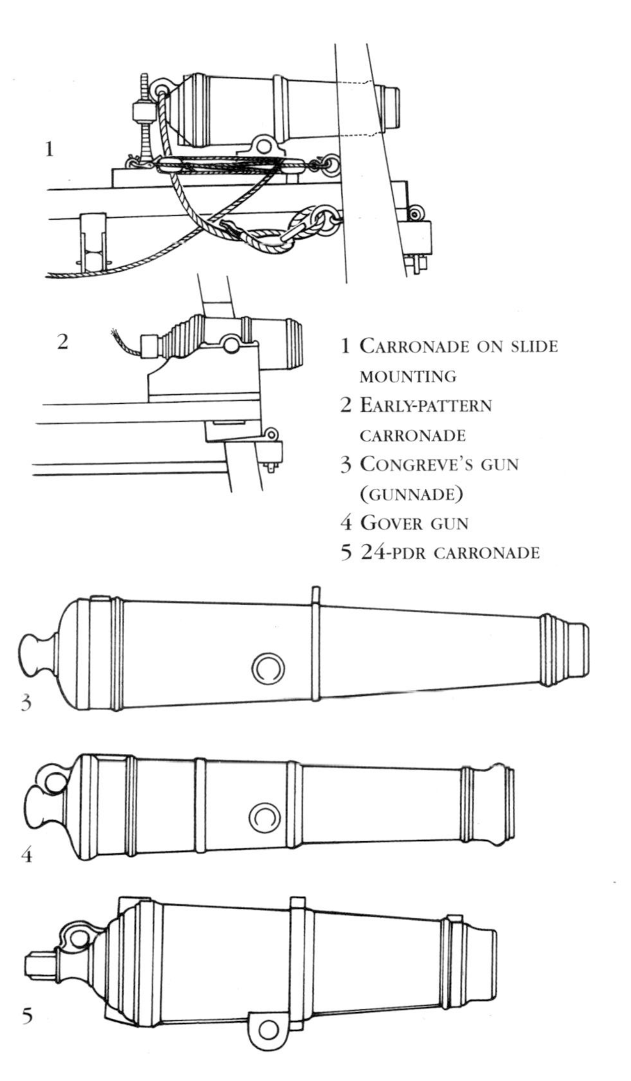

Types of Carronade. *These guns were designed to fire huge numbers of smaller balls at the crew on an enemy ship - usually to devastating effect - like a huge shot gun. They had a shorter barrel and shorter range than normal cannon. The barrels were tapered to provide more metal at the inboard end to contain the power of the explosion.*

with grain in 1794 to compensate for the failed harvest in 1793, was caught in the Channel and its escorting fleet roughly handled on the Glorious First of June. In 1797, the Spanish fleet, forced to ally with the French, was administered a sharp lesson at the battle of Cape St Vincent. French tactics therefore had to evolve afloat as they had done ashore.

Ship replacements for the imperial French fleet came largely from occupied countries. France acquired Dutch, Danish (captured by cavalry while anchored in a frozen harbour), Italian, Spanish and Venetian fleets, as well as the fleet of the Knights of St John. Through treaty, France acquired the aid of the Russian fleet and, coincidentally, the small US fleet. So, however many vessels the British captured or sank, there always seemed to be more.

Napoleon Bonaparte (1769–1821) first fired on the British when in charge of an artillery battery at the conclusion of the French siege of Toulon, which the British had occupied in support of a royalist movement. His career took him to major success on land in command of the Army of Italy and thence to the invasion of Egypt in 1798. From the point of view of the Directory – the Revolutionary governing council in Paris – the operation against Egypt would both threaten Britain's trade with India, a major source of the country's wealth, and take Bonaparte out of the political equation in Paris. Napoleon assembled around 35,000 men from the Army of Italy at various Italian ports and an escorting fleet of warships from Toulon. They rendezvoused at Malta, which was held by the Holy Order of the Knights of St John, an anachronism left over from the medieval crusades.

The troops were landed on 10 June at four separate locations. After token resistance from a single galley and two small galleots, the undermanned garrison of the island surrendered in less than 24 hours. The French armada of 13 ships of the line and around 400 transports sailed within a week, eastwards first to the southern coast of Crete, then southeast to Alexandria, arriving on 1 July.

The lack of charts, in contrast to the beautiful cartography available for Malta, and of purpose-built landing craft made the landings a shambles. The British fleet under Rear-Admiral Sir Horatio Nelson (1758–1805) had been on the coast two

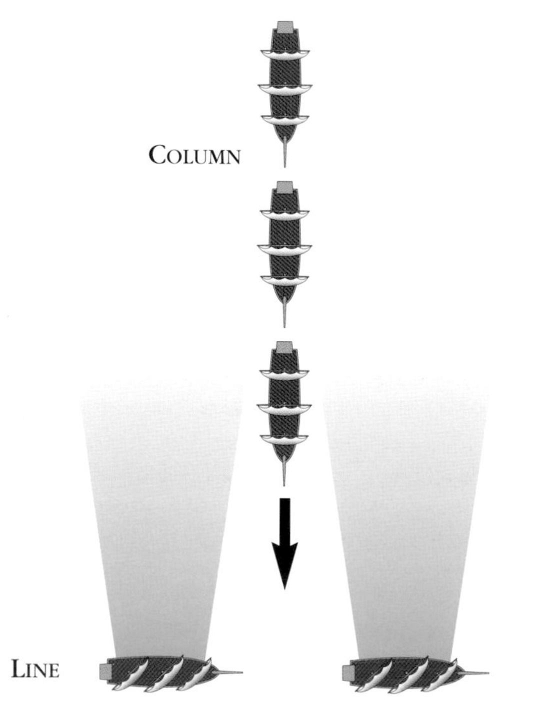

LINE VERSUS COLUMN. *The attacking column has passed through the firing arcs of the ships in line and now has a few moments peace before unleashing broadsides, at point blank range, into the vulnerable stems and sterns of the enemy.*

THE BATTLE OF THE NILE *saw, in the midst of 22 years of world war, the biggest man-made explosion of the era when the magazine on* L'Orient *exploded. It stunned and horrified both sides before the battle resumed.*

days before and could return at any moment. Napoleon had to get his men off the ships and capture Alexandria urgently - for its water supply if nothing else. They captured the port and marched on Cairo, meeting the Mameluke army on 21 July at the battle of the Pyramids, decisively won by the French. So where were Nelson and the British fleet? His absence can be explained by the unavailability of current news - an intelligence shortfall. First, although the British knew an invasion was being prepared, they did not know it was intended for Egypt. The signing-over to France of control of the Spanish fleet and the union of the two fleets at Toulon had prompted the outnumbered British to evacuate the Mediterranean by the end of 1797. News of the massing of an invasion army and escorting fleet filtered through to London in April, although its intended target was unclear. Perhaps it was to be another invasion of Ireland or Wales.

This chronology highlights the difficulties:

29 April - London orders Mediterranean fleet to scout in strength for news of invasion fleet.

30 April - Nelson arrives with Mediterranean fleet off Cadiz, southwest Spain.

2 May - Nelson dispatched with three battleships, three frigates and a sloop from Lisbon to scout the Mediterranean.

10 May - Order dated 29 April arrives at Mediterranean fleet.

17 May - Nelson captures French corvette but no definite information.

19 May - French escorting fleet leaves Toulon.

20 May - Severe storm scatters Nelson's frigates and nearly wrecks his flagship; four days to repair in Sardinia. The frigates were never able to rejoin Nelson's squadron.

24 May - eight battleship reinforcements arrive with Mediterranean fleet, then blockading Cadiz. Ten 74-gun battleships plus the *Leander*, 50 guns, sail from the Tagus River in Portugal to reinforce Nelson.

1 June - Nelson, off Toulon, mistakenly believes French fleet to still be in harbour. The harbour is screened by numerous rocks and small islands.

5 June - News of reinforcements reaches Nelson off Toulon.

6 June – French transport fleet arrives off Malta.
7 June – Reinforcements arrive off Toulon.
8 June – Nelson departs Toulon.
9 June – French escorting fleet arrives off Malta.
10 June – French land on Malta.
11 June – Holy Order of the Knights of St John surrenders to Napoleon.
12 June – Nelson off Corsica.
17 June – Nelson off Naples.
18 June – French fleet departs Malta.
20 June – Nelson, off Messina, learns that Malta has been captured.
22 June – Nelson, off Cape Passaro, learns that the French have quit Malta and are now sailing southeast.
25 June – Napoleon, off Candia, hears confirmation of Nelson's fleet searching for him. Orders fleet to Cape Aza, west of Alexandria.
28 June – Nelson's fleet cruises off Alexandria; no sign of French. Leaves, heading north.
29 June – French fleet off Cape Aza.
1 July – French fleet arrives off Alexandria.
4 July – Nelson off southern Turkey.
19 July – Nelson resupplies at Syracuse in Sicily.
24 July – Nelson leaves Syracuse bound for Morea en route to Alexandria.
28 July – Nelson, off Coron, learns French were off Candia four weeks before and sailing southeast, towards Alexandria.
1 August – 10 a.m. Nelson arrives at Alexandria. French transports in harbour but no large warships.
1 August – 1 p.m. French warships are spotted in Aboukir Bay, 24km (15 miles) east of Alexandria.

So, Nelson overtook the French fleet, which had slipped out of the way into a bay on the African coast, and then spent a month searching for it.

The Battle of the Nile: 1 August 1798

Having landed the army, which comprised 24,000 infantry, 4000 cavalry and 3000 artillerymen and their guns, the French escorting fleet had then anchored at Aboukir Bay to the east of the Nile Delta and Alexandria. The harbour at Alexandria was both full of transports and too shallow for the larger ships to enter. The admiral of the fleet, François Brueys (1753–98), no doubt pleased at having made it thus far without battle, and not having seen the English fleet for several months, relaxed. Napoleon was out of the way in Cairo. The sun was shining; the sea was calm. The ships had disgorged their share of the Army of the Orient.

Brueys had not, at that stage, even taken the precaution of ordering his fleet anchored to springs, an arrangement of cables attached to the anchor hawse that enabled the crew to alter the angle of the ship, and thus its field of fire, relative to the wind and tide (see below). Had he done so, all could have fired out to sea. Instead, the ships were held to a single anchor and therefore needed sea-room to swing at the wind's bidding. As the wind was from the north, also the direction Nelson came from, the ships could only fire east or west. However, as Brueys relaxed, so did his captains and so did his crew.

Some crewmen were ashore in Alexandria, helping the merchant ships' crews manhandle their cargo onto the dockside. Deck awnings and other paraphernalia of a slow voyage in those hot climes were left erected. Rubbish was allowed to accumulate on the lower gun decks. No patrolling squadron was established to give advance warning of an approaching enemy. So even when the British fleet sneaked a peak into Alexandria harbour, no one told the admiral 27km (17 miles) along the coast at Aboukir Bay.

Brueys had anchored his fleet in the following order, from west to east:

In the first line:

Guerrier (74 guns)	*Conquérant* (74)
Spartiate (74)	*Aquilon* (74)
Peuple Souverain (74)	*Franklin* (80) Rear-Admiral Blanquet du Chayla
Orient (120) Vice-Admiral Brueys	
Tonnant (80)	*Heureux* (74)
Mercure (74)	*Guillaume Tell* (80) Rear-Admiral Villeneuve
Généreux (74)	*Timoléon* (74)

In the second line (frigates):

Sérieuse (36)	*Artémise* (40)
Diane (40)	*Justice* (40)

An uncounted and unnamed group of smaller vessels was anchored further inshore, protected by the fleet.

The French anchorage was found by *Zealous* at 1 p.m. Nelson's reaction was typically decisive. His ships crammed on more sail and headed east. His plan was simple. He split his force into two columns, one to sail on the seaward side of the enemy fleet, the other to go inshore.

Nelson's inshore column, leading in sequence:

Goliath (74 guns) *Zealous* (74)
Orion (74) *Audacious* (74)
Theseus (74)

Nelson's offshore column:

Vanguard (74) *Minotaur* (74)
Defence (74) *Bellerophon* (74)
Majestic (74) *Leander* (50)

To the north:

Culloden (74)

To the west and making best possible speed:

Alexander (74) *Swiftsure* (74)

And hanging back so as not to get pulverized – the 18-gun brig *Mutine.*

Brueys Stands To

The French would thus be caught between two fires. As the wind would be behind his fleet when it attacked, Nelson ordered his ships to rig stern anchors. This meant they could halt, batter an enemy ship into submission, then move on to the next one. Like the French, the British suffered from poor charts of the area and were uncertain exactly where there was enough depth for them to sail. As they sailed eastwards, there was a tantalizing glimpse of the enemy as the gap between the fort of Aboukir and the islet of Aboukir opened and then closed. The ordinary seamen tending sails aloft in the British ships would have seen a positive forest of over 60 masts belonging to a long, menacing line of ships all a-bustle getting ready to receive the Royal Navy.

Nevertheless, the gap between fort and islet was deceptively shallow and the British fleet had to sail around the latter. What the British seamen could not see was the battery of four 12-pounder guns and two 33cm (13in) mortars Brueys had

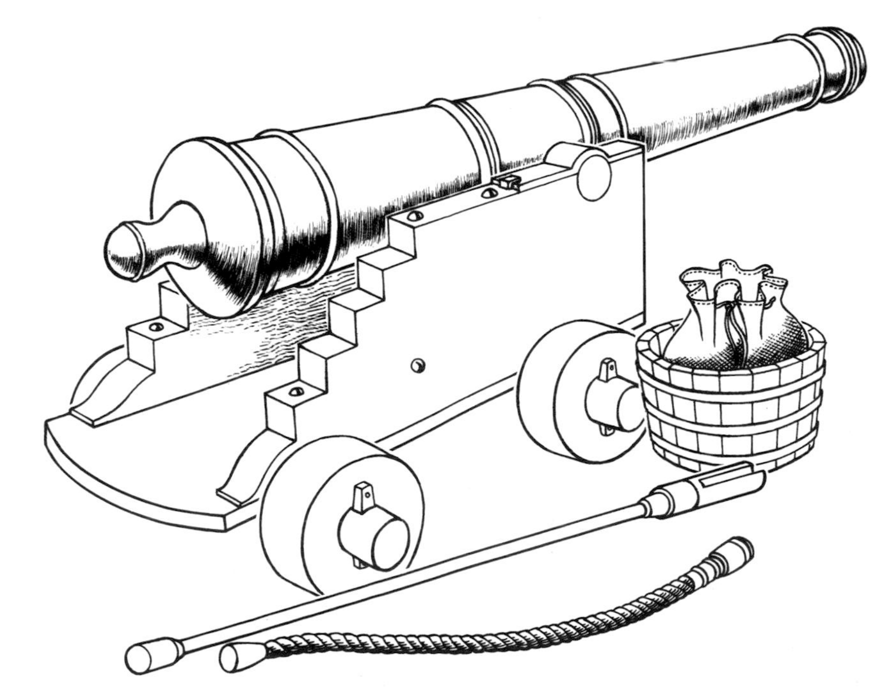

A SPANISH 24-PDR GUN. *After firing, the gun recoils back into the ship. The barrel first has to be sponged out to prevent any residue igniting the next charge. Then, a canvas bag with the next charge is rammed down the barrel, followed by the ball and, finally, wadding to keep the ball in contact with the charge. The gunner then pierces the bag through the touch hole with a metal spike and places a quill of fine powder in the touch hole. The gun is then run out and ready to fire. It takes about eight crew to keep the momentum going and is exhausting work.*

Battle of the Nile

1 August 1798

Nelson discovered the French fleet at anchor unprepared for battle and only partially manned. Although the French did much to improve their disastrous situation, it wasn't nearly enough.
The British ships concentrated on the Western end of their line and pounded one after another of their ships with no interference from the easternmost ships. As the British continued their grim work, the French flag ship, *L'Orient*, blew up. Three French line of battleships cut their anchors and ran aground, their crews providing replacements for Napoleon's army. Only Vice-Admiral Villeneuve and two ships escaped. The destruction of the French fleet trapped the army but not Napoleon. He evaded British ships and returned to France, where he was declared First Consul for life. The remnants of the French Army were defeated by combining one British/Indian army from India with another from Europe – with further aid from the Ottoman Empire.

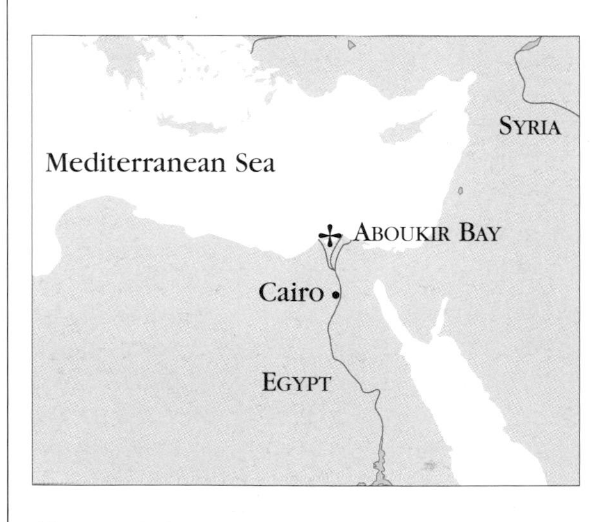

The French Directory were anxious about holding onto power and so agreed to send their most able general – Napoleon – off on a mad scheme to conquer Egypt. Napoleon proved his detractors wrong and conquered the country, but could not hold his gains due to lack of resupply from France.

ABOUKIR CASTLE

1 Having delivered the French Army to the harbour at Alexandria, the French fleet moved to a 'safe' anchorage at Aboukir Bay.

6 Three French ships cut their cables and run ashore while Vice-Admiral Villeneuve escapes with just two ships.

FRENCH FRIGATES

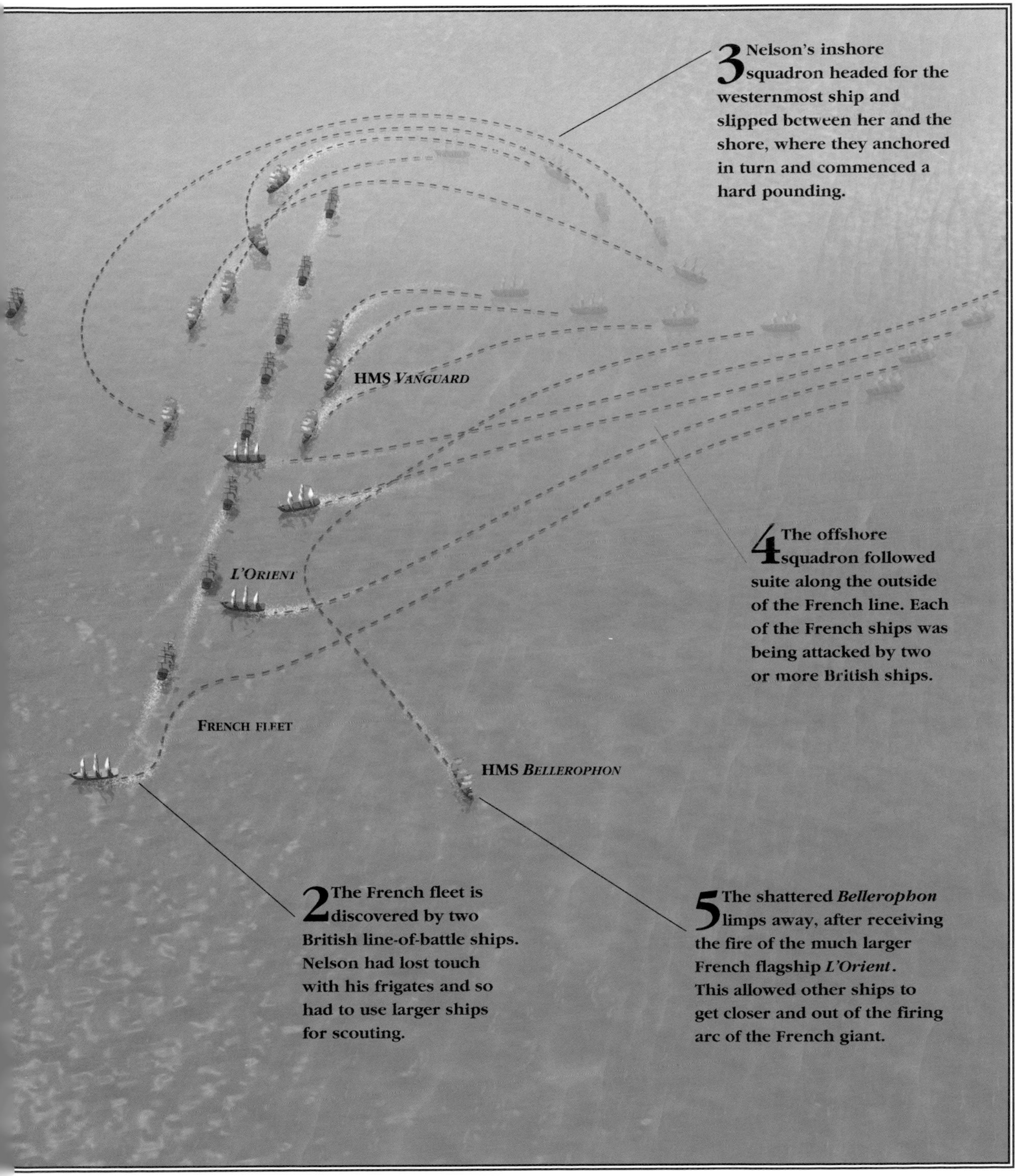

HMS VANGUARD

L'ORIENT

FRENCH FLEET

HMS BELLEROPHON

3 Nelson's inshore squadron headed for the westernmost ship and slipped between her and the shore, where they anchored in turn and commenced a hard pounding.

4 The offshore squadron followed suite along the outside of the French line. Each of the French ships was being attacked by two or more British ships.

2 The French fleet is discovered by two British line-of-battle ships. Nelson had lost touch with his frigates and so had to use larger ships for scouting.

5 The shattered *Bellerophon* limps away, after receiving the fire of the much larger French flagship *L'Orient*. This allowed other ships to get closer and out of the firing arc of the French giant.

mounted on the other side of the islet, positioned to rake any enemy vessels sailing parallel to the anchored French fleet. The French were indeed busy. When Vice-Admiral Brueys was told of the approaching English around 2 p.m., he ordered the decks cleared for action. He realized that with reduced crew levels he could not hope to hoist sail and get his fleet to sea in any kind of line of battle. He chose instead to fight with his ships at anchor.

Brueys instructed his captains to rig a cable to the ship lying astern. If this was intended to prevent the British breaking their line, the plan did not work.

However, he also ordered springs to be rigged to the anchor cables. This entailed running a rope from the bow of the ship to the anchor line and another likewise from the stern. It would have taken a long time and many men lugging a long rope, perhaps 20cm (8in) in diameter, out through bow or stern ports and along the outside of the ship to be made fast to the anchor hawse. Rigging springs did allow his reduced crews to alter the angle of their ships relative to the wind so that their guns could be brought to bear on the enemy. Regrettably for the French, there was not enough time for the reduced crews to do all this and properly clear the decks.

Consequently, the residual clutter hampered their ability to operate the guns, particularly on the port side facing the land. Brueys had created a veritable Maginot Line afloat. Sadly, the lesson was missed 120 years later. He also deployed two brigs, *Railleur* and *Alerte,* to loiter near the shallows between the islet and the mainland in an attempt to lure the British across them, where they would surely go aground.

The first shot was fired at 6.20 p.m. This was nearly five and a half hours after the French had been sighted by *Zealous,* an indication of how poor the ships of the time were at sailing into the wind. Nevertheless, as the British fleet rounded

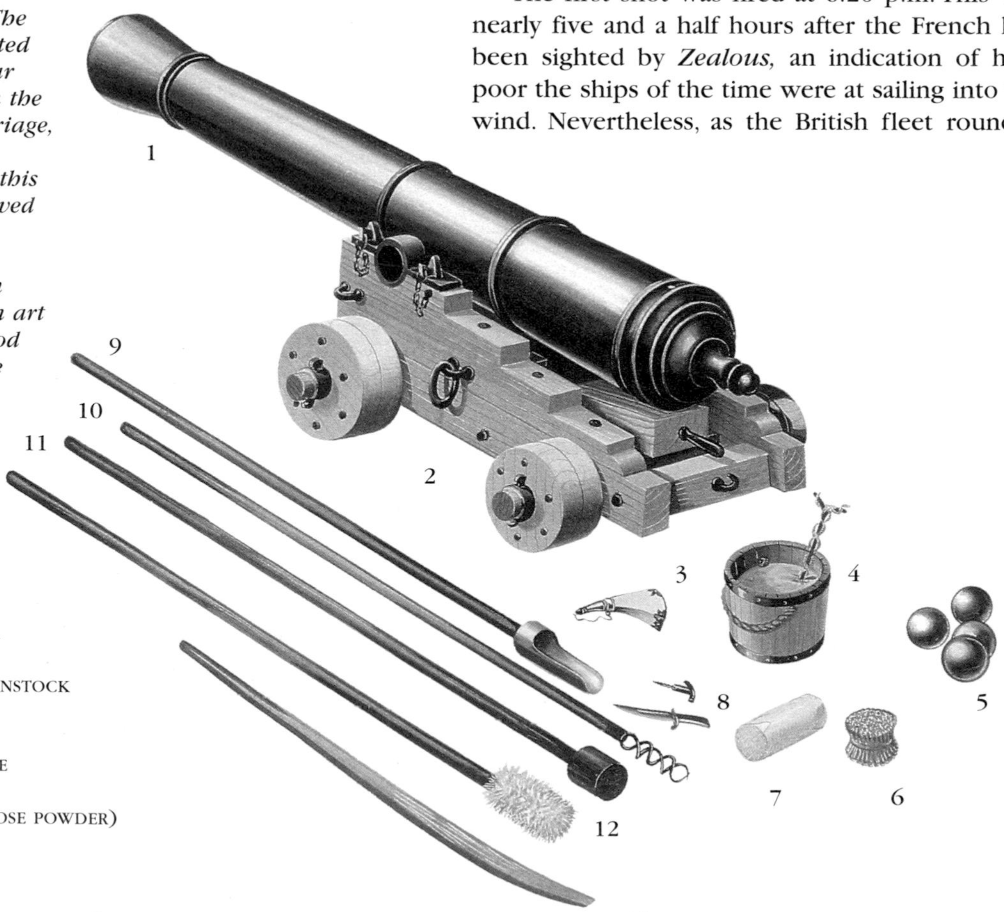

NAVAL CANNON. *The barrel is weighted towards the rear where, between the barrel and carriage, there is a large wedge. Moving this in or out achieved the required elevation, but aiming the gun was more of an art and needed good timing with the roll of the ship. Virtually the same carriage was used in fortress guns ashore.*

1 BARREL
2 WOODEN TRUCK
3 POWDER HORN
4 BUCKET WITH LINSTOCK
5 ROUND SHOT
6 GRAPE SHOT
7 POWDER CHARGE
8 KNIVES
9 SCOOP (FOR LOOSE POWDER)
10 WORM
11 RAMROD
12 SPONGE
13 LEVER (USED TO AIM GUN)

the islet, the wind came onto their sterns. Both columns turned to starboard and sailed across the wind. The inshore column headed towards the western end of the French line.

Nelson Sails In

Goliath, in the lead, took the first shots from the French ship *Guerrier* and the battery on the islet. She then crossed the bow of the *Guerrier* and blasted her at her most vulnerable point. *Goliath* was then slow in letting her anchor go, so came to rest on the left rear quarter of the *Conquérant*, with the French frigate *Sérieuse* to her front right. Vigorous broadsides were exchanged.The *Zealous* followed *Goliath*, and as the sun set in the west she commenced a brisk fire with the *Guerrier*, bringing down the latter's foremast and at the same time anchoring off her port bow. *Orion* followed *Zealous*, and skirted around her and *Goliath* dangerously inshore. She gave the poor frigate *Sérieuse* a full broadside, reducing her to a dismasted and sinking wreck, then dropped her stern anchor almost abreast the *Peuple Souverain*.

By now, the inshore column had lost formation, and the offshore column, having had to go further to give the inshore column sea-room, was headed more directly towards the centre of the French line and the giant 120-gun *Orient*.*Audacious* from the offshore column slipped into the gap between *Guerrier* and *Conquérant*, coming to rest less than 50m (55 yards) from the latter. *Guerrier* was now being attacked by two ships from bow and stern and had few guns that could be brought to bear. *Conquérant* was also suffering from the attentions of two ships, *Audacious* and *Goliath*. *Theseus* was next, and she sailed between *Zealous*, *Goliath* and their targets to anchor about 250m (275 yards) inshore of *Spartiate*.

On the other side of her, Nelson's flagship, *Vanguard*, halted just 75m (80 yards) away - point-blank range. *Minotaur* was next in the British line and came into position against *Aquilon*. *Defence*, following *Minotaur*, lined up against *Peuple Souverain,* which already had *Orion* on her other side. *Bellerophon* passed the French vessel *Franklin* and ended up adjacent to the giant *Orient*, almost twice her weight of broadside. Following Nelson's orders, the *Majestic*

SAILOR FIRING A SMALL CARRONADE *from the fighting tops down onto the enemy deck. He had to be careful that the blast from the gun did not set fire to the sails of his own ship. There was limited space for ammunition this high up, so it had to be brought up from below decks during a prolonged engagement.*

drew up to exchange broadsides with *Tonnant*. It had taken nearly an hour for the British ships to get in position, and although they were doling out a great deal of punishment, they were not having things all their own way.

Unfortunately, in his enthusiasm to join the fray, the captain of the *Culloden* clipped the shoals by the islet rather too heavily and went aground. *Leander* stayed to give what help she could, but *Culloden*'s rudder came off in the small hours of the following morning. She was out of the fight. *Leander*, having lent what help she could to *Culloden*, arrived amidst the battle of giants at around 8 p.m. She wafted into the gap left by the *Peuple Souverain*, which had drifted out of line. As she did so, she passed the dismasted *Bellerophon* drifting away from the mighty *Orient*. *Leander*'s broadsides now piled misery into the decks of the *Franklin* to port and the *Aquilon* to starboard. *Leander* was followed by *Swiftsure* and *Alexander*. The former anchored off the starboard bow of *Orient,* and the latter off *Orient*'s port stern quarter. In this position the British ships would have a full target for their broadsides, while the French could only reply with part of theirs.

Nelson's plan was now complete. His smaller fleet had succeeded in concentrating its available force against a section of the French fleet half its own size. It was now up to Brueys to bring his greater number of ships and even greater superiority in firepower to bear on the British fleet. He had the resources and the British were fully committed with no reserves. However, with cannonballs flying around like swifts in summer, Brueys was killed not long after the arrival of *Swiftsure* and *Alexander.* His flag captain was also fatally wounded shortly afterwards.

'Victory is not a name strong enough for such a scene.'

– Admiral Nelson, surveying the floating carnage the day after the Battle of the Nile

It is also not surprising that the *Orient* caught fire. Between 8 and 9 p.m., the engaged and locally outnumbered French ships were dropping like flies. *Guerrier* surrendered after three hours of the most fearful firefight. *Conquérant* lasted just 12 minutes - two out of three of her masts were shot away and she was a spent force. *Spartiate* capitulated at around 9 p.m., having suffered the attentions of no less than four separate British suitors.

The *Aquilon* stuck it out until 9.25 p.m., by which time she had lost all her masts and much of her crew. The *Peuple Souverain* had drifted out of line after her cable had parted but re-anchored abreast the *Orient.* The flagship had already caught fire and at about 10 p.m. the fire must have reached the magazine, for she blew up with an enormous explosion that stunned both sides, firing pausing from sheer shock and awe. Falling, flaming debris started fires on the French *Franklin* and British *Alexander.* Both ships managed to put them out. The *Franklin* surrendered a little while later.

The *Tonnant*, immediately astern of *Orient,* had been successfully exchanging shots with the *Majestic*, whose main and mizzen masts she had downed. Mention has to be made of her captain, Aristide-Aubert Dupetit Thouars (1760–98). He lost first his right arm, then his left, then a leg, but continued to command whilst propped up in a barrel of bran before succumbing to loss of blood. The next two French ships slipped out of line, then beached themselves, surrendering to the *Alexander* and *Leander.* The frigate *Artémise* fired a token broadside into *Theseus,* then struck her colours, but she was already on fire and blew up. The French frigate *Justice* set sail and attempted to capture the *Bellerophon* but was dissuaded by *Zealous.*

The French *Timoléon* also ran aground trying to get away. Just four French ships made good their escape: *Guillaume Tell*, *Généreux*, *Diane* and *Justice*, along with Rear-Admiral Pierre-Charles Villeneuve (1763–1806). Seventeen ships soundly beaten by just 13 is a glorious victory by any account. Nelson had dealt with a strong but static linear defence by going round the end and applying overwhelming force to just a small area. It trapped a French army in the Middle East, as well as a certain troublesome young general.

Napoleon Slips Away

However, such troublesome young generals are not always inclined to be so easily trapped. Having repeatedly defeated Egyptian attempts to oust his occupying force, and failing to fight his way through the whole Ottoman Empire around the eastern end of the Mediterranean, Napoleon was forced to desert his army in secret. He returned to France on a single ship with a few senior colleagues. France's war effort had gone considerably downhill in his absence. Virtually all of his gains in Italy had been lost, and an alliance known as the Second Coalition had formed against France. This brought together Austria, Britain, Naples, Portugal, the Ottoman Empire, Russia and the Vatican. France was being assaulted on all

LORD HORATIO NELSON, *as painted by Sir William Beechey (1753-1839), the English landscape and portrait painter.*

fronts. Attack being the best form of defence, under Napoleon no alternative strategy was ever considered. Italy was regained and the other adversaries thrown back.

In 1802, the Peace of Amiens gave Europe a breathing space, but it did not last. With political help from his friends, Napoleon executed one of the most complete and long-lasting *coups d'état* in history. The new regime that replaced the Directory was the Consulate. There were three consuls, of whom Napoleon was First Consul, and he effectively held the power. War with Britain was renewed, and, as ever, Napoleon intended to attack. The 'Army of England', 160,000 strong, was assembled at Boulogne, and work began on building a fleet of invasion barges. There was real panic in England. A census was called of able-bodied men and potential weapons; in the Channel ports, even chisels were included. Bonaparte became the bogeyman of choice to scare children to do their parents' bidding.

For the barge fleet to arrive safely on English shores required, at the very least, temporary naval superiority in the English Channel. Napoleon's plan was to lure the English blockading squadrons away from the French coast and launch the invasion before they got back. This plan would be put into effect by the French fleets from Toulon and Brest, plus the Spanish fleets from Cartagena and Cadiz. They would sail off, separately, to the West Indies, where they would join forces to make a huge fleet of possibly 40 ships of the line. This overwhelming force would return to the Channel, swamp the British Channel patrols and escort the barges across to England. To some extent the plan worked.

The Battle of Trafalgar: 21 October 1805

The man in charge at Toulon was Villeneuve, survivor of Aboukir Bay, and he led his fleet out first; he had eleven ships of the line and six frigates. This departure was noted by two British frigates, which sailed to report to Lord Nelson (he was raised to the peerage after the Nile), who was biding his time off Sardinia. Villeneuve paused at Cartagena for 12 hours, just long enough to make his presence known and to issue orders. Then he set off, passed Gibraltar and anchored off Cadiz. Again he issued orders and pressed on. The rendezvous was at Martinique in the Caribbean. There, Villeneuve was joined by the fleet from Cadiz - a further seven ships of the line. Two more ships arrived from Rochefort later with instructions for him to return to Europe and unite with the fleet (12 ships) in Ferrol , northwestern Spain, then proceed northwards to Brest (21 ships) on the Brittany peninsula.

Whilst he carried out these orders, Nelson gave chase. But with Villeneuve well beyond the horizon, Nelson guessed at Gibraltar as his destination, and was sadly south of the mark. After

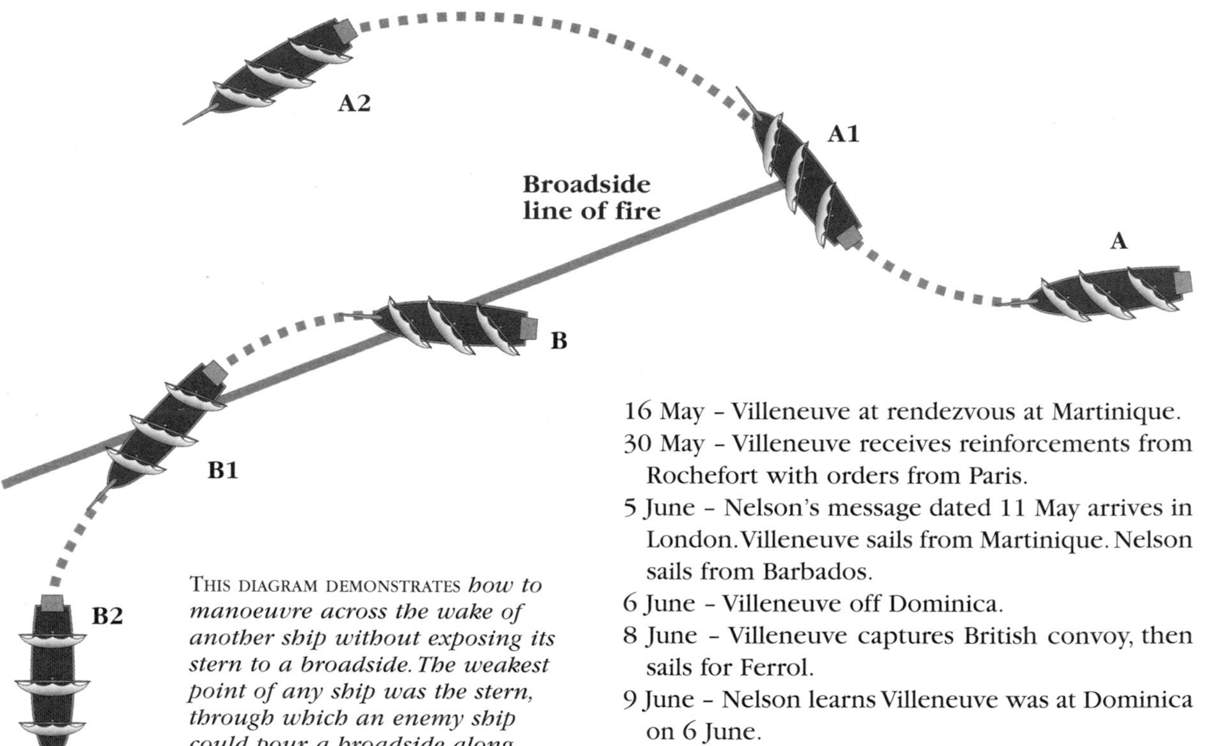

THIS DIAGRAM DEMONSTRATES *how to manoeuvre across the wake of another ship without exposing its stern to a broadside. The weakest point of any ship was the stern, through which an enemy ship could pour a broadside along the length of the vessel.*

a brush with Vice-Admiral Sir Robert Calder (1745–1818), just west of Ferrol, Villeneuve managed to achieve his aim of sailing into Ferrol and uniting his fleet with the 12 ships based there. Taking into account losses, he now had 28 under his command, and while he had been shadowed by Calder with just 15 ships, the latter decided discretion was the better part of valour and withdrew to unite his fleet with the British ships at Ushant.

Evasion and Chase

The following timetable shows the sequence of events of Villeneuve's and Nelson's cat-and-mouse operations during the spring and summer of 1805:

30 March 1805 – Villeneuve sails from Toulon.
7 April – Villeneuve off Cartagena.
9 April – Villeneuve passes Gibraltar.
9 April – Villeneuve anchors off Cadiz.
18 April – Nelson, off Sardinia, learns of French passing Gibraltar.
11 May – Nelson, off Lagos, Portugal, sails in pursuit of Villeneuve.
16 May – Villeneuve at rendezvous at Martinique.
30 May – Villeneuve receives reinforcements from Rochefort with orders from Paris.
5 June – Nelson's message dated 11 May arrives in London. Villeneuve sails from Martinique. Nelson sails from Barbados.
6 June – Villeneuve off Dominica.
8 June – Villeneuve captures British convoy, then sails for Ferrol.
9 June – Nelson learns Villeneuve was at Dominica on 6 June.
12 June – Nelson off Antigua, sails for Gibraltar.
6 July – British Channel fleet learns Villeneuve in Martinique.
17 July – Commodore Allemand breaks out of Rochefort with five ships of the line.
18 July – Nelson arrives off Cadiz and heads home on leave. He had been at sea in HMS *Victory* for over two years.
22 July – Villeneuve arrives east of Ferrol with 20 ships of the line and joins battle with Calder's squadron of 15 ships of the line. Two Spanish ships captured, two more badly damaged. Bad weather stops battle.
25 July – Villeneuve leaves the two damaged ships in Vigo Bay and sails for Ferrol.
31 July – Villeneuve arrives at Ferrol, bringing his total number of line-of-battle ships to 28. So far, so good.
9 August – Villeneuve sails with whole fleet to try and locate Allemand, who is at sea with a further five ships.

The Turning Point

Villeneuve was unable to locate Commodore Allemand. If he had done so, he might have turned north towards Brest and released the 21 French ships blockaded there. This would have brought his total fleet to 55 ships, less any losses that might have occurred. It is difficult to see how the British fleet, then off Cadiz, could have caught up with this move. It would certainly have triggered the embarkation of the 'Army of England' and its departure for southern England. However, it was not to be. Villeneuve turned south to Cadiz, where a useful six more Spanish ships were blockaded by Vice-Admiral Cuthbert Collingwood's (1748–1810) small squadron. On 20 August, Villeneuve arrived at Cadiz, bringing his fleet to 34 ships.

This result for Napoleon brought forth a suitable response from the Royal Navy. Calder, with 20 ships, was moved from Ferrol to reinforce Collingwood at Cadiz. Nelson left England with reinforcements to relieve Collingwood, arriving off Cadiz on 28 September and bringing the fleet there to 29 ships. Six of these were in urgent need of food and water replenishment. Nelson's notion of blockade differed from the traditional 'keep it close and don't let them out' idea. He preferred to let frigates do the watching from a distance and keep the fleet over the horizon where it could pounce on any brave enough to venture forth. But it was not a watertight blockade. The strategy had led to Villeneuve's escaping from Toulon and busying himself in the vastness of the Atlantic. By following Napoleon's plan, he had now built his fleet from 11 ships to the 34 now in Cadiz.

On 17 September Villeneuve received an order from Napoleon instructing him to transport the troops he had brought back from the West Indies to Naples and collect even more ships from Toulon and Genoa. This was an attempt to nip in the bud a growing Third Coalition then building against France, and in particular Russian and British cooperation in Italy.

'The business of the English commander-in-chief being first to bring an enemy fleet to battle on the most advantageous terms to himself, ... and secondly to continue them there until the business is decided.

— Nelson

Accordingly, the combined fleets were made ready to sail on 10 October. Villeneuve had also got wind of the news that Napoleon had decided to replace him and the new man was on the way. A good victory over the British would surely enable him to keep his job.

Despite receiving a further two ships, Nelson had been obliged to let five go to Gibraltar for replenishment, leaving him with just 26 ships. His orders before the battle are preserved and set out commands for three columns. One column was to break through by the twelfth ship from the rear of the enemy line, whilst his own column would aim for the centre, where he expected to find the French commander-in-chief. The third column, or Advanced Squadron, was in effect a reserve to attack as directed. He presumed the enemy vanguard would be unable to turn in time to affect the outcome. This is also what Villeneuve expected. He too had planned for a reserve squadron of roughly one-third his strength, leaving his main battle line with 22 ships.

The French and Spanish fleets started to make sail on 19 October, and the watching British ships reported the news to Nelson about 9.30 a.m. as he was cruising 80km (50 miles) to the west. He ordered 'General Chase' and then 'Prepare for Battle'. Matters, however, moved slowly. The wind was light and it was 3 p.m. before just 12 of the Franco-Spanish fleet cleared the port. The rest followed in the small hours. The wind, from the south-southwest, grew in strength, forcing Villeneuve's fleet to sail across the wind and in a northwesterly direction. Nelson, heading eastwards for the Straits, was briefly unaware of this until informed by his chain of scouting frigates.

There was much manoeuvring on 20 October, and during that night the French reserve chased off the shadowing British frigates, in the process

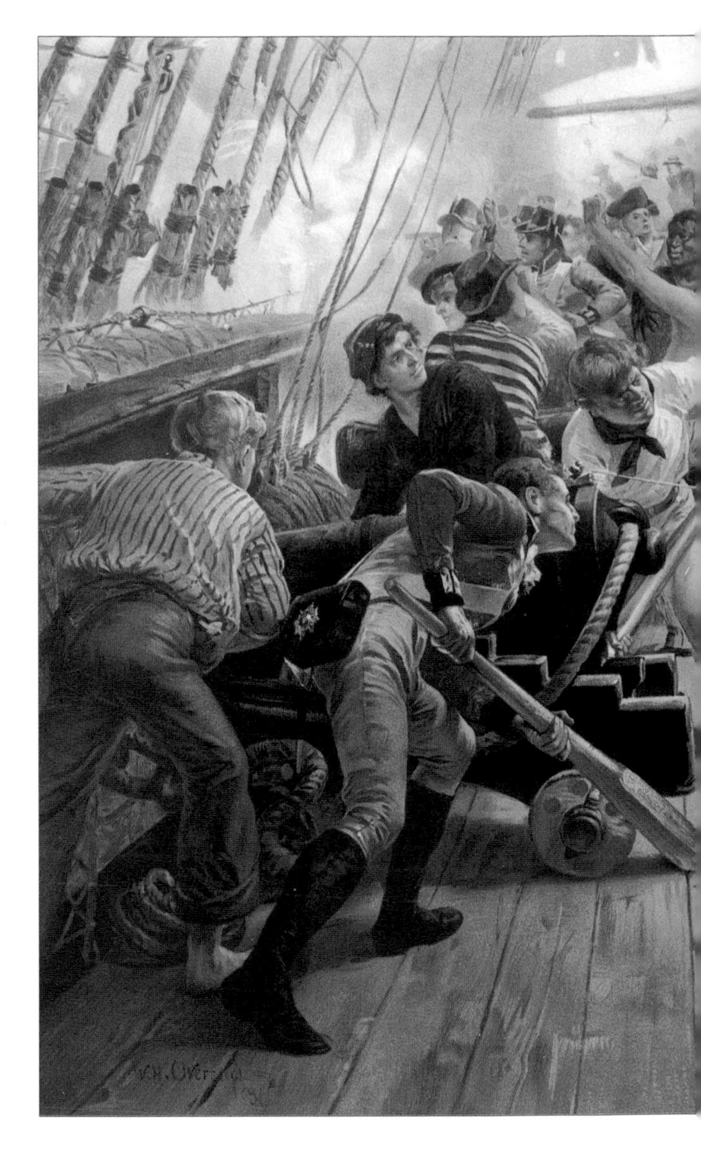

THIS PRINT, *after the painting, 'Trafalgar' by William Overend, was published in the* Illustrated Sporting and Dramatic News *in 1905 with the title, '"The Hero of Trafalgar" Nelson on Board the Victory, October 21st 1805'. Nelson is shown standing on the right on the deck of the* Victory, *facing fixedly ahead while the battle rages around him.*

glimpsing part of the British line of battle. By dawn the next day, the fleets were just 18km (11 miles) apart, about 32km (20 miles) west and slightly north from Cape Trafalgar. The British were upwind of Villeneuve's fleet. Both admirals appear to have abandoned the idea of a reserve: the French formed a single line, the British two columns. Nelson had already planned to crowd on full sail, instead of the easy sail normal for a battle, to minimize the number of broadsides his ships would receive before they reached the enemy line. Villeneuve, veteran of several battles against the British, had already given up any hope of influencing the battle. He had to rely on his captains' 'courage and thirst for glory' rather than a dependence on the signals of their commander-in-chief.

The battle lines for Trafalgar are set out below. Ships are listed in the order in which they sailed on the day of the battle:

Nelson's Weather (left-hand) Column:

Victory (100 guns) *Temeraire* (98)
Neptune (98) *Leviathan* (74)
Britannia (100) *Conqueror* (74)
Africa (64) *Agamemnon* (64)
Ajax (74) *Orion* (74)
Minotaur (74) *Spartiate* (74)

Vice-Admiral Collingwood's Leeward Column:

Royal Sovereign (100) *Belleisle* (74)
Mars (74) *Tonnant* (80)
Bellerophon (74) *Colossus* (74)
Achille (74) *Dreadnought* (98)
Polyphemus (64) *Revenge* (74)
Swiftsure (74) *Defiance* (74)
Thunderer (74) *Defence* (74)
Prince (98)

plus four frigates and two smaller boats.

Villeneuve's fleet:

Neptuno (80 guns) *Scipion* (74)
Rayo (100) *Formidable* (80)
Duguay Trouin (74) *San Francisco de Asis* (74)
Mont Blanc (74) *San Agustin* (74)
Héros (74) *Santisima Trinidad* (136)
Bucentaure (80) *Neptune* (84)
San Leandro (64) *Redoutable* (74)
Intrépide (74) *San Justo* (74)
Indomptable (80) *Santa Ana* (112)
Fougueux (74) *Monarca* (74)
Pluton (74) *Algesiras* (74)
Bahama (74) *Aigle* (74)
Swiftsure (74) *Argonaute* (74)
Montanez (74) *Argonauta* (80)

Berwick (74) *Achille* (74)
San Ildefonso (74)
Principe de Asturias (112)
San Juan Nepomuceno (74)
plus five frigates and two smaller boats.

The Fleets Engage

The British perceived Villeneuve's fleet as forming a curved line with them at its centre. This may be simply the effect of viewing a line perhaps 3km (2 miles) long across the curvature of the earth. The sailing was also seen as rather ragged. The battle line appeared to be formed with gaps in places and bunching in others. This is rather like a motorway with too many cars, when you first slow to a stop, then speed up for no apparent reason. The more ships in the line, the harder it was to iron out these glitches. Other sources attribute this phenomenon to Villeneuve's plan to brigade four French and three Spanish ships in five squadrons.

Meanwhile, Nelson's columns bore down on a point ahead of the Franco-Spanish line. Villeneuve's fleet was sailing northwards, so if the British had sailed directly towards the gap they wanted, they would have ended up chasing the enemy line instead of approaching it at right-angles. The unsung hero of the battle was the navigator who judged the speed, direction and distance of the Franco-Spanish fleet, deciding the course that would ensure the execution of Nelson's plan. By 11 a.m., the fleets were just 4.8km (3 miles) from one another and making just 3 knots, roughly 4.8km/h (3mph). The British had every sail set; the French were under easy sail only.

The first broadside came from the French *Fougueux* and was aimed at Vice-Admiral Collingwood's *Royal Sovereign,* leading the lee squadron and ahead of Nelson's section. The two British columns were now on slightly converging courses. Nelson's section was just about on target to hit the *Bucentaure,* with Admiral Villeneuve aboard. Collingwood and the *Royal Sovereign,* however, were heading a bit too far to the north. Instead of forcing a gap through at the twelfth ship, he instead broke through between the *Santa Ana* and the *Fougueux,* seventeenth in the Franco-Spanish line.

The British columns piled into the French line. The downwind French ships tended to bear away to starboard so as to bring their broadside guns to bear and even rake the British ships as they burst through the line. Both sides lost their formation, and the battle became an uncontrollable scrum, exactly as both admirals had predicted. In such circumstances each ship fights its nearest neighbour, and each man has to rely on the friends at his back. Unfortunately for the French, the British sailors had been better trained by their captains, and the captains had been better trained by their admiral. Also, the arrival of successive British ships at more or less the same spot meant the enemy ships in that immediate location were overwhelmed, just as they had been at the Nile.

Undaunted, Collingwood in the *Royal Sovereign* passed to the rear of the *Santa Ana* at 12.10 p.m., raked her savagely with a double-shotted broadside (two cannonballs in each gun) and loosed her starboard broadside at the *Fougueux.* The *Royal Sovereign* then came up alongside the starboard side of the *Santa Ana* and, while trading shots toe to toe, was herself raked from the stern by the *Fougueux* and from the bow by the *San Leandro.* However, these two ships were also hitting the *Santa Ana* and each other, so they moved away to attack other British ships, which started to arrive with an awful inevitability.

As more British ships became involved, vessels from the rear of the Franco-Spanish line also began to arrive at the central mêlée. The *Royal Sovereign* had raced ahead of her column and so

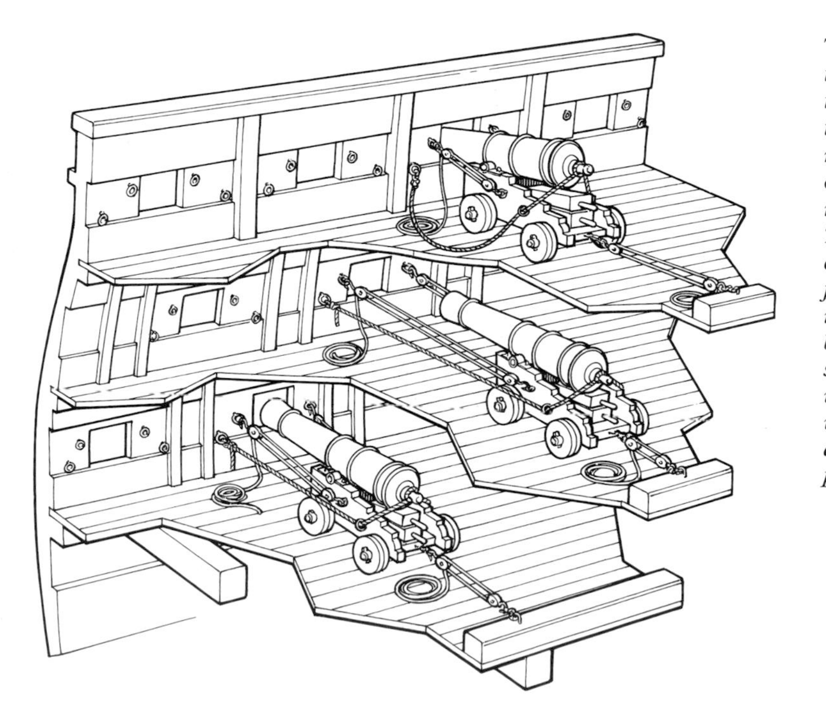

THREE-TIERED GUNDECKS *marked the 'First Rate' capital ships of the Age of Fighting Sail. On the top deck, the loaded cannon is run out on its truck through the open gun port, ready to fire upon the approaching enemy. The middle deck depicts a fired cannon rolling back into ship from the recoil of its shot, where it will be cleaned and reloaded by the gun crew. The lowest deck shows a gun secured for sea worthiness. A 'loose cannon' was more than metaphorically dangerous in a ship rolling and pitching in heavy weather.*

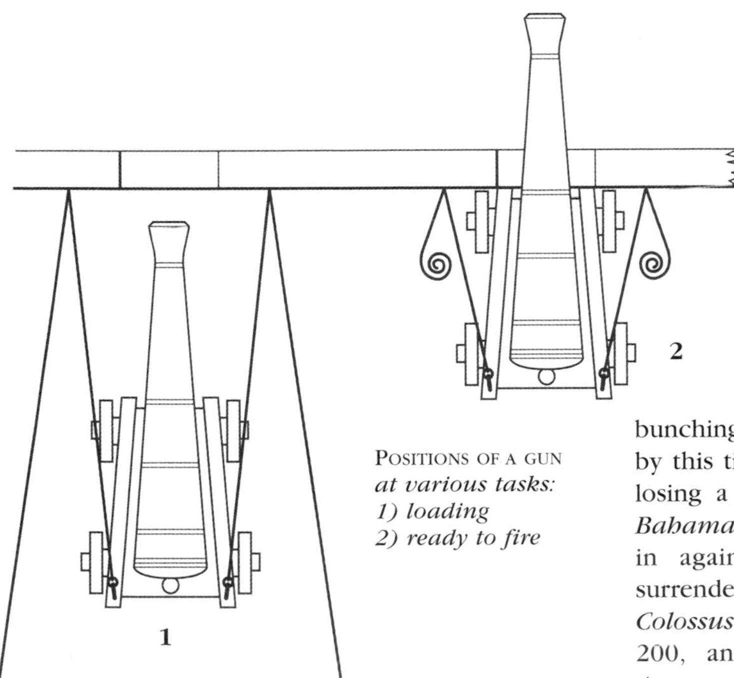

POSITIONS OF A GUN *at various tasks: 1) loading 2) ready to fire*

battled away alone for about 15 minutes before the next in line, *Belleisle,* arrived to take some of the pressure. She poured a broadside into the port quarter of the *Santa Ana,* then slipped around the stern of the *Indomptable* and got involved in a deadly duel with the *Fougueux.* In fact, *Belleisle* became a target for many Franco-Spanish ships as they came up from the rear, and had the dubious honour of ending the battle as the most damaged ship in Nelson's fleet.

Mars was next in line, and in trying to avoid a collision with the *Santa Ana* she exposed her stern to raking fire. *Tonnant,* following, came to her aid and went on to battle against the *Algesiras* and *San Juan Nepomuceno.* The former made several attempts to board but all were repelled; both later surrendered. *Bellerophon* then arrived 30 minutes after the *Royal Sovereign* and fought the *Monarca,* which had previously surrendered to the *Mars*; since the British had not been able to send a party over to take possession, *Monarca* had rejoined the fight. In the increasingly confused scrum, the *Bellerophon*'s rigging became entangled with that of the *Aigle.* She was thus engaged on both sides, lost her main and mizzen topmasts and had her captain killed. *Aigle* drifted astern and brought a raking fire to bear on *Bellerophon* until the *Revenge* appeared out of the smoke to rake the *Aigle* in turn. *Monarca* surrendered to *Bellerophon* shortly after.

Colossus, having followed the others in her column, joined the fray around 1 p.m. and found herself pitched against two ships from the rear of the Franco-Spanish line, *Bahama* and *Swiftsure.* The bunching had brought the line to three ranks deep by this time. *Colossus* blasted both ships despite losing a large part of her rigging. The Spanish *Bahama* surrendered and the British *Orion* joined in against the *Swiftsure,* which also then surrendered. If *Belleisle* suffered most damage, *Colossus* suffered most British casualties, around 200, and later had to be towed by the *Agamemnon.* Instead of following their leader directly into the same spot in the line, several of Collingwood's column moved to attack directly the rearward ships of the enemy's line in order to defeat several parts of it simultaneously. Within about two hours, the rear of the Franco-Spanish line was beaten.

Nelson Felled

In steadily fading wind, Nelson in *Victory* did not arrive at the Franco-Spanish line until a full 40 minutes after Collingwood. *Victory* had kept her studding sails flying right up to the last minute, squeezing every ounce of speed she could and taking fire from the enemy ships as she came on. The fire became increasingly accurate as she got closer, and her mizzen topmast and wheel were both shot away.

However, as soon as she passed between the *Bucentaure* and *Redoutable*, she returned the compliment, double- and triple-shotted guns tearing open the stern of the French flagship. The ships were so close, the *Victory*'s rigging touched that of the French ship as she passed. She fired her starboard guns into *Redoutable*'s bow, then ran alongside her starboard side. While her gun batteries continued to fire upon both ships,

Battle of Trafalgar

21 October 1805

Battles are won and lost by people not machines. Nelson made sure that all his commanders knew what the plan would be: two columns and sail straight into the middle. When he finally found the combined fleet at sea, there was no hesitation. His sailors and officers knew their work well. The columns were formed and maximum sail hoisted to minimize the number of broadsides they would have to suffer. When they were upon the enemy, surplus sails were cut away to save time and the captains directed their ships to the most opportune enemy target. Villeneuve had no answer other than to rely on the bravery of his officers and crews in what proved to be a bloody and protracted exchange of fire.

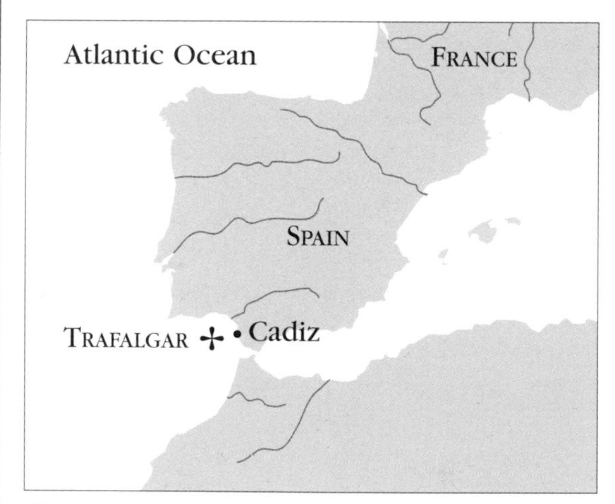

Most naval battles have been fought within 80km (50 miles) of the coast. Usually, one side does not want to fight and gets caught trying to do something else, just as at Trafalgar. Villeneuve's desire to gather up even more line-of-battle ships to lift the blockade at Brest allowed him to get caught by the aggressive British fleet.

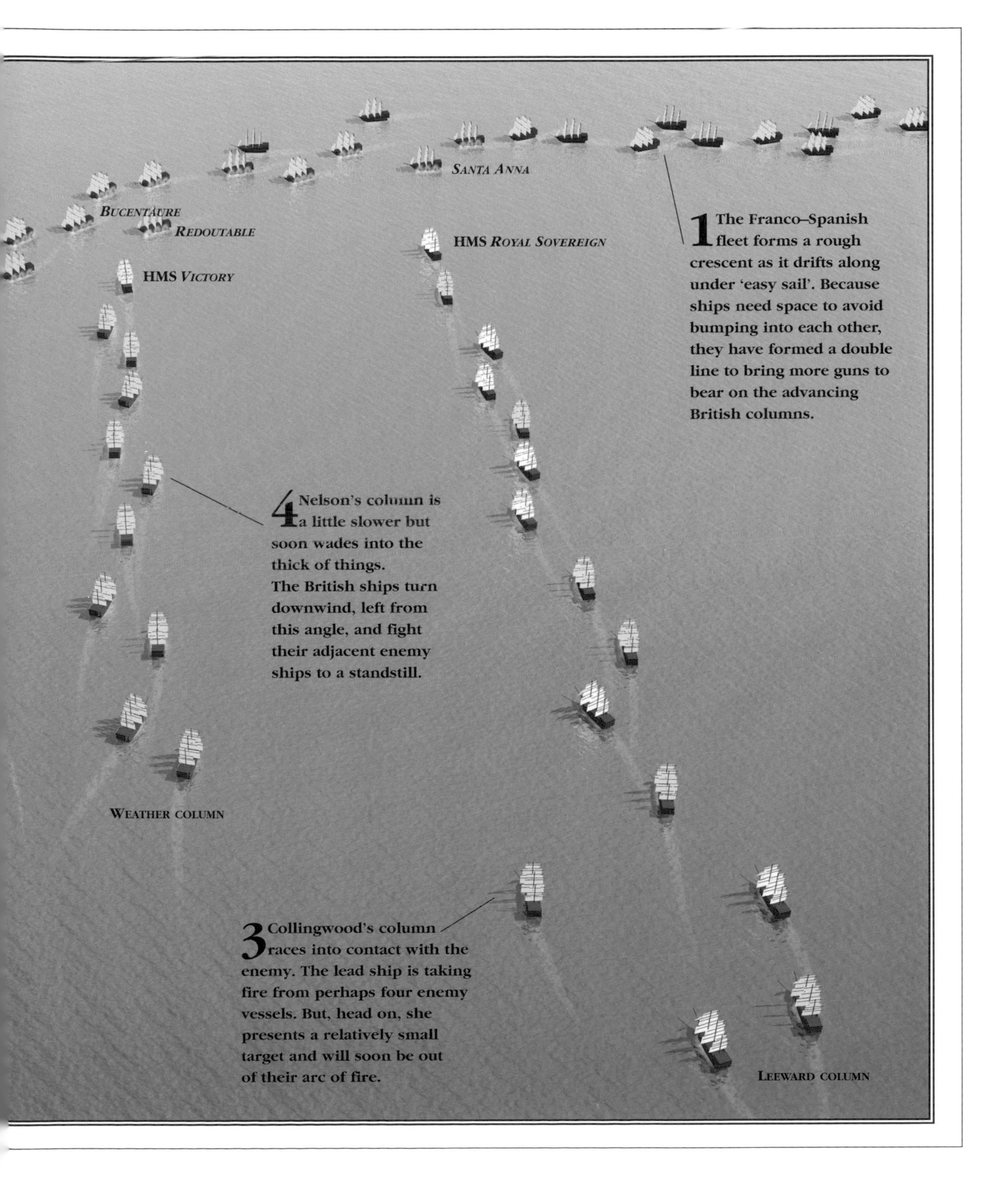
SANTA ANNA
BUCENTAURE
REDOUTABLE
HMS ROYAL SOVEREIGN
HMS VICTORY
1 The Franco–Spanish fleet forms a rough crescent as it drifts along under 'easy sail'. Because ships need space to avoid bumping into each other, they have formed a double line to bring more guns to bear on the advancing British columns.
4 Nelson's column is a little slower but soon wades into the thick of things. The British ships turn downwind, left from this angle, and fight their adjacent enemy ships to a standstill.
WEATHER COLUMN
3 Collingwood's column races into contact with the enemy. The lead ship is taking fire from perhaps four enemy vessels. But, head on, she presents a relatively small target and will soon be out of their arc of fire.
LEEWARD COLUMN

BRITISH 32-PDR. *The gun has been loaded and run out, and the gunner is aiming it. The crew, starting clockwise from the far right: powder monkey with bagged charge; runner-out holding rope; rammer; gunner; layer; loader with cannon ball; and sponger. The gunner will leap aside at the last moment and pull a lanyard to trigger the flintlock firing mechanism.*

Victory's exposed gun deck came under fire from the marksmen in the fighting tops of the *Redoutable*. It was from there that Nelson was shot around 1.25 p.m., along with many of those on the upper deck. *Victory* only just managed to save herself from being boarded by sailors and marines coming up from below.

Victory was followed by *Temeraire,* which was badly raked by the *Neptune* firing from an improvised second line. This left *Temeraire* drifting and out of control. Her gun crews kept firing as targets presented themselves, and she thus contributed her weight of shot against the *Redoutable* to her right and the *Neptune,* then on her port bow. About 1.40 p.m. the *Redoutable* drifted into *Temeraire* and was tied on by the British crew with no way of answering her fire. *Reboutable* was boarded and captured. The *Temeraire* then perceived the French *Fougueux* coming at her through the smoke and unleashed her starboard broadside at close range. The already damaged French ship collided with *Temeraire*'s starboard bow. The *Temeraire*'s crew lashed the *Fougueux*'s fallen mizzen mast to their own ship and used it as a gang plank to board and capture her, too.

Neptune came up next and laid herself alongside the towering *Santisima Trinidad,* her 98 guns on three decks pitted against the Spanish giant's 136 guns on four. They may have seemed impossible odds, but the British were undaunted, and *Santisima Trinidad,* too, was forced to surrender. *Neptune*'s course had taken her past the *Bucentaure,* into which she delivered a broadside, as did the *Leviathan* and *Conqueror.* Inside, the French flagship must have been like a vision of hell. She surrendered, and a marine captain was sent to take charge of her. He also took charge of the French commander-in-chief, Villeneuve, who was completely unharmed, delivering him to the *Mars.*

Despite the damage received on both sides, the Franco-Spanish force clearly had more ships. If these fresh forces could be committed to the fray, the British would find themselves severely pressed. Villeneuve had issued orders before he surrendered that these ships should turn and support the centre. Yet there was so little wind, they had to use their boats to turn their bows in the right direction, and they moved but slowly towards the centre.

Five ships came out of the Franco-Spanish line towards the west to take Nelson's flotilla in the flank. By the time their action was noticed, *Agamemnon* and *Ajax* were about to enter the main scrum in the centre. Nevertheless, they both fired broadsides at the approaching foe. The last two ships in Nelson's section were the *Minotaur* and *Spartiate*. They turned towards the wind and crossed the tee of the advancing line, raking the bow of *Formidable*, flagship of Rear-Admiral Pierre Dumanoir le Pelley (1770–1829). They then took up position between Dumanoir's ships and where the main centre of the battle had been and where so many badly damaged British ships lay. It seems Dumanoir intended to aid the rear of the original line and sailed on. Then, seeing that Collingwood had been able to order six British ships to form a rough line of battle to meet him, and that Vice-Admiral Federico Gravina (1756–1806) of the rearmost Franco-Spanish squadron had already quit the battle, Dumanoir sailed on towards Gibraltar but then turned again and later headed for Rochefort. Gravina made it into the safety of Cadiz with 10 ships.

The close of the battle of Trafalgar was marked by the explosion of the French ship *Achille*. She had been closely engaged with the *Prince* when her foretop caught fire. The next broadside brought the main mast down, and the fire became widespread. From then on, the explosion was inevitable. *Prince* tried to get clear and launched her boats to rescue the French sailors, despite the guns being fired by the immense heat of the fire. The explosion occurred around 5.45 p.m. and just 100 of the *Achille*'s 500 crew were saved.

Both commanders were right in their prediction of the end result. The British captured or destroyed no less than 18 of Napoleon's battleships - Nelson had hoped for 20. The victory did not come cheap. The leading British ships had suffered badly; many were dismasted and had to be towed back to base. Nelson's weather column suffered 571 casualties, Collingwood's lee column 1120 and the Franco-Spanish allies somewhere in excess of 6000. The precise figure was never recorded. Spain lost 8 of its 30 battleships, France 13 of its 70, Britain none at all. The repercussions for Spain were long-lasting and prevented the country from suppressing independence movements in its South American colonies. France was less damaged. It retained sufficient naval potential to force the British to maintain an expensive blockade of its remaining squadrons and restrict the Royal Navy's ability to hunt down and eliminate frigate squadrons and privateers that

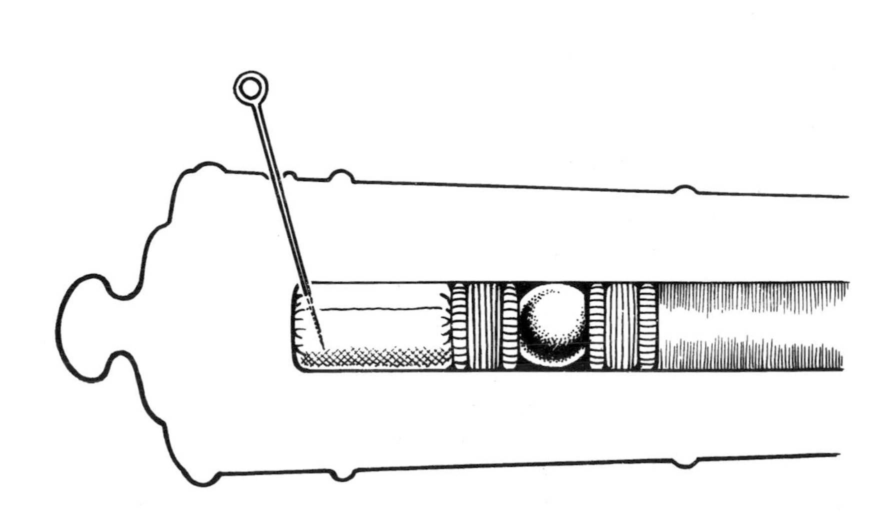

THE INTERNAL BORE *of a smooth-bore gun. Here, a round-shot cannon ball is packed with a wad either side. The pricker pierces the bag of gunpowder, is then withdrawn and replaced with a quill of finer powder. To fire the cannon, the gunner ignites the powder in the quill with his lighted linstock. The fire follows the fine powder down the touch hole to the bagged charge, which then explodes. A portion of the explosion carries back up the touch hole, making a spectacular jet of flame more than a foot high from the top of the cannon.*

preyed on international trade. Also, British workmen in British-owned yards at home and abroad were kept busy for months repairing the battle-damaged ships that eventually limped back to port.

Analysis

The success of Nelson's strategy begs the question: was there any answer to British columns cutting the French line? Certainly, cutting the line effectively prevented those ships downwind of the 'cut' from quickly returning to join in the fray. Yet, on land, the British infantry line habitually defeated the French column. At sea, guns from the line were unable to fire on the nearest enemy vessel after it got too close to the gap necessary for safe sailing of the ships in line. For the line to be able to beat the column at sea, ships adjacent to the 'cut' needed to be able to bring their guns to bear just as the British vessels reached the line. Without major design changes to the ships, enabling the guns to point more to the fore or aft, this required the Franco-Spanish vessels to break formation and sail parallel to the British ships. To a degree, some did exactly this. The *Fougueux* did in the first moments of the battle, raking the *Royal Sovereign* as she went alongside the *Santa Ana.* In the moments in which such tactics were used, the battle became a more evenly matched scrum. But as more and more British ships arrived, their numbers counted and the Franco-Spanish ships were swamped.

An alternative tactic would have been for Villeneuve to employ a twin-column formation, with the second line forming a chequerboard pattern with the first. The second line could then

MAIN NAVAL BASES *in the Napoleonic Wars. Napoleon controlled more than 20 naval bases and more battleships than Britain. However, this numerical strength was also a weakness, since he was unable to unite his dispersed fleet to defeat the superior Royal Navy.*

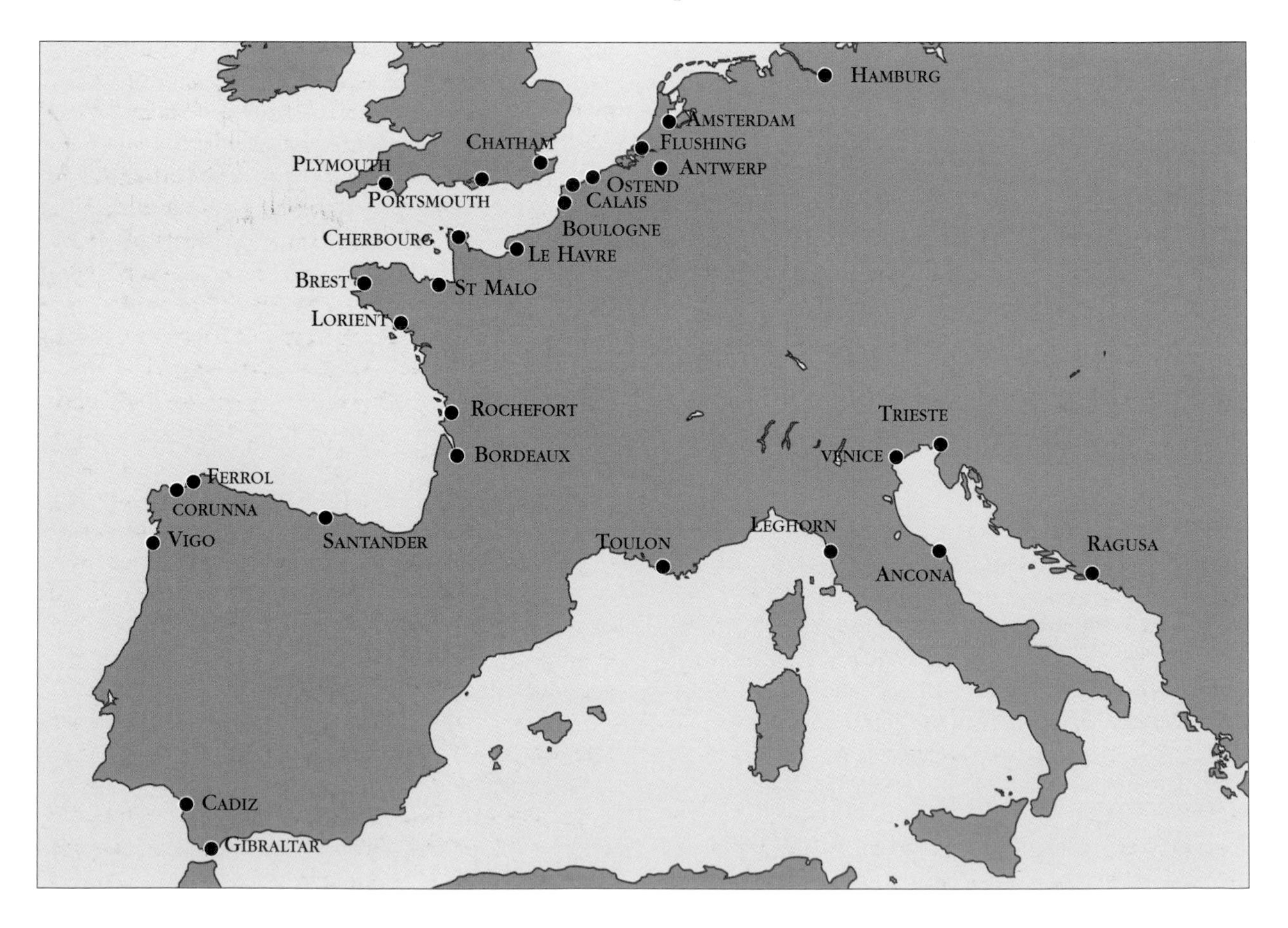

NELSON IS SHOT! *Gunpowder creates vast clouds of grey smoke, which would have obscured much of this scene. The ship's boats, centre top, were launched to reduce splinters and already the* Victory *had suffered much damage as well as many lower-ranked and unremarked casualties.*

rake the British ships as they raked the Franco-Spanish first line. The bunching at the tail end of the Franco-Spanish line at Trafalgar had this effect, but it made no difference. Nelson's plan wrested the initiative - he chose where to attack and concentrated a large portion of his fleet at a much smaller portion of the enemy's in a relatively short period of time.

He also had the supreme advantage of having at his disposal a better-trained and much more experienced force. Unfortunately for the French, Villeneuve, despite executing Napoleon's plan to concentrate his ships, was just not up to finding the solution to a problem he had clearly recognized. Neither of the strategies outlined above was ever really tested. Trafalgar was the last major battle of the age of square-rigged sailing ships.

Farther Afield

That is not to say that there were no smaller engagements that offered valuable lessons to the all-conquering Royal Navy. France and its allies still had lots of ships, and the Royal Navy was keen to flex its dominant strength. Napoleon, however, had affairs ashore to preoccupy him, and so grand naval projects slipped onto his backburner. While the major British squadrons maintained a substantial and watchful presence outside those bases where the imperial fleets bided their time, frigate captains sought prey of their own size.

It was a long-established custom of naval warfare that small armed ships would obtain 'letters of marque'. These gave them the legal right to attack enemy vessels and take what goods or ships they could as their reward; without these letters, their actions were considered piracy. The captains of such ships would cruise a chosen trade route until their holds were full or their crew lists were empty through illness or through the need to provide men to sail captured ships home. Trade having become global, these privateers sailed the world in pursuit of booty.

Britain, being the greatest global trader, suffered much from their depredations and, having bent her naval energies to line of battle ships to defeat those of France, did not have enough of the smaller ships required to counter privateers everywhere. However, expeditions were mounted with the resources available, with the aim of lancing the boil of French overseas bases.

The trade route to India - south around Africa and northeast across the vast Indian Ocean - was well known and of great importance. Conveniently astride this route lay the Dutch colony of South Africa, and further on Mauritius and the island of Réunion. Inconveniently, Holland was now part of Napoleon's European empire, and Mauritius was held by the French and harboured a very active privateer squadron. British troops were landed at Cape Town and that colony captured with a mere show of force. A more active plan was devised to take over Mauritius and the island of Réunion. In a nineteenth-century-style combined operation, the British would deliver a force of infantry - British state troops plus British and Indian troops of the Honourable East India Company (HEIC) - to capture and garrison shore bases, whilst naval elements dealt with enemy ships and provided support. However, this was not a new scheme - the British and other European powers had been doing it for over 200 years.

By mid-1810 the French had three frigates in the area - *Bellone* (40 guns), *Minerve* (40) and *Victor* (22). On 3 July, they attacked three 813-tonne (800-ton) ships of the HEIC. These were among the biggest merchantmen of the time, with some built larger, up to 1422 tonnes (1400 tons). In addition, their construction was stronger than that of naval frigates, with iron instead of oak knees and fittings. More than half the HEIC fleet was rated at 1422 tonnes (1400 tons), and increasing numbers of their ships were built in Bombay using teak, which was better than oak in tropical waters - besides HMS *Victory*, the oldest serving ship of the period was an Indian-built frigate.

Although larger than a conventional frigate as a vessel, an Indiaman's armament was slightly lighter. An 813-tonne (800-ton) Indiaman would expect to carry 32 18-pounder cannon. This was quite a respectable armament, except that the vessel did not have the crew numbers or space to operate as a true warship because of the cargo she carried, which was her real *raison d'être*. The French squadron captured two of these East Indiamen, the *Ceylon* and the *Windham*. The third made good her escape under cover of darkness.

Yet rescue was already in hand. Even before the vessels' capture a fleet was assembling at the island of Rodriguez, 720km (450 miles) east of Mauritius. The frigates *Boadicea* (38 guns) and *Nereide* (36) were to escort transports, bringing 3650 British and Indian troops. They sailed the same day as the three ships were captured - a fortuitous coincidence. Three days later the flotilla

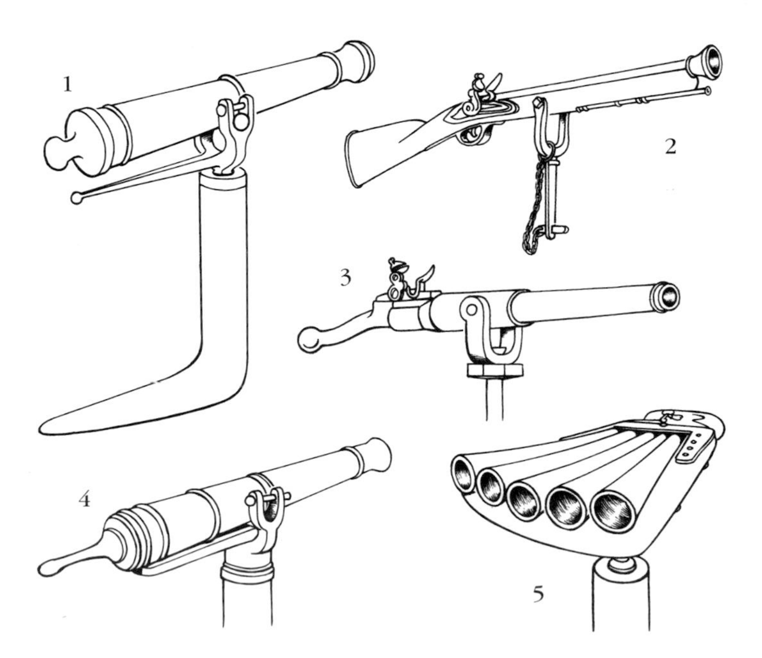

TYPES OF LIGHT GUNS. *Defence against boarding was a serious matter. Crews would mass behind their bulwarks and leap across the moment ships came alongside. These small guns were intended to wreak havoc on an attacking crew. They were mounted on top of the bulwarks and were often loaded with small shot - pellets like those used in shotguns.*

1 FRENCH 1786 PATTERN SWIVEL GUN
2 ENGLISH MUSKETOON
3 *ESPINGOLE*
4 BRONZE SWIVEL GUN
5 ORGUE MULTI-BARRELLED GUN

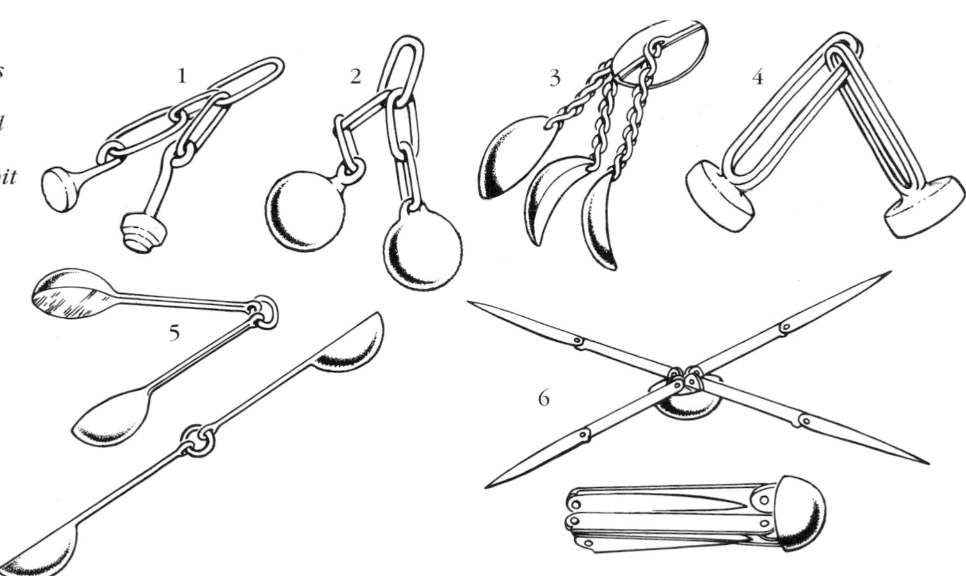

TYPES OF NAVAL SHOT. *Sailing ships use miles and miles of rope to hold the masts up and control the sails. These would be difficult to hit with a simple round ball. These devices increased the chances of a hit that could damage rigging, slowing the ship, and even bring down a mast.*

1 LINK SHOT
2 CHAIN SHOT
3 & 4 LINKED BAR SHOT
5 EXPANDING SHOT
6 KNIFE-BLADED SHOT

rendezvoused with more warships: *Sirius* (36 guns), *Iphigenia* (36), and *Magicienne* (36). The troops were landed at different points around Réunion, and the isand was captured with minimum loss of life. The bulk of the squadron moved on to harass the Ile de Passe to the southeast of Réunion, opposite Grand Port. This, it was planned, would form a secure base of operations against the rest of the adjacent island. It was duly captured after some resistance and the squadron dispersed to continue their harassing attacks, leaving just the *Nereide*, under Captain (later Rear-Admiral) Nesbit Willoughby (1777–1849), at Ile de Passe on 14 August.

The Battle of Réunion: 1810

Just six days later, on 20 August, the French squadron returned with its two East Indiamen prizes, heading for the anchorage off Grand Port; it was a flotilla of five frigate-sized ships. Captain Willoughby of the *Nereide*, the senior British officer and an old India hand, used a *ruse de guerre* to induce the French into the anchorage, where he attacked the leading ship, which also happened to be the smallest – the 22-gun *Victor.* She surrendered almost immediately and anchored nearby. *Victor* was followed in by the *Minerve,* which ordered the *Victor* to rejoin, which she did. *Nereide* and the fort on Ile de Passe – now under British control – traded shots with the *Minerve*, *Ceylon* and *Victor*, with the *Minerve* concentrating on the fort, causing an explosion and damaging the some of the guns. Some of the *Nereide*'s crew were ashore and had a narrow escape. They were rowing back to their ship and were nearly cut off by the advancing French. Fortuitously they were ignored and got back safely. In due course, the *Bellone* also sailed into the bay and anchored. The *Windham,* meanwhile, headed off to the west.

Willoughby was now in a very weak position. He held the island and he had his ship. The French had four ships, albeit with reduced crews, and the better anchorage. Willoughby sent a lieutenant off in a 7m (24ft) single-masted launch to bring news of the French arrival to the rest of his squadron. The frigates *Sirius* and *Iphigenia* and the brig *Staunch* were off Port Louis, the capital, on the other side of the island. Here, they had blockaded several privateering French ships in the harbour. Undaunted, Willoughby had the mortars on the island test the range against the French ships at anchor. Although it was too far, the French moved just in case. He also demanded the return of the *Victor,* which had surrendered earlier.

The *Windham*, meanwhile, was having no luck. Sent off to the west with a crew of 30 to warn the French in Port Louis, she was spotted by

Battle of Réunion

1810

One of the downsides to repeated success is overconfidence. After nearly 16 years of continuous victory, the captains of the Royal Navy seemed to expect to win whatever the odds and whatever the circumstances. Simply going headlong at the enemy was presumed to be enough to ensure victory. The British officer in command at Réunion failed to note the route taken by the returning French ships and failed to order the depth checked as his flotilla sailed in to battle. As his leading ships grounded, he was deprived of the opportunity to manoeuvre and thereby to concentrate against a capable foe. The crews pounded away at the enemy as best they could but no amount of hard work at the guns could mitigate their senior officer's mistakes.

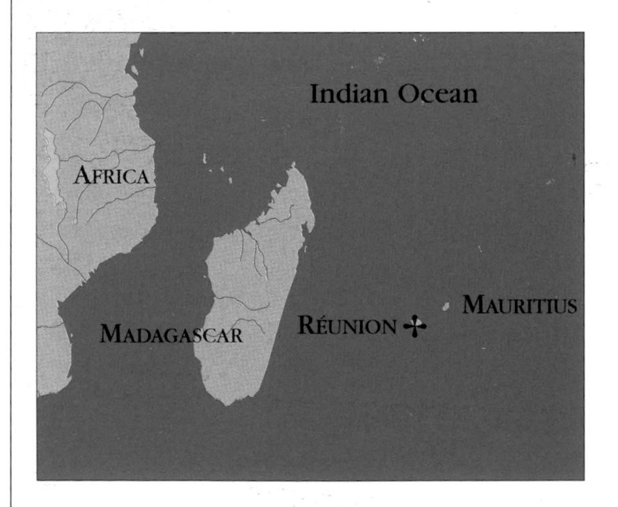

War is an expensive business and Britain needed trade to provide much of the required funds. The French naval threat in the Indian Ocean had to be met by the Royal Navy to safeguard merchant shipping from India and the Far East.

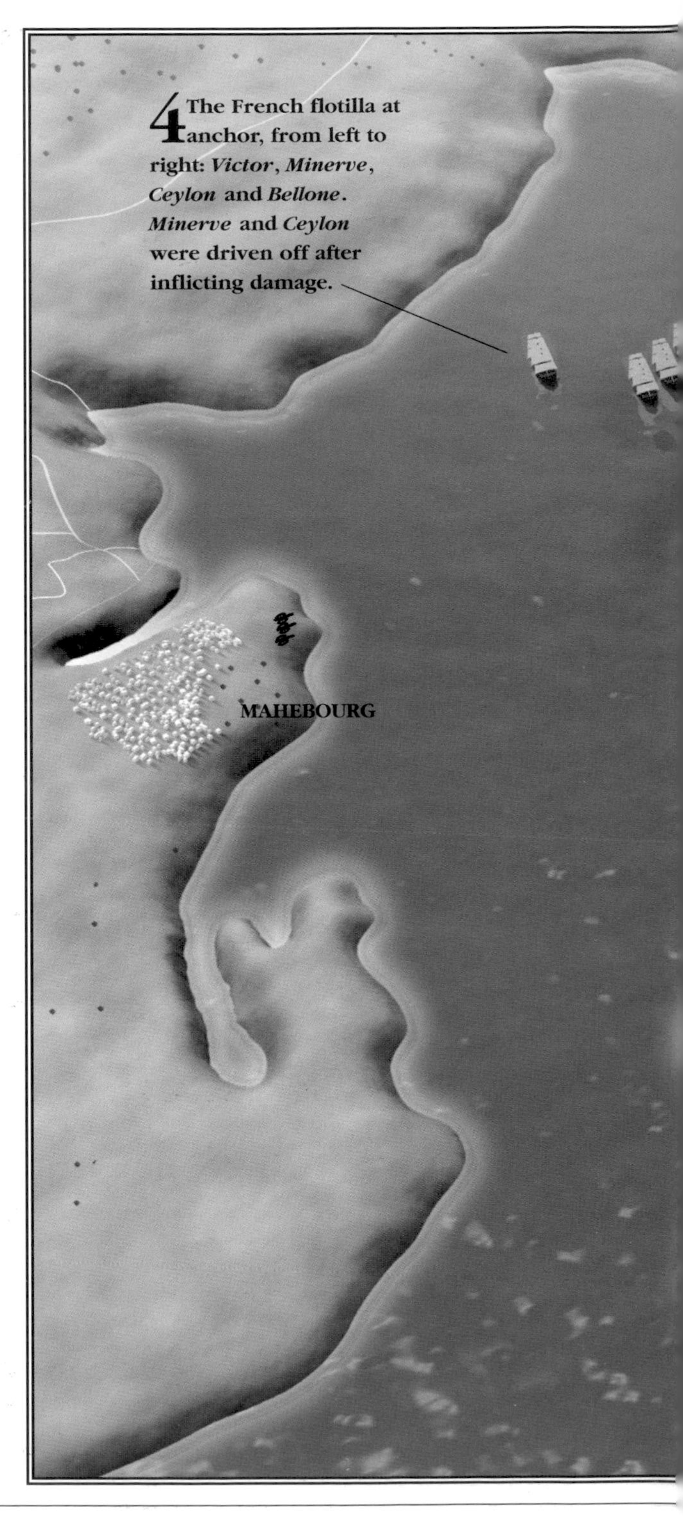

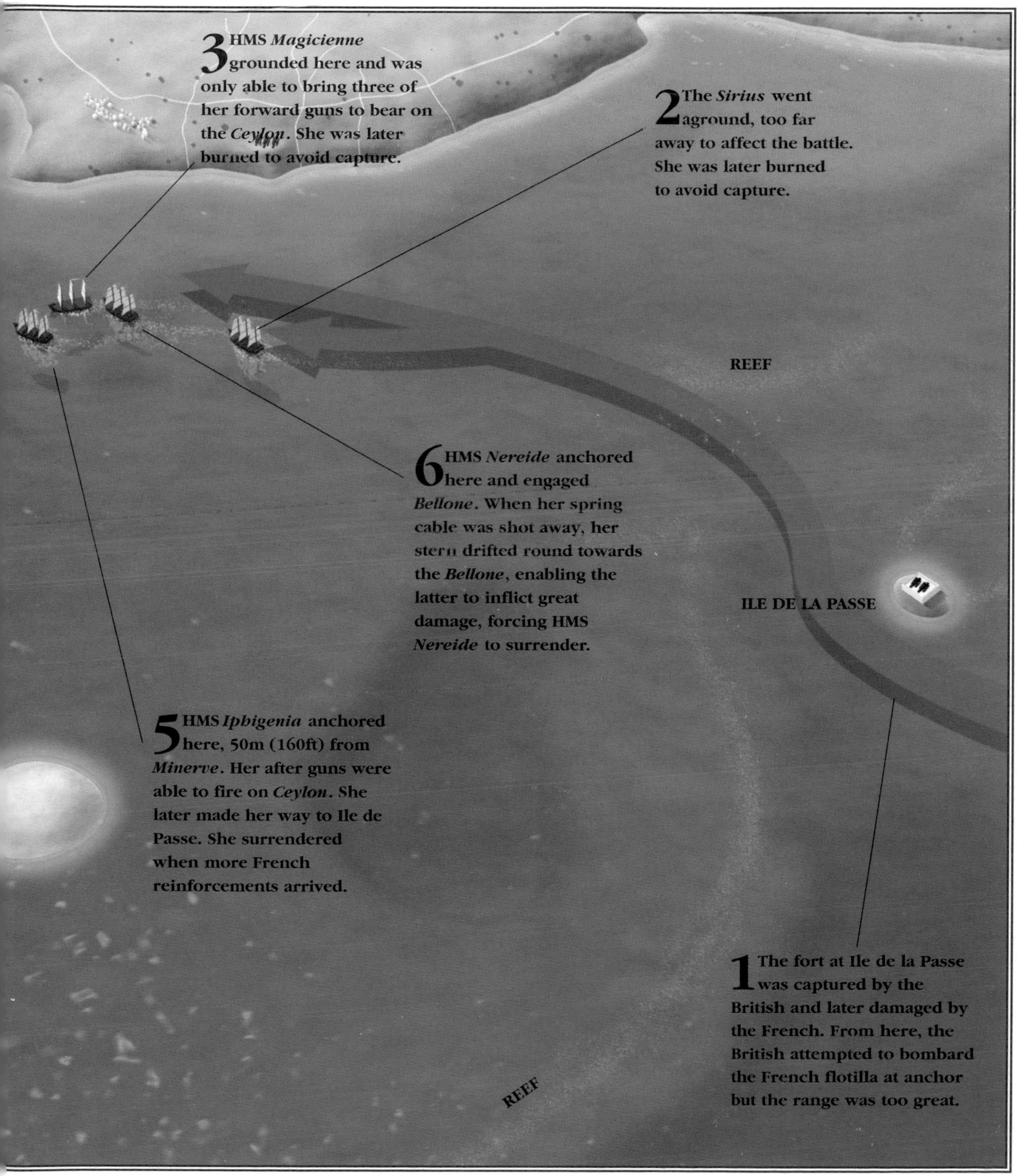

1 The fort at Ile de la Passe was captured by the British and later damaged by the French. From here, the British attempted to bombard the French flotilla at anchor but the range was too great.

2 The *Sirius* went aground, too far away to affect the battle. She was later burned to avoid capture.

3 HMS *Magicienne* grounded here and was only able to bring three of her forward guns to bear on the *Ceylon*. She was later burned to avoid capture.

5 HMS *Iphigenia* anchored here, 50m (160ft) from *Minerve*. Her after guns were able to fire on *Ceylon*. She later made her way to Ile de Passe. She surrendered when more French reinforcements arrived.

6 HMS *Nereide* anchored here and engaged *Bellone*. When her spring cable was shot away, her stern drifted round towards the *Bellone*, enabling the latter to inflict great damage, forcing HMS *Nereide* to surrender.

REEF

ILE DE LA PASSE

REEF

the frigate *Sirius* and would have been chased. However, the wind died completely and she was eventually captured by 10 men in two small rowing boats who had forgotten to take any weapons with them. The captain of the *Sirius* thus discovered the events that had taken place at Ile de Passe and dispatched the now thrice-owned *Windham* to Port Louis to rouse the rest of the squadron. The *Sirius* proceeded direct to Ile de Passe by the southerly route, arriving on 22 August. Willoughby was all for an immediate attack and they sallied forth together. Regrettably the *Sirius* grounded on a shoal adjacent to the south of the channel but was off by the following morning.

The *Iphigenia* and *Magicienne* arrived shortly after 2 p.m., also anchoring in the channel. Around 4.30 p.m., all four ships hauled their anchors and sailed into the anchorage, planning to drop anchor between the enemy ships and blast them into submission, in much the same way as Nelson had the French at the Nile. The order of sail was *Nereide*, *Sirius*, *Magicienne* and *Iphigenia*. *Nereide* managed to sail in and anchor by the *Bellone* and began to bombard her. *Sirius* sailed onto another rock before she got into range. The *Magicienne* ran aground and only three of her guns could bear.

Iphigenia, though, managed to keep to the plan and anchored to fire upon the *Minerve* at about 50m (55 yards) range. At 6.15 p.m., the *Ceylon*, taking fire from the bow chasers of the *Magicienne* and the after guns of the *Iphigenia*, struck her tricolour and sailed herself ashore. At 6.30 p.m., the *Minerve*'s anchor hawse was shot away, and she too sailed to run aground. Either the *Ceylon* or the *Minerve* got entangled with the *Bellone*, forcing her also to cut her cable and run aground.

The *Bellone*, however, could still deliver a full broadside. At around 7 p.m. the *Nereide*'s spring cable was shot away and her stern swung round to take the full effect of *Bellone*'s guns. Her guns silenced and with a 'terrible carnage on board', *Nereide* struck her colours around 1.30 the following morning. She was next visited by a boat

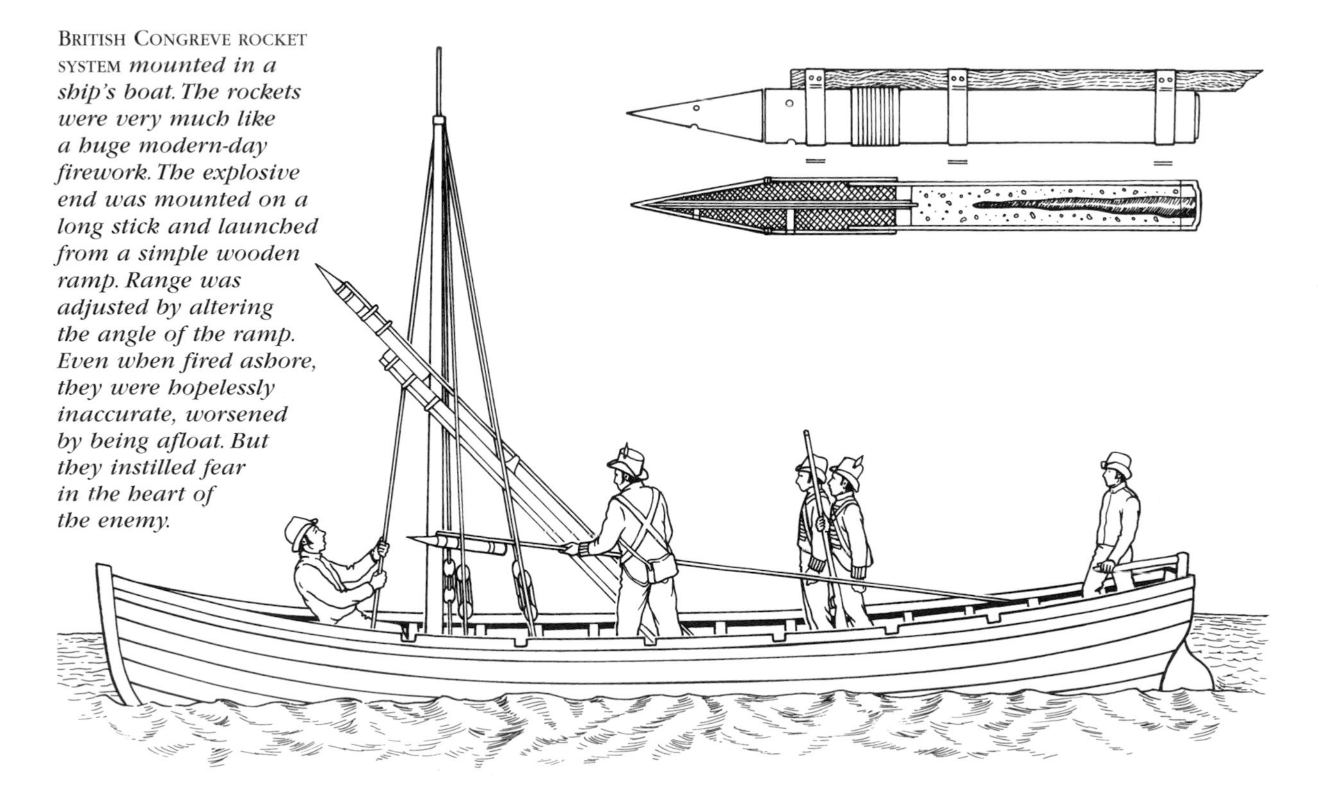

BRITISH CONGREVE ROCKET SYSTEM *mounted in a ship's boat. The rockets were very much like a huge modern-day firework. The explosive end was mounted on a long stick and launched from a simple wooden ramp. Range was adjusted by altering the angle of the ramp. Even when fired ashore, they were hopelessly inaccurate, worsened by being afloat. But they instilled fear in the heart of the enemy.*

from the commodore's ship, *Sirius,* aground and out of range, asking why she had ceased firing.

The *Magicienne* was set on fire to prevent capture, and the crew abandoned her around 5 a.m.; she blew up at 11.30 a.m. At 9 a.m., the *Sirius* was set on fire by her own crew and abandoned. The *Iphigenia* managed to extricate herself by dropping anchors at a distance from the ship using her boats, then hauling on the cables to warp herself over to the Ile de Passe. However, her troubles were not over. Three more 40-gun frigates, *Vénus*, *Astrée* and *Manche* arrived outside the reef from Port Louis. Faced with such odds, the *Iphigenia*'s commander, Captain Henry Lambert, had no real alternative. He negotiated the best deal he could, which was that the officers and crew should be returned to the Cape or to England and should not serve again until exchanged for French prisoners of war. Unfortunately, this never came to fruition, and they had to wait for a year incarcerated on the island until a further force was sent the following year.

'Our great inferiority in naval strength, does not permit us to meet them on this ground without hazarding the precious gem of our national glory. We have, however, the means of creating a powerful diversion, and of turning the scale of annoyance against the enemy.'

– William Jones, US Secretary of the Navy

The American Factor

Despite the Franco-Spanish disaster at Trafalgar, there was still plenty of fight in Napoleon's European empire. He had to reaffirm the superiority of French arms over Austria and Prussia, and finally in 1812 he marched the *Grande Armée* into Russia. While this army was marching to a frosty fate, other French and Italian troops were battling against Spanish guerrillas and a tricky Anglo-Portuguese army. Against this backdrop of grand schemes, a flea jumped on the bandwagon. Just 30 years old, the group of Great Britain's tiny former colonies now known as the United States of America had set itself of a course of expansion with minimum pretext. The United States attacked and conquered additional territory from the southern Native Americans and amongst the Spanish colonies of Florida and Miami. It negotiated the purchase of New Orleans from France and turned its avaricious gaze northwards to Canada. True, here there was some provocation. Britain had been mounting an effective blockade of Continental Europe, with whom the United States wanted to trade. Also, US merchantmen had been stopped and searched by the Royal Navy, looking for seamen deserters. A small but grand plan was devised. Super-strong frigates would be built to a standard normally reserved for line of battle ships. These would challenge such ships as could be isolated from the British fleet. Two armies would also be assembled on the border with Canada.

Matters went badly from the start. Militia units failed to turn up, and in the end only one of the two armies advanced. Meanwhile, the land campaign proceeded with forces of less than a division per side, with the more numerous Americans being repulsed. Large parts of the US-Canadian border passed through the Great Lakes area, and here the action was transferred to the water. The forces involved consisted of small ships carrying small guns. At the beginning of hostilities, the British had the 'Provincial Navy', consisting of just two small armed ships, the *Royal George* and the *Earl of Moira*, plus two schooners on Lake Ontario and a ship, a brig, a schooner and an armed merchantman on Lake Erie. The United States was even less well equipped, boasting the brig *Oneida* and an army transport brig that was captured and burnt in October 1812.

President James Madison (1751–1836) ordered the US Navy to build squadrons on both lakes to

Battle of Lake Erie

10 September 1813

On 10 September, the British under Commodore Robert Heriot Barclay and the Americans under Perry met in battle near Put-in-Bay, Ohio. The British squadron consisted of six ships with 63 cannons, while the American flotilla comprised nine vessels and 54 guns. The British were armed mostly with long guns, the traditional naval weapon, which could throw a cannonball approximately 1.6km (1 mile). The American ships were armed primarily with carronades. Perry's flagship *Lawrence* engaged her counterpart, while *Niagara* did not initially close with the enemy. After the *Lawrence* was completely disabled, Perry transferred by boat to the undamaged *Niagara*, sailed her into close action, broke the British battle line and forced Barclay to surrender. Later, Commodore Perry wrote his famous report to General William Henry Harrison: 'We have met the enemy and they are ours: two ships, two brigs, one schooner, and one sloop.'

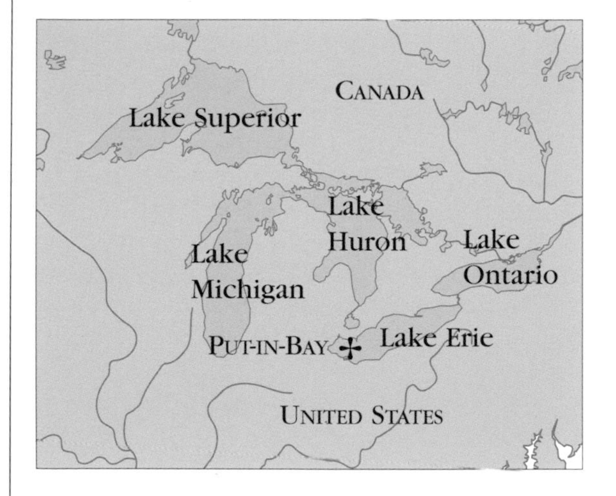

The Great Lakes and the St Lawrence River formed both the extent of the populated border between Canada and the United States of America as well as the principal means of communication for both sides in that area. Their control was vital for the successful defence and attack ambitions of both sides.

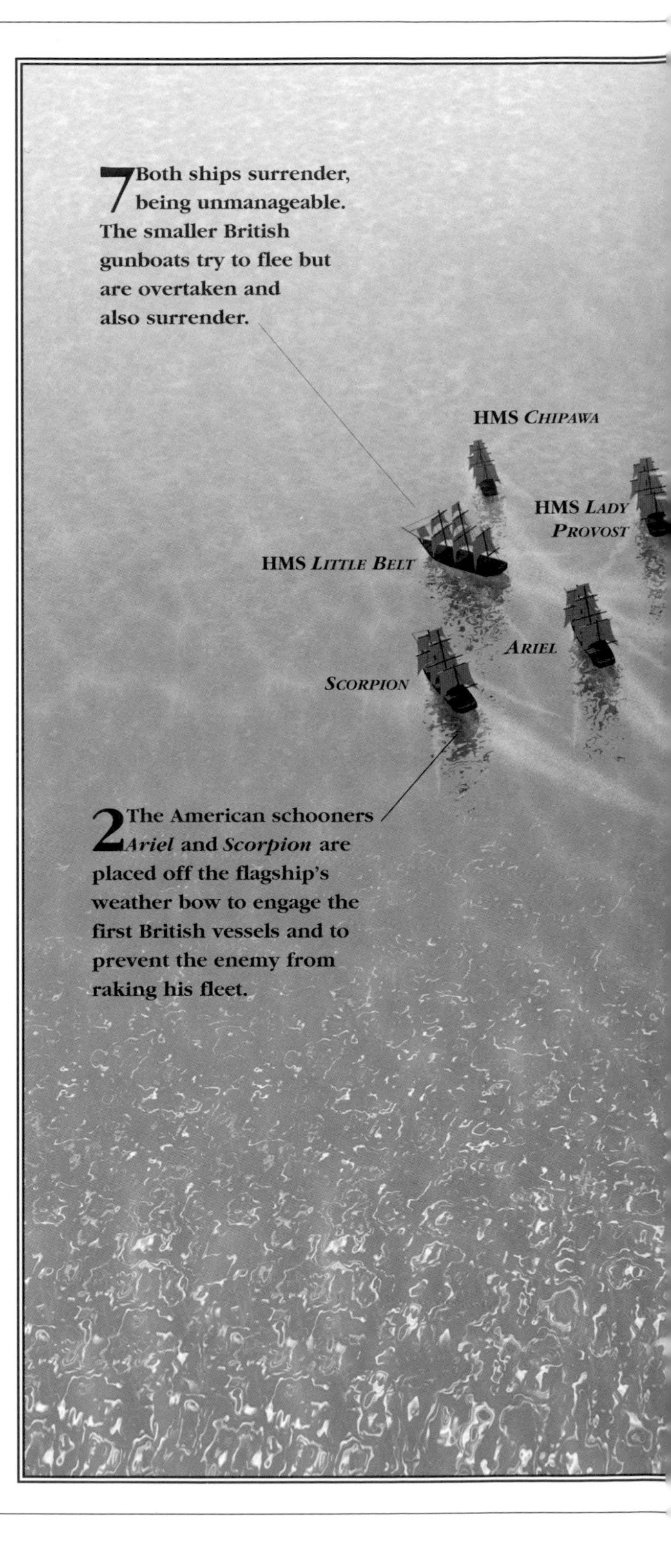

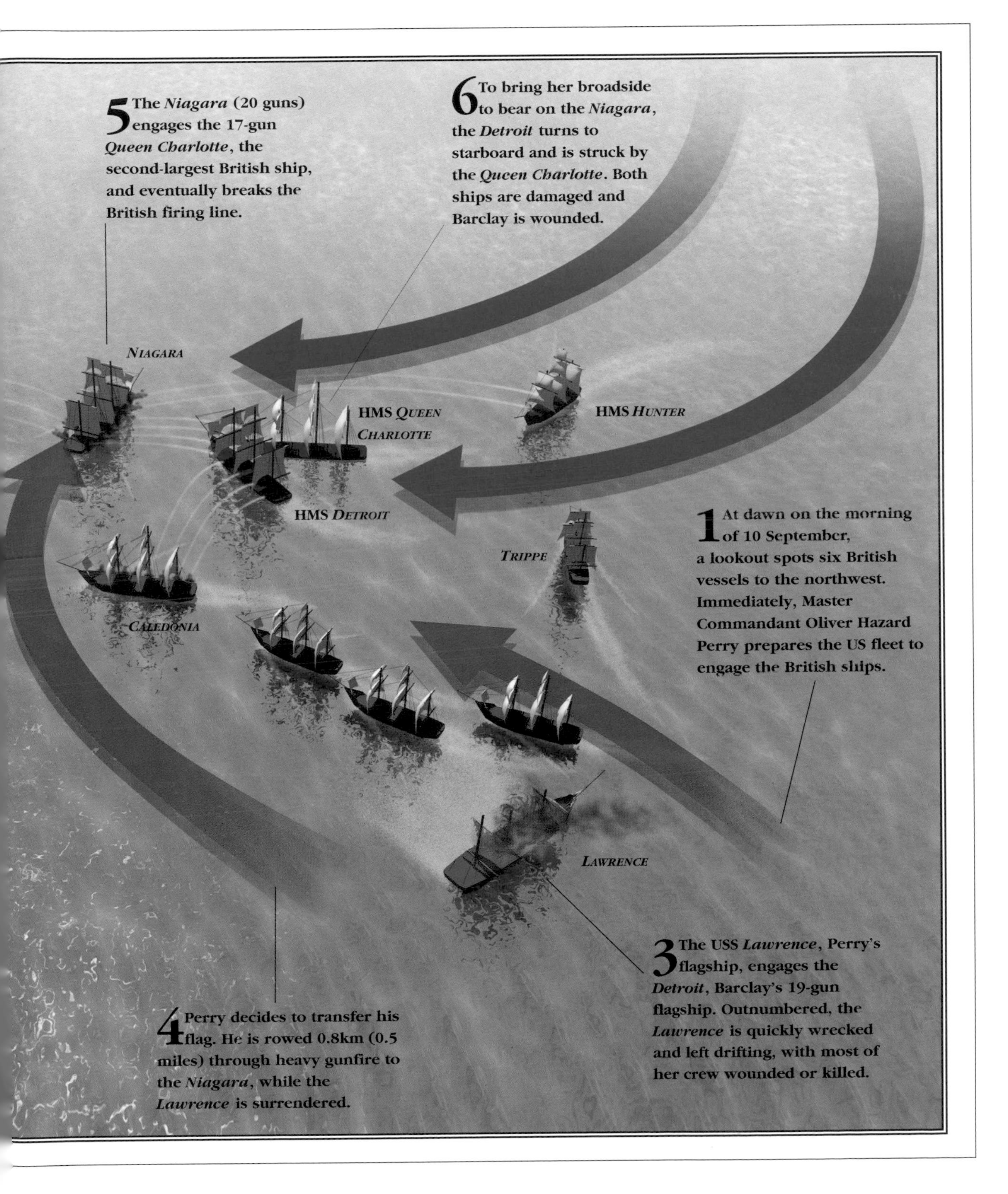
5 The *Niagara* (20 guns) engages the 17-gun *Queen Charlotte*, the second-largest British ship, and eventually breaks the British firing line.
6 To bring her broadside to bear on the *Niagara*, the *Detroit* turns to starboard and is struck by the *Queen Charlotte*. Both ships are damaged and Barclay is wounded.
NIAGARA
HMS QUEEN CHARLOTTE
HMS HUNTER
HMS DETROIT
TRIPPE
1 At dawn on the morning of 10 September, a lookout spots six British vessels to the northwest. Immediately, Master Commandant Oliver Hazard Perry prepares the US fleet to engage the British ships.
CALEDONIA
LAWRENCE
3 The USS *Lawrence*, Perry's flagship, engages the *Detroit*, Barclay's 19-gun flagship. Outnumbered, the *Lawrence* is quickly wrecked and left drifting, with most of her crew wounded or killed.
4 Perry decides to transfer his flag. He is rowed 0.8km (0.5 miles) through heavy gunfire to the *Niagara*, while the *Lawrence* is surrendered.

wrest naval superiority from the British. The new force, comprising the *Oneida* and six adapted lake ships, was ready on 8 November. The force chased but did not catch the two British ships. As winter closed in, both sides directed their energies to their shipyards and built more vessels. The British responded by constructing a 30-gun frigate and two corvettes and transferring 450 experienced sailors from the Royal Navy.

The Americans pressed ahead with building a new corvette, the 24-gun *Madison,* modifying the *Lady of the Lake* and starting work on their own frigate of 26 guns. Both sides also equipped several sail- and oar-powered launches with a single gun in the bows. By August 1813 both sides were ready to begin operations.

Great Lakes operations: Lake Erie, 10 September 1813

The Americans and the British now had squadrons of warships on both Lake Ontario and Lake Erie. On the former lake, the American force consisted of *General Pike* (26 guns), *Madison* (24), *Oneida* (18), plus 10 converted lake ships; they were equipped with a mix of guns and carronades. The British contingent comprised *Wolfe* (23 guns), *Royal George* (20), *Earl of Moira* (16), *Lord Melville* (14), *Lord Beresford* (12) and *Sir Sidney Smith* (12); they were mostly fitted with carronades. On Lake Erie, meanwhile, the Americans had *Lawrence* (20 guns) and *Niagara* (20), plus seven converted lake ships. Between them they mounted 15 long guns and 39 carronades. The British squadron contained *Queen Charlotte* (18 guns), *Lady Prevost* (12) and *General Hunter* (6), plus two schooners and a sloop. The squadron's total armament was 35 long guns and 28 smaller carronades, and one further vessel, the 20-gun *Detroit*, was still under construction.

The American commander, Master-Commandant Oliver Hazard Perry (1785–1819), began by cruising off the Detroit River, trying to provoke a response from the British flotilla. It eventually had the desired effect. The British emerged on 9 September with a favourable breeze, and their two lead ships concentrated on the *Lawrence,* Perry's flagship. The next in the American line, the *Caledonia,* was lagging behind. Within just a few minutes, the American *Lawrence* was a wreck, with two-thirds of her crew casualties. Perry got himself rowed over to the *Niagara* to continue the battle. However, the British officer corps was suffering badly from the American gunnery. *Detroit*, *Queen Charlotte*, *Hunter* and *Prevost* all lost their first lieutenants, and the British commander-in-chief was also mortally wounded. As the British attempted to sort themselves out, Perry charged his ship into their line, firing broadsides in both directions. The *Detroit* attempted to turn downwind to bring her broadside to bear but was run into by the *Queen Charlotte*, which had not responded similarly. This was clearly a mess, and with eight US ships in the immediate vicinity compared with four serviceable vessels in the British flotilla, the latter surrendered.

Lake Champlain

The Americans followed up with another substantial victory on Lake Champlain two days later. This was a combined operation on the lake in support of a land attack against Plattsburg. In this instance the Americans anchored in a line reminiscent of the French at Aboukir Bay. Both flotillas numbered 16 ships. Each was lead by a frigate, the British sporting 37 guns in the *Confiance*, the smaller American 26 guns in the *Saratoga.* The twelve British gunboats suffered badly from the American ships in their approach over open water and were forced to withdraw. At least one of the British cutters was wrecked on an Islet before closing, leaving just three ships to take on the 16 British. The British ship *Linnet* attempted to sail around the rear of the *Saratoga,* which held the left of the American line, while she was assaulted by the *Confiance* broadside to broadside. The *Linnet*, however, was countered by a force of 10 gunboats emerging from the river. The battle raged for two and a half hours before the British ship *Confiance* struck her colours to the *Saratoga.*

The ships used by both sides were much more lightly built than their ocean going cousins. They carried smaller armaments and were faster to manoeuvre and, because they could not sustain so much damage, faster to sink. These battles resembled more an armed dinghy race than the stately advance of small islands under clouds of sail.

The usefulness of the gunboats cannot be underestimated. Shallow drafted, they could operate where the bigger ships could not. Their single, large fore and aft sail meant they were better at sailing into the wind than their larger ship rigged compatriots. The large reserve of crew required to man the oars also gave them the ability to launch substantial boarding or raiding actions. Plus they could move directly into the wind or when there was no wind at all. They could manoeuvre themselves into a position where they could fire at an enemy who could not respond with broadside or bow or stern guns. Despite these advantages, the gun boats were little more than big rowing boats and were highly vulnerable to even a single hit from a ship's cannon and a carronade could utterly devastate ship and crew.

The British and Americans remained at war until 1815. Britain roaming at will along the American seaboard landing troops and seamen to destroy shipping and batteries and even the capitol building itself. In the deep South, at the battle of New Orleans, the British used 45 ships, boats and barges, like the gun boats on the Great Lakes, to deliver the army across 96.5km (60 miles) of shallow water, in the face of armed opposition. In some places the water was so shallow that the crew had to jump out and half carry the vessels across to deeper water.

The ships that fought these battles were built by hand in the old pre-industrial way. However, the writing was already on the wall. The Royal Navy's need for pulley blocks was satisfied only through the use of early machine tools. The steam engine had already taken to the water before Napoleon meet his nemesis at Waterloo in 1815. Forty years later, the American Civil War would see the rails from railway tracks used as crude armour to form ironclad ships. Iron cannon balls ricocheting off this protection sounded the death knell of small islands under clouds of sail.

MASTER-COMMANDANT OH PERRY *transferring his flag from the* Lawrence *to the* Niagara. *This was not cowardice but a practical solution to the problem of trying to command from a disabled ship.*

Select Bibliography

Blaze, Elzéar. *Military Life Under Napoleon. Chicago*. The Emperor's Press, 1995.

Blond, Georges. *La Grande Armée*. London: Arms & Armour Press, 1995.

Boulart, Bon. *Memoires Militaires du General Bon Boulart sur les Guerres de La Republique et de L'Empire*. Paris: La Librarie Illustree, nd.

Bowden, Scott. *Napoleon's Grande Armee of 1813*. Chicago: The Emperor's Press, 1990.

_____. 'Napoleon's Finest: Marshal Davout and His 3d Corps', *Combat Journal of Operations, 1805-1807*. Military History Press, 2006.

Brandt, Heinrich von. *In the Legions of Napoleon: The Memoirs of a Polish Officer in Spain and Russia, 1808-1813*. London: Greenhill Books, 1999.

_____. *Carnet de la Sabretache.* Paris, nd.
Volume 3, 1895: 'Le 7e Corps a Eylau', page 3.
Volume 4, 1896: 'Bataille d'Eylau,' page 81.
Volume 5, 1897: 'Bataille de Friedland', 'Journal d'operations du 1st corps de la Grande Armee', page 325.
Volume 15, 1907: 'Le Centenaire de Friedland', page 321; and 'Soldats d'Heilsberg et de Friedland,' page 354.

Caulaincourt, Armand de. *With Napoleon in Russia*. New York: Dover Publications, 2005.

Chandler, David. *The Campaigns of Napoleon*. New York: Macmillan, 1966.

_____. (editor). *The Military Maxims of Napoleon*. London: Greenhill Books, 1987.

Chesney, Charles. *Waterloo Lectures.* London: Greenhill Books, 1997.

Chlapowski, Dezydery. *Memoirs of a Polish Lancer*. Chicago: The Emperor's Press, 1992.

Clowes, William Laird. *The Royal Navy, a History from Earliest Times* (volumes four and five). London: Chatham Publishing, 1997.

Detaille, Edouard. *L'Armée Française: An Illustrated History of the French Army, 1790-1885*. New York: Waxtel & Hasenauer, 1992.

Du Teil, Jean. *The New Use of Artillery in Field Wars: Necessary Knowledge*. The Nafziger Collection, 2003.

Elting, John R. *Swords Around A Throne: Napoleon's Grande Armee*. New York: The Free Press, 1988.

Esposito, Vincent J. and Elting, John R. *A Military History and Atlas of the Napoleonic Wars*, London: Greenhill, 1999.

Fletcher, Ian. *Galloping at Everything: The British Cavalry in the Peninsular War and at Waterloo 1808-1815*. Mechanicsburg, PA: Stackpole Books, 1999.

Forrest, Alan. *Conscripts and Deserters: The Army and French Society during the Revolution and Empire.* New York: Oxford University Press, 1989.

Gallaher, John G. *The Iron Marshal: A Biography of Louis N. Davout*. London: Feffer & Simons, Inc., 1976.

Gardiner, Robert, editor. *Nelson against Napoleon, from Copenhagen to the Nile, 1798-1801*. London: Chatham Publishing Ltd, 1997.

_____. *Fleet Battle and Blockade: the French Revolutionary War 1793-1797*. London: Chatham Publishing Ltd, 1996.

Gill, John H. *With Eagles to Glory.* London: Greenhill Books, 1992.

Girod de l'Ain, Maurice. *Grands Artilleurs: Drouot, Senarmont, Eble*. Paris, 1895.

Goodwin, Peter. *The 20 Gun Ship* (Blandford Anatomy of the Ship series). London: Conway Maritime Press, 1988.

Graves, Donald E., editor (trans by Jonathan Williams). *De Scheel's Treatise on Artillery*. Museum Resoration Service, 1984.

Griffith, Paddy. *The Art of War in Revolutionary France, 1792-1802.* London: Greenhill Books, 1998.

Gruppe, Henry E. editor. *The Frigates* (The Seafarers series). Amsterdam: Time-Life Books, 1979.

_____. *Fighting Sail*. (The Seafarers series). Amsterdam: Time-Life Books, 1979.

_____. *The East Indiamen*. (The Seafarers series). Amsterdam: Time-Life Books, 1979.

Harbron, John D. *Trafalgar and the Spanish Navy*. London: Conway Maritime Press, 1988.

Haythornthwaite, Philip J. *Napoleon's Military Machine*. Tunbridge Wells: Spellmount Publishing Ltd., 1988.

Horricks, Raymond. *Marshal Ney*. London: Archway Publishing, 1988.

Johnson, David. *Napoleon's Cavalry and Its Leaders*. New York: Holmes & Meier Publishers, 1978.

_____. *The French Cavalry, 1792-1815*. London: Belmont Publishing, 1989.

Kiley, Kevin. *Artillery of the Napoleonic Wars.* London: Greenhill Books, 2006.

Lachouque, Henry and Anne S.K. Brown. *The Anatomy of Glory: Napoleon and his Guard*. London: Greenhill Books, 1997.

Lavery, Brian. *Jack Aubrey Commands, An Historical companion to the Naval World of Patrick O'Brian*. London: Conway Maritime Press, 2003.

_____. *The Arming and Fitting of English Ships of War 1600-1815*. London: Conway Maritime Press, 1987.

Luvaas, Jay (editor). *Napoleon on the Art of War*. New York:The Free Press, 1999.

Markham, J. David (editor). *Imperial Glory: The Bulletins of Napoleon's Grande Armée, 1805-1814*. London: Greenhill Books, 2003.

Muir, Rory. *Salamanca 1812*. New Haven: Yale University Press, 2001.

_____. *Tactics and the Experience of Battle in the Age of Napoleon*. New Haven:Yale University Press, 1998.

Nafziger, George. *Imperial Bayonets*. London: Greenhill, 1996.

Nardin, Pierre. *Gribeauval Lieutenant General des Armees du Roi (1715-1789)*. Paris, nd.

Nosworthy, Brent. *With Musket, Cannon and Sword: Battle Tactics of Napoleon and His Enemies*. New York: Sarpedon, 1996

Oman, Charles. *A History of the Peninsular War* (Volume V). London: Greenhill, 2005.

Paret, Peter. *Yorck and the Era of Prussian Reform*. Princeton: Princeton University Press, 1966.

Petre, F. Lorraine. *Napoleon's Last Campaign in Germany: 1813*. London:Arms and Armour Press, 1974.

Quimby, Robert. *The Background of Napoleonic Warfare: the Theory of Military tactics in Eighteenth Century France*. New York: Columbia University Press, 1957.

Regenbogen, Lucian. *Napoléon a Dit:Aphorismes, citations et opinions*. Paris: Les Belles Lettres, 1998.

Ross, Steven. *From Flintlock to Rifle: Infantry Tactics, 1740-1866*. London: Frank Cass, 1996.

Rothenberg, Gunther. *The Art of Warfare in the Age of Napoleon*. Bloomington: Indiana University Press, 1978.

Schneid, Frederick. *Napoleon's Italian Campaigns: 1805-1815*.Westport: Praeger, 2002.

Ségur, Philippe de. *Memoirs of an Aide-de-Camp of Napoleon, 1800-1812*. Gloucestershire: Nonsuch Publishing, 2005.

_____. *History of the Expedition to Russia* (2 volumes). Gloucestershire: Nonsuch Publishing, 2005.

Siborne, William. *History of the Waterloo Campaign*. London: Greenhill Books, 1995.

Six, Georges. *Dictionnaire Biographique des Generaux & Amiraux Francais de la Revolution et de L'Empire (1792-1814)*. Paris: Bordas, 1947.

Sutton, Jean. *Lords of the East, the East India Company and its ships (1600-1874)*. London: Conway Maritime Press, 1981.

Tousard, Louis de. *American Artillerist's Companion*. New York: Greenwood Press, 1969.

White, David. *The Frigate Diana* (Anatomy of the Ship series). London: Conway Maritime Press, 1987.

Wilson, Sir Robert. *The Campaigns in Poland in 1806 and 1807*. London:Worley Publications, 2000.

Zhmodikov, Leonidovich. *Tactics of the Russian Army in the Napoleonic Wars* (two volumes).The Nafziger Collection, 2003.

Picture and Illustration Credits

All maps and black-and-white line artworks produced by **JB Illustrations** © Amber Books Ltd.

Art-Tech/Aerospace: 65

Art-Tech/John Batchelor: 224

Art-Tech/MARS: 6/7, 12, 21, 30/31, 32, 35, 44, 47, 48, 56, 58, 59, 60, 66/67, 68, 69, 70/71, 76, 86, 88, 96/97, 102, 105, 107, 118/119, 121, 126, 133, 145, 155, 156, 172, 175, 201, 204/205, 206, 212/213, 215, 239

Bridgeman Art Library: 114/115 (State Central Artillery Museum, St. Petersburg, Russia)

Anne S. K. Brown Military Collection, Brown University Library: 14, 15, 24, 40, 46, 51, 52

Corbis: 42/43 (Historical Picture Archive), 78 (Bettmann), 80/81 (Historical Picture Archive), 90/91 (Archivo Iconografico), 116 (Alexander Burkatovski), 127 (Stapleton Collection), 230/231 (Fine Art Photographic Library)

Mary Evans Picture Library: 79, 152, 162, 168, 186/187, 191 (Rue des Archives), 192/193

Getty Images: 10/11 (MPI), 16 (Hulton Archive)

Heritage Images: 19 (Art Media), 26 (Art Media), 134 (Art Media), 197 (Art Media), 227 (Corporation of London)

Library of Congress: 249

Photo12.com: 75 (ARJ), 170/171 (Foundation Napoleon), 182/183 (Foundation Napoleon)

Photos.com: 13, 37, 41, 130/131, 219

Popperfoto: 151

TopFoto: 109 (RIA Novosti)

Index

Page numbers in *italics* refer to illustrations, those in **bold** type refer to information displays with maps and text. Abbreviations are as follows: (B) - battle; (NB) - naval battle; (S) - siege.